I

SHAMANISM

AND THE

DRUG

PROPAGANDA

THE BIRTH OF PATRIARCHY
AND THE DRUG WAR

INCLUDING A SUMMARY, IN HER OWN
WORDS, OF JANE ELLEN HARRISON'S
PROLEGOMENA AND *EPILEGOMENA TO
THE STUDY OF GREEK RELIGION*

DAN RUSSELL

Kalyx.com

Kalyx.com
P.O. Box 417, Camden, NY 13316
www.kalyx.com
ISBN: 0-9650253-1-4
Library of Congress Catalog Card Number:
98-91312

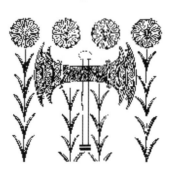

Shamanism and the Drug Propaganda   *VI*

Contents

BONE 1
COPPER 32
KNOSSOS 51
BRONZE 61
THE DOVE 76
PHOENISSA 83
PHOINIKEIA 93
MYKENAIKOS 101
IRON 108
DIONYSOS 125
MNEMOSYNE 157
DRAMA 169
ORPHEUS 175
ASSAYA 200
BALSAM 256
IDOLATRY 266
GNOSIS 295
BIBLIOGRAPHY 311
NOTES 327

BONE

The central sacrament of all Paleolithic, Neolithic and Bronze Age cultures known is an inebriative herb, a plant totem, which became metaphoric of the communal epiphany. These herbs, herbal concoctions and herbal metaphors are at the heart of all mythologies. They include such familiar images as the Burning Bush, the Tree of Life, the Cross, the Golden Bough, the Forbidden Fruit, the Blood of Christ, the Blood of Dionysos, the Holy Grail (or rather its contents), the Chalice (*Kalyx*:'flower cup'), the Golden Flower (*Chrysanthemon*), Ambrosia (*Ambrotos*:'immortal'), Nectar (*Nektar*:'overcomes death'), the Sacred Lotus, the Golden Apples, the Mystic Mandrake, the Mystic Rose, the Divine Mushroom (*teonanacatl*), the Divine Water Lily, Soma, Ayahuasca ('Vine of the Soul'), Kava, Iboga, Mama Coca and Peyote Woman.

They are the archetypal - the emotionally, the instantaneously understood - symbols at the center of the drug propaganda. A sexually attractive man or woman is an archetypal image, the basis of most advertising. A loaf of bread is an archetypal image. The emotional impact of the sacramental herbal images, or, rather, the historical confusion of their natural function, is central to the successful manipulation of mass emotion and individual self-image.

Jung: "An image which frequently appears among the archetypal configurations of the unconscious is that of the tree or the wonder-working plant." When people reproduce these dream images they often take the form of a mandala. Jung calls the mandala "a symbol of the self in cross section," comparing it to the tree, which represents the evolving self, the self as a process of growth.[1]

"Like all archetypal symbols, the symbol of the tree has undergone a development of meaning in the course of the centuries. It is far removed from the original meaning of the shamanistic tree, even though certain basic features prove to be unalterable."[2]

"...it is the decisive factors in the unconscious psyche, the archetypes, which constitute the structure of the collective unconscious. The latter represents a psyche that is identical in all individuals....The archetypes are formal factors responsible for the organization of unconscious psychic processes: they are 'patterns of behaviour.'"[3]

Those patterns of behavior are rooted in our evolutionary biology as surely as is the shape of our body. Inebriative behavior is an oral behavior, related, physiologically and psychologically, to eating and sex. It is as instinctive in people as socializing or music making. I doubt there is a solvent culture on earth in which breakfast isn't accompanied by a traditional herbal stimulant, or in which some herbal inebriant isn't wildly popular.

Inebriation - ritual, social, alimentary and medical - is basic to all cultures, ancient and modern. Traditional cultures don't separate inebriative herbalism from any of the other 'archaic techniques of ecstacy' - dancing, musicalizing, socializing, ritualizing, fasting, curing, ordeal - which are part of the same shamanic behavior complex; nor do they separate medicine from food.

This book deals with the ancient, the *unconscious* roots of the Drug War. We are no longer overtly racist, in our public laws at least, but we are still brutally anti-tribal, in many ways institutionally unloving, structurally violent, to millions of our children, our tribal primitives, and to our shamanic adults. This is a *psychological* inheritance from the ancient slave states, as well as a legal one. This internalized industrial fascism, this proscription, *causes* drug problems, in the same way that violent sexual puritanism causes sexual problems. The ancient tribal wisdom prevents them. There are many cultures, both tribal and industrial, the Vicosinos of Peru and the Dutch, for instance, that don't have anything like our current disaster, and they all apply prescription rather than proscription.

Rome, the last of the great ancient slave states, institutionalized the conquistador ethos of industrial conformity in Western culture. That ethos translates itself today as irrational fear of the shamanic experience; fear, that is, of the unconscious itself and of primitivity in general. The industrial process, and its concomitant inquisitorial neurosis, has been as successful in burying conscious knowledge of the archaic techniques of ecstacy as it has been in burying the wolf, and those that understood it. Unconscious knowledge, on the other hand, is a tad more difficult to manipulate, as the neurotic lurching of so many of our public figures demonstrates; "just say no,"after all, was promulgated by an alcoholic.

We don't escape the thrall of our dreams. The *psychology* of contemporary politics, 'history,' moves much more slowly than technology, which is a mechanical, not a biological process. We will cease to live in the world of the ancients only when sex, birth, hunger and death become different for us than they were for them. Our dream language, our spectacular automatic creativity, is, of course, archetypal imagery, the evolutionarily-determined picture-language that is the same for all peoples, regardless of culture, just as the human body and emotions are the same.

Let us go to monkeyland, then, before Babel, and listen to our ancestors, who are omnivorous primates. Just as the ancient shamanism gave birth to empirical science, so too, now, can empirical science give our latent earthly powers rebirth. Empirical intellect always was an organic part of the archaic techniques of ecstacy, as much a technique for achieving automatic creativity as dancing, singing or holy smoking. "...mind would then be understood as a *system of adaptation determined by the conditions of an earthly environment.*"[4]

The profound distinction between the known upright apes of two and three million years ago is meat eating. *Australopithecus robustus* and *A. boisei*, vegetarian australopithecines ('southern apes'-Dart) are not ancestral to the human race. *Boisei* is below left. *Australopithecus africanus*, below right, the omnivorous hunting australopithecine, is directly ancestral. That's why the younger, or related, forms of *africanus* are known as *Homo habilis* ('skillful man'-Leakey).

The distinctions between the 'robust' *robustus* and *boisei*, and the 'gracile' *africanus* and *habilis* are easy to spot. The massive postcanine teeth of *robustus* have huge roots set in heavy jawbones, strung together with thick musculature to operate the vegetable grinding apparatus. The architecture of *Homo*'s skull is completely different. Homey has no skull-top crest to hang huge grinding muscles from, and has not only smaller and lighter postcanine teeth and jaws, like ours, but teeth specifically adapted for cutting, not grinding.[5]

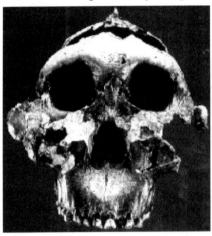 

Although sharing a common ancestor with *Homo habilis*, it appears that *robustus* was on Homey's menu, as was just about everything else. Chimpanzees and baboons, the primates whose ecology most closely resembles that of the early hominids, are the most carnivorous of living primates. Chimps come close to being hunting omnivores.[6] With the exception of chimps and baboons, vegetarianism is the basic dietary adaptation of all known primates, living and dead, except the line ancestral to man and its near offshoots.

The fierce, omnivorous ape *Proconsul*, below, a likely proto-australopithecine of twenty million years ago, shares common monkey ancestors with baboons.[7] The Miocene-Pliocene drought, starting about fifteen million years ago, which laid down the Kalahari sands of central and southern Africa, replaced forest habitat with grass savanna, slowly, over the course of millions of years.[8] As the forests shrank, the brachiator was forced to the ground, freeing those grasping hands he was accustomed to using with such power and intelligence. The combination of depth-perception, essential to a brachiator, and acute tactile control made that hand an awesome tool when evolution released it from the branches. The power conferred by wielding a club must have made the early australopithecines feel that they were waving trees in the air.

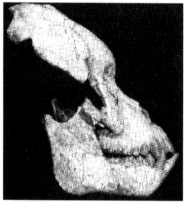

Just as baboons and chimps do, *Proconsul* supplemented his basic roots, tubers, grasses, fruits and insects with whatever meat chance put in his way. As the dry season became more and more difficult to deal with, so too the seasonal meat-eating became fixed in the ancestral biology and behavior; taking the occassional egg or fawn evolved into conscious hunting.

Like the australopithecines, but unlike all other monkeys, the African baboons and their near relatives, the Asian macaques, do most of their feeding on the ground. Baboon troop size is larger than that of other monkeys, and they are more aggressive and dominance-oriented, able to live in a wider variety of environments and control a much larger territory. In this they resemble chimpanzees, the ape that is our other great evolutionary mirror.

The baboon troop is a feeding and fighting unit, a family army on the move. The most dominant males occupy the center, the mothers and infants sharing the center with them. The less dominant males, older juveniles and pregnant or estrus females occupy the periphery. When the troop moves, the boldest, and biologically most expendable, less dominant males take the lead, the rear and do the scouting. A predator would have to get past not only the peripheral males but the fierce dominant males in the troop center before it could get to the mothers and infants.

Sexual dimorphism is evolutionarily, that is to say psychologically, basic to humans. Here is how DeVore and Washburn, the zoologists whose baboon work I have been summarizing, explain baboon dimorphism: "Selection has favored the evolution of males which weigh more than twice as much as females, and the advantage to the troop of these large animals is clear, but it is not obvious why it is advantageous for the females to be small. The answer to the degree of sex differences appears to be that this is the optimum distribution of the biomass of the species. If the average adult male weighs approximately 75 pounds and the average adult female 30 pounds, each adult male requires more than twice the food of a female. If the food supply is a major factor in limiting the number of baboons, and if survival is more likely if there are many individuals, and if the roles of male and female are different - then selection will favor a sex difference in average body size which allows the largest number of animals compatible with the different social roles of the troop."

"Interadult male antagonism results in a social order which both protects females and young and reduces feeding competition with females and young. Without altruism, the dominance behavior of a small number of males keeps a feeding space available to subordinate animals."[9] Older juvenile females don't engage in the serious mock fighting that absorbs the boys, and are socialized to expect a more protected place in the troop.

Johanson's discovery of 'Lucy,' an older form of *africanus* known as *Australopithecus afarensis*, was spectacular because he found 40% of her skeleton, including enough of the lower half to demonstrate that she was completely bipedal. The forward placement of the foramen magnum, the hole where the spine connects to the skull, also confirmed bipedalism. Her pelvis, femur and tibia were virtually identical to most of the somewhat younger *Australopithecus africanus/Homo habilis* evidence we have, although the skull was far more chimplike. That is, the bones were, like ours, adapted for bipedal movement and were completely different than those of any quadrupedal ape. They were 3.2 million years old. Lucy was 25 years old, stood 3'6" tall and weighed about 62 pounds. To date Johanson has unearthed 13 individuals in Ethiopia. Most of the adult males are a foot taller than Lucy, displaying a baboon-like sexual dimorphism.

Another interesting observation of DeVore and Washburn is the specificity of baboon herbal knowledge, extending to the seasonal recognition of usually unavailable foods and the rejection of bitter or poisonous foods. Marais, who lived with a troop of 300 chacma baboons for three years at the turn of the century, observed his baboons sparingly using powerful emetic plants for their medicinal effects. The baboons also recognized the seasonal fermentation of overripe fruit on the vine. Goodall observed her chimps going out of their way first thing every morning to find the Aspilia leaves, which contain a powerful oil that kills common parasites in the gut. Rodrgiguez and Wrangham followed up Goodall's tip, introducing 'zoopharmacognosy' at the 1992 meeting of the American Association for the Advancement of Science.[10]

Similar pharmacological cognition has been observed in Kodiak bears and coatis. The Indian mongoose, it is said, seeks mungo root when bitten by a cobra. Siegel's team observed Malayan spider monkeys carefully spitting out the poisonous seeds of the Strychnos fruit while enjoying the pulp.[11] Gorillas will regulate their ingestion of the alkaloids in Lobelia by avoiding the stems, where the concentration of alkaloid is too high for safety. Reindeer are famous for competing with Siberian shamans for the deliciously inebriating but seasonally rare Soma mushrooms. The point is, of course, that self-medication is instinctively associated with eating.

The infectious yawning reflex, which transmits a sense of fatigue, is common to primates and humans, as is glancing around every third or fourth bite (originally as a protection from food theft and predation). The baby's smile, the female or male flirtation gestures, the raised eyebrows of recognition, reliance on sight and hearing rather than smell, shock and avoidance gestures, social mood transfer and spacing, frustration displacement activities, fascination with fire, learning by imitation, as well as various reproductive behaviors are all instinctive patterns we share with the other primates.[12]

Professor Churchland: "Finally, it is useful to know that neurons and their modus operandi are essentially the same in all nervous systems - our neurons and the neurons of slugs, worms, and spiders share a fundamental similarity. There are differences between vertebrates and invertebrates, but these differences pale beside the preponderant similarities. Even our neurochemistry is fundamentally similar to that of the humblest organism slithering about on the ocean floor."[13]

The body's basic painkillers are a family of peptide chains known as endorphins, which is short for endogenous morphines.[14] They cluster in various parts of the brain and spinal cord, and are so similar in structure to morphine, one of opium sap's alkaloids, that the brain is provided with chemically-specific opiate receptor mechanisms. That is, the plant alkaloid and the brain compounds are virtually identical.[15] Of course, opium has more than three dozen alkaloids, including morphine, the most prevalent, and the brain can do even better than that.[16] This is a complex and technical biochemical mystery, but there is no doubt that the brain produces opiate alkaloids, including some virtually identical to morphine, and these bond to the brain's chemically-specific opiate receptor mechanisms.

Serotonin, an essential neurotransmitter shown to be basic to the brain's ability to produce imagery, is a tryptamine derivative, structurally related to psilocybin and LSD. That is, it is a psychedelic, an entheogenic alkaloid (generator of *entheos*, 'divine enthusiasm').[17] The FDA-approved mood-enhancer Prozac works by gently blocking the reabsorption of serotonin, thereby increasing serotonin levels in the bloodstream.

Shamans have been practicing this kind of psychopharmacology for millennia. Ibogaine, isolated from the sacred Iboga root of Gabon, also blocks the reabsorption of serotonin. Freud consciously based his invention of modern psychopharmacology on traditional shamanism, although he wasn't clear on the profound distinction between the traditional psychoactive herbs and the much more powerful, though easier to measure, newly-invented refined alkaloids.

Another evolutionarily basic electro-chemical brain connection, norepinephrine, is a phenylethylamine derivative, very closely related in structure and behavior to mescaline, another psychoactive plant alkaloid. By blocking norepinephrine receptors, commonly prescribed beta blockers combat anxiety and high blood pressure. Coca, cocaine and the amphetamines enhance norepinephrine reception. Dopamine induces euphoria, epinephrine (adrenaline) speeds up the autonomic nervous system, and GABA functions as a downer.[18] Of the eleven undisputed neurotransmitters so far identified, most are either chemical or functional copies of plant alkaloids with which the primates share their evolution.[19]

Selective pressures favored tool use for our newly upright ancestor, since tools not only vastly increased the amount of tubers and bulbs one could dig up, but rendered the capture and consumption of prey easier. *Robustus*, the gathering vegetarian, shows a much smaller brain than *Homo habilis*, who hunted him. As hominid brain volume increased, the brain area for the hand and mouth increased disproportionately, suggesting that tool use was the engine of both brain volume increase and the invention of language.[20] The evolutionary utility of free hands, then, favored the selection of intelligence and uprightness as well.[21]

The only place where the motor apparatii of speech are wired together is the cerebral cortex, the youngest part of the brain. Almost all the apparatii of speech were originally used for completely different functions. As posture became erect, the head moved forward, the larynx descended and a long, flexible mouth cavity developed. But physiology that would enable human speech as we know it today didn't emerge until, at most, 125,000 years ago.

Both tool-using and speaking are localized in the same general area of the brain, and both tool-using and sign language, instinctive gesticulation, use the hands. This is a physiological explanation of the power of imagery, signs. We know, from contemporary experiments like the ones with the gorilla Washoe and the chimps Moja, Pili and Sarah, that primates with less brain power than the australopithecines are capable of spontaneous, intelligent, affective speech in American Sign Language.[22] We also know that gibbons, dense-forest brachiators who can't rely on sight, have upwards of 150 vocal signs.

The australopithecines were true bipeds, with hands free for carrying and using the stone and bone tools found in such abundance in their deposits. The tools that have survived are mostly concussion-flaked rock hammers, cutters and daggers. What didn't survive was the simple vegetable or animal-part slings and jugs that those tools fashioned. The ability to carry food and water, something the quadrupedal baboons can't do, is itself a great technological revolution, since it opens the way to long hunts, storage, and conscious division of labor. Baboons must stay within two miles of water.

Raw meat is far more nutritionally concentrated than raw vegetable food (with the exception of honey and nuts), so the regular availability of meat meant portable rations. Among most monkeys and apes - vegetarians, adult males never provide food for females and young, as they do among hyenas, wolves and other large carnivores. Carnivore females are hunters. Since hunting is a cooperative activity, it encourages the conscious sharing of both animal and vegetable food by both sexes. This, of course, facilitates social cooperation on all levels - in the care of the young, for instance. Chimpanzees, the most carnivorous of contemporary primates, are also the most inclined to share food.

A major reason why sexual dimorphism is far less pronounced in *Homo sapiens* than in the early hominids is probably the evolutionary success in food gathering of our ancestral australopithecines. Their hand-held tools made them not only more efficient root diggers, but expert baboon and antelope hunters as well. The decreased sexual dimorphism led to a greater interchange of roles, including considerable female hunting and male child care. The result of this adaptive flexibility was, in Paleolithic terms, a very high infant survival rate.

The more mouths to feed, of course, the more pressure for the big kill and the cooperative hunt - as practiced by lions and hyenas, a basic carnivorous adaptation. As the one, two, three and four million year-old sites excavated by Dart, the Leakeys, Broom, Robinson, Johanson, White and the others demonstrate, even the oldest australopithecine sites yield the remains of large and dangerous prey animals, with, in fact, a surprising lack of small and easy prey. In Bed One at Olduvai, for instance, the Leakeys found the remains of a meal made from an extinct type of giant oryx, whose closest living relative, the gemsbok, can easily disembowel lion or man with its rapier horns.[23]

At the one and a half million year-old australopithecine kitchen midden excavated by Dart at Makapansgat, 92% of the bone fragments were antelope, indicating a dietary preference for the Bovidae that takes us up through the entire fossil record all the way to MacDonald's.[24] A consistent sign indicating tool use is the hammering open of hard bones to get at the marrow. The physical anthropologists have demonstrated the multimillion year antiquity of intentional tool making, with regular bone, tooth, antler and stone tools dating back at least three million years. Sharp stone skin cutters and bone needles, for instance, became very important to antelope hunters who knew how to sew a water jug from antelope hide and sinew.

There is even less variation in *Homo erectus* fossils of a million years ago, whether found in China or Africa, than in australopithecine fossils. *Erectus* was technologically adaptable enough to occupy an area which ground monkeys like the baboon-macaques can occupy only by evolving into at least a dozen different species.[25] Unlike baboons, the wide ranging hominine groups interbred with one another, sharing knowledge and skills, cooperating in the hunt and warfare, inventing trade and language.

Their large-brained babies were born less and less mature, as their group ecology favored a long learning period over early independence. Since estrus is incompatible with continuing child care and long-term familial cooperation, hominid females dispensed with the come-one-come-all hot week of baboon ladies. Sex thus became the facilitator of social organization.

The women, the herb gatherers, small game hunters, healers and teachers, generally maintained home base, wherein were kept the tools, foods and medicines. A wild primate will die when separated from the troop by fever or a broken bone. But with a home base that allowed for safe rest and medicine, hominids could invade new territory without first building immunity to local diseases, confident that all but the worst afflictions could be overcome.[26]

Hominid culture of seven hundred thousand years ago made clubs, handaxes, knives and scrapers, and could work stone, bone, skin and sinew with fluency. At Zhoukoudian, near Beijing, along with discarded animal bones, mostly deer, more than forty *Homo erectus* skulls were collected in a kitchen midden - collected, that is, by *Homo erectus*. There were no body bones, only heads. All the heads had been crushed by blows and opened at the base to extract the brains. The paleontologist who reconstructed the Zhoukoudian skulls couldn't find a single fragment of the skull base around the neck (foramen magnum) of any of the forty skulls.[27] The ecstacy of a successful hunt was an epiphany confirming survival. The ritual victim could either be a lead bull, a territorial competitor or a sacrificial magician who took personal responsibility for the plight of the group.

The Zhoukoudian caves were a refuge from the Second Glaciation, and it is here, and in a site in Thailand, that the oldest undoubted human hearths are recorded. Charred bone and antler, seams of finely divided charcoal, and baked clay floors have been found throughout the earliest occupation levels.[28] "'They never seem to think of fire as a means of imparting warmth - their lamps are used for cooking, light, melting snow and drying clothes rather than to warm the air.' Their use of blubber as both fuel and food reminds us that its heating value is theoretically the same whether burned or digested. The mammoth hunters of Moravia apparently fed their fires with marrow dripping from mammoth legbones, broken in half for the purpose, but there is little doubt that the same material would have been equally valued as food."[29] Obviously many otherwise undigestable vegetable foods are rendered edible by cooking.

The best tinder available to the northern inventors of regular firemaking was dried *Fomes fomentarius*, the shelf fungus found on birch; it bursts into flame when hit by a hot spark. When flint, a very hard variety of quartz, is struck by a nodule of iron pyrites, pyritic as well as flint sparks are created. Unlike flint sparks, the metallic sparks stay hot. Nodular iron pyrites and worn pyrite hammerstones have been found repeatedly in *neanderthal* and *sapiens* sites. Northern *neanderthals* were spear hunters of wooly rhinoceros and mammoth. Discarded meat bones, many split for marrow, many burnt, are common in Mousterian occupation layers. *Fomes fomentarius* has been repeatedly found with hearthstones or nodules of iron pyrites in Paleolithic sites, some dating back fifty thousand years.[30]

Wasson: "Speaking of the Uighur, a Mongolian tribe, Marco Polo tells us that 'They say of their Khan who first ruled over them that he was not of human origin, but was born of one of those excrescences on the bark of trees, and that we call esca. From him descended all the other Khans.' In another version of the same myth we learn that two trees played a part in procreating the royal family of the Uighurs, a birch and an evergreen resembling a pine. Esca is the Italian word for 'punk,' in Siberia *Fomes fomentarius*."[31]

The birch, pine and fir, around the polar cap worldwide, host *Amanita muscaria*, the subtly powerful fall mushroom greedily consumed by reindeer and shamans. R. Gordon Wasson, the brilliant founder of the branch of ethnobotany known as ethnomycology, has shown that this is the Soma of the *Rg Veda*. The birch and the pine are the trees of life in Siberian myth. Some Siberian Evenks say that the magic reindeer split a pine, from which emerged a singing woman.[32]

Some *neanderthals* are directly ancestral to *sapiens*, some not. The Steinheim skull, which combines *erectus* or 'pre-*neanderthal*'and *sapiens* features, is estimated to be 300,000 years old. As at Zhoukoudian, he had been murdered with a blow to the head, decapitated, and the base of the skull artificially widened for extraction of the brains. The Ehringsdorf skull, 140,000 years old, seems to have more *sapiens* features. He too had been murdered, decapitated, and had the base of his skull widened for extraction of the brains.

The 55,000 year-old Monte Circeo male was about 45 when he too was murdered by a blow to the head. The skull was found surrounded by a circle of stones, with the base carefully and symmetrically cut away, turned upward for use as a cup. Evidence of ritual brain eating has been found so regularly throughout the 200,000 years of Mousterian culture that it is defined as a traditional feature.[33] The Monte Circeo ritual floor had been emptied of extraneous bones and the skull surrounded by carefully piled bones of wild pig, deer, and bull. The ritual sacrifices of the classical Mediterranean have very deep roots. There are no Paleolithic hunters known, *neanderthal* or *sapiens*, for whom the sacrifice of man or beast wasn't central to the culture.

At the 45,000 year-old Shanidar Cave site in northern Iraq an adult male skeleton was found with a curing shaman's medicine kit. Seven of the eight plants represented by pollen grains were found to be medicinal plants still in use in the area, including yarrow, hollyhock, groundsel and horsetail.[34] Whether this ancient shaman must be defined as *neanderthal* or *sapiens* is open to debate. There is no sharp distinction between *neanderthal* and the following early *sapiens* industries, although the two groups became genetically separated and competitive. Some Siberian hunters say that "man was born from a tree. There was a tree, it split in two. Two people came out. One was a man, the other a woman. Until a child was born they were covered with hair. The first child was born without hair."[35]

Ceremonial or magical bone and antler batons, with holes carved in one end for finger or thong, are found throughout the 25,000 years of Upper Paleolithic remains in both Western and Eastern Europe. The technique had been to carve the sometimes intricate and realistic, othertimes notational engravings in the round, so that they seemed to tell a sequential story, like the later clay cylinder seals. In *The Roots of Civilization*, Alexander Marshack has unrolled these bones to show the recurrent use of pictographic symbols in conjunction with realistic animals and plants. The astonishing thing about the bone batons is the consistency of the symbolism employed over the course of millennia.

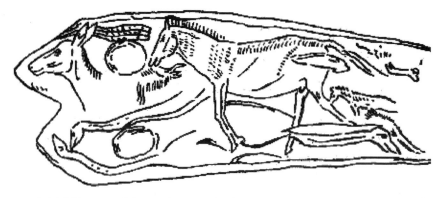

A 15,000 year-old reindeer antler baton from Montgaudier, France, realistically depicts the salmon running upriver in spring, with ecstatic seals in hot pursuit. The snakes or eels could also be spring signs for the seal hunters, as could the carefully drawn plants, bud and sprout. Between the bud and the sprout is a schematized ibex head, with crescent horns and large ears.[36] All these symbols recur in similar contexts throughout Upper Paleolithic art.

One of the things Marshack's microscopic analysis was able to prove was that much of this mobiliary art was used in a time-factored way. That is, different points were used to engrave different symbols over or next to one another at different times. Since the imagery is often seasonal, such as a bellowing bull, a pregnant doe or a snake eating birds eggs, and since many of the same symbols, such as an ibex, a trident, a v, an x or a plant, recur repeatedly, the imagery may be assumed to be storied, that is, mythological.

A bone slate from Upper Magdalenian (c.12,000 BP) France, above, clearly depicts a tribal ritual around a sacrificial bull. The trident baton or medicine lance and ceremonially carried spears can be seen in the hands of schematic human figures dancing around a huge bison head and spine. A baton from La Madeleine, below, pictures itself in the hands of a dancer, with two enormous horses, a giant snake, and a lunar calendar counting off two months by days (grouped slash marks).[37]

These late Paleolithic examples of calendrical counting, grouping the days by the phases of the moon, continue a tradition of scratching slash marks into bone that dates back thirty thousand years. Another large horse and snake are depicted on an Upper Magdalenian baton from northwest Spain. The 34 carefully grouped slash marks appear to count from one phase of the moon to another.

Marshack's 'Rosetta Stone' was a broken Upper Magdalenian bone baton from Asturias, Spain. The complex engraving combines the schematic ibex and plant signs with monthly slash-mark calendars: "If the ibex head that is struck through is indicative of an early spring rite or sacrifice, as implied in the Montgaudier and La Vache examples, then it may here represent a first spring sacrifice in the time of the thaw....Face two in this reading runs from August through October with a different plant image for each month. The August image looks like a plant in full summer growth...while September seems to be a reed and October seems to represent the nut-cone-fruit-seed image of a particular species....The technique of running a series of day-units (or month- or year-units) horizontally along an edge, with symbols juxtaposed above the days (or months or years) to indicate moments of significant rite, myth, observation, or seasonal change, appears in the historic Greco-Roman calendars, the Scandinavian calendar rune stick, the English Clogg almanac, the Siberian Yakut calendar, and on certain American Indian record sticks. Our early analysis of the engraved mammoth tusk from Gontzi, with a calendric notation along a line and with symbols above and at the end of sequences, seems to be an early example of this cognitive style."[38]

In the beautiful 17,000 year-old (Lower Magdalenian) cave paintings at Lascaux, horses, cows and buffalo are depicted with specific, stressed plant images. A 14,000 year-old carved mammoth ivory from Czechoslovakia depicts a grain plant on one side and a snake on the other. A 12,000 year-old engraved flat bone from La Vache in the French Pyrenees shows a realistic bellowing bull and a doe, apparently in early fall, the rutting season. The associated bare branches and drooping flower may confirm the season. That is also the season of the Amanitas, the Soma mushrooms, above, which may be what is depicted below the conifer branches.[39] The pictorial accentuation of meaningful plants is even more dramatic in the 12,000 year-old bone fragment showing the schematized stag head and a particular kind of flower. The complex fragment below, combining plant and animal images, was a sort of Paleolithic notebook.

Eyes floating in mid-air, shaped like diamonds, can be seen arresting the attention of a majestic stag crossing a river in which realistic salmon are leaping on a beautiful Upper Magdalenian bone baton from the Pyrenees, below. Another bone shows floating eyes attending a bear's head bleeding from the mouth, the sacrificial symbolism. The floating eye motif, in conjunction with snakes, sacred plants and ecstatic people, is repeated in Bronze Age temple-palaces from Teotihuacán to Knossos, as is the sacrificial animal motif.[40]

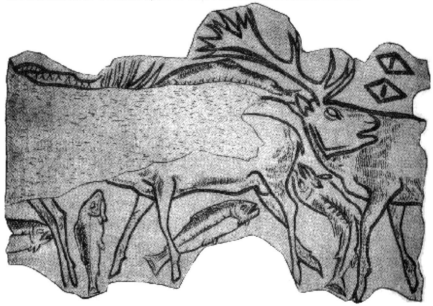

A shaman wearing a horned chamois head can be seen three times in an Upper Magdalenian baton from Dordogne, along with a large sacrificial horse (x marks the spot), a doe, and schematized snakes and birds. At Lascaux, a bird-headed, ithyphallic shaman is seen along with trident baton, bird-head baton, and a wounded buffalo with its guts trailing out.[41]

The single most common image found throughout the 25,000-year span of Upper Paleolithic art is that of an adult woman. Female images are found majestically cut into cave entrances, below right, as shaped reindeer antler batons, and as bone, stone or coal statuettes and amulets. The 20,000 year-old soft stone Venus of Willendorf, Austria, below left, was coated with red ochre (ferrous clay), as were many ceremonial batons and statuettes. A 25,000 year-old mammoth ivory calendar-baton from Moravia is a highly stylized bone stick with counting notches and pendulous breasts.

Many of these monthly counters with breast or vulva images show signs of frequent handling, which could indicate they were used as menstrual or pregnancy measures. The stress on either breasts or vulva could indicate differing aspects of womanhood. Abstracted female symbols appear on counting sticks, pendants, statuettes and cave walls from the very earliest Aurignacian levels (32,000 B.P.) onward.

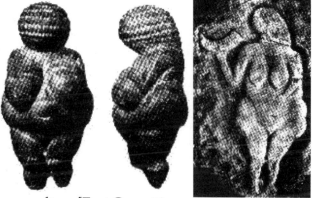

"The same culture [East Gravettian mammoth and reindeer hunters from Moravia, Czechoslovakia, 25,000 B.P.] that made the symbols of the double breasts, the isolated vulva, and the comprehensive non-pregnant 'mother goddess' made this image of a real woman in pregnancy. It is the same culture that made the quick, realistic clay images of bear and lion for the apparent ritual purposes of 'killing'and the long-term image of the decorative lion. This young woman seems to be in the tradition of the quick image made for some immediate storied purpose, perhaps participation in approaching delivery or birth."[42]

The 22,000 year-old red-ochred sculpted reliefs at the rock shelter of Laussel, France, above, one to three feet high, realistically depict a goddess holding up a crescent horn with thirteen notches on it, a god hurling a lance, a horse, a deer and other animals.[43] The thirteen notches probably count off a lunar year of 29-day months, new moon to new moon. The female image with the crescent moon is repeated over and over in both Paleolithic and Neolithic artifact and mythology. Frolov: "Perhaps the Siberian peoples possess the key to that phenomenon; their women calculate child-birth by the phases of the moon... Pregnancy has a duration of exactly 10 lunar months, and the woman keeps a sort of lunar calendar (it was always the woman who was the custodian of the lunar calendar among these nationalities)."[44]

The oldest female figurine we have is a flint sculpture from the Lower Paleolithic, more than 500,000 years old, at least 350,000 years older than anything that could be called *Homo sapiens*. Triangular stones, used in the Upper Paleolithic and Neolithic to represent the Goddess' pubic triangle, the doorway to the eternal, have been found placed on 100,000 year-old graves.[45]

Much of the schematized female imagery is combined with chevrons, angles, meanders and serpentine or spiral images identical or almost identical to the imagery found on Neolithic pottery and grave markings worldwide.[46] These designs match the eye's natural phosphenes, geometric designs produced by the eye subjectively in the absence of light, under manual pressure, or under the influence of entheogenic plants.

Dr. Max Knoll used electrical impulses to generate phosphenes experimentally in more than 1,000 people. Knoll categorized the designs reproduced by his subjects, showing more than half to be identical to the traditional magical designs of the Paleolithic and Neolithic. Professor Reichel-Dolmatoff discussed this in relation to the profuse imagery produced under the influence of the 'vine of the soul,' *ayahuasca* or *yajé*, by contemporary Tukano shamans of the Amazon, imagery in every way identical to the ancient designs.

"We must turn briefly to this second stage of the yajé trance, characterized, according to the Indians, by visions interpreted as mythological scenes. While the first stage is one of phosphenes, the second stage seems to be one of true hallucinations....This second stage of the yajé experience was discussed in detail with many informants and from their comments it appears that this stage is interpreted, in all essence, as a return to the maternal womb. It is a visit to the place of Creation, the *fons et origo* of everything that exists, and the viewer thus becomes an eyewitness and a participant in the Creation story and the moral concepts it contains. The yajé vessel is said to be a female body, the maternal body, and by drinking its contents the individual is enabled to enter it through the 'door,' the vagina one often sees depicted at the base of the container."

"If we observe the close relationship between drug-induced hallucination and such aspects as mythology, social organization, and artistic creation, we must conclude that the study of hallucinogenic plants and their use by native shamans provides the key to an understanding of many basic cultural processes. It is the hallucinatory experience which, at least among the Tukano, constitutes the common basis of most cultural activities, and the same is probably true for many other native cultures in which ecstatic states are known to be part of shamanistic practice."[47]

Ecstatic states are known to be part of shamanistic practice in every other Paleolithic and Neolithic culture known. A floating eye appears above the vulva of a 15,000 year-old schematic female figure from Dordogne, engraved on bone along with a fish, a seal's tail and a block of slash marks.[48] Etched in the bone above the entire figure is a floating mushroom.

Insight into Paleo-Siberian shamanism, typical of the ancestral cultures of all North European and Amerindian peoples, has been preserved in Tsistsistas (Cheyenne) tradition (the word Cheyenne is derived from the Lakota for 'outsider'). In *The Wolves of Heaven* anthropologist Karl Schlesier has painstakingly reconstructed the ancient central rite of this culture from the extensive archeological record, the last few ceremonial First Hunts reported by serious observers, and his own long participation in contemporary Tsistsistas life.

Tsistsistas tribal memory represents the classic thought of the Algonquian language family, from which most Amerindian dialects descend. The Tsistsistas date their founding ritual to North Dakota, 2500 years ago, after their ancestors came down from Canada as part of the general northern Algonquian migration that settled southern Canada, the Great Lakes and the western Plains. Their transition from spear-thrower to bow dates to approximately the same time, as does their acquisition of copper metallurgy. The tradition remembered, then, is that of Upper Paleolithic hunters in the process of developing the foundations of Mesolithic technology.

The First Hunt was originated by the Daughter of Thunder and Earth, the buffalo maiden incarnated as a beautiful young woman, who gave the earth to the Tsistsistas. It was she, a member of the Young Wolf Society, who chose Thunder Woman and Earth Grandmother, and together they chose the contrary shaman who represented the Original Prophet. The Original Prophet chose a Companion, who represented the tribe during the First Hunt ceremonies.

After sweat lodge purification, the five ritual performers were painted with red ochre, the color of the blood of life. After selecting a sacrificial tree, sacred herbs were smoked in deer bone pipes to communicate to the tree spirit the necessity of the tree's sacrifice. The World Tree was then felled and set up in the center of the camp circle. The Young Wolf Maidens raised the wolf lodge around the World Tree, aligning the four-post frame to the four sacred directions. The World Tree, with seven branches left at the top, protruded through the smoke hole.

Eliade: "What must be noted as of particular importance is the presence of the World Tree in every Dayak village and even in every Dayak house. And the Tree is represented with seven branches. That it symbolizes the World Axis and hence the road to the sky is proved by the fact that a similar World Tree is always found in the Indonesian 'ships of the dead,' which are believed to transport the deceased to the celestial beyond. This tree...sometimes takes the form of a lance decorated with the same symbols that serve to designate the 'shaman's ladder,' by which he climbs to the sky to bring back the patient's fugitive soul."[49]

That is, we are dealing with archetypes here that are common to Paleolithic hunting cultures worldwide, basic to human evolution and therefore to human psychology. These are archetypal symbols of the mind's relation to the earth, which relationship is the wellspring of sanity and vision. Related images are the Center of the World, the World Axis, the Navel of the World, and all the architecture that imitated the Cosmic Mountain, such as the Ziggurat and the Pyramid.

All are the Center from which the shaman climbs to communication with the sky spirits, as in the canonical foundation myth of Judeo-Christian culture, that of Moses receiving the Ten Commandments from the Burning Bush on the Mountain. It was the entheogen, the Burning Bush, that communicated God's Word. Mount Tabor in Israel is likely related to Hebrew *tabbur*, 'navel,' and Mount Gerizim is referred to in Judges (9:37) as the 'navel of the earth.' Other heavenly ladders include the ascending fire or smoke, the vine, rope, arrows, sunbeam or rainbow.[50]

Eliade: "Some features of the Australian initiation are already familiar to us: the candidate's death and resurrection, the insertion of magical objects into his body. It is interesting to note that the initiatory master, magically changing himself into a skeleton, reduces the apprentice's stature to that of a newborn infant; both these feats symbolize the abolition of profane time and the restoration of a mythical time, the Australian 'Dream Time.' The ascent is made by way of the rainbow, mythically imagined as a huge snake, on whose back the master climbs as on a rope."[51]

Tribal rites of renewal are dominated by the ancestor spirits of the dream-time, the *alcheringa* time, when we were one with the plant and animal spirits, our ancestors. The spirits are most often joined by entering a pharmacologically-induced state of temporary 'death.' This primal therapy induces a re-visioning that abolishes the separation between conscious and unconcious, re-minding the individual, and the tribe, of its roots in the earth. By unleashing its animal emotions and instincts, the tribe awakens its creativity, thereby validating the power of its symbols and traditions. Initiates are 'reborn' to a world full of meaning.

The seven branches of the World Tree are identified by the Tsistsistas with the Seven Brothers, the Pleiades. The Original Prophet, in the role of the Creator God, decorated the lodge with a red sun disk and a blue-black crescent moon. Returning inside, he painted Thunder Man, with whom he identified, with horns and eagle talons for feet. Daughter of Thunder then placed a buffalo skull facing the World Tree. The skins of a red male wolf, a white female wolf and a female kit fox were then placed on the sage north of the buffalo skull.

The Original Prophet painted the buffalo skull black for night, white for day and red for earth. A solid blue geometric star representing Rigel, the blue star of midsummer dawn, was placed between the horns. A red sun disk on the right jaw and a black crescent moon on the left completed Our Grandmother Earth, who was then ritually present. Our Grandmother's ritual skull was then buried in the Earth, her home. At that moment, the medicine lodge became a wolf den in the Sacred Mountain; not Olympos or Sinai, but Bear Butte in the Black Hills of Dakota.

The next day Daughter of Thunder ritually married the Tsistsistas companion of Thunder Man, also known as Sweet Root Standing or Sweet Medicine. She took the deer bone pipe lit by Thunder Woman and smoked it alone, signifying her acceptance of the marriage to the tribe. The pipe was then shared by the five ritual performers to facilitate communication with the spirits they represented.

The male Red Wolf, the female White Wolf and the Kit Fox hides were then carefully prepared with their complex symbolism. The Red Wolf was a manifestation of Thunder Man, the sky, day; the White Wolf was a manifestation of Our Grandmother, the earth, night. Together they were the gamekeepers who controlled hunting by all predators, including the Tsistsistas. It was they who sent the giant male animal protectors to punish abusive hunters, and animal-part talismans to reward the worthy. Kit Fox served the Master Wolves because she is associated with the dawn stars Rigel and Venus that mark the beginning of hunting time for the Plains wolves.

The original food of the Powerful Spirits was the great horned water serpent hunted by Thunder Man - a monster outside Our Grandmother's care. Since the respected sled dog, otherwise never eaten, was also outside Grandmother's care, because domesticated, its meat represented the serpent during the First Hunt. Domestication implied a diminution of the original spiritual power of the species - plant, animal or human.

Because game animals sustain themselves on wild plants, their flesh made humans part of the world community. After death humans fed the plants and animals. Chosen plants represented foods and medicines from above and below ground. The sacred foods were cooked for the wolf lodge by the androgynous Spirit Lancers, crazy or contrary shamans who, after their secret transformation ceremony, united the opposites of the world. The night was closed with the burning of sweet grass and the singing of spirit songs.

The next day was spent preparing the lodges representing the dens of the animal spirits. Each participant worked at transforming into his or her own spirit animal or familiar, using shamanic techniques that included pharmacology, music and theatre. Lavish animal costumes were an integral part of game-calling ceremonies in all northern Paleolithic hunting cultures; Halloween stirs deep memories.

The sacred deer-bone pipe used to call the spirit animals was then prepared. It was wrapped in sinew and covered with red ochre, then stuffed with sacramental herbs mixed with buffalo kidney fat and placed next to the buried buffalo skull.

Seven Young Wolf Women, representing the wolf spirit helpers, then went outside to construct the chute or pound into which the Master Wolves would drive the spirit animals. Daughter of Thunder and her Tsistsistas husband then ritually ushered the Master Wolves, Red and White, and Kit Fox into the world. All the Tsistsistas, except the spirit animals, who stayed in their lodges, came to see. After individually circling the earth and making the calling song, Red Wolf and White Wolf returned to the wolf den.

That night and the next day were spent calling the animal spirits with song, ceremony, symbol and sacrament. The rising of Rigel, the blue star of dawn, marked the beginning of the First Hunt.

The 2,000 year-old stone Medicine Wheel at Moose Mountain, Saskatchewan, has been shown by astronomer John Eddy to have cairn alignments pointing to the sun-associated risings of Rigel, Aldebaran and Sirius. The four hundred year-old Bighorn Mountain Medicine Wheel in Wyoming, with 28 stone spokes counting off a lunar month, also had cairn alignments toward the heliacal risings of Rigel, Aldebaran and Sirius.[52] Hawkins has shown that Stonehenge (c.1600 BC) was also aligned around the marker of midsummer sunrise, the start of wolf hunting time, so that at dawn of the summer solstice the sun rose in dead line with the altar and heel stone, the other stones marking rising or setting at the solstice or equinox of the other seasons.[53] Brennan has shown alignment to lunar risings in the megalithic monuments of Old Europe, and the oldest Sumerian temples, dating to 5000 BC, have their corners aligned to the cardinal points of the compass (Tepe Gawra), as do most later ziggurats.[54]

Just south of Saskatchewan, in the Powder River Basin on the Montana-Dakota border, the 1800 year-old Ruby site revealed a buffalo chute with the corral subtly built into the natural architecture of an arroyo. Six feet from the buffalo chute was a 39'x15' medicine lodge with eight carefully placed buffalo skulls around the southern postholes. The only other bones found in the lodge were ritually buried buffalo vertebrae, archeologically reenacting the buffalo spine scene pictured on p.14. The oldest ceremonial site in North America, the 10,000 year-old Jones-Miller site near the Montana-Wyoming border, reveals a medicine pole in a buffalo pound associated with ceremonial objects.[55]

The First Hunt continued as Our Grandmother gave the Sacred Pipe to Daughter of Thunder, who took it to the entrance of the corral and called to the animals, "I am the star of dawn." The costumed, masked and painted impersonators of the buffalo, deer, otter, wolf, bear, cougar, badger and other animals then came out of their dens. Both the herd and solitary animals were accurately portrayed and impersonated - 'contacted.'

After more calling songs, the Master Wolves and Kit Fox, aided by Spirit Lancers, went out to hunt the costumed spirit animals. Spirit animals were slain with much theatrical blood and gore, but immediately came back to life. That is, those killed came back to life by nourishing and healing humans. Anyone who wanted healing from either the animal spirits or their shaman hunters was offered it at this time.

A medicine lance which had been prepared by a shaman in the animal lodges was then placed next to a sheet of buffalo meat. By donning his skin, Daughter of Thunder asserted her dominance over Red Wolf and the animals. She and Grandmother conducted three more ritual hunts, demonstrating success using the medicine lance and the dried meat. The skin was then returned to the Red Wolf runner, who used the medicine lance and meat to demonstrate his own dominion over game. The Spirit Lancers then distributed wafers of the sanctified meat to all. The first buffalo killed in the real hunt would be smoked and sacramentally shared as well.[56]

Coyote, servant of Red Wolf, and the Spirit Lancers then led all the spirit animals in an encirclement of the camp, then into the drive lane of the chute and corral. On completion of their ritual capture, all brushed off with white sage, so as to return to ordinary consciousness.

Daughter of Thunder then gave the sacred pipe, full of powerful entheogenic herbs, to the Original Prophet, who broke the seal and lit it. The pipe was slowly smoked by all the main ritual performers, then extinguished. After more song and meditation, Thunder Man erased the sand painting of the universe and brushed all with white sage. Since spiritual communication had been achieved, the next hunt would be real.

The powerfully psychoactive beanlike seeds of the flowering shrub *Sophora secundiflora,* mescal beans, were found associated with Peyote, Mexican buckeye and shamanistic rock paintings at the 9,000 year-old Fate Bell Shelter site in Texas. They were also found at the equally old Frightful Cave site, and at the 10,000 year-old Bonfire Shelter site. At Frightful Cave mescal beans were found in every occupation level from 9500 B.P. to 570 C.E.[57]

"The use of the hallucinogenic *natema* drink [*yajé, ayahuasca*] among the Jivaro makes it possible for almost anyone to achieve the trance state essential for the practice of shamanism. Given the presence of the drug and the felt need to contact the 'real,' or supernatural, world, it is not surprising that approximately one out of every four Jivaro men is a shaman. Any adult, male or female, who desires to become such a practitioner, simply presents a gift to an already practicing shaman, who administers the *Banisteriopsis* drink and gives some of his own supernatural power - in the form of spirit helpers, or *tsentsak* - to the apprentice."[58]

All tribal cultures were shamanic, and all shamanic cultures, even the shamanically promiscuous Jivaro, distinguish between the heroic professionalism of healers and leaders, whose sophisticated psychopharmacology and yoga require hard work, and the ordinary communion of celebration and healing, which is, and always has been, the most common form of public ecstatic behavior engaged in by humans. Eliade: "...shamans do not differ from other members of the collectivity by their quest for the sacred - which is normal and universal behavior - but by their capacity for ecstatic experience, which, for the most part, is equivalent to a vocation."[59]

'Shamanism,' then, as an archetypal, that is, instinctive behavior pattern, has come down through evolutionary history both as the refined specialty of the medico-spiritual professional, and as the ordinary communion of the occasional participant. "Every Indian can obtain a 'tutelary spirit' or a 'power' of some sort that makes him capable of 'visions' and augments his reserves of the sacred; but only the shaman, by virtue of his relations with the spirits, is able to enter deeply into the supernatural world; in other words, he alone succeeds in acquiring a technique that enables him to undertake ecstatic journeys at will."[60]

Initiation into secret or functional societies, common among tribal peoples worldwide, often includes inebriation and ordeal, and is halfway between professional shamanism and ordinary communion. The Tsistsistas Spirit Lance Society was composed equally of men and women. Some of the most powerful Lightning Lancers were transvestites who united in themselves the opposites of the universe. Turn of the century observers such as Mooney, Petter and Curtis, as well as Tsistsistas participants, all mention "remarkable if not supernatural feats, such as lifting great weights, jumping extraordinary distances, throwing their fellow men about as though they were without weight, taking objects from the bottom of kettles filled with boiling soup, and dancing barefoot on hot coals. The Indians state that they used internally some herb to make it possible for them to perform these superhuman feats of strength."[61]

The eastern Algonquian Penobscot word for shaman translates as 'drum sound person.' Achterberg noted that much shaman drumming imitates the heartbeat, and pointed to studies which demonstrated that the frequency range of much shaman drumming matches the brain's theta rhythms, the measurable EEG waves associated with creativity, unusual problem-solving, vivid imagery and states of reverie.[62] "'The drum is our horse,' the shamans say."[63]

The Tungusic word 'shaman,' 'spirit person,' given academic status by the Russian anthropologists, is in fact the youngest and least complex of the Tungusic terms. Some of the others translate as 'to inhale helping spirits,' 'to reach for the soul of a sick person,' 'to induce spirit helpers to enter one's body,' and 'to perform by the campfire.'[64] Eliade's classic short definition of shamanism is "archaic techniques of ecstacy," and he stresses that the shaman's chief functions are healing and leading magico-religious rites.[65]

Ackernecht: "In a certain sense, the primitive psychotherapist uses more and stronger weapons than the modern psychotherapist. He works not only with the strength of his own personality. His rite is part of the common faith of the whole community which not seldom assists *in corpore* at his healing act or even participates in singing and dancing. The whole weight of the tribe's religion, myths, history and community spirit enters into the treatment. Inside and outside the patient he can mobilize strong psychic energies no longer available in modern medicine."[66]

The ancient world didn't separate ecstacy from healing and vision, and healing among Paleolithic peoples, worldwide, almost always includes the communal use of powerful entheogenic herbs, to which access to the animal powers of the earth is attributed. The *pharmakon*, as the Greeks called it, causes transformation. This communal transformation, this waking dreaming, can call up esoteric cultural knowledge - the identification of healing plants, for instance - that might otherwise be unavailable. Because it unleashes the brain's automatic creativity, pharmaco-shamanic ecstacy is often empirical and encyclopedic.

The Siberian Evenks, bear, moose and reindeer hunters, practiced a ritual First Hunt almost identical to that of the Tsistsistas, thus culturally confirming the archeological evidence of very ancient common ancestry with the Algonquian buffalo hunters. Anthropologists have traced bear ceremonialism from northern Scandinavia across Eurasia to the northern half of North America. Evenk ceremonialism celebrates the North Asian brown bear, as does the most ancient Tsistsistas tradition.

The cosmic bear, half animal, half human, mythologically linked with the first ancestor, was universally regarded by Siberian hunters as the source of the shaman's power of transformation. Nearly all Paleo-Siberian hunting groups buried the omnivorous bear with ritual otherwise reserved for humans. "In Siberian thought, the bear, a visitor in the middle world especially beneficial to humans, is associated with both the world above and the world below....But because the sacred mountains are entrances to the world below, in the symbolism of shamans' costumes, he represents this region of the universe more deeply than any other animal spirit. The underground dwellings of the Selkup Earth Mother, *Ylyunda kotta*, for example, are guarded by her two protectors, half-bear, half-man.... Vasilevich...believes that shamanism was originally a woman's prerogative. Anisimov...mentions that the robe of an Evenk shaman is always cut in the characteristic design of a woman's garment."[67]

The last of the Mahican bear sacrifices was held as a combination Munsee-Mahican Big House-Bear Sacrifice ritual on the Six Nations reserve (Ontario) in 1850. The ceremony required that a powerful woman dreamer be contacted by the bear spirit, who revealed the den of the sacrificial bear. Twelve ritual hunters and a leader then went to the hibernation place divined by the dreamer and led the bear to the Big House where he was ceremonially slain by the chief. The Big House itself was a projection of Ursa Major, Great Mother Bear, the ceremonial officials occupying the places of the stars. The sacred food, the bear's flesh, was the only food eaten during the twelve nights of the ceremony. Powerful herbs, transformation and rebirth were shared by all.

The Oklahoma Unami earth-renewal was initiated by a transformed bear shaman wearing a bearskin body suit. It was this bear, mounted on a buck, who herded the deer for hunters throughout the year.[68] The Yuroks of northwestern California, the westernmost Algonquian speakers, also practiced an annual medicine hunt, corralling salmon in traps built into dams spanning the annual spawning run. They say it is the "old woman who lives in the earth"and her

spirits, the animals, trees and rocks, who force women to become shamans, whereas male shamans are usually, but not always, associated
with a younger creator spirit.

"Once I was asleep on my sick-bed, when a spirit approached me.
It was a very beautiful woman....Other shamans say they have had
the vision of a woman with one-half of her face black, and the other
half red. She said: 'I am the "ayami"of your ancestors, the Shamans. I
taught them shamaning. Now I am going to teach you. The old
shamans have died off, and there is no one to heal people. You are to
become a shaman....I love you, I have no husband now, you will be
my husband and I shall be a wife unto you...' Sometimes she comes
under the aspect of an old woman, and sometimes under that of a
wolf, so she is terrible to look at. Sometimes she comes as a winged
tiger. I mount it and she takes me to show me different countries....She
has given me three assistants - ...the panther...the bear...and the tiger.
They come to me in my dreams, and appear whenever I summon
them while shamaning."[69]

Anthropologists have identified four transformation animals
among Siberian shamans: the bear, the reindeer, the deer and the
birds.[70] Just as pictured on the cave wall at Les Trois Freres, p.31, the
transformation is total, the shaman's skeleton, head, torso, arms and
legs becoming those of the animal protector or familiar. The bear is
generally associated with the powers of the earth, the bird with those
of the sky, the versatile deer with both, as well as with the middle
world. A male deer shaman's drum will be buckskin, a female deer
shaman's, doeskin. Transformation, for purposes both perceptible and
incomprehensible to the modern observer, was the object of the professional shaman.

Just as most moderns couldn't begin to approach the strength,
stamina, perceptivity and resourcefulness of an accomplished Paleolithic hunter, so too the sophisticated psychopharmacology and yoga
of accomplished shamans is well beyond the reach of most moderns.
A modern observer couldn't tell, for instance, if the buffalo shaman
actually succeeeded somehow in calling the buffalo, or if their appearance at the appointed time and place was simply an accident or
an educated guess. Shamans of all cultures insist that the communication is direct and intentional. Grinnell reports seeing two shamans
walk into a herd of buffalo and simply lead it into camp using eagle
wing fans.[71] Anthropologists consistently report very ancient methods of divination and augury used for game location which would
seem incomprehensible or ridiculous to the modern observer, and

which, nonetheless, are apparently effective.

Neihardt, who had spent years with Black Elk, was amazed to see him intentionally, and emotionally, create rain on a hilltop on an otherwise cloudless day.[72] I myself, in my early twenties, had a well-known elderly mestizo Peruvian curandero teach me, over the course of a few months, in the hills above Los Angeles, how to intentionally call the wind. Most mechanistic moderns would insist that is impossible, having completely forgotten their biological connection to the earth. It is possible, but it requires a state of consciousness not ordinarily achievable under industrial conditions. It also requires the realization that the Earth is Gaia, not merely a collection of raw materials. Calling the wind is not a parlor trick, it is yoga. Feats of healing, such as closing open wounds, can be accomplished in such a transformed state.

Schultes: "Among the Tukanoans of the northwestern Amazon, for example, older shamans assume the guise of jaguars and are feared above all others. A jaguar that attacks a human being is thought to be shaman, and any shaman suspected of such an attack may himself be killed. The spirit of the murdered shaman, however, enters another jaguar, so the danger continues. In the Colombian Putumayo, Indians turn into jaguars after taking the hallucinogenic yajé and chase deer and tapirs in the forest with great ease. Beautiful ceramic vessels from the Chavin Culture of Peru, at least three thousand years old, clearly depict jaguars in association with the narcotic San Pedro cactus. Throughout South America, a number of indigenous names for 'varieties'of hallucinogens refer to the jaguar, as among the Kamsa of Colombia, who call one of their strongest hallucinogenic plants *mits-kway borrachero* (intoxicant of the jaguar). The Kubeo of the Colombian Amazon relate that caapi-intoxication causes the men to see people in the bright colors of the jaguar."[73]

Churchland: "The classical distinction into 'five senses' is notoriously inept, since there are receptors not only for taste, smell, sound, sight, and touch but for a miscellany of other things as well. There are proprioceptors for detecting changes in position of the head, kinesthetic receptors in the muscles and the tendons to detect stretch, receptors for visceral distension and for lung stretch, and receptors in the carotid arteries to detect levels of oxygen in the arterial blood....the category 'touch' rakes together diverse perceptions, including light touch, erotic sensations, light and deep pressure, vibration, a variety of temperature sensations, and a wide assortment of painful sensations."

"Snug within the confines of our own perceptual world, it is jolting to realize that other animals are richly receptive where we are stony blind. Bees can detect ultraviolet light; snakes have pits for electromagnetic waves in the infrared range; flies have gyroscopic strain gauges; aquatic vertebrates can detect water displacement by means of lateral-line organs; pigeons have ferromagnets for orienting with respect to the earth's magnetic field, sharks can pick up and use low frequency (0.1-20 Hz) electric fields; electric fish are sensitive to high frequency (50-5,000 Hz) current. A human submerging into the ocean depths finds an engulfing silence, but for an electric fish the watery world is rich in electro-magnetic events, and it uses electrolocation and electrocommunication to great advantage... The world as perceived by humans is not the world as perceived by any organism. Rather, it is that narrow dimension of the world evolution has permitted our specialized receptors to detect."[74] "If the doors of perception were cleansed," wrote the great shaman William Blake, "every thing would appear to man as it is, infinite."[75]

Eliade: "All over the world learning the language of animals, especially of birds, is equivalent to knowing the secrets of nature and hence to being able to prophesy. Bird language is usually learned by eating snake or some other reputedly magical animal. These animals can reveal the secrets of the future because they are thought to be receptacles of the souls of the dead or epiphanies of the gods. Learning their language, imitating their voice, is equivalent to ability to communicate with the beyond and the heavens. We shall again come upon this same identification with an animal, especially a bird, when we discuss the shaman's costume and magical flight. Birds are psychopomps. Becoming a bird oneself or being accompanied by a bird indicates the capacity, while still alive, to undertake the ecstatic journey to the sky and the beyond."[76]

Contemporary neuroscience has no idea where the distinction between cognitive and noncognitive processes lies. The best working model Professor Churchland can suggest for the brain is a living hologram.[77] The historical achievements of Paleolithic shamanism are strong empirical proof that both extrasensory perception, which can be empirically demonstrated but not explained, and creative genius are at work. They include the discovery of virtually all known medicinal plants and innumerable ways of employing them, the invention of local and general anesthesia, midwifery, surgery, transfusion, organ replacement, vaccination, hypodermic injection and acupuncture.

Auric vision is a power consistently attributed to the ancient shamans. Auric (Kirlian) photography confirmed the reality of the acupuncture points in 1957; ancient Chinese shamans drew accurate schematics of the dozens of bodily points, which show up as white light on the Kirlian photographs, thousands of years ago. Obviously, they were using their 'biological technology' to see the white light.

The intellectual, social and technological contribution of Paleolithic shamanism is immeasurable. Virtually all the surviving Bronze Age mythology, for instance, attributes the discovery of astronomy, mythology, writing and metallurgy to the shamans. Anthropologists are consistently amazed at the encyclopedic genius, botanical or poetical, they encounter in many shamans. One anthropologist reported an Amazonian shaman who could accurately discuss the properties of more than 2000 plants.

The many Iron Age shamans known as Homer could sing both *The Iliad* and *The Odyssey* from memory. These book-length epic poems, which date from the events they describe, are hundreds of years older than the Ionian Homers who finally set them down in writing. They could not have survived to have been recorded in the eighth century BC had they not been memorized by singing shamans over the course of generations. Imagine the power of the intellect that could sing *The Iliad* from memory. The anthropological literature is full of examples of shamans capable of as much as a hundred continuous hours of repeatable versification, a feat very few, if any, moderns could match.[78] Poetry, of course, is the shamanic invention *par excellence*. *Strophe* (verse) means 'a turning,' and the Latin *ballare*, from which ballad, means 'to dance.'

COPPER

As the European glaciers receded at the end of the Paleolithic, the sea level rose and the vegetation ceased to support great herds of reindeer, bison and horse. Pine forest replaced tundra and deciduous forest replaced pine. Tundra team hunters became individual forest hunters, employing dogs (wolves) and a sharpened kill technology. This included nets, spear-throwers, fish hooks, toggling harpoons and the awesome bow and arrow. Elusive red and roe deer, boar, fish and aquatic mammals replaced the great herds on the Mesolithic menu, and plants were gathered more assiduously.

Climatic factors, however, don't explain the independent rise of agriculture in those areas that didn't experience major climatic change, such as the Near East and Mesoamerica. The evolution of human technology and trade seems to have played a major role in the 'Neolithic Revolution,' as did the population pressure inherent in successful adaptation.

Hunter-gatherers obviously take advantage of the easiest pickings, following a herd or crop in season. The broader the spectrum of food sources in a given area, the less need to pull up stakes in search of food. The richest food areas are good fishing grounds and mountainous regions with adjacent valleys and plains. Obviously montane areas bordering good fishing grounds are ideal. The Mesolithic is characterized by rich, semi-sedentary communities supported by a broad spectrum of wild resources: acquatic foods, wild fowl, small and large game and a very wide array of plants.

Their environmental manipulation included animal domestication, improved ground stone technology, sophisticated techniques of food storage and better traps and tools. The earliest woven cord we have dates to 15,000 BC, from Lascaux, and the earliest netting and cloth to c.7500 BC in the Near East and c.8500 in the Americas. The plant fibers employed include hemp, flax, nettle, ramie, jute, sisal, elm, linden, willow, esparto, maguey, yucca and innumerable others; animal hair was also popular.[79]

In 1967, Harlan, with a flint sickle, harvested enough wild wheat in one hour to yield one kilo of clean grain - grain twice as rich in protein as domestic wheat.[80] In three weeks a family could harvest a metric ton of clean wheat, more than it could eat in a year. Mesolithic communities are found with a profusion of reaping knives, querns, pestles, mortars and clay-lined storage pits for processing and storing wild grains, nuts, roots and berries.

It is likely that the rich coastal or montane communities themselves first evolved agriculture, which was then used more intensively by culturally connected offshoots. The then well-watered hill country of Southwestern Asia reveals the ancestors of many early cultigens. It was the daughter groups of these well-established, often overpopulated Mesolithic communities, expanding to areas less well-supplied by nature, that felt the pressure to rely on domesticates.

Some of our most ancient samples (c.7500 BC) of morphologically domesticated grain, emmer wheat, come from areas of southwest Iran well outside the plant's present wild range, indicating deliberate attempts to reproduce the dense natural stands necessary for profitable harvest. Our first evidence of irrigation comes from the same area, the lowland steppe of Khuzistan, south of ancient Susa, east of Mesopotamia, a dry, treeless plain that produces drought-resistant, portable seeds with a very long shelf-life. It was in hearth areas like this that the improved Mesolithic subsistence technology became the first human industrial engine - agriculture. Favorable mutations, such as multiple grain heads, toughening of the spine, ears which didn't shatter on ripening and softening of the chaff were seized upon, as was tameness and wooliness in sheep.

One way to look at the birth of agriculture is simply to list the areas of origin in *The Oxford Book of Food Plants*. These plants are both the economic and ecological foundation of human industrial culture. Obviously the attribution of any one cultigen is both technical and debatable, and connecting areas overlap. This is just a broad sketch of the general consensus:

W.Asia	Asia Mnr-Medit	Europe/Arctic	East Asia
Wheats	Einkorn Wheat	Oat	Rice
Common Millet	Olive	Barley	Foxtl.Millet
Chick Pea	Rye	Carrot	Lotus
Garlic	Hazelnut	Sweet Chestnut	Ch.W.Chestnt
Soybean	Pine Kernels	Broad Bean	Peach
Grapes	Sweet Cherry	Medlar	Apricot
Fig	Bay Laurel	Raspberry	Orange
Mulberry	Saffron	Blackberry	Lemon
Pomegranate	Capers	Gooseberry	Citron
Horseradish	Fenugreek	English Wheat	Kumquat
Chervil	Coriander	Black Mustard	Persimmon
Quince	Cumin	Hop	Wineberry
Emmer Wheat	Fennel	Dill	Tangerine
Pistachio	Marjoram	Sage	Litchi
Barley	Thyme	Tarragon	Tea
Almond	Leek	Filbert	Hemp

W.Asia	Asia Mnr-Medit	Europe/Arctic	East Asia
Pea	Rosemary	Chamomile	Endive
Lentil	Summer Savory	Parsley	Ch. Cabbage
Date Palm	Lemon Balm	Angelica	Welsh Onion
	Globe Artichoke	Chicory	
		Wild Cabbage	
		Cauliflower	
		Broccoli	
		Kohlrabi	
		Rhubarb	
		Asparagus	
		Turnip	
		Parsnip	
		Chervil	

Americas	Africa	India-Trop.Asia	Mltiple/Unkn
Maize	Sorghum	Finger Millet	Walnut
Peanut	Bulrush Millet	Lotus	Apples
Sunflower	Oil Palm	Mung Bean	Pears
Black Walnut	Sesame	Lime	Rape
Pecan	Pigeon Pea	Mango	Currants
Brazil	Cowpea	Tea	Cranberry
Cashew	Coffee	Cucumber	Squash
Runner Bean	Water Melon	Egg Plant	Plums
Pumpkins	Okra	Banana	Licorice
Kidney Bean	Melons	Sugar Cane	Caraway
Butter Bean		Coconut	Celery
Strawberry		Macadamia	Lettuce
Blueberry		Lablab	Spinach
Grapefruit		Rambutan	Onion
Pineapple		Palmyra Palm	Chives
Cocoa		Black Pepper	Beet
Papaya		Nutmeg	Radish
Avocado		Cinnamon	Flax
Gherkin		Cardamoms	
Tomato		Cloves	
Jack Bean		Ginger	
Passion Fruit		Turmeric	
Guava		Basil	
Sweet Pepper		Yam	
Red Pepper			
Vanilla			
Allspice			
Potato			
Jerusalem Artichoke			
Cassava			
Sweet Potato			

Early hunter-gatherer-farmer settlements had a very long life, thousands of years, revealing no sharp break between the evolved hunter-gatherer subsistence patterns and early farming. Rather a very slow increase in reliance on domesticates is revealed. The desert valley of Tehuacán, 150 miles south of Mexico City, shows a slowly growing population between 8000 and 500 BC, finally culminating in the critical mass necessary to support a stratified industrial society.

Originally, nomadic family groups gathered together to form macrobands in the lush wet season, to effectively compete for the wild harvest with the animals. Twelve recent sites of major excavation provide clear evidence of a gradual increase in reliance on domesticated plants and animals, and the slow conversion of Tehuacán culture into permanent macrobands. By 1000 BC the evolved Tehuacán villages of up to 300 people reveal a matristic religion, with mostly female Goddess figurines and rich female burials. This indicates a matrilineal culture, just as in Neolithic Europe, the Near East and Asia.[81] Trade and craft specialization evolved, as well as a complex agriculture susceptible to centralized management.

Throughout the Near East and Europe, obsidian, the black volcanic glass, sharp and hard as a rock, was prized for spearheads, daggers, arrowheads and mirrors. Long distance trade in obsidian, which can be mined in only a few places, can be demonstrated as far back as 9,000 BC. Jericho, in 8300 BC, traded for the same Anatolian obsidian, from Catal Huyuk, as did Khuzistan, thus the cultural contact, from Israel to Turkey to Iran, can be shown to predate agriculture. Jericho, an international entrepot, commanded the Red Sea resources of salt, bitumen (tar/glue) and sulphur ('brimstone'for firing/pigment/metallurgy).[82] It supported about 2500 people, and its wealth made it a military target, hence the thick walls, first built c.7500 BC and repeatedly rebuilt.

Obsidian from Melos, in the Greek Cyclades, found its way throughout Crete, Italy and Egypt in Neolithic times, as did emery, the corrosive polishing stone essential for lapidary work, from Melos' sister island of Naxos.[83] The first proof of long-distance trade in finished products in Khuzistan are the many highly-polished limestone and alabaster mushroom stones, identical to those found in graves hundreds of miles to the west near the Tigris River.[84] Thus the early cultigens found a ready international market.

Pottery making represents the evolution of working clay into figurines, weaving, container-making, coloring with mineral pigments and firing, all techniques used for millennia prior to the first appearance of pottery, about 6500 BC in Iran and Anatolia. When the red ore cuprite, the green ore malachite or the blue ore azurite is heated, bright globules of pure copper drip out. The earliest known metal artifacts are copper, lead and gold beads, tubes, pins and needles from Catal Huyuk in Anatolia, near the metal- and mineral-rich Taurus Mountains, c.6500 BC.

Was it the pottery kiln that became the metal smelter, or the smelter the kiln? Did the bread oven give birth to both? The priestesses at Catal Huyuk could tell you. Some of the metal and stone work done at Catal Huyuk, such as the polishing of obsidian to a smooth mirror sheen and the drilling of hair-thin holes through solid rock, was so sophisticated that archeologists still can't figure out how they did it. At its height, c.5800 BC, the 30-acre town supported 7,000 inhabitants. It was the greatest trading center of the Western Neolithic. Despite its size, there is no evidence of totalitarian stratification, although there is plenty of evidence of long-distance trade in minerals, especially obsidian, which they exchanged for Syrian flint.

Their organization was tribal and collectivist, revealing very little class structure, but considerable craft specialization, such as farming, herding, hunting, potting, carpentry, weaving, painting and metallurgy.[85] Of 300 excavated rooms, 88 had painted walls, most indicating a religious function. Gimbutas: "There are no depictions of arms (weapons used against other humans) in Paleolithic cave paintings, nor are there remains of weapons used by man against man during the Neolithic of Old Europe. From some hundred and fifty paintings that survived at Catal Huyuk, there is not one scene of conflict or fighting, or of war or torture."[86] The same can be said for the scores of frescoes found at the sprawling Neolithic-Bronze Age Cretan center of Knossos, where the artistic concentration, as at Catal Huyuk, was on pharmaco-shamanic transformation and communion with the beauty and power of nature.

There are no male graves at Catal Huyuk, or anywhere else in Neolithic Europe, to match the rich graves of prominent older women or royal girls. This indicates a matrilineal culture, as does the surviving mythology. Throughout Neolithic Europe temples were placed close to other houses, indicating a familial religion, not one of domination. There are no acropolises, prominent central buildings, heavy fortifications or military burials of prominent male chiefs. There are main houses around which the community focused, but they seem to have been simply those of stem families of matrilineal descent.

The voluminous evidence from burials indicates very little distinction between rich and poor, as if the gap wasn't that great. Men were honored with maces, flint firestones (often with sulphur or pyrite hammerstones in a leather kit), stone chisels, seashell jewelry (valued objects of trade), flint scrapers and obsidian knives and arrowheads, indicating a respect for their fighting, woodworking, trading and hunting skills. Males were also found with quernstones for grinding grain and females were found with woodworking tools. Generally, female graves were found with tools for sewing, basketry and farming, jewelry, obsidian mirrors, cosmetics, pottery, ochre, quernstones and symbolic religious items.[87]

The most frequent image seen at Catal Huyuk is a frog-shaped woman giving birth, a figure of cthonic (underground, earthly, vegetal) transformation and rebirth. It is a shamanic image remarkably similar to the *yajé* imagery produced by contemporary Tukano shamans, and to the stone amulets found throughout the European Upper Paleolithic. As in the Amazon, the Goddess' transformation animals were vultures, leopards and deer.

The priestesses at Catal Huyuk dressed as vultures. Seven huge Griffon vultures are painted on the walls of an early-level shrine, dating to c.6200 BC. They are shown picking over the bones of the decapitated dead as a preliminary to their rebirth.[88] On the wall of one shrine, between the huge bull head and the shrine post, a pair of plaster female breasts was suspended. Each breast contained the complete skull of a Griffon vulture, the beak protruding through each nipple, offering 'vulture milk' to the communicants, entheogenic milk for visitation with the dead.[89] To this day the Southern Kwakiutl of British Columbia dance with the 'cannibal birds' during their winter communion with the ancestor spirits, wearing masks, and taking entheogens similar to those of the vulture priestesses of Catal Huyuk.[90] Under the largest temple at Catal Huyuk, a Queen-Priestess was found buried with the jaws of three tusked wild boars, truly ferocious scavengers of death, arranged around her head.

James Mellaart, excavator of Catal Huyuk: "As a symbol of male fertility an aurochs bull or a large ram was more impressive than man himself and the power of wild life and death was suitably symbolized by the leopard, the largest and fiercest wild animal in the region; in the destructive ferocity of the boar or in the impressive spectacle of flocks of Griffon vultures."[91] Few anthropomorphic male gods were found; males were usually, but not always, depicted as rams or bulls.

Human skulls were found buried beneath the wild bull skulls which had been prominently set into many of the shrine walls at Catal Huyuk. One large Goddess figure shows her giving birth to a bull's head; others show her giving birth to rams. A large clay figurine from the shrine in Level II (5750 BC) shows the Goddess supported by two leopards giving birth.[92] A limestone holy trinity was found: the Mother Goddess and her adult daughter, standing next to their leopards, and a boy god, riding his leopard.[93] A small stone plaque shows an adult man and woman embracing in one frame, and the woman is shown with her child in the other. Anthropomorphic male gods are shown procreating, riding their bulls and hunting in leopard-skin caps.

Mellaart: "As it seems extremely unlikely that the entire population, or even all the males, were dressed in leopard-skins, we may assume that the hunters here represented were a small section of the populace entitled to this ceremonial dress, in other words the priesthood. It seems unlikely that at this period the entire able manhood of Catal Huyuk, which must run into the thousands, partook in annual hunting-rites and it is far more likely that the conduct of such rites was entrusted to a select body of priests. That this shrine was devoted to the hunt seems beyond reasonable doubt and it may be significant that the second shrine nearby was entirely decorated with floral symbols and kilims [woven mats], symbols of agriculture and weaving, occupations pre-eminently associated with women....Sometime during the fifty-eighth century BC agriculture finally triumphed over the age old occupation of hunting and with it the power of woman increased: this much is clear from the almost total disappearance of male statues in the cult, a process which, beginning in Catal Huyuk II [5750 BC], reaches its climax in the somewhat later cultures of Hacilar."[94]

The Neolithic impulse stresses the creative hearth and human-engineered fertility, the special sphere of women. Agriculture, weaving, pottery, metallurgy, medicine, astronomy, calendrical counting, mythology and writing are largely matristic inventions. As agriculture was equated with the Goddess, the bull was equated with the androgynous principle of fertility that comes to life in the womb, which it resembles. The horns can be seen as the fallopian tubes and the head as the uterus; the shapes are an exact match.[95] This is, of course, a logical extension of the thought of Paleolithic hunting culture, which depended on the herds for life. Bull heads were often reproduced in the Goddess' womb, or shown giving birth, between the horns, to the Butterfly or Bee Goddess, a female shaman in a state of ecstatic transformation.[96] This is a common Cretan image.

Another common Cretan expression of divine possession was the depiction of a votary seated in a swing (p.77) which is suspended from two huge bull horns, with a dove, symbolizing the visitation of the Holy Spirit, perched on each horn.[97] A Creto-Mycenaean 'bull-flower' krater shows two bulls with bulging 'floating' eyes joining horns over a large magical plant exuding numinous dots; the bulls are covered with magical signs, and other numinous plants grow toward them.[98] Thousands of bull-head images have been recovered from Neolithic to Iron Age levels. They are consistently shown sprouting transformed shamans and magical plants, many with holes between the horns for the insertion of the stem of the sacramental plant itself.

Of the Goddess symbolism recovered from Europe's hundreds of well-excavated sites, an enormous percentage is painted or engraved on drinking vessels. Virtually all the drinking vessels display entheogenic symbolism, and virtually all Neolithic and Bronze Age temples and shrines yield a profusion of cups, bowls, vases, funnels and ladles. In fact most Neolithic houses reveal a corner shrine with the same paraphernalia. Archeologists often call these 'libation' vessels, when, in fact, they are clearly communal drinking vessels.

One communion bowl from Romania, c.4400 BC, has a voluptuous bird-headed woman rising out of the center of the bowl, as if the contents of the bowl were identical to the magical milk from her breasts.[99] One vase-mug from Yugoslavia, c.5000 BC, is shaped like a stout woman, with chubby legs and prominent vulva. Whoever drank from that was drinking from the belly of the Goddess herself.[100]

Sir Arthur Evans, the seminal genius who excavated Knossos, Crete's sprawling complex of Neolithic and Bronze Age palaces, noticed that "The plant designs of the frescoes are in their essence simply accessories to the main subjects presented, which are human or animal figures. On the pottery, however, this essential feature is omitted, and only the vegetable details are selected for reproduction."[101] These included entheogens and anodynes like bearded barley, opium poppies and the psychoactive bulbs - lilies, hyacinths and saffron.

"Moreover," adds Gimbutas, "the symbolism of Old Europe, 6500-3500 BC, provides an essential key to understanding Paleolithic religion, since many of the images are continuous."[102] It was she who pointed out to Wasson that, down to the present, *Amanita muscaria* ('Soma') is enjoyed at wedding feasts and other celebrations in parts of her native rural Lithuania, and that the Lithuanians had an ancient tradition of exporting quantities of the mushrooms to Lapp shamans in the Far North.[103]

Most Neolithic cultures, as most Upper Paleolithic, engaged in the widespread secondary ritual burial of skulls and the use of red ochre on human bones. Given the undoubted continuity of Neolithic European culture with the Upper Paleolithic, it is obvious that the Neolithic vases and goblets, as the Paleolithic, were designed more for ingestion than libation. 'Libation,' as a substitute for ingestion, is an historically late symbolic trick of God-Kings, or Queens, who insisted that only they or their minions were allowed to ingest the empowering entheogens. If any 'libation' was offered to Grandmother

Earth by tribal Neolithic people, it was offered as a share in the communal drinking and smoking. The ritual vase below is from Knossos.

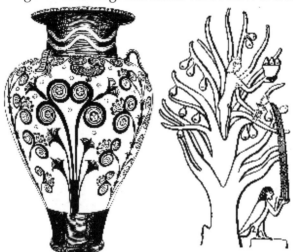

Throughout southern Neolithic Europe, in the lakeshore villages of north Italy and Switzerland, for instance, opium was a major crop, and its association with Cretan and Greek ecstatic rites is certain.[104] Hemp rope was found in substantial quantities in Narva settlements between the Baltic Sea and the Bay of Finland, dating to c.3500 BC.[105]

The Indo-European word for hemp, *kannabis*, is preserved in Greek, Albanian, Germanic, Slavic and Baltic, but is unknown among eastern Indo-European speakers. 'Poppy' likewise has a limited Indo-European linguistic range. Since the linguistic distribution coincides with the archeological evidence of cultivation, Gimbutas suggests that this indicates the original area of cultivation encountered by the Indo-European invaders.[106] This, of course, doesn't settle the question of the 'origin' of hemp, which is also known from Neolithic China. But Neolithic people didn't grow pot or opium, brew barley[107] or pick mushrooms to 'libate' - they smoked and drank. As the ancient *Rg Veda* says of Soma, "...thou sittest in the vessels, having been pressed for Indra, inebriating drink, which inebriates, supreme mainstay of heaven."[108]

The bear-legged, ring-handled mugs from the Danilo culture of the Balkan Adriatic coast, c.6000 BC, were designed to feed 'bear-juice' to the communicants, not to 'offer' anything to some theological abstraction. A delightful terracotta bear from the Cyclades, c.2700 BC, himself drinks from the bowl he is holding.[109] Equally shamanic are the Vinca remains of the central Balkans, c.5200 BC, revealing the Bird Goddess as the main deity, often as a vase. We see Snake Goddesses,

Bear Mothers - that is, transformed bear-headed women holding human babies - and Bird Mothers. The Vinca remains also include male satyrs almost identical to the 17,000 year-old transformed shamans drawn on the cave walls at Les Trois Freres (p. 31). There are also owl-faced ritual vases, that is, vases with floating eyes. In many cases these drinking vessels were painstakingly carved from their most expensive stones - marble, alabaster and opalite.

Another consistent feature of the Neolithic temple and shrine assemblages are kernoi, ceremonial footed dishes with a large central bowl encircled by many small cups, obviously for sharing the contents of the central bowl.[110] Above left from Malia, Crete, c. 1500 BC, above right from the island of Samos, c. 650 BC. Below left from Melos, also c.650 BC. Below right is the famous kernos found at Classical Eleusis. It was also the symbol of initiation carved into the walls of the great temple. Wasson, Ruck and Hofmann have shown that the kernos was used for sharing entheogenic brew made from the microscopic mushroom *Claviceps purpurea*, the mold that grows on barley and wheat, mainstay crops of Old Europe. The Athenian Eleusinian rite, according to both its own mythology and the archeological record, was a Mycenaean import from Crete, the last island survival of the great Old European, pre-Indo-European, civilizations.

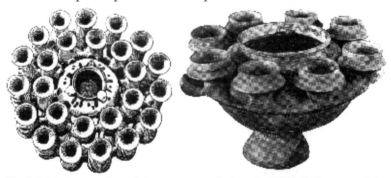

'Delphi,' the ancient Mycenaean shrine (c.1350 BC) turned into a Classical Greek institution, means 'womb,' *delphys*. The word is also related to *delphis*, 'dolphin,' the incarnation of the sea, the womb from which Crete sprang. Some Neolithic Goddess figurines have a small plant in place of the vulva, an overt reference to the food of the Goddess used to travel to the *fons et origo*.[111] The Hagar Qim temple on Malta, dating to about 3300 BC, housed a triangular altar stone, symbolic of the Goddess' pubic triangle. The Goddess' womb is also frequently associated with fish and snakes, other archetypal symbols of death and ecstatic regeneration.

That the Neolithic temple was conceived as the womb of the Goddess is indisputable. The dolmens, the narrow stone entrances of the 'anthropomorphic' megalithic tombs of West Europe, c.4500-3000 BC, were used as passages of 'rebirth' after 'incubation' in the tomb/womb, just as in Melanesia; they were stone birth canals.[112] Most Neolithic graves are seed- egg- or womb-shaped, indicating 'planting' for rebirth. Many of the ancient clay temple models we have show the temple as the belly of the Goddess, whose head is the chimney.[113] The *omphalos*, the stone 'navel' of the earth, was conceived as the center of Neolithic shrines, the place from which new life arose. I still remember cracking my mother up, when, as a 5-year-old, I described my birth as punching through her belly button. The thought came naturally.

Within the Hagar Qim temple was a stone table-altar into which had been carved a bowl. It was decorated in front with a tree of life growing from a pot, an obvious reference to the contents of the bowl. Next to it was a standing slab, a 'baetylic pillar,' with floating eyes, double-spiral 'oculi' out of which grew sacred plants. In the temple's central courtyard were two large, carefully carved mushroom-shaped limestone altars with cups carved into the stone mushroom caps, obviously to hold the sacred mushroom juice.[114]

Sacred mushroom stones, dead ringers in size and shape for un-opened *Amanita muscaria* mushrooms (above), complete with the un-usual stem and foot and the cap's unique striations, were found in the passage graves of Portugal, c.3000 BC.[115] I have taken *Amanita muscaria* mushrooms once a year for many years. It certainly doesn't surprise me that they were assumed to be useful to those needing rebirth. Many of the mushroom stones of the Maya highlands depict an ecstatic shaman in the mushroom's stem with a halo, extending to the mushroom's cap, around the head. That is, the shaman, as above, is pictured as an ecstatic mushroom.

Wasson discussed the Aztec sculpture Xochipilli, 'Prince of Flow-ers,' below, on display in Mexico's National Museum of Anthropol-ogy.[116] A mesmerized shaman, squatting atop a rectangular stone base, stares skyward. Both the base and the shaman are covered with im-ages of floating mushrooms and other identifiable entheogenic flow-ers. The statue comes from the slopes of Popocatepetl, from whence Heim introduced the traditional Mexican entheogen *Psilocybe aztecorum* to science. The mushrooms on the Aztec sculpture are dead ringers for Heim's *Psilocybe* mushrooms.[117] The base also depicts a butterfly, archetypal symbol of the soul, feasting on a mushroom, and numerous other clear naturalistic carvings of uniquely identifiable entheogens, such as morning glories.

Vinca mushroom stones, from near Belgrade, c.5000 BC, were made from their most valued green rock crystal.[118] One painting in the Levantine rock art from southeastern Spain, c.7000 BC, shows about 20 ecstatic women, men, children, goats and dogs dancing around two tree-size mushrooms.[119] A virtually identical scene, sculpted in clay, survives, as do many mushroom stones, from the Mexico of 2,500 years ago.[120]

Evans unearthed a gold signet ring from Knossos, below, c.1500 BC, which shows a young male God, floating in mid-air, greeting the Great Goddess. Inside her sanctuary, on top of which grows a sacred tree, stands a mushroom, as large as the young male God, as the central object.[121] The 'baetylic pillar,' as archeologists call it, is often depicted as a mushroom.

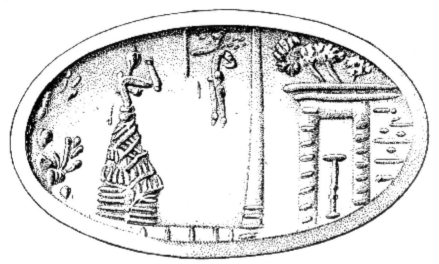

A giant dancing Cow Goddess, an African woman twenty times larger than her fellow dancers, wearing huge bull horns from which emanate a sparkling aura, painted as numinous white dots, was left on the cliff walls of Tassili, in a once-green central Sahara. Another great painting left by these nomadic cattle herders, c.2000 BC, shows a transformed mushroom-shaman with bulging bee eyes and antennae, a human body sprouting mushrooms from every pore, literally outlined in mushrooms, and a fantastic aura.

Many warm-weather psychoactive mushrooms, such as the *Psilocybe* varieties, *Stropharia cubensis* and *Paneolus sphinctrinus* strongly prefer cow dung as a medium. The natives of Bali cultivate *Copelandia cyanescens* on cow and buffalo dung in their gardens for their most joyful religious festivals.[122] One Tassili rock painting shows a line of dancing mushroom-headed people, each holding a mushroom, in a field of floating mushooms, quite like Disney's dancing mushrooms in *Fantasia*. The Tassili shamans were expressing one more reason why the Cow Goddess was viewed as the Mother of All Gifts, Hathor, Pandora.[123]

The artistic level achieved by many Neolithic cultures is extraordinary. The graphite- and gold-painted pottery produced by the Karanovo civilization of central Bulgaria in 4700 BC proves the existence of very sophisticated firing techniques. The Karanovo and Cucuteni cultures traded copper and gold artifacts and precious stones as well as their extraordinary pottery with each other. The largest Cucuteni town in western Ukraine, dating to about 3700 BC, contained 2,000 houses, about 16,000 people.

Ceramic workshops were found there in two-story buildings, the top floors of which were apparently temples. The many clay temple models recovered show only women producing pottery in the downstairs temple workshops. Cucuteni pottery, employing the wheel, rivals anything the world produced for the next thousand years. Wheeled vehicles are depicted in both Cucuteni and Karanovo layers from about 4500 BC. A basic element of Cucuteni pottery design was the caduceus, or at least two s-shaped snakes creating an 'energy field,' drawn as floating lines, where their heads met.[124]

The snake, archetypal symbol of earthly regeneration and herbal healing, was a major motif of Neolithic art, both sacred and secular. An 8,000 year-old cult vessel from Yugoslavia has two bird-headed snakes guarding the contents of a ritual bowl.[125] A 6500 year-old vase from Romania shows snakes encircling the concentric circles of the world, "making the world roll" as Gimbutas says.

Horned snakes, or horned animals in association with snakes, or bird-headed Goddesses wrapped in snakes, or Goddesses with snakes for hair, or schematic snakes, are reproduced on sacred drinking vessels, shrine Goddesses and pottery more frequently than any other imagery, from the Ukraine to Crete, from 8,000 to 1500 BC. "The pregnant figurines of the seventh and sixth millennia BC are nude, while the pregnant ladies of the fifth and fourth millennia are exquisitely clothed except for the abdomen, which is exposed and on which lies a sacred snake."[126]

Female Neolithic images, many with the head of a snake or bird, outnumber male images 30 to 1.[127] Like the bison-men of the Upper Paleolithic caves, the male god's principal Neolithic manifestation was in the form of a bull or bull-man, the Son of His Mother. The Snake-Bird Goddess, a figure of cthonic transformation and ecstatic resurrection, was the original Creatrix.

Evans: "The Gournia...relics dedicated to the snake cult are associated with small clay figures of doves and a relief showing the Double Axe./These conjunctions are singularly illuminating since they reveal the fact that the Snake Goddess herself represents only another aspect of the Minoan Lady of the Dove, while the Double Axe itself was connected with both. Just as the celestial inspiration descends in bird form either on the image of the divinity itself or on that of its votary...so the spirit of the Nether World, in serpent form, makes its ascent to a similar position from the earth itself."[128] The Double Axe, then, cuts both ways.[129]

Jung: "Archetypes are systems of readiness for action, and at the same time images and emotions. They are inherited with the brain structure - indeed, they are its psychic aspect. They represent, on the one hand, a very strong instinctive conservatism, while on the other hand they are the most effective means conceivable of instinctive adaptation. They are thus, essentially, the cthonic portion of the psyche, if we may use such an expression - that portion through which the psyche is attached to nature, or in which its link with the earth and the world appears at its most tangible. The psychic influence of the earth and its laws is seen most clearly in these primordial images."[130]

Primary among them, the snake, archetypal image of ecstatic creativity and the life force, of evolutionary adaptation, in all Neolithic cultures known. Gimbutas: "The snake is a transfunctional symbol; it permeates all themes of Old European symbolism. Its vital influence was felt not only in life creation, but also in fertility and increase, and particularly in the regeneration of dying life energy. Combined with magical plants, the snake's powers were potent in healing and creating life anew. A vertically winding snake symbolized ascending life force, viewed as a column of life rising from caves and tombs, and was an interchangeable symbol with the tree of life and spinal cord."[131]

The snake, the phallus, the mushroom and the bull, of course, aren't really separable images, as both Neolithic art and contemporary dreams suggest. Gimbutas: "The whole group of interconnected symbols - phallus (or cylinder, mushroom and conical cap), ithyphallic animal-masked man, goat-man and the bull-man - represents a male stimulating principle in nature without whose influence nothing would grow and thrive....The 'bisexualism' of the water-bird divinity is apparent in the emphasis on the long neck of the bird symbolically linked with the phallus or the snake from Upper Paleolithic times and onwards through many millennia....The image of a phallic Bird Goddess dominates during the seventh and sixth millennia in the Aegean and the Balkans. Sometimes she is a life-like erect phallus with small wings and a posterior of a woman, which, if seen in profile, is readily identifiable as a bird's body and tail....'Bisexualism' is reflected in bird-shaped vases with cylindrical necks and....in representations of hermaphroditic figurines of the Vinca culture having male genital organs and female breasts." (Parenthesis hers.)

"The 'Fertility Goddess' or 'Mother Goddess' is a more complex image than most people think. She was not only the Mother Goddess who commands fertility, or the Lady of the Beasts who governs the fecundity of animals and all wild nature, or the frightening Mother Terrible, but a composite image with traits accumulated from both the pre-agricultural and agricultural eras....Throughout the Neolithic period her head is phallus-shaped suggesting her androgynous nature, and its derivation from Paleolithic times...divine bisexuality stresses her absolute power."[132]

Marshack reproduces a 20,000 year-old lunar counting bone which is simply a phallic head with two pendulous breasts. A 16,000 year-old lunar counting baton from France is a phallic bone with a vulva. A Goddess figure from Hungary, c.5400 BC, is shaped like a penis and testicles.[133] Just as it was obvious that life came from the womb or egg, so it was obvious that the conjunction of the sexes produced a numinous power. Respect for the power of the Bull was in no way contrary to respect for the Goddess, who bore the Bull.

Many of the magical signs found on Old European pottery from 6000 to 4000 BC are direct descendants of Upper Paleolithic symbols, such as the V sign, used to indicate the Goddess' pubic triangle on

19,000 year-old ivory figurines from the Ukraine. The inverted V sign was used to indicate the cap of sacred mushrooms. Snakes, flowers, eyes, ears, waves, chevrons and x's are equally ancient. These signs evolved into linguistic magical signs, consistently found in all Old European cultures. They include moon-counting lines and circles, triangles, meanders, v's, m's, n's, squares, s's, diamonds, arcs, y's, +'s, tridents, bidents, swastikas, bird's feet, concentric circles, houses and numerous other geometric and schematic patterns.[134]

The 'sacral' ivy-leaf, a standard device of Cretan potters for millennia, became a letter in both Linear A and B.[135] Gimbutas, organizing linguistic work that began with Evans, has graphed 68 Old European signs that can be shown to be identical to either Cretan Linear A or Classical Cypriot syllabic phonemes, the two great island survivals of this Old European, pre-Indo-European, language.[136] This script, which predates the earliest evolved temple-palace script of Old Sumer by 2000 years, isn't a bureaucratic device designed to manage the tax rolls, as in Sumer, but magical script, produced only on religious items. The Near Eastern scripts, of course, also originated in their predecessor Neolithic communities, thus the evolution is contemporaneous.

The Egyptian name for their hieroglyphs, originally used only for sacral purposes, was 'speech of the gods.'[137] We have 8,000 year-old stamp seals from Macedonia designed to leave their geometric impressions in wet clay, that is, moveable type. We also have Macedonian cylinder seals, designed to be rolled over the wet clay. This script is found only on figurines, thrones, temple models, altars, communion vases, sacred bread models, pendants, plaques and spindle whorls found in temples. Its purpose was to trigger magical communication, automatic speech, not accounting. Spindle whorls were often used as temple ornaments since the Goddess, like the Spider, the Wasp and the Bee, was a weaver of, and carried the sting of, magical plants. Below is a Queen's pendant, Knossos, c.2000 BC.

KNOSSOS

The Cretan Queens of Knossos were consistently portrayed, for thousands of years, as winged wasps or bee-headed women surrounded by floating eyes and snakes. They were also depicted as bare-breasted shamans, in a flounced skirt, with a flower crown and outstretched arms holding a cobra in each hand.[138] They cast spells. Their flower crowns were sometimes capped by the image of a panther, the premier transformation beast.[139]

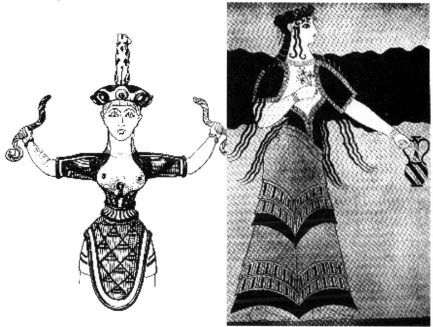

The throne of the Queen of Knossos was found in its original position against the north wall of the Throne Room. It was flanked by intensely colorful frescoes of huge eagle-headed lions, wingless griffins, below, sprouting peacock plumes to indicate their benevolent character. They are couchant amongst the sacramental papyrus reeds. At their heart, near their lion's shoulder blade, are spiraliform rosettes, symbolic entheogens.[140]

A cup from the Phaistos palace in Crete, below, c.2100 BC, shows two women with bee bodies floating in mid-air above an open blossom and a huge, pillar-like bud. They are adoring a live fish happily wriggling atop the baetylic bud.[141] This is an indication of the ecstatic effects the ladies of the palace expected from the contents of the cup, which were expressed, no doubt, from the sacramental bud.

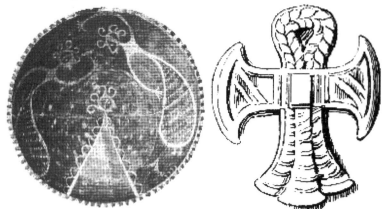

Palace ladies were portrayed wearing a 'sacral knot' on their collar at the back of the neck. Explains Evans: "The religious significance of this knot in connection with Minoan cult is further brought out by the signet... The central theme of this design [p.50] is a scene of divine communion, where a female figure, probably a votary, partakes of the fruit of a sacred tree, which inspires her with ecstatic frenzy. To the right is a Minoan shield - itself, like the *Ancilia*, a medium of religious 'possession'- with an object attached to it which we must certainly recognize as a version of the sacral knot....A remarkable comparison supplied by a small ivory relief from Palaikastro [above]...shows...the sacred Double Axe....The Knot itself may be supposed in this case to be inside the socket of the axe, the ritual adjunct being here substituted for the shaft. This symbolic arrangement became the prototype for a decorative device of the later Late Minoan I ceramic style....Of the dedication of articles of apparel we have direct evidence in the votive robes for suspension found among the faience relics of the Temple Repositories of Knossos. To attach a part of the dress round the baetylic object or actually to tie it round it is a regular part of the rite of 'sleeping in', or 'incubation', in sanctuaries."[142] The Cretan/Greek word for 'Double Axe,' *labrys,* is related to *labyrinthos,* indicating descent into one's personal underworld.

The beautifully etched solid gold Ring of Minos, below, found at Knossos, weighing almost a full ounce, dates to about 1550 BC. It was used as a correspondence seal by a royal personage. It depicts the Goddess, seated at the left shrine near a set of sacral horns, who has just journeyed over the sea in a sea-horse boat, which is in the center foreground. The boat is steered by a bare-breasted, bee-headed woman and carries two baetylic pillars upon which rest sacral horns. To the left of the Goddess, who faces us, at the central and right-hand shrines, two voluptuous naked maenads each bend a sacred tree growing from the top of a shrine and offer its fruit to the Goddess. One maenad, at the central shrine, hands a pitcher of the fruit-juice to another who floats in the air above the Goddess. All three shrines are supported by huge sprouting bulbs.[143]

The most famous examples of Cretan Linear A are spiral magic texts, spells, carved on communion cups from the temple palace at Knossos.[144] Cretan Linear A, descended directly from Neolithic Cretan levels, was heavily influenced by Luvian (S.Anatolian/N.Phoenician) immigrants, c.1750 BC, the so-called Minoans, and was used both for magical and accounting purposes.

Evans also found magical inscriptions in Linear A on the black steatite Libation Table, above, from the Cave Sanctuary of Psychro on Mount Lasithi, near Knossos, which dates to c.1550 BC. This is the very cave where Hesiod tells us that Rhea gave birth to Zeus.[145] On a small bronze tablet from the votive deposit of the cave, above, which depicts an ecstatic male dancer, Evans found early pictographic Linear A signs for 'snake' and 'dolphin.' The libation table itself consists of two bowls built into either side of the top of a large pitcher, which extends below the table top into which it is built.[146] The ritual ladle dipped into the pitcher, as the one below, was probably leaf-shaped.

Cretan goldsmiths, like their Egyptian and Babylonian contemporaries, with whom they traded, excelled in the reproduction of flowers and foliage.[147] The Princess of the Lilies, a centrally located seven foot tall painted plaster relief which introduces the Central Court of the Palace at Knossos, depicts an athletic teenage girl, probably leading a sacred animal by a rope.[148] Surrounded by flowers and butterflies, the Princess, in bull-leaping costume, wears a crown of lilies and ostrich plumes and a necklace of lilies.[149] The lily *Nymphaea ampla*, the probable 'precious water flower' of Mexico, from which entheogenic alkaloids have been isolated, was repeatedly pictured in Mayan frescoes as the adornment of divine manifestations.[150]

The most elaborate fresco in the Palace at Knossos, composed of hundreds of figures, follows the Corridor of the Procession. Celebrants carry musical instruments and vases to a central Goddess or Priestess painted on a larger scale and in more detail than the others. Her attendants, all women, are also larger and more detailed than the other women and men in the crowd. That is to say, the central female figures are distinguished by sacred function, not by sex alone.

Ceremonial Cretan ships, in which royal women were given the place of honor, were depicted with huge entheogenic flowers on the bow and stern, sixteen-petalled rosettes, where later there would be rams.[151] A sixteen-petalled rosette is the ancient symbol of the Japanese royal family, identified as a Chrysanthemum, a 'golden flower.'[152] The family Compositae, to which chrysanthemums belong, is one of the largest families of flowering plants. Numerous Compositae have been identified as entheogens.[153] A cylinder seal from Sumer, c.3500 BC, depicts a shaman floating above a ship almost identical to the Cretan ships, the bow and stern of which are magical plants. Communicants on the shore offer similar plants at a shrine.[154]

CAH: "The open-air shrines were still used [in Crete]... If the court and the country landowners shared in services at these shrines, as evidence from the Kamares grotto shows, then this suggests that the object of worship was common to the palace and the countryside. The mother goddess was also worshipped in crypts, and this is probably connected with her worship in caves....The goddess...was probably believed to appear by invocation of the worshippers, and a tree or pillar may have been the sacred place where she appeared. That she revealed herself in the form of a bird or snake is shown by a great deal of later evidence... A painted clay bowl from Phaestus indicates that already in this early period the goddess could reveal herself in human form in moments of ecstacy. Clay pipes, partially provided with moulded snakes, which have been found in the later palace chapels, are also to be connected with the epiphany of the goddess, and their use may go back to the Early Palace Period....the cult in Crete differs from the cults in Egypt and the Near East just in this respect that provision is made for more active participation by the worshippers...sacrifices of bulls occurred at this period in preparation for the epiphany of the goddess."[155] Just such a bull sacrifice, conducted by priestesses, is pictured (p.63) on a fresco panel of the Cretan Hagia Triada sarcophagus, c.1500 BC.[156]

Many stone and clay sacramental tripods, that is, cooking pots on three legs, painted red, white and black, the moon's colors, have been unearthed in Crete. Many others come from just across the Cretan Sea in Mycenae, in southern Greece, along with their leaf-shaped ladles.[157] Evans: "These vessels [below], which have a pointed spade-like outline and a shallow basin within...have the appearance of ladles... Clay ladles, some with comparatively short handles, are of frequent occurence in the Neolithic deposits of Knossos and they appear amongst other vessels of ritual usage [including beautiful chalices, as below, and tripods] besides primitive 'horns of consecration' in the Early Minoan [c.3300 BC] votive deposit of Mochlos."

"What is specially interesting to note in this connexion is that a vessel of the same chalice-like form, with the triple ring clearly marked, is seen in the hand of the Goddess...seated on a folding-stool on the great signet-ring [below] of the 'Tiryns Treasure'[the Peloponnesian coast just south of Mycenae, c.1400 BC]....Here...the liquid contents of the cup are supplied by a succession of four Genii, of the leonine Minoan kind [lion-headed satyrs with folded bee wings], holding up the spouted ewers - with which they are so often associated in scenes of libation....we seem here to have before us a series of scenes of a sacramental nature in which chalices that may, as we shall see, have contained the juice of a Sacred Tree, were passed from hand to hand, to be sipped by the seated votaries, to whom something of the divine essence was thus communicated."[158]

"May not the Goddess herself have been depicted as participating in this ritual refection?/On the Tiryns signet and a series of seal types referred to below, we have pictorial examples of drink-offerings made to her, either by ministrants in human form or by the lion-shaped Genii. Among these the best clue to the actual character of the liquid offering itself is supplied by the large gold signet-ring.../In this case the Goddess is seated on a stepped altar of isodomic masonry, and beckons to a youthful male satellite, who, with one arm, pulls down the branch of a sacred tree, rising from within a small pillared enclosure, and in the other holds a 'rhyton'of the pear-shaped kind that evidently served to hold the juice expressed from its fruit....on...a series of clay signet impressions....a female ministrant approaches her, bearing in one hand what may be a two-handled 'rhyton', with its orifice temporarily stopped, and in this case the sacred nature of the contents are indicated by a ring [floating] above, symbolizing a celestial orb."[159] "On a gold signet from the same tomb a similar orgiastic figure receives the source of her inspiration in the fruit of a sacred tree through the hands of her minister."[160]

The Gold Ring of Isopata, near Knossos, p.50, dating to c.1500 BC, explicitly depicts bee-headed women dancing in ecstacy, surrounded by beautifully drawn floating plants, possibly entheogenic lilies, a disembodied 'Cleopatra' eye and floating snakes.[161] This is a depiction of *ekstasis*, animal transformation and the disembodied flight of the soul. Evans: "...a design on a remarkable gold signet-ring found in a built tomb at Isopata, where a similar eye appears in the background of a scene depicting a ritual dance held in honour of the Goddess as the visible impersonation of the all-seeing presence of the divinity. The 'Eye of Horus', so familiar in Egyptian relgious Art, seems to have supplied a suggestion of this symbolic usage... On another signet [below] it is coupled with the [floating] ear which also recurs in the background of a Minoan cult scene with an analogous reference to an all-hearing Power."[162]

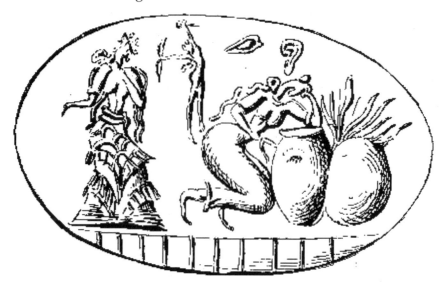

Murals from the great Maya city of Teotihuacán, c.450-650 CE, clearly depict almost identical floating eyes in the sap dripping out of identifiable entheogenic flowers.[163] Incredibly, cultural contact between Europe, the Near East, the Far East and Mexico seems to have happened by this time, according to the very serious evidence Cyrus

Gordon, Henriette Mertz and Carl Sauer are able to offer.[164] But, since floating eyes appear worldwide from the Paleolithic to the Iron Age in virtually all cultures, we may assume that the floating eye motif is a natural product of the human mind, the normal way to express entheogenic ecstacy.

In most ancient cultures, including Mesoamerican and Hellenic, the butterfly represents the soul; a common Greek word for butterfly is *psyche*, soul.[165] Many contemporary Mazatecs and Cretans alike still regard butterflies as the souls of the departed. Some clay seal impressions from Knossos, one of which is on p.50, show the dots in the wings of a butterfly actually transformed into floating eyes.[166]

In both cultures the butterfly is equated with the bee. Like the wasp, the power of the bee's sting came from the power of the plants it pollinated. A Mycenaean gem of Minoan workmanship, below, c.1400 BC, pictures a large sacred plant growing from horns of conse-cration, supported by a chalice. The plant is ceremonially flanked by two lion-headed satyrs in bee skins, that is two shamans, each hold-ing aloft, directly over the plant, a jug of sacramental drink.[167] The bees not only made honey for the honey-beer, but pollinated the magi-cal flowers the mead was spiked with, thus transforming the sha-mans themselves into buzzing lion-headed bees.

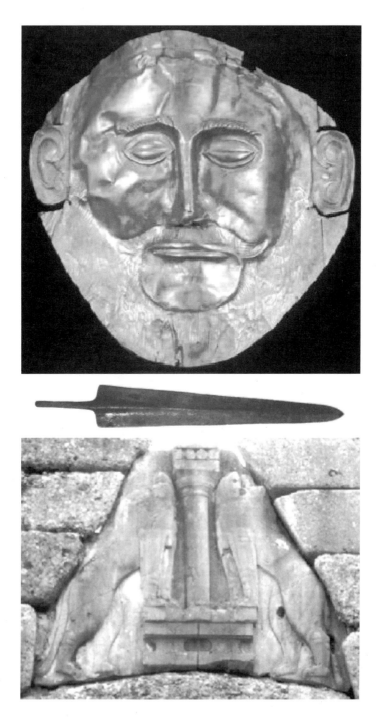

THE GOLD MASK OF AGAMEMNON, BRONZE SWORD,
AND THE LION GATE, MYCENAE, C.1500 BC

BRONZE

Between 6500 and 4500 BC, throughout well-populated Neolithic Europe, there is a complete absence of hill forts, and an almost complete absence of fortifications, although communal violence did occur. Hunting weapons, such as the slingshot, bow, lance and spear served for communal self-defense.[168] A daughter community of Catal Huyuk, Hacilar, was repeatedly put to the torch in the mid sixth millenium and became a walled fortress, as did another daughter community, Mersin. Catal Huyuk itself was deserted by 5500 BC, as was Hacilar by 5000 and Mersin by 3500.[169] As at Jericho, accumulated wealth and strategic trade location seems to have lured the marauders.

The horse, the tarpan, was first tamed as an engine of war and high-speed travel by fierce nomadic pastoralists from the Ukraine and Kazakhstan about 5300 BC, using antler-tine bridles. Their economy was based on very large horse herds used for milk, meat, hide and sinew, which they didn't hesitate to drive into new territory. Since they relied on conquest, their mobile society was militarized and hierarchical, and their mythology stressed the role of the warrior as Creator. They carried bows and arrows, spears, long daggers and, later, short metal swords.

Since they left barrow or tumulus graves, individual pits covered by a low cairn or mound, *kurgan* in Russian, Gimbutas adopted this as the general name for the various steppe peoples sharing this culture. Kurgan hordes flooded Old Europe in three successive waves, c.4400 BC, c.3500 BC and c.3000 BC. These are the 'Proto-Indo-European' speakers whose language became the basis of the Greek, Celtic, Germanic, Italic, Albanian, Slavic, Armenian, Iranian and Indic language groups.[170]

Kurgan warriors could travel at least five times faster than the sedentary competition, and soon controlled the trade routes over vast areas of Southeastern Europe. For the first time, rich male graves, replete with weapons and horse-head sceptres, appear in Europe, indicating chieftancy and patriarchal organization. Kurgan values are expressed not only in the numerous sites of massacre uncovered, but in the institutionalization of suttee, the sacrifice of the chief's wife or entire family, including the children, on the death of the honcho. Numerous examples of child sacrifice have been uncovered. The chief's body was laid in the middle of the mortuary house along with his prestigious metal weaponry, his sacrificed wife next to him, the children around the edges, and the servants and animals in the next room. These gruesome scenes are a regular feature of Kurgan culture, found over and over again. There is no Neolithic evidence of regular human sacrifice until the Kurgans, then it never stopped.

Over the centuries Europe's Neolithic villages became socially stratified, with the bulk of the Mediterranean-type population ruled by a warrior-elite of Kurgan, proto-Europid type. Hilltop forts appear, along with a pastoral economy, signs of violence, and patriarchal religious symbols emphasizing the sun. For the first time, throughout the Alpine valleys, Bulgaria, Romania, the Black Sea region and the Caucasus, heavily-armed male gods appear on stone stelae along with their solar symbolism.

By 3500 BC the official solar symbolism replaced the beautifully executed sacred script on Cucuteni pottery. The building of Cucuteni temples, the making of graceful communion vessels and the writing of the Old European script came to an end. Trade in metals and metal weaponry burgeoned. Daggers, shaft-hole axes and flat axes of arsenic bronze are found throughout the Pontic region, along with metal workshops containing clay bivalve molds. Northwest Yugoslavia, southwest Hungary, Slovenia and Slovakia yield an impressive chain of hill forts, where most of the metallurgy took place.[171]

The well-established Neolithic cultures of Old Europe didn't just die out overnight; those that remained unconquered adapted to the new environment. Sacred monarchy, a military institution, was born. As the ecology militarized, the loving Mother-Queen found herself managing constant warfare. She became a Mother-Terrible, a *SHE* Who Must Be Obeyed, as H. Ryder Haggard put it. As the Bull's blood once was, so the Warrior's blood became - the source of life for the tribe. More and more authority devolved to the war shamans, as their responsibility for the survival of the tribe increased. They still ruled by deputizing for the Queen, for the Mother remained the Source of life. It was She, and her Priestesses, who sacrificed the Bull, or the Warrior-Bull, at the solstices.

Since initiation is mock death and resurrection, and since plants became 'plant-man' and bulls became 'bull-man,' the 'sacrifice' would have been symbolic or entheogenic in most cases, since, most often, the Queen and her entourage would be 'killing' the old year and bringing in the new, as in the Bull sacrifice on the Cretan Hagia Triada sarcophagus, c. 1500 BC, below. Island Crete, however, until the Mycenaean-Dorian age, was militarily secure. Times of terror came to mainland Europe much earlier. And in such times, extreme unction was demanded, one way or the other, of the war shaman, as it was among Paleolithic tribes.

The first conception of a 'king' was as the sacrificial servant of the people, the war shaman who would lay down his life. Like the ritual Bull and the *pharmakon* which were traditionally consumed together, the king would sacrifice himself for the common good. The *pharmakos*, the sacrificial king, replaced the *pharmakon* more and more often as competition for the land increased. The Paleolithic Bull became a Warrior sacrificed to an emerging ethos of warfare, to an ecology of territorial competition and functional specialization - to a glorification of servitude and sacrifice that would have been alien to most Neolithic communities, except in extreme circumstances. The evolution, then, was from tribal to theacratic, to theocratic, to militaristic.

All the great originary city-states of Mesopotamia, China, Mesoamerica, Peru, Africa, India and Europe ended up 'militaristic,' that is, completely absorbed in internecine warfare. Cultural anthropologists classify the stages in the development of early civilizations as Incipient Farming, Formative, Florescent, Theocratic Irrigation-Trade State, and Militaristic State. Although there are regional and sub-regional differences - irrigation, for instance, was less important in some areas than in others - the pattern of creative, matristic, tribal, egalitiarian Neolithic villages enslaved by warrior tribes, or transfixed by internecine warfare, holds throughout. 'Militaristic' is used as a *synonym* for 'historical' by cultural anthropologists. This is not merely a function of the nastiness of those darn men, since increased agricultural efficiency itself produces intense population pressures and competition for resources. The resultant internecine warfare automatically produces the need for an effective defense.

Braidwood and Reed estimate 0.125 people per square mile in Late Paleolithic Iraq, c.10,000 BC.[172] Flannery estimates 0-1 person per square kilometre in southwestern Iran, bordering Iraq, in the Late Paleolithic, growing to more than 6 people after large-scale irrigation appears, c.3000 BC - a sixty-fold increase.[173] Agriculture, then, is a cybernetic engine, creating its own pressure for increased production and territorial expansion. This was the exact opposite of the Neolithic process, which stressed the powerful hearth skills of women. The Bronze Age process stressed the confrontational skills of the warrior.

Furthermore, humans have an inherently carnivorous psychology. Even the tribal Neolithic communities lived by hunting and practicing animal sacrifice, which they uniformly associated with religious epiphany. Animal sacrifice, as the Cretan rite illustrates, was a major function of Neolithic priestesses. Blood was considered nourishing, entheogenic, and the entheogenic or curative sap of plants was regarded as their 'blood.' Wealth-managing bureaucracies, of course, which the Neolithic communities lacked, were careful to generate reasons for acquiring more wealth. In this sense, Early Bronze Age city-states can be seen as military institutions.

The introduction of domestic sheep, goats, cattle and irrigated flax (linseed, linen and nets) in Khuzistan, about 5500 BC, is marked by a decrease in hide-working tools and flints and an increase in spindle-whorls, looms and pot sherds, indicating an increasing reliance on domesticates over hunting. Over the course of the next 1500 years Khuzistan evolved sophisticated irrigation combined with cattle drawn plows. The resultant excess wealth led to the military consolidation of the previously unwalled towns, since surplus food, by definition, supports standing armies.[174]

Khuzistan was a direct ancestor of the first great military-industrial complexes up and down the Tigris and Euphrates, from Eridu, Ur (Ubaid), Uruk and Kish in the south to Nippur, Samarra, Nineveh and Diyarbakir, 'Copperland,' in the north. The Halaf culture in northern Iraq, conquered by the Mesopotamians, introduced them to metal weaponry from 'Copperland.'[175] The names of those towns aren't Sumerian, nor are the names of the Tigris and the Euphrates. The Khuzistan Neolithic farmers and their trading partners, the 'Ubaid' people as they are called, named the geography.

The post-Flood Sumerian rulers have Semitic names, indicating conquest from the west. Influence from aggressive pastoralists from the east, over the Zagros Mountains through Khuzistan, is also indicated. Khuzistan six-row barley, tolerant to low rainfall and high salinity, became the basic cultivated cereal of irrigated lowland Mesopotamia, as its flax became the basic cloth and oil crop and its sheep the basic animal.

Eridu, in the extreme south, couldn't have been occupied without an efficiently managed irrigation system. For the irrigation-masters, this automatically entailed ruthless political control. As in Europe, metallurgy was controlled by the conquistadors. Before the (Early Bronze Age) Flood, says Sumerian legend, metal came from Bad-tibira, 'the fortress of the metal smiths.'[176] Eridu, according to both archeology and the Sumerian King List, was equally ancient, home of the first antediluvian king.

The kings of Early Dynastic Sumer claimed descent from the Goddess, whose figurines still predominate in the finds of 4300-3500 BC. "A-Anne-pada king of Ur, son of Mes-Anne-pada king of Ur, has built a temple for Ninhursag."[177] Enlil was in the ascendancy, but he was still the son of Ninhursag, the Horned Mother. On a seal from Gawra, near Nineveh, c.4000 BC, a horned rainmaker is shown followed by an ibex. Another shows two shamans stirring a cauldron, around which is a row of dancers, a man with a bident, other shamans in animal masks and communicants having intercourse in the company of snakes.[178] Gimme that old time religion.

Sumerian kings were celebrated for opening breweries under the direction of Ninkasi, 'the lady who fills the mouth....bakes with lofty shovel the sprouted barley....mixes the *bappir*-malt with sweet aromatics."[179] A shrine from Uruk 4, 3100 BC, pictures itself as a trough out of which the flock of Inanna, all the important domesticated animals, are drinking. Her symbol is shown as a magical plant, an eight-petalled rosette.[180]

Sumerian kings rationalized their military consolidation in

pharmaco-shamanic terms. The first King of Kish, Etana, "he who stabilized all the lands," was cursed with childlessness for his efforts. In order to lift the curse, Etana rescued an eagle that had been cast into a pit by a serpent whose friendship it had betrayed by devouring its young. The grateful eagle then transported Etana to heaven to obtain 'the plant of birth,' thus enabling the continuance of his line.[181] Etana's image, perched on the back of the eagle, remained a standard device of Sumerian cylinder seal cutters for millennia. Another very early Sumerian king, Dumuzi, mentioned on the King List as a near contemporary of Etana, became Tammuz, the Sumerian Dionysos. The Sumerian King List was dug up at Larsa, and dates to c.2000 BC. The next king it mentions, the warrior-king Gilgamesh, became the most famous hero of the Babylonian world.

No sooner had the first dynasties of Sumer been established than they fell to warring with each other like junk yard dogs. This caused, as the King List says, the kingship to be carried off to Awan, near Susa. This was the great Elamite center bordering Khuzistan, which was coveted for its mineral wealth. But then "Awan was smitten with weapons" and the kingship once again "was carried off to Kish."[182]

The solid-wheeled war-chariot, pulled by asses and supplied with bronze weaponry, was their tank.[183] The kings of Ur were buried in their tanks, drenched in material wealth, and surrounded by their sacrificed family and large retinue.[184] By 3000 BC, Kish and Uruk, thanks to large-scale irrigation, each housed 20-30,000 people, at least half of whom were serfs or slaves of the temple-palaces. A thousand years later the population would increase tenfold.[185]

Below is a sample of the pictographic cuneiform writing from an obelisk of the king of Kish, c. 2600 BC. This writing is fully deciphered. Most of what we know of the organization of ancient Mesopotamia comes from the tax rolls of the temple palaces. Thus we know that of the 1200 members of the Baba temple community in Girsu, c.2500 BC, more than 100 were fishermen. The temple, not the fishermen, owned the fish. There was private property, but most of that fell into the hands of the military aristocracy. Citizens were divided by law into nobility, commoners, serfs and slaves. Slaves were legally defined as farm animals and fed half the rations of free workers.

The voracious bureaucracy, under the pretext of national security, confiscated or taxed everything in sight. "Who transgress the established norms, violate contracts..../Who having eaten did not say 'I have eaten it,'/Who having drunk, did not say 'I have drunk it,'/Who said 'I would eat that which is forbidden,'/Who said 'I would drink that which is forbidden.'"[186]

At Lagash, shearing, the basis of Sumer's essential textile industry, could be done legally only at the palace, which charged for the service. There were birth taxes, marriage taxes, divorce taxes, death taxes, sales taxes and transport taxes. The nuclear family was no longer a tribal but a taxable unit. Credit was extended on the security of personal freedom, and the husband's obligations fell upon the wife and children, as the wife's upon the husband. The restriction of female property rights not only rendered the nuclear family a more tractable tax unit, but further detribalized culture as well. Sexual equality before the law would have meant that obligations weren't transferable.

Those who had been reduced to slavery for non-payment of debts or taxes, as well as prisoners of war, were often blinded to prevent escape, and then worked to death as draft animals. The political allegiance of the common folk was shaken to such a degree that Urukagina, king of Lagash in about 2350 BC, promulgated reforms which repealed much of the taxation. For the first time in history the word 'freedom' was used in a political document: the word is *amargi*, and it means, literally, 'return to the mother.'[187]

According to the ancient tablets, Ninhursag, 'Lady of the Mountain,' caused eight great plants to grow in Dilmun (Eden), the 'Land of the Living' east of Sumer, where neither sickness nor death was known. The eight great plants of the Land of the Living were grown through three generations of Goddesses, all born of the water. But Enki, the Sumerian Apollo, whose name means 'heaven-earth,' *An-Ki*, sent his satyr to pick the plants, so that he could eat them. The enraged

Ninhursag cursed Enki with death, and then disappeared.

Enki's eight precious organs began to deteriorate as he started to die, and even Enlil, 'heaven's breath,' couldn't save him. Whereupon the fox volunteered to find Ninhursag in exchange for a boon. At the fox's bidding the Goddess returned, and seated Enki by her womb. She caused eight healing Goddesses to come forth, each offering the magical herb specific to each of Enki's deteriorating organs. The last organ to be healed, without which Enki would die, was the rib. For the rib, *ti*, 'the Lady of the Rib,' Ninti, was brought into being. *Ti* also means 'to make live,' because Ninti offered Enki the fruit that completed his healing process. Ninti was 'the Lady Who Makes Live.' That is the literal meaning of 'Eve,' the Lady of the Rib. That is also the original function of Eve's fruit.[188]

A major trading partner of the Sumerian and succeeding Akkadian powers was Egypt. Each Neolithic village of Egypt had identifed itself by a magical plant or animal totem. The Bronze Age process of amalgamation left 22 totemic districts in Upper (southern) Egypt and 20 in the Delta to be organized by the early dynasts. Throughout the Egypt of this period images of the Goddess predominate. The king of the first great Egyptian state, in Upper Egypt, wore a tall white helmet symbolizing a sacred plant, usually called a lotus, though it is botanically unidentified. The king of Lower Egypt wore a red wicker diadem; the botanical identification of the 'red crown' is also lost.

The green papyrus sedge, the *waz*, an economically important plant, obviously wasn't the original totem plant symbolized by the red crown, but it became the symbol of Lower Egypt. The Delta Goddess Wazet, wearing the Red Crown and sitting atop her symbolic papyrus, is pictured above as a cobra. Mut, Mother Vulture, wears the White Crown as she perches atop her lotus plants.[189] These plants were turned into huge pillars at Karnak, symbolically supporting the realm. The lotus and the papyrus knotted together symbolized Egypt, known throughout the ancient world as 'the two Egypts.'[190]

Three lotus flowers grew out of the head of Hapi, the God of the Nile, depicted as a kneeling man with breasts holding out a tray with drinking mugs on it. His hieroglyphic symbols included a pipe.[191]

During the Early Dynastic Period, c.3000-2700 BC, succession to the throne was matrilineal, through 'She who united the Two Lords,' 'She who Sees Horus and Seth,' and the 'Mother of the King's Children.' Every early king bore the title Falcon-God (Horus), associating him with the Sun, but he is often shown sitting infant-like on the knee of a huge Isis.[192] He wore a long lion's tail from the back of his belt. He was the *ka-mutef*, the Bull of his Mother.[193] The slate palette of Narmer, the first unifier of Egypt, c.3000 BC, below, shows him as both the Falcon, perched on magical flowers, and the Conquering Bull. Narmer's name is framed between two giant horned heads of Hathor, the Cow-Goddess, Wazet, Delta Queen.[194]

The Old Kingdom is also called the Pyramid Age, 2700-2200 BC. Khufu's (Cheops) pyramid, the most awesome of the lot, piled 2,300,000 blocks of limestone, each weighing about 2.5 tons, up to a height of nearly 500 feet. It took slave teams of 100,000 men, each working three-month shifts, 30 years to complete the job.[195] The people, says Herodotus, were "worn down to the extremity of misery."[196]

The Uraeus, the maternal asp or cobra whose hieroglyphic sign was the mystic floating eye, was worn on the heads of Pharoahs and Queens alike - as a threat. The cobra was poised to strike, as the Greek name *ouraios*, expressive of animal fury, 'quivering tail,' implies.[197]

Says the Pyramid Text, *To the Crown of Lower Egypt*, c.2500 BC: "O Net-crown, O In-crown, O Great Crown, O Sorceress, O Serpent! Let the slaughter that he maketh be as the slaughter that thou makest! Let the fear of him be as the fear of thee!" As a poem to King Amenemhet III (1842-1797 BC) put it, "He is Bastet, that protecteth the Two Lands; he that revereth him shall escape his arm. (But) he is Sekhmet against him that transgresseth his command."[198] Bast, the Lion-headed 'Lady of Life,' was the producer of vegetation; she wore the Uraeus on her head. Sekhmet was the goddess of war.

The Pyramid Text *The Deceased Devours the Gods* (c.2500 BC) seems to describe Pharoah's powers in pharmaco-shamanic terms: "He is the Bull of the Sky, with his heart bent on thrusting (?), that liveth on the being of every god, that eateth their...limbs, when (?) they have filled their bellies with magic on the island of Nesisi....He it is that eateth their magic and swalloweth their lordliness....He hath eaten the Red Crown, he hath swallowed the Green One. He feedeth on the lungs of the Wise Ones; he is satisfied with living on hearts and their magic....He hath swallowed the understanding of every god."[199]

The Red Crown could refer to the red-crowned mushroom *Amanita muscaria*, the Soma of the *Rg Veda*, just as the Green Crown could refer to another entheogenic mushroom, now considered the exclusive property of Pharoah. In any case, the language of the overtly pharmaco-shamanic *Rg Veda* of c.1500 BC is virtually identical: "This bull, heaven's head, Soma, when pressed, is escorted by masterly men into the vessels, he the all-knowing....thou sittest in the vessels, having been pressed for Indra, inebriating drink, which inebriates, supreme mainstay of heaven, [Soma] who gazes in the far distance."[200]

From the Pyramid Text *The Goddesses Suckle the Deceased*: "He hath trampled for himself these thy rays into a ramp beneath his feet, that he may go up thereon unto his mother, the living snake that is upon Re. She hath compassion on him, she giveth him her breast, that he may suck it, O king."[201] Snake milk was always the *pharmakon* of the gods.[202] The *Tale of the Shipwrecked Sailor*, c.2000 BC, has our Egyptian hero washed up on an island inhabited by a kindly giant prophetic snake with brows and beard of lapis-lazuli. As soon as the sailor left it, to make the lapis snake's prophesies come true, the island disappeared.

The large-scale mining of lapis lazuli, turquoise, marble, alabaster, diorite, carnelian, jasper, obsidian, amber, copper, gold, silver, cinnabar, lead, tin, iron, zinc, manganese, arsenic, sulphur and salt drove the invention of chattel slavery. State monopolies of the copper trade, practiced by most ancient empires, allowed control of the production of weapons. The discoveries that molten arsenic and tin would turn copper into bronze, that silver could be extracted from both lead and copper ore, and gold from quartz, only served to increase the value of slaves. So did the great municipal building projects. Slaves became as important to the state trading monopolies as the precious metals themselves. The Cretan tribute-bearers below, depicted on the Tomb of Rekmara (c.1460 BC), offer blooming magical flowers to Pharoah, to grease the wheels of international commerce.[203]

Hammurabi's Code (Babylon c.1700 BC), and the virtually identical earlier Sumerian codes we have, are typical of the law codes of most of Babylon's trading partners. They are largely concerned with management of the slave system and protection of governmental fiscal prerogatives.[204] Society was divided into 'men, subjects, and slaves' in Hammurabi's 300 paragraph code. These were subdivided into official guilds: craft, priestly, military, farm, etc. The guilds were occupation-specific; there were architects, painters, potters, sculptors, smiths, fowlers, wainwrights and launderers. Membership in a guild was usually hereditary, an element of clan identification, and failure to fulfill an hereditary obligation could be punished by death or reduction to slavery.

Chief among the military guilds were the Indo-European chari-oteers, the *maryannu*, Southwest Asia's mobile mercenaries. In the seventeenth century BC a confederation of these horsemen, calling themselves the Hyksos, 'Shepherd-Kings,' conquered Egypt, proving to the world that the horse-drawn light chariot, with its revolutionary spoked wheels, was far superior to the ass-drawn heavy chariot with its cumbersome solid wheels.

Although the principle of 'an eye for an eye' is enshrined in Hammurabi's Code, this applied only to parties of equal rank. If an aristocrat, a 'man,' knocked out the tooth of a commoner, a 'subject,' he owed him a little money, not his own tooth. Not only major of-fenses such as murder, kidnapping, theft and false accusation, but relatively minor offenses such as filial disobedience, adultery, breach of contract and failure to pay the oppressive taxes were punished with death, reduction to slavery and/or vicious lashing or mutilation.

"15: If a *man* has helped either a...*slave* of the state or...a...*slave* of a private citizen to escape through the city gate, he shall be put to death. 16: If a *man* has harbored in his house...a *slave*...and has not brought him forth at the summons of the police, that householder shall be put to death. 109: If *outlaws* have congregated in the establishment of a woman wine seller and she has not arrested those outlaws and did not take them to the palace, that wine seller shall be put to death. 195: If a son has struck his father, they shall cut off his hand. 209: If a *man* struck another *man's* daughter and has caused her to have a miscarriage, he shall pay ten shekels for her foetus. 210: If that woman has died, they shall put his daughter to death [it was also a son for a son]. 212: If by a blow he had caused a *subject's* daughter to have a miscarriage, he shall pay five shekels of silver [two for a *slave*]. 212: If that woman has died, he shall pay one-half mina of silver [one-third mina for a *slave*]. 226: If a brander cut off the slave-mark of a *slave* not his own without the consent of the *owner* of the *slave*, they shall cut off the hand of that brander. 282: If a male *slave* has said to his *master*, 'You are not my master,' his *master* shall prove him to be his *slave* and cut off his ear."[205]

Another legal document puts it succinctly: "Sin-balti, a Hebrew woman, on her own initiative has entered the house of Tehip-tilla as a *slave*. Now if Sin-balti defaults and goes into the house of another, Tehip-tilla shall pluck out the eyes of Sin-balti and sell her."[206] The vast bulk of the Mesopotamian population were either slaves or serfs. About 100 of the 300 paragraphs of Hammurabi's Code refer directly to the rules governing slavery.

A considerable class of international traders, merchant-warriors with large armed retinues, also existed. Abraham was one of these. The Code gave them the right to enslave their debtors for non-payment. These licensed government operatives were enjoined to ransom captive Babylonian soldiers and to return runaway slaves for punishment.

The king of Mari, Zimri-Lim, left over 20,000 neat, legible clay tablets to us, including his correspondence with Hammurabi (1728-1686 BC). That and thousands of other tablets prove that among the elite, literacy, and a very high level of medical, chemical, geological and mathematical knowledge was common. His stela shows a genuflecting Hammurabi receiving the law from Marduk. Below that is some of the original text.

THE DOVE

Babylonian royal women were often given the title of High Priestess and were strictly forbidden by Hammurabi's Code, on pain of death, to mix with the common folk. Aristocratic women, however, were encouraged to become a wife of the God who administered civil affairs. As such they often functioned as a Goddess of Love in the temple, so as to increase the fertility of the realm.[207] Union with a temple priestess, in an ecstatic state after preparatory ritual, was a sacred marriage with the Goddess.

One Babylonian incantation explains the role of the priestess: "O *kukru, kukru, kukru,* in the pure, holy mountains thou hast engendered 'little-ones' by a sacred prostitute, 'seeds of a Pine' by a vestal..." The priestess' sympathetic procreation engendered sacred 'pine seeds,' which likely refers to the entheogenic *Amanita muscaria*, which grows only in association with pine, fir and birch. *Kukru* means 'pod' or 'womb.' Pliny says that "the fungi...are all derived from the gum that exudes from trees." Theophrastus says that the gum of the silver fir tree (*Elate`*) "is what the prophets call 'the menses of Eileithyia.'"[208]

The Cretan Eileithyia was understood to be the Babylonian Ishtar, a later incarnation of the Sumerian Iahu. She was also called Aphrodite ('Born of Sea-Foam') or Dictynna ('She of the Fishing Nets') by the Cretans, who traded extensively with the Sumerians and Babylonians, often through Phoenicia, where she was called Asherah or Astarte. The common epithet applied to the Goddess throughout this shared Semitic cultural orbit was 'the Exalted Dove.' In Cretan tradition, Eileithyia, the Goddess who was 'child-bearing,' came from the womb of Hera. Hera's womb was identified as the holy cave of Amnisos on the Cretan coast, the trading harbor of Knossos.[209] Our word 'amniotic' comes from *amnias*, 'woman of Amnisos,' an epithet of the Exalted Dove.

Evans: "In the present case, the central object of cult, emphasized by the disproportionate scale on which it is drawn, and saluted by the votary, is the dove perched on the symbolic tree. This is of the greatest religious moment. It is the ritual equivalent of the birds perched on the leafy shafts of the sacred Double Axes on the Hagia Triada Sarcophagus [p.47], of the doves resting on the capitals of the miniature pillar shrine, and of those which in the case of the gold relics from the Mycenae Shaft Grave poise, not only on the altar horns, but on the actual votary. [The votary opposite, swinging on the dove-blessed horns, comes from Knossos.] In all these instances, as pointed out above, we must recognize by the light of primitive religious ideas the visible sign of possession by the divinity, who, on the tablet and the pillar shrines is no other than the Great Minoan Goddess in her aspect as Lady of the Dove, while the fish brings in her marine attribution. The celestial signs above help to complete her attributes."

"The prominence here of the tree cult illustrated by the sprays rising between the horns, and the central tree behind the altar - apparently a pine - is noteworthy. It points to a time when the forest growth of *Pinus maritima* that still clothes part of the Lasethi uplands had stretched about the Cave Sanctuary itself and supplied the Goddess with a sacred Grove./The tree, dove, and fish, which here appear as the vehicles of divine possession, aptly symbolize her dominion of earth, air, and sea."[210]

Iahu, the Sumerian Exalted Dove, was the daughter of Tiamat, the primeval waters. As the renowned linguist Professor John Allegro, Secretary of the Dead Sea Scrolls Fund and one of the original translators of the Scrolls, teaches, IA, in Sumerian, means 'juice' or 'strong water.' The root idea of U, according to its usage in words like 'copulate,' 'mount,' 'create,' and 'vegetation,' is 'fertility,' thus 'Iahu' means 'juice of fertility.'[211] That is the name of an entheogen, the fruit of 'the menses of Eileithyia.' The Sumerian Goddess was also called Inanna. 'Ishtar,' the Akkadian-Babylonian name, is derived from the Sumerian USh-TAR, 'uterus' in Latin. 'Dove,' peristera in Greek, also means 'womb,' as does its Semitic cognate yonah, Jonah.

The Akkadian era of Lower Mesopotamia (southern Iraq) was founded by Sargon of Agade or Akkad, c.2360 BC. Bab-ilu, 'the Gate of God,' Hammurabi's capitol city, inherited the political ascendancy about 600 years later. In Hammurabi's Babylon, the Exalted Dove was cut in two by Marduk. "You, Marduk, are the most revered of the awesome gods. Your fiat is unequalled, your dictate is Anu. From this day forward your pronouncements shall be unalterable. Your hands shall have the power to raise up or bring down. Your word shall be prophetic, your command shall be unrivalled. None of the gods shall be above you!"

"Let any downtrodden man with a cause present himself to my statue , for I am the king of justice. Let him read my inscribed words carefully, and ponder their meaning, for these will make his case clear to him, and give peace to his troubled mind! 'He is Hammurabi, the King, a father to all the people. He has heard the word of Marduk, his lord, and thus has guaranteed the prosperity of the people forever, leading the land into righteousness' - let my supplicant proclaim this, praying with his whole heart and soul for me!"[212]

Enuma Elish, 'When on High,' has the unrivalled Marduk creating order out of the corpse of Tiamat, the Primordial Ocean-Woman, specifically called a woman in the myth and portrayed as an enraged shaman, like Hera, creating poisonous monsters for self-protection. Marduk, Tiamat's son, volunteers to rescue the rest of her rebellious progeny from the enraged Goddess: "He looked toward the enraged Tiamat, with a spell on his lips. He carried a magical plant to ward off her poison....After slaying Tiamat the lord rested, pondering what to do with her dead body. He resolved to undo this abortion by creating ingenious things with it. Like a clam, her split her in two, setting half of her to form the sky as a roof for our earthly house."[213]

Tiamat, above center, became the *Tehom* of Genesis. 'Firmament' means 'what is spread out,' and is a reference to the body of Tiamat. Marduk is Yahweh to Tiamat's Tehom.[214] Marduk, or his hero Gilgamesh, was craftily portrayed as a winged shaman bringing the herb of immortality from heaven to earth, thus usurping the function of Tiamat's daughter Iahu, the original Yahweh, the Exalted Dove. Gilgamesh brings magical opium poppies to earth on the relief, below right, from the palace of Ashurnasirpal II,c. 875 BC.

Marduk's rite involved ceremoniously cutting a dove in two at the Spring Equinox, an enormously powerful image for a culture that understood the meaning of the dove. Henceforth the wings belonged to Marduk, who proved as useful to Nebuchadnezzar in 600 BC as to Hammurabi in 1700 BC.[215]

Hammurabi's Code became the common law of the Near East, officially adopted or copied by all the powers for the next 700 years. Hammurabi also popularized the Gilgamesh Epic, adopted by his

Babylonians from their cultural mother, Sumer. Gilgamesh was the Babylonian Odysseus. The earliest representations we have of this ritual legend were carved on Sumerian stone, c.3000 BC, and fragments of it were found in numerous sites, including Megiddo, Amarna and Khattusha, all dating to c.1400 BC. The library of Ashurbanipal at Nineveh yielded the most complete version of the Gilgamesh epic, in Akkadian cuneiform, dating to c.650 BC. Gilgamesh's quest is specifically entheogenic, as is the quest of Eve in Genesis. There are many variations of this popular sacramental motif.

Gilgamesh slew the snake living at the base of the magical *huluppu* tree planted by Inanna, causing Lilith, the 'Screech Owl,' to tear down her house, in the midst of the tree, and flee. The image of Lilith below dates to the time of Hammurabi. Having usurped Lilith's prophetic and transformative powers, Gilgamesh was enabled to present her tree to Inanna, who turned it into a shaman's drum and drumstick for Gilgamesh. But Gilgamesh plunged Uruk into unending warfare, therefore, "because of the cries of the young maidens," his drum and drumstick fell into the netherworld. Enkidu, the king's bold warrior, bravely descended to retrieve the drum, but was unable to return alive.[216]

Grief stricken, Gilgamesh then set out on his odyssey in search of the secret possessed by Utnapishtim, 'Day of Life ,' the Ark-building Noah who had achieved immortality in the land of the magical fruit trees. On meeting the travelling Gilgamesh, the scorpion-man says to his wife, "The body of him who has come to us is flesh of the gods." The scorpion man below, about to share some goat juice, was engraved on a Sumerian harp.

On reaching him, Utnapishtim's wife is moved to ask what boon he will bestow on Gilgamesh for the heroic effort he has made to arrive at the land of the magical fruit trees. "'I will reveal a secret of the gods to you: a thorny plant that will prick your hands like a rose. But if you can get your hands on it, it will give you life anew! As soon as Gilgemesh heard this, he lit his water pipe, he tied heavy stones to his feet. The stones pulled him under to the bottom of the ocean, where he found the magical plant. He grabbed it, not minding the thorns. He cut the weights from his feet, so that the sea cast him up on the beach." Gilgamesh explained to his waiting boatman Urshanabi that the plant is so powerful that its name must be "Old Man Becomes Young." But on the way home, as Gilgamesh stopped to bathe at a well, a giant snake, alerted by the magical plant's aroma, arose from the depths and stole the plant of immortality.[217]

The plant-stealing snakes below were carved onto a green stone vase used to hold the sacramental drink in one of Hammurabi's temples. Like the scorpion men, their bite escorted Babylonians to the land of the magical fruit trees, there to visit Utnapishtim.

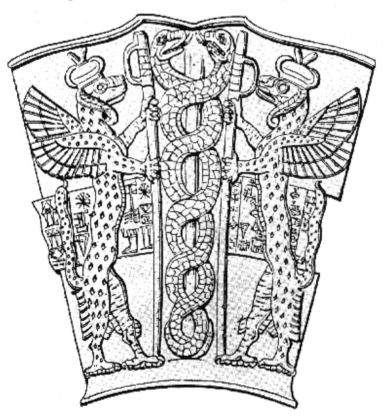

PHOENISSA

The Theban Thutmose III (1490-1436 BC) became the greatest conqueror in Egyptian history. The Theban Ram Amon, originally an ithyphallic satyr, was combined with the Old Kingdom Sun-God Re to become Amon-Re, bringer of victory over the hated Hyksos to the Theban dynasts of the Empire Period (1567-1320 BC). Among the peoples Thutmose enslaved were many from the newly-conquered lands in Canaan.

The vaunted solar monotheism of Akhenaten, his grandson, who ruled this vast empire eighty years later, was simply the revised logo of the Theban dynasty, the traditional Re-Horus of the Horizon, the falcon combined with the sun, the Aten, the 'Disc.' Akhenaten removed the falcon, and gave the Sun hands holding the ankh, the bulb-topped crucifix, a schematized image of the Goddess with arms outstretched, a symbol of life similar to the sacral knot. Akhenaten represented himself not with a falcon but with a shepherd's crook.[218] Akhenaten worshipped the Aten; everyone else worshipped Akhenaten, 'Beautiful Child of the Aten,' 'Son of God.'

Akhenaten used his revised logo to commit both cultural and actual genocide in the process of political regimentation. Other manipulations of the archetypal imagery included the substitution of phonetic symbols for the ancient pictographs. 'Law' was formerly indicated by the figure of a squatting woman with a feather in her hair, the Goddess Maet. Akhenaten substituted phonetic abstractions based on pictures of other things. 'Mother' was formerly indicated by the hieroglyph of the vulture, symbol of the Goddess Mut.[219] Mut, mother vulture, also meant 'time' and 'sky,' indicating her shamanic associations. The psychopompic priestesses at Catal Huyuk were vultures who granted death and rebirth, 'time.'

This demythification of the ancient matristic imagery coincided with confiscation of the Goddess' temple wealth by Akhenaten. Official prayers could be addressed to Aten only through the agency of The Sacred Shepherd, who taxed and impressed the population for grandiose projects, ignored foreign policy as the empire crumbled, and attacked the traditional cults, literally chiseling the names of Amon, Horus, Ptah and Mut off their monuments. Akhenaten's personal effigy replaced Horus even in services for the dead. The result was near civil war with the army, the priesthood and the people, and a tactical retreat for 'monotheism' on Akhenaten's death.[220]

Parts of Akhenaten's *Great Hymn to the Aten* are repeated almost word for word in Psalm 104, either transmitted through the Canaanites or simply remembered from the days when the children of Israel were Akhenaten's slaves. The *Hymn* is very similar to earlier hymns to Amon and Osiris, differing from them mostly in ignoring the existence of the other deities, now restored to their traditional places. The only full-length copy of the *Hymn* was found in the Amarna tomb of Ay, d.1348 BC, Akhenaten's Master of the Horse, who succeeded Tutankhamon, Akhenaten's son-in-law, as Pharoah.[221] Tutankhamon's spectacular untouched tomb was found by Carter in 1922.

The Contending of Horus and Seth, a twelfth century BC manuscript, tells of the battle between Horus, son of Isis and Osiris, and Seth, evil brother of Osiris, for the divine kingship. Isis poses as a seductress to trick Seth and then transforms herself into a prophetic bird. Despite this magical help from his mother, Horus cuts off her head and turns her into a decapitated flint statue.[222]

By the end of the reign of Ramses III (1198-1166 BC), the last great imperial pharoah, the temples owned about a fifth of the people and a third of the land outright. Amon-Re of Thebes, the imperial temple, owned three quarters of that, and only the temples were exempt from taxation and the draft.[223] The afterlife of Amon, for all except Pharoah, the incarnation of Amon, was no shamanic ecstacy, but one in which a man was "registered for work which is to be done in the Underworld as a man under obligation, to cultivate the fields, to irrigate the banks, to transport sand of the east and of the west."[224]

State slavery was a major factor in the economy of all the powers. Since international trade was virtually a state monopoly, national debts and tribute were often paid in slaves. Capture in warfare was a virtual guarantee of enslavement. A major object of Theban imperialism was Phoenicia - Syria and Canaan. In the Phoenician Epic of Kret, a literary precursor to *The Iliad*, King Pebel of Edom plays the role of King Priam. He tries to buy Kret off his insistence on Hurrai (Helen) with an offer of "silver and yellow gold, / A portion of her estate and perpetual slaves."[225] It was a sincere offer.

Phoenissa, the Bloody One, was the mother of the Phoenicians. *Phoinis*, crimson, Tyrian purple, the color of congealed and menstrual blood, was the unique sea-shell dye for which the Phoenician coast was long famous.[226] Menstrual blood was considered life-giving. Its Latin description, *purpura*, purple, means 'very very pure,' *purus*. The Greek Phoenix was the transformed *Phoenissa*, the Snake-Bird Goddess.

The Phoenician port of Gubla, the Greek *Byblos*, was the entrepot for Egyptian papyrus, from which was made ships' ropes, sails, clothing and writing linen.[227] *Byblos*, papyrus, gave the Greeks their word for books, *biblia*, from which Bible. Unlike the more expensive parchment or vellum, skins, papyrus has a short life, and little has survived outside the dry deserts of North Africa.

The greatest Phoenician trading center from 1800 to 1200 BC was the port city of Ugarit in North Syria, modern Ras Shamra, a metropolis connecting Crete, Cyprus and Greece with Egypt, Babylonia, Khatti (Turkey) and Assyria (northeast Iraq, south Turkey).[228] Syrian, Anatolian, Cretan and Cypriot copper, tin, wine, grain, opium, kannabis, olive oil, dyed wool, timber, rare stone, minerals, finished metal products and ships were traded for Babylonian, Egyptian, Somali and Ethiopian copper, gold, grain, wool, fabrics, incense, ivory, ebony, wine, beer, foodstuffs, medicines, jewelry and cosmetics.

Ugarit left behind a wealth of diplomatic, commercial and liturgical archives on clay tablets, written in the alphabetic cuneiform called Ugaritic. Other scripts found include Cypro-Minoan Linear A, Mycenaean Linear B, Egyptian hieroglyphs, Hurrian (Mitannian-Syrian) cuneiform and Hittite hieroglyphs.

Tablets with Akkadian syllabic cuneiform, the diplomatic *lingua franca* used by all the powers, were also found in great abundance. Since we have their vocabulary lists, we know that advanced scribes had to qualify in four languages, including the ancient Sumerian, from which Akkadian was derived. The commercial motivation to simplify this confusing array of scripts was very strong.

'Akkadian' refers to the phonetic transliteration of Sumerian writing into the Semitic Akkadian tongue. The Akkadian era of Lower Mesopotamia (southern Iraq) was founded by Sargon of Agade or Akkad, c.2360 BC. Old Akkadian is derived from Sumerian as written English is derived from Greek. Bab-ilu, 'the Gate of God,' Hammurabi's capitol city, inherited the political ascendancy about 600 years after Akkad. The Assyrians, to whom power devolved 600 years after that, were originally from Assur in northern Mesopotamia, on Phoenicia's eastern border. Culturally, Ugarit looked to ancient Sumer the way classical Greece looked to ancient Crete. For that matter, Israel looked to ancient Sumer much the same way.

The two main Ugaritic scripts were the diplomatic Akkadian and the more common everyday Ugaritic, both 'cuneiform,' that is, 'wedge-shaped' simplified pictographs (pp. 67 & 75). They were inscribed with a stylus on clay. In use for thousands of years, these proto-syllables took on completely abstract phonetic values, and were thus transferable from one language to another. The Ugaritic Phoenician cuneiform tablets we have were dug up in the library of the high priest near Ugarit's two main temples (to Baal and Dagon, the Bull and the Fish). They were baked hard in the conflagration (earthquake, invasion?) that destroyed the town, c.1200 BC. The 500 or so Amarna letters, Akhenaten's diplomatic archive, were found at his capitol of Akhetaten, known today as Tell el-Amarna. They date to c.1400 BC, and are written mostly in conventional Akkadian by Phoenician scribes who injected much of their own grammar and vocabulary.[229]

Dagon, the Fish-Man, was also worshipped in Crete, as Daguna in the Hagia Triada tablets, and as Proteus by the Greeks. *The Epic of Kret*, the eponymous Cretan hero, was a direct literary ancestor of both the Bible and Homer. It was dug up in El's hometown, Ugarit. "Kret was disturbed by his dream, in which El, the Father of Man, descended. In his vision the Father of Man drew near, asking 'Why does my son, the Son of El, weep? Does he covet the kingdom of his father the Bull, or dominion like the Father of Man?' Pour wine from a silver cup; and from a gold cup, honey. Ride the top of the high tower. Exalt the heavens. Sacrifice the Bull to your father, El, the Bull.

Win over Baal, Dagon's son, with your sacrificial offering."

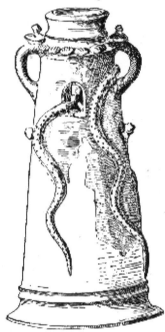

Hebrew law (Lev:2:11) makes a point of prohibiting burnt offerings of meat with honey, consistent with the ritual demonization of a conquered mother culture (and the historical diminution of Israeli cuisine). Interesting also is the Hebrew demonization of transvestism (Deut:22:5), portrayed in the Canaanite *Epic of Aqhat* as a sign of power. Serpents, given a place of honor in all Canaanite temples,[230] as they were on Crete, were demonized right along with "Ashtoreth the abomination of the Sidonians."(2:Kings:23:13) The snake tube above came from the House of Ashtoreth at Beth Shan. Politically, of course, the Phoenicians were ruthless piratical slavers who practiced child sacrifice, that is, political terror, giving Israelite moral disgust a firm foundation in fact.[231] In the hands of Phoenician tyrants, Ashtoreth was anything but a loving village Great Mother.

The Bible calls the Phoenicians 'Canaanites,' a variation of the Akkadian *kinahhu*, also meaning crimson or purple. *Aqhat* translates to Hebrew as *Qehat*, the name of Levi's son, called *Kohath* in the erudite King James bible.[232] One of the priestly guilds of Ugarit was the *Kohanim*, the direct ancestor of Israel's great priestly guild. In Sumerian, from whence cometh the word *Kohanim*, GU-EN-NA means 'guardian of the holy juice' or 'guardian of the holy semen.'[233] Fertility, vegetal or human, was high on the Sumerian list of priorities.

The *Kohanim* competed for legitimacy in Israel with the 'pagan' priests of *Kadesh*, the Syrian Hathor, pictured above in Egyptian relief handing sacramental plants to her votaries. The *Kadesh* were concerned with physical sacramentalism - vegetal, animal or human. They were wiped out, but to this day their name means 'blessing'or 'holy' in Hebrew. *Kadesh*, according to Professor Allegro, is derived from Sumerian US-KUD and US-TAR, Ishtar. 'Rabbi' is apparently derived from Akkadian *rabi*, administrator.

Virtually all of Israel's agricultural festivals were Phoenician in origin, as was much of the language, law, industrial arts, music and architecture. The Old Testament never refers to the 'Hebrew' or 'Israelite' language, but to the 'language of Canaan.'[234] Jerusalem (Uru-Salim), Solomon, Salaam, Salome, Salmon, Absolom, Salem and Salmaah (the Kenite Dionysos) can all be traced, through the path of the ancient writings, to the Willow Goddess Sal-Ma, also known as Circe or Belili, whose related place names are of great antiquity throughout the Aegean and Mediterranean.[235]

Solomon's Temple was built on the traditional Phoenician model, a virtually identical example of which was uncovered in 1936 in north Syria (Tell Ta'inat) dating to about 900 BC, dedicated to Astarte, to whom Solomon also built temples. (2:Kings:23:13) Israel, Moses, Abraham and Daniel are all Canaanite names. Daniel is the hero of the Canaanite *Epic of Aqhat*. *Dan* means 'to judge,' and *El* means 'a god.'

Sarah means 'princess' in Hebrew and 'queen' in Akkadian-Phoenician (Asherah). Jezebel, wife of King Ahab (874-852 BC), was a high priestess of Asherah. Until Josiah put a stop to it (2:Kings:23:7),

Asherah was considered El's wife in Judah. "To Rewashsha [Egyptian Prince of Taanach, near Mediddo, c.1460 BC]: Thus Guli-Adad. Live well! May the gods take note of thy welfare...Thou hast written to me concerning silver and behold I will give fifty of silver, truly I will do!/Further, and if there is a wizard [Akkadian *ummanu*;Hebrew *omman*] of Asherah, let him tell our fortunes and let me hear quickly, and the omen and the interpretation sent to me./As for thy daughter who is in the town of Rubutu, let me know concerning her welfare; and if she grows up thou shalt give her to become a singer, or to a husband."[236]

One Ugaritic text reveals Mot, Baal's evil twin, God of the Underworld, enraged at Baal's conquest of the seven-headed Leviathan. Mot repays Baal with terror and death, but not before Baal copulates with a heifer, who bears him a Bull. Thereupon Baal dies and the Earth becomes barren. Anath decides to avenge her brother Baal: "She cleaves Mot with a sword. She winnows him with a fan. She burns him with fire. She grinds him in the millstones. She plants him in the fields."[237] As if by seed, Baal is resurrected in the renewed Earth. Shapsh, the Sun Goddess who sees all, is dispatched by El to find Baal, who is once more battling with Mot. After seven years, Mot will have yet another victory. The rites enacted by Anath are a virtual duplicate of the rites enacted by Demeter in the *Hymn to Demeter*, the etiological myth of the Eleusinian Mysteries. Baal's struggle, that is, was pharmaco-shamanic, a sacramental ritual, as the stela on p.87, from Ugarit, c.1600 BC, indicates.

Another text of the Baal and Anath cycle, the 'Anath' text, has this Phoenician Diana, in the midst of battle, receive "The message of Aliyan Baal, the word of Aliy the Mighty: 'Bury hatred in the dust of past battles. Bury mandrakes as a peace offering in the earth. For I have the whisper of the tree in the wind, and the word of the stone. I hear the sound of the deep starry heavens. I have the power of the lightning unknown to heaven. Nor do the earthly multitudes understand my power. Come with me, and I, the God of Saphon, shall reveal it, in the midst of my Mountain of Power. Who can rise against Baal, the Rider of Clouds? I have sacked the house of El-Zebub, and regained my gold from those who once drove Baal from the heights of Saphon.'" In Psalm 68, Yahweh is the 'Rider of Clouds.'

As in *The Iliad*, the God is willing to share his shamanic powers in return for a *quid pro quo* from the Goddess: he wants her to talk Asherah ('Lady Asherah of the Sea,' Hera) into asking El (Zeus) to authorize Kothar-and-Hasis (Hephaistos) to build him a palace. Anath assures

Baal that "My father El, the Bull, will yield, for my sake as well as for his own. For if he refuses to grant Baal a proper house I will pound him into the ground like a defenseless sheep. I will make his grey hair and beard flow with his own blood, lest he grant Baal a house of the gods, a proper court like a true son of Asherah!"

This physical self-confidence is an indication of the psychological pre-eminence of the Goddesses in the Ugaritic pantheon, despite their patriarchal demotion to 'daughters' and 'wives.' Ultimately, often as transvestites, they are the source of real power.

'Baal' and 'Phallus' have the same Sumerian root, the verb AL, to 'bore' or 'drill.'[238] Baal's house, the text tells us, was built of cedars from Lebanon covered with worked precious metals, the actual building materials of the First Temple. Kothar-and-Hasis comes from Caphtor, Crete, as does Hephaistos. Crete, and all the surrounding islands, were as much a home of 'Lady Asherah of the Sea' as Phoenicia. The fierce Asherah opposite comes from the Ionian island of Corfu, c.600 BC. Corfu's Greek name, *Kerkira*, means 'the Island of Circe,' 'the weaver' who stings like a bee and bites like a snake.

92　*Shamanism and the Drug Propaganda*

PHOINIKEIA

Ba'al's mother was Ba'alat, the Lady, the Mistress, called Hathor, the Horned Mother, by the Egyptians, Lady of the Turquoise. She was worshipped in the southern Sinai in 1500 BC by the Egyptians and the Semitic turquoise miners they employed. It is here that the earliest Proto-Sinaitic inscriptions, Hebrew phonemes derived from pictures, are found. This is a Semitic extrapolation of a linguistic advance already made by the Egyptians and the Akkadians. Thus the oval, *ro*, 'mouth' in Egyptian, stood for 'r'; *zt*, 'snake,' for 'z'; and the rectangle, *shy*, 'lake,' for 'sh.' These phonetic pictographs were combined to form completely abstract words.[239]

An inherent conceptual advantage of Egyptian writing was that it was painted on papyrus paper, not gouged into clay. The scribes below were immortalized in limestone c.1350 BC. New Kingdom literature, c.1500-1000 BC, written in the New Egyptian phonetic pictographs popularized by Akhenaten, which Erman calls "cursive hieroglyphics," is full of loan words from Phoenicia and Canaan, indicating close two-way contact.

The pictograph of 'house,' the Semitic *bayt*, gives the letter b; 'eye,' *'ayn*, gives ' (*yodh*); a 'curved line/lamp,' *lamed*, gives l; and a 'cross,' *taw*, gives t, giving b-'-l-t, Our Lady of the Turquoise.[240]

It is a simplification to say that modern languages, based on Greek, Hebrew and Aramaic, developed from Phoenician, since Phoenician itself is partly derived from Egyptian, Cretan, Akkadian and Hittite-Luvian (Anatolian). Moses' nemesis, Ramses II (c.1295-1224), who owned a considerable part of Phoenicia, actually built a special temple for the Phoenician Asherah in his residence.[241] Early Egyptian pictographs themselves were heavily influenced by those of its trading partners, Sumer and Crete.[242] And Egyptian, Cretan and Sumerian, moreover, are derived from their magical Neolithic mothers.

Both the Greek and Hebrew alphabets were immediately derived from Phoenician, and Phoenician was immediately derived from Ugaritic. In fact Ugarit was discovered, in 1928, when a Syrian farmer plowed into a Mycenaean Greek tomb.[243] Although it is 'alphabetic,' that is, phonetically pictographic, the 22-letter Phoenician alphabet is an exact match of its 27-letter cuneiform Ugaritic mother, after the extra five phonemes, which converged with other Phoenician sounds, are eliminated. Hebrew coincides exactly with Phoenician, in the same order, and Greek almost exactly:aleph, beth, gimel, daleth:alpha, beta, gamma, delta:ox, house, camel, door. From Phoenician, or, as they used to be called, 'Moabite' phonemes, developed not only Greek, Hebrew and Aramaic, but Latin, Arabic, Ethiopic, Cyrillic and, ultimately, the written forms of all Western and Semitic languages. In fact a,b,d,h,k,l,m,n,p,q,r,t in English are in the same order as in Ugaritic.[244]

Greek, an Indo-European language, and Hebrew, a Semitic language, thus have common ancestors not only in Phoenician, a Semitic language, but in Hittite, an Indo-European language; Akkadian, an originary Semitic language; Egyptian, a Hamitic language; Sumerian, a Semitic-influenced Ural-Altaic language; and Cretan, an Old European language.

The definitions, therefore, of 'Semitic' and 'Indo-European,' are, evolutionarily, artificial boundaries, since cultural contact was contiguous and intense.[245] The distinction between English and Greek is also artificial, since much English is in fact Greek, and much Greek is in fact Sumerian, Egyptian, Akkadian, Cretan or Hittite-Luvian. The Cretan hieroglyph for 'wine,' found in the originary Greek writing called Mycenaean Linear B, is almost identical to the Egyptian hieroglyph for wine, recalling the type of grape arbor used in Egypt during the 1500's BC.[246]

Gelb has pointed out that many signs in apparently unconnected systems, such as Ugaritic, Korean, Brahmi, Yezidi, Old Hungarian, Numidian, Runic and Somali, are identical. Since the explanation isn't likely to be cultural contact, we are left with the archetypal patterns of the human mind.[247] Jung discovered the same thing when he noted the identity of originary pictographs, and the drawings of children, in unconnected cultures. A nine year-old Dutch girl, asked to compose an original alphabet, came up with signs found in Phoenician, Sinaitic, Cretan and Cypriot. Cultural contact is thus fed by the archetypes.

Cretan		Sinaitic	Moabite	Palestinian		Ionic	Attic	Corinthian	Chalcidian
⩔ ∀		ⴹ	ⴲ	ⴲ ⴲ s.		A	ⴲ A	A ⴲ	A
ⴲ	ⴲ	◻	ⴲ	ⴲ		ⴲ	ⴲ	ⴲ ⴲ	B
ⴲ			ⴲ	ⴲ		ⴲ	ⴲ	))	⟨
ⴲ	ⴲ		ⴲ	ⴲ ⴲ s.		ⴲ	ⴲ	ⴲ	D
ⴲⴲ	ⴲ		ⴲ	ⴲ		ⴲ	ⴲ	ⴲⴲⴲ	ⴲ
	ⴲ	ⴲ	ⴲ	ⴲ				ⴲ	F
ⴲ	ⴲ	ⴲ	ⴲ	ⴲ ⴲ s.		I	I	I ⴲ	I
ⴲ	ⴲⴲ		ⴲ	ⴲ ⴲ ⴲⴲ ⴲa.		ⴲ	ⴲ	ⴲ	ⴲ
ⴲ	ⴲ		ⴲ	ⴲG.		ⴲ	ⴲ	ⴲ	ⴲ
ⴲ	ⴲ	ⴲ	ⴲ	ⴲ		I	ⴲ I	ⴲ	I
	ⴲ	ⴲ	ⴲ	ⴲ		ⴲ	ⴲ	ⴲ	k
ⴲ	ⴲ	ⴲ	ⴲ	ⴲ		ⴲ	ⴲⴲ	ⴲ	L
		ⴲ	ⴲ	ⴲ		ⴲ	ⴲ	ⴲ	ⴲ
ⴲ	ⴲⴲ	ⴲ ⴲ	ⴲ	ⴲ		ⴲ	ⴲ	ⴲ	ⴲ
ⴲ	ⴲ		ⴲ	ⴲ s. ⴲ a.		ⴲ		ⴲ	ⴲ
ⴲⴲ	ⴲⴲ	ⴲ	ⴲ	ⴲ		ⴲ	ⴲ	ⴲ	ⴲ
ⴲ		ⴲ	ⴲ	ⴲ ⴲG.		ⴲ	ⴲ	ⴲ	P
ⴲⴲ	ⴲⴲ		ⴲ	ⴲ ⴲ s. ⴲ G.				ⴲ	ⴲⴲ
ⴲⴲ			ⴲ	ⴲ ⴲ s. ⴲ s.		ⴲ	ⴲ	ⴲ	ⴲ
	ⴲ	ⴲ	ⴲ	ⴲ		ⴲ	ⴲ	ⴲ	P
ⴲ		ⴲ	ⴲ	ⴲ		ⴲⴲ	ⴲⴲ		⟨
ⴲ	ⴲ	ⴲ	ⴲ	ⴲ		T	T	T	T

'Etymology' in Greek means 'the *logos* of the truth,' from *etymos*, 'true.' By tracing the original meaning of a word we contact the archetypal picture, the unconscious content or bio-historical truth connected to the earth, our automatic selves. The Egyptian hieroglyph for 'King' is a beautifully drawn bee, thus indicting that it was originally the hieroglyph for 'Queen.'[248] There are no king bees, as Egyptian beekeepers knew perfectly well.

Graves: "And from the inability to think poetically - to resolve speech into its original images and rhythms and re-combine these on several simultaneous levels of thought into a multiple sense - derives the failure to think clearly in prose."[249] By poetically, Graves means automatically, which, ultimately, means empirically, but in an evolutionary not a phenomenological sense. *Historein*, 'history,' is a combination of *histor*, 'to judge or measure,' and *idein*, 'to see or apprehend.' The Greeks understood etymology as history: *phoinikeia*, 'phonemes,' 'letters,' literally means 'Phoenicians.'

Herodotus: "These Phoenicians who came with Cadmus...brought to Greece, when they settled in it, various matters of learning and, very notably, the alphabet, which, in my opinion, had not been known to the Greeks before....The Greeks who lived round about the Phoenicians at this time were mostly Ionians [Mycenaeans]. They learned the alphabet from the Phoenicians, and, making a few changes in the form of the letters, they used them and, in using them, they called the letters 'Phoenicians' (*Phoinikeia*)....The Ionians also from ancient times called books 'skins' because, from lack of papyrus, they used goat- and sheepskins. Still in my time many of the barbarians write on skins in this fashion./I myself have seen Cadmean letters in the shrine of Ismenian Apollo in Thebes in Boeotia. These are engraved on certain tripods and in many respects are akin to Ionic letters."[250]

Cadmus, 'East' in Phoenician, was brother to Europa, 'West,' the Princess of Phoenician Tyre. She was taken to Crete by the Bull Zeus, who made her the mother of King Minos, who established the Cretan Palatial Epoch, c.1750 BC.[251] It is notable that the Phoenician incursion into Crete seems to have taken place without warfare, and that Cretan culture continued to prosper, as if there had been extensive prior cultural contact.

Willetts: "In art Europa is frequently shown on the bull, holding his fertilizing horn in one hand and in the other the flower, at once the symbol of her own fertility and the sign of her origin in herbal magic before agriculture and cattle-raising deified the bull."[252]

The Ionic amphora below, picturing Hermes stealing the cow Io from the giant Argos, makes Willetts' point graphically. The Greeks who stole Crete from the Minoans, c.1450 BC, the Mycenaeans, Homer's Achaeans, were the children of Danae, the mother of Perseus, founder of Mycenae. They were an *ad hoc* military confederacy which included Mycenae, Pylos, Tiryns, Argos, Corinth, Sparta, Thebes, Athens and many of the other powerful tribes of Greater

Greece. They introduced their bronze weaponry, their internecine warfare and their military autocracy to Crete, but absorbed much of the 'Minoan' genius as well, deriving their phonetic Greek Linear B from Cretan Linear A, as refined by Europa of Tyre.

Mycenaean pottery was renowned for its high artistic and technical quality. Mycenaean transports hauled copper ingots, bronze weapons, fine stones, textiles, pottery, slaves, olive oil, wine, opium, 'unguent' and kannabis throughout the Mediterranean.[253] *Kannabis*, as Professor Allegro teaches, is derived from Sumerian BI-US, 'erect,' and GAN, 'mushroom head' or 'penis.' It is related to *Panacia*, 'offerings of all kinds of fruits and cakes.' That is, *kannabis* is a Mycenaean sacramental name.[254] Their rigging and nets were also made from it, a habit they picked up from the Cretans and Egyptians.[255]

The Mycenaeans and the Welsh are related via the Tuatha de Danaan, the 'People of the Goddess Danae,' Mycenaean settlers of Denmark and Britain, c.1500 BC. 'Denmark' is 'the Kingdom of the Danaans.'[256] The eldest of the Danaid priestesses, Albina, 'The White Goddess,' gave her name to Albion, as Britain was called by the ancients. This is the same Druidic Albion that imported Egyptian beads from Akhenaten's capitol city into Salisbury Plain, along with the Egyptian astronomical sophistication evident at Stonehenge.[257] The floating mushrooms, below, were engraved on stone #53 by Stonehenge's builders. The Rillaton gold cup, c.1450 BC, taken from a chief's grave in Cornwall, is virtually identical to the gold cups taken from the shaft graves at Mycenae.[258] The Celtic Arianrhod was the Mycenaean/Cretan Ariadne.

Over the centuries Britain was visited with numerous Greek immigrations, including that of the Milesians, who hit Ireland in about 1250 BC. As Apollodorus put it, Iason, 'the man of the drug,' "built a ship of fifty oars named Argo after its builder; and at the prow Athena fitted in a speaking timber from the oak of Dodona."[259] 'Oak' is *drys* in Greek, *derwen* in Welsh, *dur* in Gaelic. The Gaelic plural *duir*, *derwydd* in Welsh, 'Druid,' means 'oak-seer.' The Druids buried their dead in oak boats, like the one described by Apollodorus.[260] Odysseus was a Druid: "The man himself had gone up to Dodona/to ask the spelling leaves of the old oak/what Zeus would have him do - how to return to Ithaka/after so many years - by stealth or openly."(*Od*:19:290)

In *The Song of Amergin*, which Graves dates to the Milesian invasion of Ireland, *Duir*, the Oak-God, says "I am a god who sets the head afire with smoke."[261] The Celtic shamans wrote the *Beth-Luis-Nion*, the 'Birch-Rowan-Ash,' the originary Welsh/Irish Tree Alphabet consisting of Birch-Rowan-Ash-Alder-Willow-Hawthorn-Oak-Holly-Hazel-Vine-Ivy-Dwarf Elder and Elder, according to O'Flaherty, plus five vowel trees. An interested monk, c.1250 CE, preserved enough of the ancient Druidic *Battle of the Trees*, still recited by the bards, to enable O'Flaherty to rescue the ancient tree alphabet for modern times. Robert Graves: "I noticed almost at once that the consonants of this alphabet form a calendar of seasonal tree-magic, and that all the trees figure prominently in European folklore."

In all Celtic languages, *trees* means *letters;* to cast a *spell* thus had pharmaco-shamanic as well as phonetic implications. The Druidic mysteries consisted largely of the correct use of the various berries, leaves, barks, saps and woods in the appropriate season. Graves' decipherment of the tree alphabet is largely pharmaco-mythological analysis designed to determine which trees were substituted for which in the sometimes political process of transmission.

The five vowels denote the five stations of the year: New Year's Day plus the four 13-week seasons, which correspond to Birth, Initiation, Mating, Sleep and Death. The first vowel tree, *Ailm*, silver fir, was the tree of Druantia, the Gallic Fir-Goddess, 'Queen of the Druids,' whom the Greeks called Eileithyia.[262] Theophrastus specifically says that the silver fir is Eileithyia. Druantia's day was the first of the year, the extra day of the winter solstice, the day the Divine Child was born. It was celebrated by consuming Druantia's offspring, the 'seeds of a Pine,' as the Babylonians put it.

The Birch-Rowan-Ash had thirteen consonants, the same number as the notches on the crescent horn of the Paleolithic Goddess of Laussel (p.17). That is also the number of the 28-day lunar months in the Druidic year as reported by Pliny and Caesar. Also the number of consonants of the original Pelasgian (Neolithic-Luvian) alphabet (Diodorus Siculus), and the first Greek (Mycenaean-Ionian) alphabet (Aristotle).[263]

The song of the Welsh oak-seers that Graves extrapolated directly from *Battle of the Trees* is remarkably like the *Odyssey* (5). Bloduewedd, 'Flower-face,' the Welsh Kalypso, says that she was "spellbound by Gwydion," the Welsh Odysseus or Odin. He was also known as Yggr. He rode *Askr Yggr-drasill*, Yggdrasil, 'the ash tree that is the horse of Yggr.' Bloduewedd says that Gwydion "formed me from nine blossoms, / nine buds of various kind.... / From the bean in its shade bearing / A white spectral army / Of earth, of earthly kind.... / Nine powers of nine flowers, / Nine powers in me combined, / Nine buds of plant and tree. / Long and white are my fingers / As the ninth wave of the sea."[264]

As The Bhagavadgita put it: "There is a fig tree / In ancient story, / The giant Ashvattha, / The everlasting, / Rooted in heaven, / Its branches earthward; / Each of its leaves / Is a song of the Vedas, / And he who knows it / Knows all the Vedas."[265] As Revelation puts it: "On either side of the river stood a tree of life, which yields twelve crops of fruit, one for each month of the year. The leaves of the trees are for the healing of the nations."[266]

MYKENAIKOS

Professor Evans: "On the remarkable gold signet-ring, known from the place of its discovery [Mycenaean Pylos] as the 'Ring of Nestor', the scenes of inititiation into the after-life are divided by the trunk and branches of a Minoan 'Tree of the World'. Here there can be little doubt...that the plant, the shoots of which spring forth from the trunk to give shade to the lion guardian of the realms below, must be identified with the same 'Sacral Ivy' that climbs the rocky steeps in this cycle of wall paintings. The heart-shaped leaves and even the double terminal tufts of flowers are distinctly indicated. These leafy offshoots, moreover, are not shown as branches of the tree, but are clearly extraneous growths like ivy or mistletoe, but the latter is here excluded from its very different form. The tree itself is bare of foliage like the medieval 'Tree of Paradise' that prolonged the tradition of some much earlier congener of Yggdrasil. At its foot here, in place of the 'loathly serpent' Nidhoggr, crouches a dog-like animal, the Minoan prototype of Cerberus - with a single head."

"May we not perhaps go even farther? This conspicuous spray - with its green leaves picked out, as we see them in the fresco, by the bright orange outline of the sacred emblem - springing from the hoar and barren trunk of the tree that here seems to stand on the borders of the Minoan Underworld, might it not itself have possesed some mystic power? It is impossible not to recall the Golden Bough, which, when plucked by Aeneas, opened for him the passage to Avernus. But ever, as one was torn away, another branch of gleaming gold sprang in its place."[267]

This overtly pharmaco-shamanic signet ring was an actual correspondence seal used by a ruler of Mycenaean Pylos. That the later Homeric memory of Mycenaean history is descended from genuine contemporary epic has been demonstrated by the geographical details found in *The Iliad* and *The Odyssey*. Not only Evans in his excavations on Crete, but Schliemann, in his uncovering of Troy, Mycenae and Tiryns, and Blegen in his discovery of Pylos, were able to analyze the classical texts for geographical clues which led to the actual discovery of the sites. The largest cache of Linear B tablets, from the Palace of Nestor, was dug up by Blegen in 1939 at Pylos, in southern Greece. When the palace was finally destroyed by the Dorians in about 1150 BC, the palace archives, sun-dried clay tablets which otherwise might have disintegrated, were baked hard as a rock in the conflagration.

But for all its historical accuracy, the Homeric poetry is fundamentally Ionic, not Mycenaean, a romantic memory of the descendants.[268] Writing, for instance, is mentioned only once, when Bellerophon of Argos hands the King of the Lykians, who were Luvian speakers just north of Phoenicia, the probable 'Phoenicians' of Herodotus, a tablet covered with signs.[269]

Mycenae, near Pylos in the Peloponnese, was actually a literate palace culture with a high degree of industrial specialization and social stratification. It had conquered island Crete about 1450 BC. The Mycenaean system was feudal, run by barons, 'the folk,' who served under the King. The large sheep-wool-textile industry was controlled by giving each shepherd exactly one hundred sheep to bring in for shearing. The shearing was done by the trained slaves - men, women and children - who were accounted for, and fed, exactly like the sheep, as a 'flock.' The most numerous class of people mentioned in the tablets are 'slaves of the god.' The proportion of rations was 5:2:1, men:women:children, with slaves getting half the allotment of free workers. Rations were distributed monthly, so that slaves got 30 units and free workers got 60 units. This was the same system used in Sumer and Akkad.

The King, the *Wanax*, the *Pharmakos*, claimed descent from *Wanassa*, *Potnia*, 'The Lady.'[270] Zeus was promoted by the Ionic Homeric poets to a position he never had among the real Mycenaeans, for whom he was a suckling infant or youthful initiate, a *pharmakos*, animal Son,

Dionysos, the Bull of the Plant Mother. The beautiful ivory sculpture found at Mycenae depicts an infant Dionysos bouncing on the knee of The Two Queens, the *Diaskourai*.[271]

The cult room dug up in 1969 at Mycenae, dating to about 1300 BC, revealed Goddess figurines and snakes, basically a Cretan religion.[272] At Argos 'Plant-Man' was called 'Dionysos The Cretan.' One of Ventris'most interesting discoveries when he deciphered Linear B was the name of Dionysos, thus confirming what the Greeks themselves had always maintained, that Dionysos came from the womb of his Cretan mother, via the Mycenaeans, the *Mykenaikos*.[273]

The *Mykenaikos* were the people of the *mykes*, the 'mushroom.' *Myesis*, 'initiation' in Greek, *mystes*, 'initiate,' and *mysteria*, 'the festival of the mysteries,' all derive from the root of *mykes*. Pausanias: "When Perseus ('the destroyer') returned to Argos, shamed by the rumours of this murder, he persuaded Megapenthe ('much suffering'), daughter of Proitos to exchange crowns, and taking hers he founded Mycenae. This is where his *mykes* [cap, sword cap] fell off, and he believed it was the sign to build a city. I have heard too that it happened he was thirsty and pulled up a *mykes* [mushroom] from the ground, and drank the water that rushed out, and that, liking it, he called the place Mycenae."[274]

Actually, Megapenthe named the city: *mykenai* is the feminine plural, a name predating the Mycenaean arrival. Professor Ruck: "Still more explicit is the depiction of Perseus's journey that we see on a fourth-century BC *amphora* from southern Italy. The artist followed the tradition that confused the Hesperides and their golden fruit with the Hyperborean garden. He shows us Perseus in the far-off land as he beheads Medusa [Megapenthe], the primordial queen who is a manifestation of the Great Goddess to whom the Lykian god ['wolf-land' Apollo] was consort. In displacing her from her former role, Perseus, as a son of the Olympian Zeus, founded the Indo-European dynasty at Mycenae. Clearly identified as the fruit of the Medusa's magical tree on the vase painting is the mushroom."[275]

The Mycenaean stirrup jar, holding what the ancients called 'unguent' or 'ointment,' was Mycenae's most popular export.[276] Archeologists judge the commercial reach of Mycenae by the appearance of its unguent jars in the finds, from the Hazor sacked by Joshua to Akhenaten's Tell el-Amarna to Hittite Khattusha. The 'stirrups' were handles for pouring out of the circular spout, which was small enough to be easily stoppered.

One of the early full sentence Ventris was able to decipher in Linear B was "How Alxoitas gave Thyestes the unguent-boiler spices for him to boil in the unguent."[277] On investigation, it was discovered that nothing inedible was ever used in the aromatic 'unguent,' and that some ingredients, such as wine and honey, were utterly inappropriate as a skin salve. That is, the 'unguent' was for ingestion. *Kyphi*, Egyptian incense, was also used as an aromatic and an interior medicine.[278]

The ingredients listed included coriander, cyperus, henna, ginger-grass, mint, iris root, wine, honey, olive oil and 'MA.' Cyperus can be three or four plants of the genus *cyperaceae*, including papyrus, eaten like sugar cane by the Egyptians, or chufa, brewed as an aromatic tea or eaten by the root. It has been found in Egyptian tombs, c.2400 BC. Henna, the ancient red-orange hair dye, was used by the Egyptians to cure headache. Its flowers have a delicious aroma, and Egyptian ladies colored their breasts with it. The fine foxes above, shown imbibing amidst the floating fruit, were painted onto the walls of the tomb of Userhet at Thebes, c.1300 BC. Coriander, the delicious spice, is also a perfume and a tonic for the stomach. Iris root is a stomach tonic mentioned by Theophrastus and Dioscorides, and ginger grass and mint are edible aromatics.[279]

'MA' is associated in the texts with Eileithyia, the Cretan/Greek Goddess of Childbirth, obviously an aspect of Demeter, 'Earth Mother.' The Mycenaeans made a point of importing herbal infusions from Crete, in stirrup jars with Cretan place names, marked with the sacred Double-Axe sign. Since they needed neither jars nor olive oil nor herbs for their large-scale unguent manufacturing process, and, since opium had always been a major Cretan crop, as the temple-palace records show, it is likely that 'MA,' the ingredient called 'The Mother,' is *mekonion*, opium.[280]

Demeter's name is often used as a synonym for 'poppy fields' in the palace records and she is often represented as either holding or wearing bulging poppy capsules. The Opium Mother on p.107 is from Gazi on Mycenaean Crete, c.1350 BC. Inscribed Mycenaean stirrip jars dating to the same time have been found in the earliest levels at Eleusis,[281] where opium was a sacred symbol. Opium continued to be a symbol of fecundity well into Roman times.[282] Opium's contrived modern image intentionally confuses abuse of its refined alkaloids with the traditional uses of the whole sap. Whole opium sap is actually a safe, relaxing stimulant, which, given in the right dosage, would indeed be helpful in birthing.

The 'ointment,' furthermore, was distributed to all classes, including the army and the slaves, by the priests of the temples, as in Mesopotamia and Egypt. The workers building the Theban necropolis actually went on strike because "we have no ointment." The infusion was frequently used for ritual purposes, and was also a warm gift of kings, palace to palace.[283]

Mycenaean ointment jars were found in the Hittite palace at Khattusha, near Ankara, which yielded hundreds of clay tablets in the various languages of their empire in Asia Minor. These included bilingual tablets in the two major languages, Luvian (Lykian-SW Turkey) and Hittite.[284] The Phaistos Disk, below, c.1650 BC, is a circular six-inch Luvian syllabo-pictographic magic text made with stamp seals, in effect moveable type, found in a Cretan palace. Among the clear pictures are numerous different plants, an eight-petalled rosette, mushrooms and doves.[285] Professor Gordon translates a sentence from the Phaistos Disk as: "I have eaten in the temple of Hadd."[286] Hadd is the Bull, Baal. One did not go into the temple to eat doughnuts, one went in to consume potent herbal sacraments, to commune with the ineffable.

One tablet found at Khattusha has the Goddess of Magic and Healing, Kamrusepas, telling the enraged son of the Storm God, Telepinus: "Here is ointment for the heart and soul of Telepinus! Just as malt and malt-loaves become one, so let your soul become one with mankind. Just as spelt is pure, so let Telepinus' soul become pure! As cream is smooth and honey is sweet, so let Telepinus' soul become smooth and sweet! See now, O Telepinus! Your path is purified with fine oil. So walk, O Telepinus, in rapture over this purified path. Let aromatic woods and incense be at hand! Let us set thee, O Telepinus, into the right state of mind!"[287]

IRON

The Hittites of mineral-rich Khatti were the first iron-wielding superpower, jealously guarding the secrets of smelting this most common of hard metal ores with an army of mine administrators. Their neighbors to the east, the Assyrians, inherited the superpower mantle on the collapse of the Hittites, c.1200 BC. The Assyrian warrior below comes from the Palace of Sargon, c.900 BC. Ramses II, Moses' nemesis, was forced to deal with Hittite Khatti as an equal after the battle of Kadesh (1286 BC), ceding north Syria to it.[288]

The cult of Khattusha, the Hittite capitol from 1800-1200 BC, 90 miles east of Ankara, united the cults of the conquered regions of Asia Minor and Syria. Images of the conquered gods were brought to the capitol, where the conquered cult was redefined by carefully prescribed ritual. Violation of the newly prescribed ceremonial rules was said to interfere with the supernatural effectiveness of the king in preventing human suffering, and were therefore defined as 'sin.' Official state ritual included the reading of astrological and biological signs, public sacrifices and the priestly ingestion of the now restricted shamanic herbs. This ritual interceded with the sacred and demonized the profane, chief among which were the ancient usages connected with the newly conquered gods.[289]

Early Iron Age states were fierce military-industrial complexes constantly in search of metal, slaves and territory. Original Sin, the religion of the conquistador priest, has its roots in the mandatory ceremony and ritual of the Iron Age war leagues. Below are Mycenaean weapons Evans unearthed at Knossos. Troy, the fortress bottleneck through which the vast Black Sea trade emptied into the Aegean, fell to the Mycenaean war league in its twilight, about 1200 BC. Mycenae itself was destroyed less than a century later, as were the great Cretan centers the Mycenaeans ruled, probably by the Dorians.

Like the Mycenaeans before them,the Dorians, mounted pastoralists, entered the Peloponnese as conquerors. Their three main tribes were divided into 27 phratries, patrilinear brotherhoods, some of the names of which were found at Argos inscribed on water-pipes.[290] The native population of 'Helots' were enslaved as hereditary community property by the pipe-smoking brothers. Their military hierarchy tolerated no social dissent. By 800 BC Sparta controlled all Laconia, and, along with Argos, Corinth and Megara, all the Peloponnese except the mountains of Arcadia. Attica went through the same process of military consolidation under the Ionians, as did the northern regions under the Aeolians, Boeotians and Thessalians.

The demand for metal, and slaves to work the mines, played a major role in the founding of overseas trading colonies. Archaic Greek states, 800-500 BC, founded hundreds of colonies throughout Europe and North Africa.[291] The enslavement of the locals was standard colonization procedure. Slaves were at a premium since most children never saw fifteen; rare was the woman who lived past thirty or the man who lived past forty.

The canonical Boeotian Hesiod dated the ages of man by the precious metals mined by the slaves: the original golden race of the orchard garden, whose spirits "roam everywhere over the earth, clothed in mist and keep watch on judgements and cruel deeds, givers of wealth"; the matriarchal silver race destroyed by Zeus for refusing to recognize him; the flesh-eating bronze race "sprung from ash trees...terrible and strong,"who destroyed themselves in warfare; the founding fathers of Mycenae and Troy who dwell "untouched by sorrow in the islands of the blessed"; and their descendants of iron, who "never rest from labor and sorrow."[292]

Delphi for north and central Greece, Olympia for the Peloponnese, and Delos for the Cyclades and Attica became political centers of an amphictiony, a theocratic alliance.[293] *Amphiktyonis*, the Mycenaean goddess who binds together, an aspect of Demeter or Danae, gave way to *Amphiktyon* as the founder of the Dorian and Ionian leagues of neighbors; he was the son of Deucalion, 'sweet wine,' the Greek Noah.[294] Official magical sanction from the alliance's oracle was an obligatory preliminary to colonization. The colonists were sent forth with a spit from the home city and a pot with fire in it. The new colony was then joined to the mother city by communal sacrifice using the maternal spit and fire.

Nothing political happened among the Greeks that wasn't preceded by a communal sacrifice, usually followed by a sacramental meal. The warriors solicited Apollo at Delphi, Olympia or Delos with votive tripods, that is, free-standing three-legged cooking pots. The sacrificial animals were often cooked with magical herbs. They are shown arising reborn from the cauldron, often with vines growing from their bodies, or drinking from an entheogenic cup.[295] Like the chalice, the tripod's contents were originally considerably more important than its shape or its 'votive' function.[296] The Attic vase below, c.490 BC, typically pictures the tripod as a magical vehicle.

The Pythia herself is most often pictured seated in a tripod, that is, speaking entheogenically, straight from the Cretan ladle. In Classical times Greek women, with the schizophrenic exception of the Pythia, the 'Snake-Woman' herself, were forbidden to approach the tripod at Delphi. Barbarians couldn't sacrifice before Greek altars or participate in Greek assemblies or contests, nor could Greek women, who were kept away from sacrifices and blood.

Civic participation of the wives of citizens was reserved for their bloodless sacrifices or the occassional Dionysian celebration, which recognized their originary female powers.[297] This participation was politically, though not psychologically, peripheral in the culture. Greek wives were legally the juniors of their sons, couldn't share in the communal sacrifices without the intercession of their husbands, who handed them the meat, and couldn't institute legal proceedings without the same intercession.[298]

The distinction between the raw and the cooked, between the wild, with which the 'bestial' (pre-industrial) souls of women were equated,[299] and the civilized (military-industrial), with which men were equated, was profoundly important to the Greek polity. The Greeks sacrificed only their domesticated animals, just as the Tsistsistas did when they wanted to stress their internal cohesion.

It made sense to Agamemnon, according to Aischylos, c. 460 BC, to sacrifice his daughter Iphigeneia ('she who was born at dawn') to raise the winds to Troy. It also made sense to the Athenians, in the temple of Apollo at Delphi, to acquit Orestes of his mother Klytaimnestra's murder, despite the fact that Queen Klytaimnestra was simply avenging her daughter Iphigeneia when she slew Agamemnon. Orestes claimed sanctuary of Apollo because he was ritually clean "by purification of slaughtered swine," the 'first domesticate' that was the Old European symbol of the Goddess.[300]

Orestes wasn't guilty of matricide, explains Apollo, because, like the earth, "The mother of what is called her child is not its parent, but only the nurse of the newly implanted seed. The begetter is the parent, whereas she, as a stranger for a stranger, doth but preserve the sprout..."[301] Apollo then points to Athena's Hesiodic birth from the head of Zeus as empirical proof that ejaculation is more important than gestation.

The Young Wolf Women had been captured, or, rather, raped. "Such boldness has she - a woman to slay a man. What odious monster shall I fitly call her?....Brewing as it were a drug (*pharmakon*), she vows that with her wrath she will mix requittal for me, too, while she whets her sword against her lord....Woman, what poisonous herb nourished by the earth (*chthonotrephes*) hast thou tasted, what potion drawn from the flowing sea, that thou hast taken upon thyself this maddened rage and execration of the public voice?"[302] Zeus, as Harrison hilariously points out, is the "archpatriarchal *bourgeois*."

Agamemnon, the commander-in-chief, tells Teukros the archer, "if ever Zeus who holds the aegis and Athene grant me to sack outright the strong-founded citadel of Ilion, first after myself I will put into your hands some great gift of honour; a tripod, or two harnesses and the chariot with them, or else a woman, who will go up into the same bed with you."[303] Nestor's idea of revenge: "Therefore let no man be urgent to take the way homeward until after he has lain in bed with the wife of a Trojan to avenge Helen's longing to escape and her lamentations."[304]

Teucer, the Mycenaean founder of Salamis in Cyprus, is said to have introduced the regular custom of sacrificing a slave to Zeus.[305] The royal tombs of Salamis, dating to the seventh and eighth century BC, confirm that this was indeed the regular custom of the Greek military aristocracy.[306] Achilleus promises the dead Patroklos: "Before your burning pyre I shall behead twelve glorious children of the Trojans."[307] Following the usual custom, the survivors were enslaved for work in the mines.

The oracle centers themselves became objects of political competition between the fierce oligarchic city-states. The potters show the Athenian Herakles, Peisistratrus' hero, 540 BC, disputing possession of the Delphian tripod with Apollo himself, that is, with the other powers of Central Greece: Thebes, Sicyon, Thessaly, Megara, etc. The oracular rulings had the force of international law among member states of the amphictiony, especially as regards competition over colonies and trade routes.

Not only enslavement, but massacre was often the punishment for revolt or refusal to pay tribute to Apollo's representatives. The Athenian massacre of all the adult males on Melos and the enslavement of the women and children in 416 BC was a typical, not an isolated event.

Peisistratus traded slaves, metals, salt, textiles, pottery and wine through Emporiae and Massilia (Spain and France), not exaltation of the shamanic traditions of the prospective slaves. 'Spear-won' territory was property fairly won. That's what made Homer canonical to Peisistratus. Thucydides wrote that the Greeks "used to fall on communities that were unwalled and living in villages, plunder them, and make most of their living that way. This profession was not shameful as yet, and indeed was held in some esteem. Among some mainlanders even now it is a distinction to succeed in doing this; and the old poets testify to the practice, showing the regular question asked of those who arrive by sea to be: 'Are you pirates?'- on the assumption that the questioned would not deny the fact, and that those who were interested to know would not reproach them with it."[308]

Peisistratus' raiding parties consisted of helmeted hoplites, carrying *hoplons*, shields, iron-tipped spears, iron swords and bronze armor. Only the *aristoi*, the best, could afford the equipment and time for training, only they could finance the expeditions, and only they were written into the constitutions as Equals. Noble houses controlled priesthoods, and oligarchic clans had their own hereditary magistracies; factional power struggles were endemic. Thucydides: "As Greece became more powerful and made more of the acquisition of wealth than ever before, then generally tyrannies were established in the states as the revenues became greater."[309]

Herodotus: "In an oligarchy the fact that a number of men are competing for distinction in affairs of state cannot but lead to violent personal feuds; each of them wants to get to the top and to see his own proposals carried; so they quarrel. Personal quarrels lead to open dissension and then to bloodshed; and from bloodshed the result is one-man rule (*monarkhia*)."[310]

The 'oracles' would then be asked to sanctify by 'revelation' the divinity of the new monarch and his clan. The descendants of Cypselus (c.625 BC), portrayed by Herodotus as a sort of Moses, ruled the sea power Corinth and its many colonies. A golden bowl dedicated (*anethen*) as spoils from Heraclea by the 'sons of Cypselus' was found at Olympia, which had obediently confirmed the Cypselid descent from Herakles.[311] Sparta's gory victory over Argos for control of the Peloponnese (546 BC) was subsequently celebrated by an annual religious festival, as if the butchery had been an epiphany.

Aristotle: "...for at this rent they worked the fields of the rich. The whole land was in the hands of a few (*oligon*); and if they did not pay their rents they could be sold into slavery, themselves, and their children. And all borrowing was on the security of personal liberty till Solon's time; he was the first champion of the people. The heaviest and most bitter element for the many was their servitude."[312]

Solon and Peisistratus gained enormous political leverage by eliminating enslavement for debt among their own constituency while continuing to use slaves as a medium of international exchange. Much is made of Greek democracy, but citizenship was most often defined by wealth, *time*, 'honor,' and power was almost always confined to the landed aristocracy, to whom the serfs and slaves, the *atimia*, were indentured.

Although compassionate, and politically astute, both Plato and Aristotle thought slavery a perfectly moral foundation on which to build an ideal aristocratic state, and neither entertained the idea that the free laboring classes were worthy of full citizenship. In the *Laws* Plato couples slaves with children as having imperfectly developed minds, and Aristotle, in the *Politics*, regards barbarians as slaves 'by nature.' His compassion is reserved for Greeks, and his respect for aristocrats. Under Solon, the legal testimony of slaves became valid, vis-a-vis those with honor, only through torture, *basanos*, testing the mettle.

The slave burials of eighth century BC Pithecusa, in Sicily, show that slave ownership extended well down the social ladder to families of relatively humble means.[313] Slaves were as regular a commodity of the Greek traders at Ezekiel's sixth century Tyre as bronze cauldrons.[314] The naval power Chios traded its mass-produced wine, Thracian silver, Egyptian grain and slaves for resale. Nebuchadnezzar traded Israelis, Palestinians, Phoenicians, Elamites, Medes, Persians, Egyptians, Lydians and Ionians.[315]

The Law Code of Gortyn, Crete, c.500 BC, codifying yet more ancient law, charged 1200 obols for the rape of a free person by another free person, 2400 obols for rape of a free person by a slave, 30 obols for rape of a serf by a free person and 1,2 or 24 obols for rape of a slave by a free person. The 24 obol fine was imposed if the slave died.[316]

Almost every significant government from the Late Bronze Age to the nineteenth century has been a theocratic slave state in which the official rituals of the culture reinforced mass servitude. The sacred fire of the Mother City which the colonists so treasured on their arduous voyage of conquest was meant to replace that of their hosts. "Conquering gods their titles take/From the foes they captive make."

Propaganda works by way of true myth, imagery which instantly affects our emotions. This archetypal imagery is brought to life by pharmaco-shamanic rites in tribal cultures, and those rites are criminalized and coopted by their industrial conquerors. The solar monotheism, the Aten of Akhenaten, served the same purpose as the Apollo of the Delphian powers, or the Juppiter Maximus of Caesar, or the Jesus Invictus of Constantine and Charles V. The Imperial Icon facilitated the efficient management of the conquered by requiring the replacement of their culture with the Imperial syncretism. This cultural genocide effectively turned once independent people into farm animals - *andrapoda*, as the Greeks put it, 'human-footed stock.'

The archetypal matristic imagery remained an organic if diminished part of classical Olympian mythology because the Greeks remained more decentralized than either the Israelis or the Romans. King David organized all the women of royal blood into a royal harem, thus making the 'matrilineal' throne of Israel the exclusive province of the King and his line. This device was adopted in Rome on the founding of the Vestal College, but, because there was no central Greek government, and because the canonical Hesiod, early on, had, as Herodotus put it, "given the deities their titles and distinguished their several provinces and special powers,"[317] absolute theological patriarchy never reached Greece, although Olympian tradition is certainly warrior-based.

As Graves puts it, "The institution of patriarchy ends the period of true myth; historical legend then begins and fades into the light of common history."[318] That is, true myth, the archetypes of consciousness evoking evolutionary, that is behavioral, realities, instinct, the stuff of dreams, is more easily discerned through the fog of Greek legend than Israeli or the much later Roman. As Homer put it, "Two gates for ghostly dreams there are: one gateway/of honest horn, and one of ivory./Issuing by the ivory gate are dreams/of glimmering illusion, fantasies,/but those that come through solid polished horn/may be borne out, if mortals only know them."[319]

Graves says that all true poetry celebrates the thirteen lunar months of the ancient year, the birth, life, death and resurrection of the God of the Waxing year, who is the son, lover and victim of the threefold Goddess, the Muse of all true poets. "Her names and titles are innumerable. In ghost stories she often figures as 'The White Lady,' and in ancient religions, from the British Isles to the Caucasus, as the 'White Goddess.' I cannot think of any true poet, from Homer onwards who has not independently recorded his experience of her. The test of a poet's vision, one might say, is the accuracy of his portrayal of the White Goddess and of the island over which she rules. The reason why the hairs stand on end, the eyes water, the throat is constricted, the skin crawls and a shiver runs down the spine when one writes or reads a true poem is that a true poem is necessarily an invocation of the White Goddess, or Muse, the Mother of All Living, the ancient power of fright and lust - the female spider or the queen-bee whose embrace is death."[320] Sculptures of the Bone Goddess, the Stiff White Goddess of Death, are consistently found in burials throughout the Neolithic, often with entheogenic plants or snakes attached or engraved.[321]

"The Mazatecs say that the mushrooms speak. If you ask a shaman where his imagery comes from, he is likely to reply: I didn't say it, the mushrooms did....The spontaneity they liberate is not only perceptual, but linguistic, the spontaneity of speech, of fervent, lucid discourse, of the logos in activity. For the shaman, it is as if existence were uttering itself through him. From the beginning, once what they have eaten has modified their consciousness, they begin to speak and at the end of each phrase they say *tzo* - 'says' in their language - like a rhythmic punctuation of the said....'I am he who puts together,' says the medicine man to define his shamanistic function: 'he who speaks, he who searches, says. I am he who looks for the spirit of the day, says. I search where there is fright and terror. I am he who fixes, he who cures the person that is sick. Herbal medicine. Remedy of the spirit. Remedy of the atmosphere of the day, says. I am he who resolves all, says. Truly you are man enough to resolve the truth. You are he who puts together and resolves. You are he who puts together the personality. You are he who speaks with the light of day. You are he who speaks with terror.'"[322]

Jung: "Myth is the primordial language natural to these psychic processes, and no intellectual formulation comes anywhere near the richness and expressiveness of mythical imagery. Such processes are concerned with the primordial images, and these are most succinctly reproduced by figurative language."[323]

CAH: "The earliest [Greek] dedications are records that this object belonged to the god, and that X has given it in hopes of, or return for, a divine favour. The verse on the 'Dipylon Jug' identifies it as a prize offered for the best dancer, presumably at a public festivity like that in Phaeacia, when after athletic contests the young people performed dances before and after a bardic recital. Public statements designed to lodge in people's minds naturally used the mnemonic power of verse. Prose was not yet held to be an art..."[324] The oracles at Delphi were enunciated in the ancient dactylic hexameter, the automatic versification taught by the snake-women to the bards who recited *The Iliad* and *The Odyssey*. The Dipylon Jug wasn't empty; the prize wasn't the jug, which would have been of no meaning to a wild young dancer, it was its contents.[325]

Professor Harrison: "...the gist of the Oschophoria [autumn festival] is clear. It is like the race of Olympia, a race of youths, *epheboi, kouroi*, with boughs....Two epheboi chosen from each of the ten tribes, raced against one another. The ten victors, after being feasted, formed into procession, one of them leading the way as *keryx*, two following, dressed as women and carrying branches, the remaining seven forming, as at Delphi, the *choros*. The prize is...a cup of mingled drinks, manifestly not a thing of money value but of magical intent, a sort of liquid *panspermia* ['all-seeds'], or *pankarpia* ['all-fruit'], meet for a vintage feast. The blend of cheese and wine and honey may not commend itself to our modern palates, but Demeter, save for the wine, drank the same in her holy *kykeon* ['mixture']."

"In the Oschophoria the winner of the race is, as at Olympia, an *Eniautos-daimon* and a *basileus* ['king'] in one. He dies as an individual and revives as an eternally recurrent functionary....Another ritual element points to early days - the *Deipnophoroi* or foodbearers who supplied the chosen epheboi with provisions, took part in the ceremony, and then 'played the part of the mothers' of the youths on whom the lot fell... They also recited myths to encourage the youths.

We have then as an integral part of the ritual just the two factors always present in matriarchal mythology, the Mother and the Son. The mother brings food, because like Mother-Earth she is essentially the feeder, the Nurturer; the mother speaks words (*mythoi*) of exhortation and consolation such as many a mother must have spoken in ancient days to a son about to undergo initiation. Such words spoken aloud may actually have been a feature of initiation ritual."

The holy trinity above, dating to c.450 BC, was found in marble relief at Eleusis - Demeter, Persephone and the Divine Child, Dionysos, also called Triptolemos, 'threefold warrior.' "An Iowa Indian when asked about the myths and traditions of his tribe said: 'These are sacred things and I do not like to speak about them, and it is not our custom to do so except when we make a feast and collect the people and use the sacred pipe.' A pious man would no more tell out his myths than he would dance out his mysteries. Only when the tribe is assembled after solemn fasting, and holy smoking, only sometimes in a strange archaic tongue and to initiate men or novices after long and arduous preparation, can the myth with safety be uttered from the mouth; such is its sanctity, its *mana*."[326]

The rite, of course, has an ecological function in the life of the group. The entheogenic or proprioceptive state induced by 'holy smoking' or 'holy drinking' is designed to foster perception of the group's, or the individual's, place in the world. The mythology, the words of the Mother, calls up memories (*mnemosyne*-realization) of the evolutonary ecology, the roots of the mind-body. "When we realize that the myth is the plot of the *dromemon* [ritual] we no longer wonder that the plot of a drama is called its 'myth.' It would be convenient if the use of the word myth could be confined to such sequences, such stories as are involved in rites. Anyhow the primitive myth, the myth proper, is of this nature..."[327]

Graves: "My thesis is that the language of poetic myth anciently current in the Mediterranean and Northern Europe was a magical language bound up with popular religious ceremonies in honor of the Moon-goddess or Muse, some of them dating from the Old Stone Age, and that this remains the language of true poetry....The language was tampered with in late Minoan times when invaders from Central Asia began to substitute patrilinear for matrilinear institutions and remodel or falsify the myths to justify the social changes. Then came the early Greek philosophers who were strongly opposed to magical poetry as threatening their new religion of logic, and under their influence a rational poetic language (now called the Classical) was elaborated in honor of their patron Apollo and imposed on the world as the last word in spiritual illumination..."[328] The "new religion of logic," of course, was that demanded by the burgeoning military-industrial complex.

Human industry is to the ecosphere what individual consciousness is to the collective unconscious. Just as sensitivity to the ineffable ecosphere must be our teacher if we are to survive the effects of our own technology, so must sensitivity to our own ineffable logosphere, our collective unconscious, be our teacher if we are to survive the politics that technology has generated.

Jung: "Just as the day-star rises out of the nocturnal sea, so, onto-genetically and phylogenetically, consciousness is born of uncon-sciousness and sinks back every night to this primal condition. This duality of our psychic life is the prototype and archetype of the Sol-Luna symbolism."[329] "Luna is really the mother of the sun, which means, psychologically, that the unconscious is pregnant with con-sciousness and gives birth to it."[330] "The foundation of consciousness, the psyche *per se*, is unconscious, and its structure, like that of the body, is common to all, its individual features being only insignifi-cant variants."[331]

The loss of connection to the ecstatic processes, the loss of an easy bridge between the conscious and the unconscious, is the beginning of neurosis, the loss of connection to the Holy Mother, the irrational voice of our emotions, the fountainhead of our genius. The last thing Greek slaves needed was genuine inspiration, so, for them, the con-tents of the Jug became taboo. We have all become Greek slaves. The Mycenaeans, conquerors and transmitters of Cretan culture, were themselves absorbed by the southerly march of the Dorians and Ionians. Their Classical Greek imagery was then transformed by the Romans into the Orthodox Christianity which became the manda-tory religion of the late Roman slave states, of all the medieval Euro-pean slave states, and the theological underpinning of the Euro-Ameri-can industrial theocracy.

Kannabis, as the Greeks called it, sacred mushrooms, coca leaf, Peyote and the other ancient herbal sacraments are among the most easily accessible doorways to the proprioceptive and oracular avail-able. They are fountainheads of creativity and earth-consciousness industrial culture desperately needs. Without institutionalized, or at least legalized shamanism, a Paleolithic adaptive technique, human political culture risks domination by the suicidally robotic, as our re-peated acts of genocide and our virtually institutionalized ecocide tend to indicate. It is the tribal, the mammalian, the creative part of our psyche that is sensitive to our biological relationship to the earth. Is global political culture successfully dealing with the industrial de-stabilization of the ecosphere? Unmitigated industrial values are a path to evolutionary suicide.

The ancient shamanic bridges need to be rebuilt; the familial tribal cultures need to be listened to very carefully. Humanizing the evolved industrial polity will be every bit as difficult as healing the damaged ecosphere and rendering human industry ecological. "The Teleut shaman calls back the soul of a sick child in these words: 'Come back to your country!...to the yurt, by the bright fire!...Come back to your father...to your mother!...'....It is only if the soul refuses or is unable to return to its place in the body that the shaman goes to look for it and finally descends to the realm of the dead to bring it back."[332] Hence historiography.

DIONYSOS

The *Hymn To Demeter*, written down c.700 BC, is the foundation legend of Athenian culture, as the legend of Moses on the Mountain is the founding legend of Israeli culture. Classical writers and the *Hymn* itself attribute the origin of the Great Mysteries at Eleusis, 14 miles from Athens, to Crete. The archeological finds, such as the ivory depicting Demeter, Persephone and the infant Plutos ('wealth,' Dionysos, the Son, the Seed) found at Mycenae confirm this.[333]

Eleusis means 'the place of happy arrival,' 'Advent,' and is related to *Elysion*, 'the realm of the blessed.'[334] The name derives from the Cretan Goddess of Childbirth, 'child-bearing' Eileithyia, also called Eleuthyia. The name itself is not Indo-European, but Old European, Cretan or Carian, related to *lada*, 'lady' and the goddess Leto.[335]

Pausanias: "A shrine of Eileithyia stands near here. They claim she came from the Hyperboreans to Delos to help Leto in her birth-pains, and that other people got Eileithyia's name from them. The Delians do in fact offer sacrifices to Eileithyia, and sing the hymn by Olen. But the Cretans think Eileithyia was Hera's child, born at Amnisos in the country around Knossos."[336] The Cretan month of *Eleusinios* coincides with the Greek month of *Boedromion*, the harvest time of the Eleusinian mysteries.[337] The 14th century BC Mycenaean temple at Eleusis, mentioned in the *Hymn*, was unearthed in 1931.[338]

'Persephone' means 'she who brings destruction.' Her shamanic trip into winter is described in the first lines of the *Hymn To Demeter*: "I begin to sing of rich-haired Demeter, awful goddess - of her and her trim-ankled daughter whom Aidoneus rapt away, given to him by all-seeing Zeus the loud-thunderer."

"Apart from Demeter, lady of the golden sword and glorious fruits, she was playing with the deep-bosomed daughters of Okeanos and gathering flowers over a soft meadow, roses and crocuses and beautiful violets, irises also and hyacinths and the narcissus, which Earth made to grow at the will of Zeus and to please the Host of Many, to be snare for the bloom-like girl - a marvellous, radiant flower. It was a thing of awe whether for deathless gods or mortal men to see: from its root grew a hundred blooms and it smelled most sweetly, so that all wide heaven above and the whole earth and the sea's salt swell laughed for joy. And the girl was amazed and reached out with both hands to take the lovely bauble; but the wide-pathed earth yawned there in the plain of Nysa, and the lord, Host of Many, with his immortal horses sprang out upon her - the Son of Kronos, He who has many names."

"He caught her up reluctant on his golden car and bare her away lamenting. Then she cried out shrilly with her voice, calling upon her father, the Son of Kronos, who is most high and excellent. But no one, either of the deathless gods or of mortal men, heard her voice, nor yet the olive trees bearing rich fruit: only tender-hearted Hecate, bright-coiffed, the daughter of Persaios, heard the girl from her cave..."[339]

The root of *narkissos*, the fragrant 'narcissus' of a hundred blooms that ensnared Persephone, is *narki*, 'drowsiness,' likewise the root of *narkotikos*, 'narcotic.' 'Ivy' is *kissos*: Pausanias: "they speak of the Singer Dionysos and of Ivy as the same god."[340] The *Hymn*, then, describes a 'narcotic ivy' of a hundred flowers that Persephone picked on the plain of Mount Nysa, in Crete, satyric gift of the Zeus of Nysa, Dionysos.

Professor Ruck: "The etymology of Nysa is not certain, but related words seem to be *nystazo*, 'to nod and doze in sleep,' a reaction that would be attributed to the *narkissos*, and *nysos*, a Thracian word for 'bride,' and *nysso*, 'to sting.' In botanic lore, Dionysus' own plant, the *kissos* or 'ivy,' was called *nysa*... Dionysus' name is often taken to mean the 'Zeus of Nysa' or the 'Divine Bridegroom.'"[341] Homer calls Nysa "the sacrosanct and uttermost Blossom (*Anthedon*)."[342]

According to Ovid, the 'narcotic ivy' was opium.[343] Dionysos' mother, Demeter, was the Opium Goddess every bit as much as the

Grain Goddess.[344] At Gazi, in Crete, a figure of the Goddess was found (p.107) with ripe poppy heads in her headress that had specially colored incisions, dripping with sap. On a gold signet ring from the Thisbe Treasure, a standing Kore hands two bulging poppy heads to a majestically seated Demeter. On the spectacular gold signet ring from Mycenae, above, c. 1500 BC, Demeter, seated beneath the Double Axe and the World Tree, hands three bulging poppy heads to Kore.[345] The Cretan 'sleeping idol,' Demeter, from Isopata, wears a diadem of opium poppy heads, each painted with a slit for extraction of the sap. A ceremonial *krater* in the National Archeological Museum of Taranto, below, c. 450 BC, depicts Demeter's son, Dionysos, wearing a crown of opium poppies.[346] That is a comment on the ceremonial content.

A beautiful ceremonial vase, below, c.350 BC, shows the divinites adoring a huge poppy seed capsule growing out of the center of an ornate temple-tomb, surrounded by floating four-petal rosettes, symbol of the four-petalled opium flower. Persephone rushes up to the enshrined poppy, a huge speckled mushroom, Soma, the size of a parasol, in her right hand.[347] These are also references to the sacramental ceremony in which the vase was employed.

Opium is a likely ingredient of the *kykeon* ('mixture') drunk at Eleusis. Unmistakable reliefs of the uniquely shaped bulging opium capsules atop their stems were carved into the walls of the Athens Eleusinion, along with barley, myrtle, steer skulls, kernoi and eight-petalled rosettes.[348] These images were also carved on the *cista mystica* carried on the heads of the huge 'caryatids,' structural Goddess pillars, literally 'nut trees,' that supported the temple at Eleusis.

In the *Hymn*, Demeter explains to Queen Metaneira that "it was not right for her to drink red wine. She asked them to give her a drink of barley-meal and water mixed with tender pennyroyal [the *kykeon*]. She mixed the drink and gave it to the goddess, as she had asked, and mighty Deo accepted it, complying with holy custom."[349]

This is the 'sober offering' of the mysteries. One's mind became 'sober,' enlightened. The barley added to the *kykeon* became magical in the following manner: it molded, grew ergot, the sclerotia, *erysibe*, 'rust,' the 'beard' which produces tiny entheogenic mushrooms, *Claviceps purpurea*. Clay sealings have been found at Knossos which reproduce molded barley in conjunction with lion-men, and several Palace tablets take cognizance of the barley beard in their accounting. A jasper prism stamp-seal was found in Middle Minoan layers, c.1600 BC, which reproduces the 'beard' along with the barley.[350]

In the class of sac fungi, most ergot alkaloids are derivatives of lysergic acid, as sacred in Mayan morning glories as in Cretan flower wine.[351] The neurotransmitter serotonin is also a derivative of lysergic acid, which is, obviously, a clue as to how *Claviceps*, and its refined derivative LSD, works.[352] The sclerotic stage is the dormant stage, which eventually falls to the ground to release spores which grow into the reddish mushrooms.

Red letters, oracular letters, were said to be rusted, *erysibe*, the color of the hair of the spirit of possession, Aidoneus, the Son of Kronos, in the *Hymn To Demeter*. Red was also the color of Soma, which, as Persephone indicates, was also sacred to the composers of the *Hymn*.[353] Danaan *Adamos*, 'unconquerable,' related to Hebrew *adamah*, earth, and *dam*, blood, and the Semitic *Edom*, red, all mean 'the red man,' or 'made of red earth.'[354] That is, 'Aidoneus' is related to 'Adam.' This archetypal association of red with sacred power was later reversed by the conquistadors, so that the Roman Hades (Aidoneus) and the Roman Judas (Yehudah) were portrayed with red hair.

Apollodorus was quite clear on the magical powers of 'rust,' which he called *ion*, literally, 'purple drug': "Phylacus marvelled, and perceiving that he was an excellent soothsayer, he released him and invited him to say how his son Iphiclus might get children. Melampus promised to tell him, provided he got the kine. And having sacrificed two bulls and cut them in pieces he summoned the birds; and when a vulture came, he learned from it that once, when Phylacus was gelding rams, he laid down the knife, still bloody, beside Iphiclus, and that when the child was frightened and ran away, he stuck the knife in the sacred oak, and the bark encompassed the knife and hid it. He said, therefore, that if the knife were found, and he scraped off the rust (*ion*), and gave it to Iphiclus to drink for ten days, he would beget a son. Having learned these things from the vulture, Melampus found the knife, scraped the rust, and gave it to Iphiclus for ten days to drink, and a son Podarces was born to him."[355] The prophetic vulture is the one adorning the walls at Catal Huyuk.

"Ergonovine is a water-soluble alkaloid of ergot....decidedly more powerful in its effects on the uterus than are the other alkaloids of ergot; this difference is more marked on the puerperal than on the nongravid uterus....the first effect of ergonovine is a heightening of uterine tonus...its chief action is to produce rhythmical contractions."[356] (*U.S.Disp.*) As Pseudo-Dioscorides shows, this action of ergot was understood by the ancients.[357]

The barley beard was, therefore, elemental to women's mysteries:

it induced the sacred marriage with Aidoneus and aided in giving birth. Greek midwives carried the staff of the winged snake-nymph Korykia, below, the entwined psychopompic snakes that escorted their charges into the precincts of the Goddess. This is the same staff, the kerykeion, in Latin 'caduceus,' that became the symbol of modern medicine. Hippokrates got it from Korykia. Both images below date to c.500 BC. Korykia, Iris of the Rainbow, is the prototype of Hermes.

Evans says the word 'Korykia' may be derived from *krokus*, which he identifies with *Crocus sativus*, saffron, the most important Cretan dye and perfume plant. Saffron was used to dye the robes of ecstatic dancers.[358] Saffron is identified as a promoter of menstruation by Grieve, and so, possibly, is an abortifacient as well if taken in large doses. *Krokus* is the old Hebrew *karkom*. (S.of Sol:4:14) Whether Korykia's *krokus* was saffron or some other powerful bulb, it does seem that Korykia was Eileithyia, Demeter, Persephone, Artemis or Iris in her incarnation as 'Lady of the Bulb.'

Six psychoactive bulbs are pictured on an elaborate ritual cup from Knossos, c. 1450 BC, one of which is painted with the floating eyes and menacing stare of a gorgoneion, a shaman keeper of the mysteries.[359] As we have seen, sprouting Korykian bulbs are shown supporting Cretan shrines on many stamp seals and signet rings.[360] The winged Gorgon below is from the island of Rhodes, c.700 BC.

Archeologist R.F. Willetts: "Apart from Crete and the islands, Eileithyia also had a flourishing cult in Laconia. She had two temples at Sparta, according to Pausanias, who also mentions the sanctuary of Demeter Eleusinia, the Eleusinion, near Taygeton. ...Demeter and Kore...are called Eleusiniai.... We saw that the chief Minoan deity, in her capacity as moon-goddess, was associated with herbal magic, which is older than agriculture and is everywhere the province of women. In Greece, the root of the peony, the dittany, the withy, the galingale, the pomegranate, the lily and the myrtle had special associations with childbirth and menstruation. The lily and the myrtle were both sacred to Aphrodite, the lily checking menstruation and the myrtle preventing premature delivery by closing the uterus. At Boiai, in Laconia, the myrtle was sacred to Artemis Soteira ['the Saviour'] who aided women in childbirth. Just as the statue of Artemis at Agra, in Attica, was decorated with garlands of withy, and wreaths of helychryse and galingale were made by Spartan girls for Hera, so crowns of myrtle were used by Eleusinian hierophants. Like *kokkos* (pomegranate-seed), the word *myrton* (myrtle-berry) was used to mean *pudenda muliebria*. It seems safe to infer that the myrtle garland of the Hellotia [women's fertility festival] was also associated with herbal magic and therefore represents a primitive stratum of cult practice confined to women."[361] All the herbs Willetts mentions were beautifully reproduced on Bronze Age Cretan drinking vessels, as on these faience chalices from Knossos.

Life comes from Eleusis, 'the place of happy arrival,' from Delphi, 'the womb,' but to acknowledge that would be to acknowledge the primacy of *Thea*. Not Zeus, or his Only Begotten Son Apollon, nor Elohim or his Only Begotten Son *Moshiy'a/Yehoshu'a/*Jesus, but the Saviour Persephone, as she was called, the *Arrhetos Koura*, 'the ineffable maiden,' the Only Begotten Daughter, as she was called, first.

Persephone, the winged Snake Nymph Korykia, was inseparable from her herbal magic. Apollonius: "Thereupon the handmaids were making ready the chariot; and Medea meanwhile took from the hollow casket a charm which men say is called the charm of Prometheus. If a man should anoint his body therewithal, having first appeased the Maiden, the only-begotten, with sacrifice by night, surely that man could not be wounded by the stroke of bronze nor would he flinch from blazing fire; but for that day he would prove superior both in prowess and in might. It shot up first-born when the ravening eagle on the rugged flanks of Caucasus let drip to the earth the blood-like ichor of tortured Prometheus. And its flower appeared a cubit above ground in color like the Korykian crocus, rising on twin stalks; but in the earth the root was like newly-cut flesh. The dark juice of it, like the sap of a mountain-oak, she had gathered in a Caspian shell to make the charm withal, when she had first bathed in seven ever-flowing streams, and had called seven times on Brimo, nurse of youth, night-wandering Brimo, of the underworld, queen among the dead, - in the gloom of night, clad in dusky garments. And beneath, the dark earth shook and bellowed when the Titanian root was cut; and the son of Iapetos himself groaned, his soul distraught with pain. And she brought the charm forth and placed it in the fragrant band which engirdled her, just beneath her bosom, divinely fair. And going forth she mounted the swift chariot..."[362]

Iliad: "And lovely-haired Hekamede made them a potion....First she pushed up...a beautifully wrought cup which the old man brought with him from home. It was set with golden nails, the eared handles upon it were four, and on either side there were fashioned two doves of gold, feeding, and there were double bases beneath it. Another man with great effort could lift it full from the table, but Nestor, aged as he was, lifted it without strain. In this the woman like the immortals mixed them a potion with Pramneian wine, and grated goat's-milk cheese into it with a bronze grater, and scattered with her hand white barley into it."[363] Magical barley powder is reverently sprinkled into sacramental brews throughout the literature.

Demeter, of course, specifically insisted on a wineless potion; her mysteries have to do with barley, not the much later grape. The use to which this food of the Goddess is put is carefully explained in the *Hymn* by Demeter to Queen Metaneira, who has asked the disguised Goddess to nurse her boy: "'Gladly will I take the boy to my breast, as you bid me, and will nurse him. Never, I ween, through any heedlessness of his nurse shall witchcraft hurt him nor yet the Undercutter: for I know a charm far stronger than the Woodcutter, and I know an excellent safeguard against woeful witchcraft."

"When she had spoken, she took the child in her fragrant bosom with her divine hands: and his mother was glad in her heart. So the goddess nursed in the palace Demophoon, wise Celeus' goodly son whom well-girded Metaneira bare. And the child grew like some immortal being, not fed with food nor nourished at the breast: for by day rich-crowned Demeter would anoint him with ambrosia as if he were the offspring of a god and breathe sweetly upon him as she held him in her bosom. But at night she would hide him like a brand in the heart of the fire, unknown to his dear parents. And it wrought great wonder in these that he grew beyond his age; for he was like the gods face to face. And she would have made him deathless and unageing, had not well-girded Metaneira in her heedlessness kept watch by night from her sweet-smelling chamber and spied. But she wailed and smote her two hips, because she feared for her son and was greatly distraught in her heart."[364]

The founding legend of the Israelis is strikingly similar: "And the angel of the Lord appeared unto him in a flame of fire out of the midst of a bush: and he looked, and, behold, the bush burned with fire, and the bush was not consumed. And Moses said, I will now turn aside, and see this great sight, why the bush is not burnt."

"And when the Lord saw that he turned aside to see, God called unto him out of the midst of the bush, and said, Moses, Moses. And he said, Here am I. And he said, Draw not nigh hither: put off thy shoes from off thy feet; for the place wheron thou standest is holy ground. Moreover he said, I am the God of thy father, the God of Abraham, the God of Isaac, and the God of Jacob. And Moses hid his face; for he was afraid to look upon God."[365]

To Demeter: "So spake Rhea. And rich-crowned Demeter did not refuse but straightway made fruit to spring up from the rich lands, so that the whole wide earth was laden with leaves and flowers. Then she went, and to the kings who deal justice, Triptolemus and Diocles, the horse-driver, and to doughty Eumolpus and Celeus, leader of the people, she showed the conduct of her rites and taught them all her mysteries, to Triptolemus and Polyxeinus and Diocles also, - awful mysteries which no one may in any way transgress or pry into or utter, for deep awe of the gods checks the voice. Happy is he among men upon earth who has seen these mysteries; but he who is uninitiate and who has no part in them, never has lot of like good things once he is dead, down in the darkness and gloom."[366] Who may participate in the holy mysteries, of course, is a political decision, but even these late patriarchal foundation legends clearly attribute the divine communication to the agency of the 'burning bush' or 'Demeter's fire.'

The *Anthesteria*,'the Blooming,' the Greek Spring festival, the Lesser Mysteries, Easter, Passover, was divided into three parts: cask-opening, cups and pots. The huge storage jars, the Pithoi (casks), were used throughout the Mediterranean for grain and wine storage as well as for burial. Professor Harrison: "The Pithoigia of the Anthesteria is the primitive Pithoigia of the grave jars, later overlaid by the Pithoigia of the wine jars."[367] That is, the souls of the dead were evoked for the Resurrection of Spring. The joyous floral design below is from a Melian *pithos*, c.600 BC.

In the *Works and Days*, when Pandora "lifts the great lid of the *pithos*" all the misfortunes of mortality fly out. Hesiod thus equates the Mystery of the Spring Resurrection with death itself, as the Israelis did in their complex Passover legend. The winged 'All-giver,' Pandora, originally, on Crete, from whence the festival comes, instigated the rebirth of the world, not its woes.[368]

Pandora-Korykia-Persephone is the Greek equivalent of Eve, and is similarly manipulated. Eve is the Hebrew equivalent of Ishtar, whose Babylonian legend is a virtual duplicate of the legend of Persephone, as is the legend of Ishtar's Sumerian mother Inanna or Iahu, dug up at ancient Nippur. Ishtar is smitten in the underworld with sixty diseases, stopping all reproductive life on earth. Ea, the Babylonian Prometheus, extracts a magical flagon from Ereshkigal, the Babylonian Hecate, the water from which enables Ishtar to rise to the surface. Reunited with Tammuz (Dionysos), they perform the sacred rites for the dead, who restore life to the upper world as the two make love.

During 'cups,' through entheogenic and erotic ecstacy, the dead earth was brought back to life. By dancing with the ghosts, ancient Eros, the fructifying power, was reborn. After 'cups' came *Chytroi*, 'pots for the food of the dead'- gifts to encourage the ghosts to return once again to their homes underground.[369]

'Death' was a state that could be visited, one could be 'abducted' to the realm of the dead, hence the sacramental identity of Greek women with Persephone; they regularly *became* Persephone. Explains Ishtar: "On the day when Tammuz comes up to me,/When with him the lapis flute and the carnelian ring come up to me,/When with him the wailing men and the wailing women come up to me,/May the dead rise and smell the incense."[370]

"Sixty times the food of life, sixty times the water of life, they sprinkled upon it,/Inanna arose./Inanna ascends from the nether world....Verily the dead hasten ahead of her....They who preceeded Inanna,/ (Were beings who) know not food, who know not water,/Who eat not sprinkled flour,/Who drink not libated wine,/Who take away the wife from the loins of man,/Who take away the child from the breast of the nursing mother." (Nippur, c.1800 BC)

Eliade: "It certainly seems that the chief function of the dead in the granting of shamanic powers is less a matter of taking 'possession' of the subject than of helping him to become a 'dead man'- in short, of helping him to become a 'spirit' too."[371]

Harrison: "The ghosts had other work to do than to eat their supper and go. They took that 'supper,' that *panspermia* ['all seeds'], with them down to the world below and brought it back in the autumn a *pankarpia* ['all fruits']. The dead are *Cthonioi*, 'earth-people,' *Demetreioi*, ' Demeter's people,' and they do Demeter's work, her work and that of Kore the Maiden, with her Kathodos ['descent'] and Anodos ['ascent']."[372] (I have transliterated Harrison's Greek into phonetic English throughout. This and the succeeding three chapters are largely a summary, in her own words, of Professor Harrison's seminal thesis. Unintroduced quotations are hers.)

Persephone's need to return underground for a third of the year was insured by Aidoneus' gift of a single pomegranate seed. This is a symbolic entheogen: the blood red pomegranate seed, *Rhoa*, was a reference to the ancient aspect of Demeter, Rhea, whose spell cannot be broken. It is the seed that must be reborn.[373]

Whatever the sacramental vehicle was for joining the dead in their Spring Resurrection, it wasn't distinguished from the food. Greek festivals, like Winnebago festivals, regarded the meat and the herbal brew and the 'food of the dead' as a whole, as givers of *mana* (Melanesian), *wakan* (Lakota), *orenda* (Iroquois), *menos* (Greek). The

Anthesteria was considered so sacred that even slaves were allowed to participate. Below is a cult plate from Marathon, c.550 BC. Persephone holds a pomegranate flower. Aidoneus holds his horny cornucopia. The plate, to judge from its design, seems to have held sacramental bulbs.

Professor Ruck: "We can do no more than guess at the identity of the drug at the Lesser Mystery, but certain aspects of Dionysian symbolism suggest that the winter bulb [*krokus*] may have been a metaphor or analog for another plant that also seemed to grow suddenly from an egg-like bulb within the cold earth. This plant may have been the mushroom or *mykes*, the untameable fungoid sibling to the ergot of the grain harvest. *Mykes* resembles the word *mykema*, the roaring of a bull or of thunder, a pun that perhaps derives from the syllabary of the Mycenaean-Minoan period, in which the 'mu' syllable would have been written with the pictogram of a bull's head. The pun is most explicitly presented in a fragment of a fifth-century tragedy where the poet seems to have said, if the text can be trusted, that the land 'roared with mushroom-bellowing.' The verse has been thought to be part of the poet's tragedy about Perseus..."[374] Perseus, that is, of the *Mykenaikos*.

The bull's head, as the symbol of the Goddess' powers of regeneration, would be a natural symbol for the Goddess' entheogen. Euripides: "Come God-/Bromios, Bacchus, Dionysos /burst into life, burst/into being, be a mighty bull,/a hundred-headed snake,/a fire-breathing lion./Burst into smiling life, oh Bacchus!"[375] Bacchus, more accurately *bakkhos*, means 'sacred branch.' Its Sumerian derivation indicates satyrical, that is phallic, associations, fertility and pharmacology not being differentiated by those who celebrated the orgies of his rites.[376] The Anthesteria became known as the Great Dionysia.

"The Bacchoi in Crete eat of a bull, the Bacchae in Thrace and Macedon of a hill-goat; the particular animal matters little, the essential is that there should be communal feast of Raw Flesh, a *dais omophagos*....The *Feast of Raw Flesh*...was part of the rite of Bacchic initiation. We shall find that this Feast is as it were the prototype of all sacrament and sacrifice."

The Feast of the Transformation, not His, but Ours: "Etymologically there is nothing in either word [sacrifice/sacrament] that tells of a gift, nor yet of a god, no notion of renouncing, giving up to another and a greater. Sacrifice is simply either 'holy doing' or 'holy making,' *hiera rhezein*, just *sanctification*, or, to put it in primitive language, it is handling, manipulating *mana*....The *omophagia* was part of a religion, that is a system of sanctities, that knew no gods; it belongs to a social organization that preceded theology. The origin of sacrifice and sacrament alike can only be understood in relation to the social structure and its attendant mode of thinking from whence it sprang - totemism. Only in the light of totemistic thinking can it be made clear why, to become a Bacchos, the candidate must partake of a sacrament of Raw Flesh."[377]

"On the votive relief...we see the process of divinization go on as it were under our very eyes. The relief falls into three portions. In the gable at the top is a bull's head. In the center is the figure of the god to whom the relief is dedicated, Zeus of Wealth or Prosperity; he pours libation on an altar, near him is his eagle. Below, the scene represented is a Bouphonia. An ox is tethered by a ring to the ground near the blazing altar. Behind him is an Ox-smiter (Boutypos) with axe uplifted ready to strike. To the left behind the ox a girl approaches, holding in her left hand a plate of fruit and flowers."

"...if we look at the god's figure more closely we see that, if Zeus he be, it is in strange form. On his head are horns: he is *taurokeros*, bull-horned like Iacchos; he is bull-faced, *Boupropos*, like the infant Dithyrambos. Now, when these animal gods come to light, it is usual to say the god assumes the shape of a bull, or is incarnate in the form of a bull. The reverse is manifestly the case. The lower end of the ladder is on earth, planted in the reality of sacrifice. The sanctified, sacrificed animal becomes a god. He then shed his animal form, or keeps it as an attribute or a beast of burden, or, as in the case of Jupiter Dolichenus...he stands upon the animal he once was, stands in all the glory of a deified Roman Emperor with double axe and thunderbolt."

"Any animal in close relation to man, whether as food or foe, may rise to be a god, but he must first become sacred, sanctified, must first be *sacrificed*....the dedication (*anadeixis*) of the bull takes place at the beginning of the agricultural year; the bull's sanctified, though not his actual, life and that of the new year begin together."[378]

"That the Bouphonia was not merely a 'common sacrifice' but also a communal feast is certain from the name given to a family who shared it. Theophrastus mentions ...not only families of Ox-smiters (*Boutupoi*) and Goaders (*Kentriadai*), but also a family of Dividers (*Daitroi*), so called, he says, from the 'divided feast' (*Dais*) which followed the partition of the flesh."[379]

"*The death of the ox was followed by a mimic Resurrection.* When the ox had been flayed and all the flayers had tasted his flesh, Porphyry tells us 'they sewed up the hide and stuffed it out with hay and set it up just as it was when it was alive, and they yoked a plough to it as though it were ploughing....his resurrection is the *mimetic representation* of the new life of the new year and this resurrection is meant to act magically. The worshippers taste the flesh to get the *mana* of the ox, and to do that they must slay him. To taste the flesh is good, but best of all is that the ox himself should on his resurrection renew his life and strength....The simple fact is that the holy ox is before the anthropomorphic god, the communal feast (*dais*) before the gift-burnt sacrifice (*thusia*). The Bouphonia belongs to the stage of the communal feast followed by the resurrection."[380]

"Plutarch...asks 'Who is the *Hosioter* among the Delphians?...They call the *Hosioter* the animal sacrificed when a *Hosios* is designated.' It is at first sight astonishing to find the name *Hosioter-He who consecrates*, the Consecrator - applied to the victim rather than the priest. But...the Holy Bull is the source of *mana*. In him *mana* is as it were incarnate. He it is who consecrates. At Delphi he became and *was* a god - the Bull-Dionysos."

"The month Bysios was, Plutarch tells us, at the beginning of the spring, the time of the blossoming of many plants. The 8th of Bysios was the birthday of the god, and in olden times on this day only did the oracle give answers. At Magnesia the new daimon comes in at the time of sowing; at Delphi the *Thyiades* wake up the infant god Liknites at the time when the Hosioi offer their secret sacrifice, presumably first *of* and then *to* the Hosioter, the Bull. The death of the old-year daimon may be followed immediately by his resurrection as the spirit of the new year....This holy vehicle of the year's *mana*, this *eniautos*-daimon who died for the people, became at Delphi and many other places a bull-god, a divinity born of his own sacrifice, i.e. of his own sanctification.."[381]

"This strange and thoroughly mystical attitude towards the sacrificed food-animal comes out very beautifully in the Finnish *Kalevala*, where a whole canto is devoted to recounting the sacrificial feast to and of Otso the mountain bear. They chant the praises of the Holy Bear, they tell of his great strength and majesty, the splendour of his rich fur, the glory and the beauty of his 'honey-soft' paws. They lead him in festal procession, slay and cook and eat him and then, as though he were not dead, they dismiss him with valedictions to go back and live for ever, the glory of the forest. In the litany addressed to him the sacramental use of his flesh comes out very clearly. Limb by limb he is addressed: 'Now I take the nose from Otso/That my own nose may be lengthened,/But I take it not completely, And I do not take it only./Now I take the ears of Otso/That my own ears I may lengthen.'"[382]

A common word for 'goat,' 'sheep' or 'fleece' in Greek was *melon*, which also meant 'apple,' as in the Golden Apple of the Hesperides.[383] The animal and vegetal sacraments were inseparable, virtually indistinguishable, since they were always consumed together. Another word for 'fleece' was *dian*. *Dianthis* meant 'blossoming,' so that *dian*, 'fleece,' also meant 'blossom.' "'and they held in their hands the sender which was they say the kerykeion, the attribute of Hermes, and from a sender of this sort, *pompos*, and from the *dian*, the fleece...they get the word *diapompein*, divine sending.'(Eustathius)"[384] This is a Sumerian word, DA-IA-U-NA, translated by Allegro, from the usage of its constituent parts, as 'having power over fertility,' Diana.[385]

"In the *Bacchae*, when the messenger returns from Citharon, he says to Pentheus: 'I have seen the wild white women there, O king,/Whose fleet limbs darted arrow-like but now/From Thebes away, and come to tell thee how/They work strange deeds.' The 'wild white women' are in a hieratic state of holy madness, hence their miraculous magnetic powers. Photius has a curious note on the verb with which 'Potniades' is connected. He says its normal use was to express a state in which a woman 'suffered something and entreated a goddess' and 'if any one used the word of a man he was inaccurate.' By 'suffering something' he can only mean that she was possessed by the goddess (*entheos* or *katochos*)..."[386] (Harrison's parenthesis. Within a quotation, mine are square.)

Oreithyia, 'she who rages in the mountains,' was the grandmother of Eumolpus, the 'beautiful singer' who was the first hierophant at Eleusis.[387] His son was Keryx, the first herald at Eleusis. Oreithyia was one of the Hyakinthidae, 'daughters' of the *hyakinthos* flower. Explains Plato: "a blast of Boreas, the north wind, pushed her off the neighboring rocks as she was playing with Pharmakeia."[388] *Pharmakeia* means 'the use of drugs.'[389] Another Cretan name for Dionysos, the *pharmakos* who was the *pharmakon*, was *Hyakinthos*. The word is related to Greek *hysginon*, 'blue blood,' which Apollo (the Dorians) accidentally spilled. The flower was said to have grown from the blood.[390]

The juice of the Hyancinth root, according to Grieve, is an effective remedy for vaginal inflammations. The gum of the bulbs and plant were used for fixing feathers on arrows, and the fresh bulbs are a powerful intoxicant.[391] The *Hyakinthos* not only sent the hunter, but the arrows as well. *Hyakinthos* is pictured, as on p.58, floating in mid-air, armed with his bow and arrow.

The first lines of *The Bacchae*, which won for Euripides the prize at the Great Dionysia, are these: "I, Dionysos, son of Zeus, am back in Thebes./I was born here, of Semele, daughter of Cadmus,/blasted from her womb by a bolt of blazing thunder." Later the Chorus of Maenads explains: "Him,/whom his mother carried/to premature and painful birth/when in a crash of thunder/she was death-struck by a fiery bolt./But quicker than death,/Zeus swept him up and plunged him/into a makeshift womb-/secure from Hera's eyes-/in the thick of his thigh,/stitched with stitches of gold./As time ripened into fate/ he delivered the bull-horned God/and crowned him with a crown of serpents./Thus was created the custom/for thyrsos-carrying maenads/to twine snakes in their hair./Oh, Thebes, Semele's nurse,/ crest your walls with ivy./Burst into greenness, burst/into a blaze of bryony,/take up the bacchanalian beat/with branches of oak and of fir,/cover your flesh with fawnskin/fringed with silver-white fleece/ and lifting the fennel,/touch God/in a fit of sanctified frenzy./Then all at once, the whole land will dance!"[392]

Semele is, of course, Megapenthe, the *Mykes* of the *Mykenaikos*. Ruck: "With the cult name of Bromios, Dionysus was called the 'thunderer' or 'roarer' and both his mother Semele and a kind of mushroom had the same epithet relating them to the thunderbolt.... Furthermore, stone grave markers in the shape of mushrooms have been found at various Greek sites, some of them as early as the archaic period."[393]

Entheogenic mushrooms, which pop up overnight, were said to be caused by the lightning. This genesis served as an explanation of their extraordinary power. In the Maya *Popol Vuh*, just as in *The Bacchae*, the entheogen is called 'lightningbolt'(*kakulja*). Wasson: "Certain it is that these uses of *kakulja* do not mean lightningbolt at all. They refer to entheogens, the secondary meaning. The 'one-leg lightningbolt' means Soma. The 'dwarf lightningbolt' means the various entheogenic *Psilocybe* species, normally much smaller than the fly-agaric (Soma), by comparison 'dwarfs.' The 'green lightningbolt' is the entheogenic morning-glories and any other phanerogamic entheogens. These are obvious interpretations for anyone who knows the entheogens."[394] In the *Rg Veda* (Sanskrit,c.1500 BC), Parjanya, god of Thunder, is father of Soma, repeatedly referred to as 'Not-Born Single-Foot,' and often accompanied by the cthonic snake.

In the *Hippolytus*, Euripides (c.428 BC) wrote: 'O mouth of Dirce, O god-built wall/That Dirce's wells run under;/Ye know the Cyprian's fleet foot-fall,/Ye saw the heavens round her flare/When she lulled to her sleep that Mother fair/Of Twy-born Bacchus and crowned her there/The bride of the bladed thunder:/For her breath is on all that hath life, and she floats in the air/Bee-like, death-like, a wonder.'"[395]

In *The Bacchae* Euripides has Dionysos ask: "Why am I here? A god in the shape of a man,/....I danced my way throughout the East,/ spreading my rituals far and wide - a God/made manifest to men./ Of all Greek cities, Thebes is the one I chose/to rouse into a new awareness,/dressing Greek bodies in fawnskins,/planting the thyrsos in Greek hands,/....This town must learn,/even against its will, how much it costs/to scorn God's mysteries and to be purged./So shall I vindicate my virgin mother/and reveal myself to mortals as a God,/ the son of God."[396] If that sounds like Paul, that's because Paul was a Greek.

Here is Euripides on the sanctity of the wine that was the Blood of the Virgin's Son; the speaker is the old seer Teiresias, admonishing the daimonic hunter Prince Pentheus (Sufferer): "Your tongue is so nimble/one might think you had some sense, but your words/contain none at all. The powerful man/who matches insolence with glibness is worse than a fool./He is a public danger!/This new God whom you dismiss,/no words of mine can attain/the greatness of his coming power in Greece. Young man,/two are the forces most precious to mankind./The first is Demeter, the Goddess./She is the Earth - or any name you wish to call her -/and she sustains humanity with solid food./Next came the son of the virgin, Dionysos,/bringing the counterpart to bread, wine/and the blessings of life's flowing juices./His blood, the blood of the grape,/lightens the burden of our mortal misery./ When, after the daily toils, men drink their fill,/sleep comes to them, bringing release from all their troubles./There is no other cure for sorrow. Though himself a God,/it is his blood we pour out/to offer thanks to the Gods. And through him,/we are blessed."[397]

Professor Ruck points out that Pentheus, as Euripides repeatedly mentions[398] is the son of the 'serpent man' Echeion, one of the crop of serpent's fangs planted by Cadmus in founding Thebes.[399] As the son of the serpent-plant, his ancestry is clearly pharmacological; serpents were said to derive their venom from the plants they ate, and likewise the plants' powers were said to derive from the serpents that crawled amidst them. The 'thunder gong' that signalled the birth of the divine child Brimos at Eleusis was called the *echeion*; it is the same gong used by Euripides to announce the arrival of Bromios, the 'Thunderer,' the reborn Dionysos.[400]

Brimo is Thessalian for 'strong,' the northern Greek epithet for Hekate/Persephone, the destroyer, who had so many epithets because she could only be described, not named. It was the serpent-plants that were carried in the maenad's staff, the fennel-crowned *thyrsos*. Korykia's snake-staff is the symbol of the *thyrsos*. The *liknon*, the harvest basket that also served as a winnowing fan and cradle, also became a ritual herb carrier and, later, symbol of the Divine Child. Like gardeners, the Maenads nurse Bakkhos, Liknites, then consume him to raise him up again. The babe in the cradle is the *mysterion* in the *liknon*, the *pharmakos* who was the *pharmakon*.[401]

The contest between Dionysos and Pentheus in *The Bacchae*, then, is the contest between the King and his twin, both sons of the same androgynous parent, the snake-plant. Pentheus is the waning reflexive primitivity, Dionysos the waxing agrarian enlightenment. Ruck: "A similar opposition between gathered and cultivated plants involved the god Dionysus: poisonous and intoxicating wild ivy with its diminutive clusters of berries was apparently related to a cultivated plant that it resembled, the vine with its bunches of juicy grapes. This opposition is often depicted in vase paintings, where the elder Dionysus is shown confronting the younger manifestation of himself in a new generation as his own son, the boy named 'Bunch of Grapes,' who carries the vine plant, while his father holds the wild ivy....the fact that maenadic ceremonies did not occur in any relationship to the timing of the events involved in viticulture can now be understood, for these mountain rites centered not upon wine but upon the wild and intoxicating herbs gathered while the more civilized god was absent in the otherworld, undergoing the cultivation that would convert the juice of crushed grapes into an inebriant. Even wine, however, was felt to have an affinity to the toxins of wild plants, for, as we have shown, wine itself was flavored with various herbs that intensified its intoxicating qualities, hence requiring it to be diluted with several parts of water to tame it for civilized purposes."[402]

The distillation of alcohol was unknown to the Greeks (discovered c.1100 CE), who had no word for it. Their strongest wine could only have been about 14% alcohol, brandy, past which alcohol becomes fatal to the yeast which produces it, yet they constantly write of having to dilute it for safety. Obviously this is the potent flower wine of old.[403] Archilochos, the earliest known composer of dithyrambs, ecstatic songs sung to the reborn Dionysos, wrote that the songs came to him as "the wine shook my mind with lightning."[404]

Pausanias: "In this place they say Phytalos ['plant-man'] took Demeter into his house, and the goddess gave him the fig-tree as a reward. What I say is confirmed by the inscription on the grave of Phytalos: 'Here Phytalos, king and hero, received/terrible Demeter, revelation/of the first fruit of autumn:/humanity named it the sacred fig./The honors of the race of Phytalos/will not grow old'....A small shrine built along the road is called the shrine of the Bean man....Those who know the mystery of Eleusis and those who have read Orpheus will know what I am talking about."[405] The archaic Greek mirror below shows Demeter, wearing her sacral knot, handing magical plants to Phytalos, dressed as a typical initiate, an *ephebos*.

Hesiod: "Demeter, noble among goddesses, gave birth to Wealth [Iacchos], in union of intimate desire with the hero Iasius ['the man of the drug'] in a thrice-fallow field, in the rich Cretan land: broad back of the sea, and whoever encounters him, into whosoever hands he comes, he makes him rich and bestows much fortune on him."[406]

Continues Teiresias in *The Bacchae*, speaking specifically of pharmaco-shamanic ecstacy: "This God is also a prophet. Possession by his ecstacy,/his sacred frenzy, opens the soul's prophetic eyes./ Those whom his spirit takes over completely/often with frantic tongues foretell the future....A day will come when you shall see him/ straddling the rocks of Delphi amid a blaze of torches,/leaping from peak to peak, swinging and hurling high/his thyrsos, the emblem of his glory/ acclaimed throughout Greece. So Pentheus,/listen to me. Do not mistake the rule of force/for true power. Men are not shaped by force./Nor should you boast of wisdom, when everyone but you/ can see how sick your thoughts are. Instead,/welcome this God to Thebes. Exalt him with wine,/garland your head and join the Bacchic revels."[407]

Adds the chorus: "He is life's liberating force./He is release of limbs and communion through dance./He is laughter and music in flutes./He is repose from all cares - he is sleep!/When his blood bursts from the grape/and flows across tables laid in his honor/to fuse with our blood,/he gently, gradually, wraps us in shadows/of ivy-cool sleep....Look how the fire leaps/out of Semele's holy tomb!/How the lurking flame/left there once by the bolt of Zeus,/springs to life!/ Down, trembling Maenads. Fling your bodies to the ground./He rises from the ruins/of the once-mighty house,/that he himself has laid to dust./Here he comes, the son of God!"[408]

These are the central religious images of the mother culture of the authors of the Greek New Testament, written 450 years before Jesus. As Clement put it: "Euripides, the philosopher of the stage, has divined as in a riddle that the Father and the Son are one God."[409] On the island of Andros, after the winter solstice, the birth of Dionysos was celebrated as the transformation of the water of a sacred stream into wine. This transformation was attributed to the *Oinotropoi*, below, the 'wine-turners': 'wine maiden,' 'seed maiden,' and 'oil maiden,' a holy trinity.[410]

The psychology of this archetypal pharmaco-shamanism is basic to Christian theology. That is, it is basic to an understanding of Jesus as *pharmakon*, Eucharist, and basic to an understanding of the demonization of Dionysos, Jesus' Greek alter ego, his Pentheus, as Judas became his Hebrew Pentheus. Jesus' displacement of Dionysos meant, quite literally in the hands of Roman slavers, that Dionysos' sacraments were now illegal, just as Imperial Christian displacement of Tsistsistas culture meant that their sacraments are now illegal. *The Bacchae* are the Young Wolf Women.

Here are the miracles of *The Bacchae*: "First, they let their hair fall down their shoulders/and those whose fawnskins had come loose/ fastened them up, while others girdled theirs/with snakes that licked their cheeks. Some,/mothers with newborn babies left at home,/ cradled young gazelles or wild wolf cubs in their arms/and fed them at their full-blown breasts/that brimmed with milk./Then they wreathed their heads with shoots/of ivy, oak and flowering bryony./ One of them lifted a thyrsos, struck a rock/and water gushed from it as cool as mountain snow./Another drove a stick into the ground/ and at the bidding of the God,/wine came bubbling up./Those who wanted milk/just scratched the soil lightly with their fingers/and white streams flowed, while from their ivy-crested wands/sweet honey dripped like sparkling dew."[411]

Numerous Greek vases picture themselves in the hands of ecstatic Bacchae ladling out entheogenic potion from an altar sprouting roots, out of which arises a vegetal Dionysos, a human-faced tree sprouting branches. "The vine is a tree; but Dionysos is Dendrites, Tree-god, and a plant-god in a far wider sense. He is god of the fig-tree, Sykites; he is Kissos, god of the ivy; he is Anthios, god of all blossoming things; he is Phytalmios, god of growth. In this respect he differs scarcely at all from certain aspects of Poseidon, or from the young male god of Attica and the Peloponnese, Hermes....This affiliation is clearly shown by the fact that in art Hermes and Dionysos appear, as they were worshipped in cultus, as herms; the symbol of both as gods of fertility is naturally the phallos. The young Dionysos, a maturer Liknites, is not distinguishable from Hermes."[412]

Hermes Psychopompos, he of the mushroom-phallos. Hermes' Dionysiac symbol, below, is that of the mother of herbal medicine, the entwined snakes of the kerykeion. Both the maenad and the satyr facing Hermes hold the fennel-crowned herb carrier, the thyrsos, symbolized by the Korykian staff on Hermes' gown. A black-figured vase, c.550 BC, pictures itself in the hands of a bestial Silenos, leading Dionysos in his chariot, who holds a chalice, out of which pop four floating mushrooms.[413] Another Attic black-figured vase, c.500 BC, below, shows Dionysos exactly the same way, in his chariot, but this time surrounded by bunches of grapes.

"The main distinguishing factor in the religion of Dionysos is always the cult of an intoxicant, but wine is not the only intoxicant, nor in the North the most primitive. Evidence is not wanting that the cult of the vine-god was superimposed on, affiliated to, in part developed out of, a cult that had for its essence the worship of an early and northern intoxicant, cereal, not vinous."

"Dionysos is a god of many names; he is Bacchos, Baccheus, Iacchos, Bessareus, Bromios, Euios, Sabazios, Zagreus, Thyoneus, Lenaios, Eleuthereus, and the list by no means exhausts his titles....Some, like Iacchos and probably Bacchos itself...were originally only cries. Iacchos was a song even down to the time of Aristophanes, and was probably, to begin with, a ritual shout or cry kept up long after its meaning was forgotten....Sabazios is Thracian and Phyrgian, Zagreus Cretan, Bromios largely Theban, Iacchos Athenian. Some of the epithets have unquestionably shifted their meaning in the course of time."[414]

Although the name may have originated on Crete, Dionysos became a Thracian name. The Greeks called the Thracians 'ruled by women.' Dionysos, Orpheus, Mousaios and Thamyris are the mythical Thracian authors of the Homeric Hymns. The mounted Thracian (Scythian) warriors, feared archers in both Greek and Roman times, celebrated Zalmoxis, explained by Porphyry as meaning 'bearskin' and 'strange man.' Zalmoxis is related to the composite magical animal of Homer's mare-milkers, the *triquetrum*.[415]

Herodotus talks of the Scythians howling with delight at the steam bath they take in marijuana smoke.[416] Marijuana was sacred to the Greeks, who burned it, along with laurel and bearded barley, for the Pythia, and her audience, as she prophesied.[417] The Iranian word for marijuana, *bangha*, is a common term throughout Central Asia for all types of inebriation, just as 'bemushroomed' is the common word for inebriation north of Iran.[418]

Wasson: "In the Vogul language all words relating to drunkenness are derived from the word for fly-agaric (Soma), *panx*, and its innumerable variants according to the dialect. This means that Vogul speakers, when they talk of getting drunk, say that the man is 'bemushroomed.' But it is important to note that the Vogul speaker is not aware of the etymology of the word: he uses it without thinking of the fly-agaric, whether the man was 'bemushroomed' on alcohol or fly-agaric. This is similar to our use of the word 'drunk.'"[419]

The original Greek words for 'to be drunk' and 'to make drunk' are *methyein* and *methyskein*.[420] Ovid said that Dionysos invented honey, an important element of Cretan cult and the source of *methy*, mead, honey-beer. In the *Hymn to Zeus*, reflecting Cretan tradition, the infant Zeus, lying in a golden *liknon*, is suckled with honey, by a goat.

"Before he had advanced to agriculture he had a drink made of naturally fermented honey, the drink we now know as mead, which the Greeks called *methy* or *methe*. The epithet 'sweet' which they constantly apply to wine surprises us, but as a characteristic of 'mead' it is natural enough. This mead made of honey appears in ancient legends. When Zeus would intoxicate Kronos he gave him not wine, Porphyry says, for wine was not, but a honey-drink to darken his senses. Night says to Zeus: 'When prostrate 'neath the lofty oaks you see him/Lie drunken with the work of murmuring bees,/Then bind him,' and again Plato tells us how when Poros falls asleep in the garden of Zeus he is drunk not with wine but with nectar, for wine was not yet. Nectar, the ancient drink of the gods, is mead made of honey; and men know this for they offer to the primitive earth-god libations of honey (*melisponda*)....Plutarch says mead (*methy*) was used as a libation before the appearance of the vine, and 'even now those of the barbarians who do not drink wine drink honey-drink'(*meliteion*)."

"The *nephalia* [sober offerings, bloodless libations] are but intoxicants more primitive than wine. Next in order came the drinks made of cereals fermented, the various forms of beer and crude malt spirit.... The number of primitive beers - *cervisia, korma, sabaia, zythos* - is countless....All...are made of fermented grain, they appear with the introduction of agriculture, they tend to supercede mead, and are in turn superceded by wine. To put it mythologically the worship of Bromios, Braites and Sabazios pales before the Epiphany of Dionysos."[421]

"...and ambrosia, the delectable food of the gods, seems to have been a porridge of barley, oil, and chopped fruit, with which kings were pampered when their poorer subjects still subsisted on asphodel, mallow, and acorns."[422] (Graves) If the barley were molded, the king would be eating a fruit-flavored psychoactive porridge that would indeed suggest Olympos. "And while she [Penelope] slept the goddess/endowed her with immortal grace to hold/the eyes of the Akhaians. With ambrosia/she bathed her cheeks and throat and smoothed her brow -/ambrosia, used by flower-crowned Kythereia/ when she would join the rose-lipped Graces dancing."[423]

"Pantomimic dancing is of the essence of each and every mystery function. To disclose the mysteries is as Lucian puts it 'to dance out the mysteries.'....In the light of initiation ceremonies we understand why the Kouretes and Korybantes though they are real live youths are yet regarded as *daimones*, as half divine, as possessed (*entheoi*), enthusiastic, ecstatic, and why their ceremonies are characterized by Strabo as orgiastic....As *daimones* whether wholly or half divine the Kouretes *have all manner of magical capacities*."[424]

"...the Dithyramb was a ritual song sung in the winter season, probably at festivals connected with the winter solstice, of an orgiastic character and dealing with the god as an impersonation of natural forces, dealing with his sufferings (*penthous*), his death and resurrection....Dithyrambos, all philologists agree, cannot etymologically be separated from its cognate *thriambos*, which gave to the Latins their word *triumphus*. The word *thriambos* looks as if it were formed on the analogy of *iambos*.... Suidas....says 'they call the madness of poets *thriasis*.' May not *thriambos* mean the mad inspired orgiastic measure?...Mythology has left us dim hints as to the functions of certain ancient maiden prophetesses at Delphi called Thriae. May they not have been the mad maidens who sang the mad song, the *thriambos*?"

"The account of these mysterious Thriae given in the Homeric *Hymn to Hermes* (7th cent.BC) is strange and suggestive. Hermes is made to tell how his first gift of prophesy came not from Zeus, but from three maiden prophetesses: 'For there are sisters born, called Thriae, maiden things,/Three are they and they joy them in glory of swift wings./Upon their heads is sprinkled fine flour of barley white,/They dwell aloof in dwellings beneath Parnassos' height./They taught me love of soothsaying while I my herds did feed,/Being yet a boy. Of me and mine my father took no heed./And thence they flitted, now this way, now that, upon the wing,/And of all things that were to be they uttered soothsaying./What time they fed on honey fresh, food of the gods divine,/Then holy madness made their hearts to speak the truth incline,/But if from food of honeycomb they needs must keep aloof/Confused they buzz among themselves and speak no word of sooth.'"[425]

The prominent wives who celebrated the Thesmorphoria, the ancient autumn festival that culminated in the Eleusinian Mysteries, were called *Melissai*, Bees, after the Cretan fashion. Their Gorgon masks transformed them into originary furies in possession of the mystery of communal rebirth, into which no male eye may pry. At this three-day rite the originary power of the women reigned supreme, the *Melissai* performing bloody as well as bloodless sacrifices, as in Crete.

"The honey service of ancient ritual has already been noted...and the fact that not only the priestesses of Artemis at Ephesus were 'Bees,' but also those of Demeter, and, still more significant, the Delphic priestess herself was a Bee....The *thriambos* was then...the song of the Thriae or honey-priestesses, a song from the beginning like the analogous Dithyramb confused, inspired, impassioned. The title Dithyrambos ['Zeus-leap-song'] through its etymology and by its traditional use belonged to Dionysos [Zeus of Nysa], conceived of in his twofold aspect as the nature-god born anew each year, the god of plants and animals as well as of human life, and also as the spirit of intoxication."[426] The spiritual effects of the contents of the vase above, from Delphi, c.540 BC, would seem to be adequately expressed by the look on Dionysos' face.

Ovid, an ancient who knew his stuff, explains how Dionysos, he of the sacred branch, Bakkhos, got his magic, and his chariot, from the shaman Queen of the Flowers, his Mother Medea: "There were yet three nights before the horns of the moon would meet and make the round orb. When the moon shone at her fullest and looked down upon the earth with unbroken shape, Medea went forth from her house clad in flowing robes, barefoot, her hair unadorned and streaming down her shoulders; and all alone she wandered out into the deep stillness of the midnight....'O Night, faithful preserver of mysteries, and ye bright stars, whose golden beams with the moon succeed the fires of day; thou three-formed Hecate, who knows our undertakings and comes to the aid of the spells and arts of magicians; and thou, O Earth, who provides the magicians with potent herbs; ye breezes and winds, ye mountains and streams and pools; all ye gods of the groves, all ye gods of the night: be with me now. With your help when I have willed it, the streams have run back to their fountainheads, while the banks wondered; I lay the swollen and stir up the calm seas by my spell....Luna do I draw from the sky...even the chariot of the Sun, my grandsire, pales at my song; Aurora pales at my poisons....Now I have need of juices by whose aid old age may be renewed and may turn back to the bloom of youth and regain its early years. And you will give them; for not in vain have the stars gleamed in reply, not in vain is my car at hand, drawn by winged dragons.'"

"There was the chariot, sent down from the sky. When she had mounted and stroked the bridled necks of the dragon team, shaking the light reins with her hands she was whirled aloft. She looked down on Thessalian Tempe lying below, and turned her dragons toward regions that she knew. All the herbs that Ossa bore, and high Pelion, Othrys and Pindus and Olympos, greater than Pindus, she surveyed: and those that pleased her, some she plucked up by the roots and some she cut off with the curved blade of a bronze pruning-hook. Many grasses also she chose....And now nine days and nine nights had seen her traversing all lands, drawn in her car by her winged dragons, when she returned. The dragons had not been touched, save by the odor of the herbs, and yet they sloughed off their skins of many long years....plunging her knife into the throat of a black sheep, she drenched the open ditches with his blood. Next she poured upon it bowls of liquid wine, and again bowls of milk still warm, while at the same time she uttered her incantations, called up the deities of the earth, and prayed the king of the shades with his stolen bride not to be in haste to rob the old man's body of the breath of life."

"When she had appeased all these divinities by long, low-muttered prayers, she bade her people bring out under the open sky old

Aeson's worn-out body; and having buried him in a deep slumber by her spells, like one dead she stretched him out on a bed of herbs. Far hence she bade Jason go, far hence all the attendants, and warned them not to look with profane eyes upon her secret rites. They retired as she had bidden. Medea, with streaming hair after the fashion of the Bacchants, moved round the blazing altars, and dipping cloven sticks in the dark pools of blood, she lit the gory sticks at the altar flames. Thrice she purified the old man with fire, thrice with water, thrice with sulphur."

Medea is pictured working this magic on the sacramental vase below, dating to c.480 BC. The illustration is obviously a comment on the function of the sacrament, that is, the contents of the vase.

"Meanwhile the strong potion in the bronze cauldron is boiling, leaping and frothing white with the swelling foam. In this cauldron she boils roots cut in a Thessalian vale, together with seeds, flowers and strong juices. She adds to these ingredients pebbles sought for in the farthest Orient and sands which the ebbing tides of Ocean laves. She adds hoar frost gathered under the full moon, the wings of the uncanny screech-owl with the flesh as well, and the entrails of a wolf that can change at will into human form....she stirred it all up with a branch of the fruitful olive long since dry and well mixed the top and bottom together. And behold!, the old dry stick, when moved about in the hot broth, grew green at first, in a short time put forth leaves, and then suddenly was loaded with olives. And wherever the froth bubbled over from the hollow pot, and the hot drops fell upon the ground, the earth grew green and flowers and soft grass sprang up. When she saw this Medea unsheathed her knife and cut the old man's throat; then, letting the old blood all run out, she filled his veins with her brew. When Aeson had drunk this in part through his lips and part through his wound, his beard and hair lost their hoary grey and quickly became black again; his leanness vanished, away went the pallor and the look of neglect, the deep wrinkles were filled out with new flesh, his limbs had the strength of youth. Aeson was filled with wonder, and remembered that this was he forty years ago."

"Now Bakkhos had witnessed this marvel from his station in the sky, and learning from this that his own nurses might be restored to their youthful years, he obtained this boon from the Colchian."[427]

MNEMOSYNE

"The gist of the *eniautos* as distinguished from the *etos* comes out in the epithet *telesphoros* 'end bringing,' which is frequently applied to *eniautos*. The *etos* or year proper is conceived of as a circle or period that turns round. This *etos* varies...from a month to nine years or even longer. The *eniautos* is not a whole circle or period but just the point at which the revolution is completed, the end of the old *etos*, the beginning of the new....the cardinal turning point of the year... Such a day to ancient thinking must be marked out by *rites de passage*, for the issues were perilous. Such *rites de passage* are those of Closing and Opening, of Going to sleep and Waking up again, of Death and Resurrection, of killing or carrying out the Old Year and bringing in the New. To such rites it was natural, nay, necessary, to summon the Kouros."

"...we see that a weather-magician like Oinomaos ['wine-power']...goes back to a time when there was no god to be incarnated...the sky god is only a projected human reflex of this human figure of the magician, who claims to command the powers of the sky and to call down its rain and thunder by virtue of his own *mana*....The individual on whose vigour and exceptional powers the fertility of the earth depends, cannot be allowed to continue in office when his natural forces fall into decay. Hence the single combat, in which he has to make good his right to a renewed period or else to die at the hands of a more vigorous antagonist....the term of office was a 'year'- a term which...may denote a lunar or solar year or a longer period of two, four, or eight solar years - a *trieteris, penteteris,* or *ennaeteris* [the *eniautos* falls at the beginning of the third, fifth or ninth year]."

"Further, since the *eniautos* itself could be concretely conceived as a *daimon* carrying the horn of plenty...we may think of the temporary 'king' as actually being the *eniautos-daimon* or fertility spirit of his 'year.' When the year is fixed by the solar period, we get festivals of the type of the Roman Saturnalia or the Greek *Kronia* (with which the Saturnalia was regularly equated in ancient times), and the single combat appears as the driving out of winter or of the dying year by the vigorous young spirit of the New Year that is to come. It is as *eniautos-daimon*, not at first as 'incarnate god' or as king in the later political sense, that the representative of the fertility powers of nature dies at the hands of the New Year."[428]

That is, the Bull of his Mother, Kronos, yields to Zeus, Tantalus to Pelops, Pentheus to Dionysos, King to Twin, the old year to the new, at the tribal feast. The feast is centered on the magical cauldron into which the dismembered bull is thrown for resurrection, by communal ingestion, as the new year. Access to these sacraments is access to the powers of Oinomaos. *Oinos*, a Cretan word, was a generic term for any intoxicant.[429]

Herakles, 'Glory of Hera,' was Oinomaos. "We talk glibly of the 'club' of Herakles as his 'characteristic attribute' and thereby miss the real point. The 'club' of Herakles is not to begin with a thing characteristic of Herakles, a *hropalon*, the rude massive weapon of a half-barbarian hero; it is a magical bough, a *klados* rent from a living tree. The Orphic Hymn going back, as so often, to things primitive thus addresses Herakles: 'Come Blessed One, bring spells for all diseases,/ Drive out ill fates, wave in thy hand thy branch;/With magic shafts banish the noisome Keres.'" The chalice of Duris, opposite, picturing itself in the hands of Herakles, dates to c.480 BC.

"What manner of daimon this Herakles, this Daktyl ['Finger'], was is made abundantly clear from this very cult of Mycalessian Demeter to which Pausanias refers. At Mycalessos close to the Euripos Demeter had a sanctuary. 'They say that it is closed every night and opened again by Herakles, who is said to be one of the so-called Idaean Daktyls ['Fingers of Ida'- 'Ida'means 'forest']. Here a miracle is exhibited. Before the feet of the image they place whatever fruits the earth bears in autumn and these keep the bloom upon them the whole year round.' It is a *pankarpia*. Such magical fruits, with upon them a bloom that is perennial rather than immortal, does the Eniautos-daimon carry in his Eiresione [olive branch twined with wool] and hold for ever in his cornucopia."

"Herakles, the Idaean Daktyl, brought fertility to plants but also to man. His cornucopia is for fruits, but sometimes it held *phalloi* [mushrooms]....Herakles then, till saga caught and transformed him, was an Idaean Daktyl and as such own brother to the Kouretes, the Korybantes and the Satyrs. We wonder no longer that it was Herakles the eldest of the Idaean Daktyls who founded the Olympic games. It is not merely that there may have been early immigrants from Crete, it is certainly not because Herakles was the strong man of the Twelve Labours, it is because Herakles, the Idaean Daktyl, was as Megistos Kouros the fertility-daimon of the year."[430]

"Herakles is not only a seasonal fertility-daimon; he is manifestly a daimon of the Sun-Year. His Twelve Labours occupy a Great Year, *megas eniautos*....This twelfth year was not 12 months but 14, that is, it had two intercalary months necessary to equalize approximately the moon and sun cycles. The sacrifice that, together with the death of Herakles on the pyre, crowned the great calendar festival, the Eniautos-festival, had a like symbolism. Twelve 'perfect bulls' stood for the twelve years, but in all the victims were a hundred [hecatomb], to save the face of the hundred moons in the octennial moon-cycle."[431] The ritual vase bearing the illustration below dates to c.550 BC.

The Idaean Daktyloi, the 'Fingers of Mount Ida' were likely *Amanita muscaria*, Soma, the uniquely speckled entheogenic mushroom that, in southerly Crete, grew only in the higher elevations. The Cave of Zeus, near Ida's summit, twenty miles from Knossos, was a religious sanctuary for millennia.[432] The floating speckled *Amanita* opposite comes from an elaborate ritual vase dating to c.480 BC.

"The Daktyls of Crete, the initiates of Idaean Zeus...initiated Pythagoras into the thunder-rites of the Idaean cave. If Picus the Bird-King was of their company, small wonder that he could make and unmake the thunder....they were, compared to the Kouretes, a specialized society of sorcerers. Of like nature were the Telchines in Rhodes, of whom Diodorus says...'they are also said to have been magicians (*goites*), and to have had the power of inducing at their will clouds and rain-showers and hail, and they could also draw down snow, and it is said thay they could do these things just like the magi. And they could change their shapes and they were jealous in the matter of teaching their arts.'"[433] Ruck, following Hesychius, says that 'Telchine' is derived from 'melting,' *texis*, and 'enchantment,' *thelxis*.[434]

The Kouretes, the 'initiates,' were the children of Kar, the Old European Mother Goddess associated with Hecate. The word is related to *korai*, 'plant shoots.'[435] The initiates contacted the ancestors in the ancient pharmaco-shamanic rites. Eustathius, commenting on the "ancient tribe of the Kouretes"says they "were [Cretan] sorcerers and magicians. 'Of these there were two sorts: one sort craftsmen and skilled in handiwork, the other sort pernicious to all good things; these last were of fierce nature and were fabled to be the origins of squalls of wind, and they had a cup in which they used to brew magic potions from roots. They...invented statuary and discovered metals, and they were amphibious and of strange varieties of shape, some no feet, and some had webs between their fingers like geese. And they say that they were blue-eyed and black-tailed.'"[436]

Nonnos: "From Crete came grim warriors to join them, the Idaian Daktyloi, dwellers on a rocky crag, earth-born Corybants, a generation which grew up for Rhea selfmade out of the ground in the olden time. These had surrounded Zeus a newborn babe in the cavern which fostered his breeding, and danced about him shield in hand, the deceivers, raising wild songs which echoed among the rocks and maddened the air - the noise of the clanging brass resounded in the ears of Kronos high among the clouds, and concealed the infancy of Kronion with drummings."[437]

"In his treatise on the *Face in the Orb of the Moon*, Plutarch tells us that the moon is daimon-haunted, but that certain of the better sort of daimones do not always stay in the moon. 'They come down hither in order to take charge of oracles, and they are present at, and take part in, the highest order of orgiastic initiatory rites, and they are chasteners and watchers over wrong doings and they shine as saviours in battle and at sea....*Of the best of these daimones those of the age of Kronos said they themselves were. And the same of old were the Idaean Daktyls in*

Crete and the Korybantes in Phrygia and the Trophoniads in Lebadeia of Boeotia and countless others in various places...of whom the sacred rites and honours and titles remain.'"

"...the cardinal rite of tribal initiation was a mimetic Death and Resurrection. By every sort of pantomime the notion was enforced that the boy had died to his old life, had put away childish things, had in a word a new social status and soul...tribal initiation was the prototype of all social rites...the rites at birth, marriage, the making of a medicine man, death itself, were only *rites de passage*, the transit from one state to another. Change which is life itself is emphasized, represented. To consult an oracle you need a *rite de passage* just as much as to be made a member of a tribe. To know is to be in touch with *mana*, not to be *entheos*, for the *theos* is not yet formulated and projected, but to be sanctified, to pass inside the region of *tabu*; hence the preliminary purification. Lethe is but an attenuated Death; Mnemosyne, renewed consciousness, is a new Life."

"Thus, to consult an oracle, a veritable, almost physical, *rite de passage* is indispensable. The suppliant must pass out of the actual, sensible, 'objective' world, into that other world of dream, of ecstacy, of trance, with its secondary reality, the world in which emotions, hope and fear, and imagination, are blended with what we should call subjective hallucinations. He needs a *rite d'agregation* to assimilate him, and when he would return to the normal sensuous world with its other and almost alien reality he needs a *rite de segregation*....But the Mnemosyne of initiation rites, the remembering again, the *anamnesis*, of things seen in ecstacy when the soul is rapt in heavenly places, she is surely now, as ever, the fitting Mother of all things musical."[438] *Mnemosyne*, according to Hesiod, is the Mother of the Nine Muses. She could look forward as well as backward, that is, she 'remembered' how the world worked, so that she could prophesy as well as recall.[439]

"The real distinction is that heroes and cthonic divinities are Year-daimons who die to rise again. The Olympians are...and it is nowise to their credit, Immortals (*athanatoi*). It is as Year-daimons that Heroes have cthonic ritual with all its characteristic apparatus of low-lying altars, of sunset sacrifices, and above all of the *pankarpia* ['all-fruits']."[440]

"Herakles the *Ephebos, the* Kouros, is fitly wedded to *Hebe,* maiden youth in its first bloom, who is but the young form of Hera Teleia, *the* Kore. Herakles, it is abundantly clear from his cornucopia, is Agathos Daimon; but if so, we naturally ask where is his characteristic snake? He has no kerykeion, no snake-twined staff; his body never ends, like that of Cecrops, in a snake's tail. Olympos did not gladly suffer snakes, and Herakles, aiming at Olympos, wisely sloughed-off his snake-nature. While yet in his cradle he slew the two snakes that attacked him and his twin brother Iphikles....this snake-slaying is common to many heroes and...culminates as it were in the myth of the slaying of the Python of Apollo."[441]

"Another hero-daimon Saviour and Defender like Herakles was less prudent; he kept his snake and stayed outside Olympos, the great Hero-Healer with the snake-twined staff, Asklepios. Asklepios is a god but no Olympian; his art-type is modelled on that of Zeus; he is bearded, benign, venerable; he is, in fact, the Zeus of daimon-heroes. He never becomes an Olympian because he remains functional rather than personal, he is always the Saviour-Healer."

"In art as a rule the snake is twined about his staff, but in the relief...the simple truth is patent: the god in human form leans on his staff awaiting his worshippers, the holy snake behind him is his equal in stature and in majesty. It was in the precinct of Asklepios at Epidauros that the relief was found, dedicated to the Agathos Theos ['Good God'] with his cornucopia and sacred snake....the omphalos [navel-stone] at Delphi is not at Delphi only. The omphalos is of Ge rather than of Apollo, and wherever there is worship of Mother Earth there we may expect the omphalos. We find it at Eleusis, clearly figured on the Ninnion pinax, the center of the whole design. We meet it again at Phlius. Asklepios himself, then, is a snake-daimon, twined round the omphalos of Ge. He is but the daimon of the fertility of the Earth. As such he never passes wholly to the upper air of the Olympians. He remains a Saviour and a Healer, loved of the dream-oracle, very near to the earth and to man....the omphalos...according to *literary* tradition....is the grave mound of a sacred snake, *the* sacred snake of Delphi."[442]

Here is the resurrection, the initiation, of Glaukos, son of Pasiphae and Minos of Crete, as told by Apollodorus, first century BC: "But Glaukos ['grey-blue one'], while he was yet a child, in chasing a mouse fell into a jar of honey and was drowned. On his disappearance Minos made a great search and consulted diviners as to how he should find him. The Curetes told him that in his herds he had a cow of three different colours, and that the man who could best describe the cow's colour would also restore his son to him alive. So when the diviners were assembled, Polyidus ['the many-shaped'] son of Coeranus, compared the colour of the cow to the fruit of the bramble, and being compelled to seek for the child he found him by means of a sort of divination. But Minos declaring that he must recover him alive, he was shut up with the dead body. And while he was in great perplexity, he saw a serpent going toward the corpse. He threw a stone and killed it, fearing to be killed himself if any harm befel the body. But another serpent came, and, seeing the former one dead, departed and then returned, bringing a herb, and placed it on the whole body of the other; and no sooner was the herb so placed upon it than the dead serpent came to life. Surprised at this sight, Polyidus applied this same herb to the body of Glaukos and raised him from the dead. Minos had now got back his son, but even so he did not suffer Polyidus to depart to Argos until he had taught Glaukos the art of divination. Polyidus taught him on compulsion, and when he was sailing away he bade Glaukos spit into his mouth. Glaukos did so and forgot the art of divination. Thus much must suffice for my account of the descendants of Europa."[443]

The serpent mother of medicine, whose toxin comes from the plants it eats and whose plants carry the bite of the serpent, presented the *pharmakos* with his *pharmakon*. Glaukos'saviour was a slithering *dios ketesios*, a 'Zeus of household property,' the traditional mouse-catcher of the grain bin. Ovid tells this very ancient Cretan tale of death and resurrection, initiation, differently. Glaukos of Anthedon, 'the city of the flower,' is amazed to find the fish he has just caught spring back to life on accidental contact with a magical plant on the beach. "Could some god have done it, or the juices of some plant?

And yet what plant could have such power? I picked some stalks and chewed what I had picked. The juice, the unknown juice, had hardly passed my throat when suddenly I felt my heart-strings tremble and my soul consumed with yearning for that other world."[444]

Elaborate tube-shaped mugs with attached cups, sort of one-piece kernoi, were found in a Cretan house shrine. They were apparently used like hamster houses; some showed clay snakes emerging from the mug to feed from the attached cup. Figurines were found with the mugs, showing the Goddess affectionately cradling a large snake, which extended from her crotch to her chin. The umbilical cord/ snakes were symbols of the rebirth to be expected from Glaukos' snake juice. The juice was mixed in the tripod around which the figurines and mugs were all arranged. Tripod cauldrons were often depicted with snakes arising from them, and innumerable sacramental vases have molded snakes drinking from the mouth.[445]

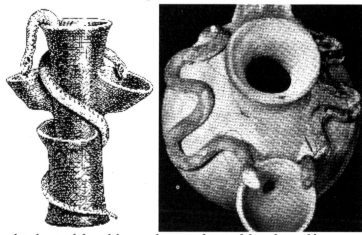

"In the days of the old month-year the goddess herself was a snake. When she took human form the snake became her 'attribute'; it was the 'symbol of wisdom.'....The snake among the Greeks was full of *mana*, was intensely sacred, not because as food he supported life, but because he is himself a life-*daimon*, a spirit of generation, even of immortality. But - and this is all-important - it is immortality of quite a peculiar kind. The individual members of the group of the Cecropidae [Athenian high-priests] die, man after man, generation after generation; Cecrops, who never lived at all, lives for ever, as a snake. He is the *daimon genus*, the spirit, the genius of the race, he stands...for the perennial renewal of life through death, for Reincarnation, for *paliggenesia*...'birth back again'....a belief in reincarnation is characteristic of totemistic peoples."[446]

Sepulchral urns from the fifth century BC show small holes through which the soul, conceived as a snake, was to crawl to get at the funeral offerings.[447] The illustration below is from an Attic black-figured funeral vase, c. 550 BC.

"It is Hermes always who attends Pandora-Anesidora, she of the pithos, when she rises from the earth. Always he carries his kerykeion with the twin twisted snakes, that kerykeion which we saw gathered in the coils of the Agathodaimon on the coins of Alexandria... We understand now why Hermes, as phallic herm, is god of fertility of flocks and herds, but also, as Psychopompos, god of ghosts and the underworld. He, a snake to begin with and carrying always the snake-staff, is the very *daimon* of reincarnation....At the Oschophoria the herald (*aggelos*) does not crown himself, he crowns his Kerykeion and his herald's staff with the two snakes entwined. This surely looks back to the time when the *Eniautos-daimon* was a snake or a pair of snakes, and the crown was for the symbol of the snake-*daimon*..."[448]

The kerykeion, that is, symbolized the cthonic power of the God-dess to bring the Anthesteria, the Blossoming, as did the oracular Korykian Cave at Delphi, where the snakes danced in underground ecstacy. Competing male rattlesnakes actually form the figure of a caduceus as they wrestle for dominance in their caves during the mating season. The kerykeion was the symbol of both Hermes Psychopompos and Asklepios, since revelation and incubation are not two different things.

The 'caduceus,' Latin for kerykeion, is the symbol of modern medicine thanks to Hippokrates of Kos, the legendary 'first physician' (d.c.377 BC). He was said to be descended from Asklepios in his incarnation as a stag. In Homer, Chiron the centaur, holding his *klados* of pine, emerged from his cave to teach Asklepios the use of herbs.

Asklepios is derived from *skalops* or *aspalax*, 'mole.' The *tholos*, the underground 'tomb' for incubation excavated at Epidauros revealed the interior structure of a molehill.[449] Barren women went to Epidauros for cure by the mole snakes. The oldest clear representation we have of incubation is the 'Sleeping Lady' of Malta, c.5000 BC., found in the cellar of a temple, the part that functioned as a tomb as well as a place of incubation.[450]

The *Epidauria* were later incorporated in the Eleusinian Mysteries, as Asklepios was identified with the Divine Child, Dionysos, the rebirth. Hippokrates' totem plant was the cypress, the staff around which the snakes curled. The Koan school of physicians published under the name of their founder. Hippokrates' second son and grandson, great healers in their own right, were both called *Drako*, 'Snake.'

The central tenet of Hippokratic healing was Eleusinian *ekstasis*. Hippokrates and his son Thessalos, designated by Athens as sons of Asklepios, *heros iatros*, hero physicians, literally 'hero druggers,' were special guests at the Eleusinian Mysteries.[451] Many modern physicians, claiming to have taken the 'Hippocratic Oath,' will tell you that *ekstasis* is 'non-medical,' because it is 'recreational.' Hippokrates would have thought that was as stupid as saying that, since eating a good meal is recreational, it is, for that reason, 'non-nutritive.'

The *ekstasis* of incubation, descent to the underground realm of Lethe, was followed by Mnemosyne, renewed consciousness, bringing with it Rebirth. The medicines used to induce this personal *Kathodos* and *Anodos* included that given by the two Goddesses of Eleusis, the sacred mushroom.

DRAMA

It was to this shamanic *enthousiasmos* that we owe the masterpieces of Classical Greece. When the shamanism died, so did the archetypal creativity. *Theama* means 'vision.' The *theatron* was 'the place of visions.' "But we are apt to forget that from the *epos*, the narrative, to the *drama*, the enactment, is a momentous step, one, so far as we know, not taken in Greece till after centuries of epic achievement, and then taken suddenly, almost in the dark, and irrevocably. All we really know of this momentous step is that it was taken sometime in the sixth century BC and taken in connection with the worship of Dionysos. Surely it is at least possible that the real impulse to the drama lay not wholly in 'goat songs' and 'circular dancing places' but also in the cardinal, the essentially dramatic, conviction of the religion of Dionysos, that the worshipper can not only worship, but can become, can *be*, his god. Athene and Zeus and Poseidon have no drama because no one, in his wildest moments, believed he could become and be Athene or Zeus or Poseidon. It is indeed only in the orgiastic religions that these splendid moments of conviction can come, and, for Greece at least, only in an orgiastic religion did the drama take its rise."[452]

"In the rites at Eleusis of which most details are known we have the very last stage of the development before the final step was actually taken, we have *dromena* [things done, ritual actions] on the very verge of *drama*. Late authors in describing the Eleusinian rites use constantly the vocabulary of the stage....Psellus is recording 'what the Greeks believe about demons'and he passes from theology to ritual. 'Yes and the mysteries of these (demons), as for example those of Eleusis, enact the double story of Deo or Demeter and her daughter Pherephatta or Kore. As in the rite of intitiation love affairs are to take place, Aphrodite of the Sea is represented as uprising. Next there is the wedding rite for Kore. And the initiated sing as an accompaniment "I have eaten from the timbrel, I have drunk from the cymbals, I have carried the *kernos* [holder of the cups of *kykeon*], I have gone down into the bridal chamber [*hieros gamos*, 'sacred marriage'].' Then also they enact the birth-pains of Deo."[453]

"The elements of the Eniautos myth are few and simple; its main characteristic is its inevitable, periodic monotony. This comes out clearly in the *dromena* of the Oschophoria. The principal factors are: (a) A contest (*agon*). In this case and also in the Karneia and in the Olympic Games the contest is a race to decide who shall carry the boughs and wear the crown. (b) A *pathos*, a death or defeat. In the Theseus myth this appears in the death of the old king. The *pathos* is formally announced by a *messenger (aggelos)* and it is followed or accompanied by a *lamentation (threnos)*. (c) A triumphant Epiphany, an appearance or crowning of the victor or the new king, with an abrupt change (*peripeteia*) from lamentation to rejoicing....The *dromenon* may of course take a somewhat simplified form. Thus the Kathodos and Anodos of Kore omits the *agon*, but probably in all cases where a human representative had to be chosen, a leader or king, the contest element was present. It is surely a fact of the highest significance that the Greek word for actor is *agonistes*, contester. The shift from sorrow to joy was integral because it was the mimetic presentation of the death of the Old Year, the birth of the New."[454]

"The *mythos*, the plot which is the life-history of an Eniautos-daimon, whether performed in winter, spring, summer or autumn, is thus doomed by its monotony to sterility. What is wanted is material cast in less rigid mould; in a word *legomena* not bound by *dromena*, plots that have cut themselves loose from rites. The dithyramb, which was the periodic festival of the spring *renouveau*, broke and blossomed so swiftly into the Attic drama because it found such plots to hand; in a word - *the forms of Attic drama are the forms of the life-history of an Eniautos-daimon; the content is the infinite variety of free and individualized heroic saga - in the largest sense of the word 'Homer.'*"[455]

"Achilles and Alexandros are tribal heroes, that is collective conceptions of conflicting tribes in Thessaly [home of Olympos]. Hector before, not after, he went to Troy was a hero-daimon in Boeotian Thebes; his comrade Melanippos had a cult in Thebes, Patroklos whom he slew was his near neighbor, like him a local daimon. It is the life-stories of heroes such as these, cut loose by the Migrations from their local cults, freed from their monotonous periodicity, that are the material of Attic drama, that form its free and plastic plots."

Below are Hektor, Andromache, Paris and Helen, from an Attic sacramental vase, c.550 BC. The names were written with magical intent, backwards, so as to come to life when viewed in a mirror. The image on Hektor's shield says something about the ritual contents of the vase, as do the wings on Paris' feet..

"When Peisistratos ordered the recitation of 'Homer' at the Panathenaea, the influence of the epos on the rude dramatic art of the time must have been immediately felt, and it only needed the birth of an Aischylos to make him seize of the *temache* that lay so close to hand. He or his predecessors took of necessity the prescribed form, the life-history of the daimon, and filled it with new content, the story of the daimon de-daimonized; an Agamemnon who, though a tribal daimon at home, was an individual hero before the walls of Troy."[456]

"If...we bear in mind these two factors, the old daimonic, magical ritual which lent the *forms*, the new 'Homeric' saga which lent the heroic *content*, the relation of the drama to the worship of Dionysos and also to the worship of the dead becomes, I think, fairly clear. The plays were performed in the theatre of Dionysos, in the precinct of the god, his image was present in the theatre, the chorus danced round his altar, his priest sat in the front and central seat among the spectators. In the face of facts so plain it seems to me impossible that the drama had its roots elsewhere than in the worship of Dionysos. Aristotle is right, tragedy arose from leaders of the Dithyramb."[457]

"Now, when we remember that Pentheus is only another form of Dionysos himself - like Zagreus, Orpheus, Osiris and the other daimons who are torn to pieces and put together again - we can see that the *Bacchae* is simply the old Sacer Ludus ['Sacred Game,' *dromenon*] itself, scarcely changed at all, except for the doubling of the hero into himself and his enemy. We have the whole sequence: Agon, Pathos and Messenger, Threnos [lamentation], Anagnorisis [acknowledgement] and Peripeteia [exaltation], and Epiphany. The daimon is fought against, torn to pieces, announced as dead, wept for, collected and recognized, and revealed in his new divine life. The *Bacchae* is a most instructive instance of the formation of drama out of ritual. It shows us how slight a step was necessary for Thespis or another to turn the Year-Ritual into real drama....The extremely close connection between the mysteries and the Year-daimon will be in the minds of all..."[458]

Ruck: "We must imagine an audience in somewhat less than a perfectly rational state pharmacologically, for, as Philochorus, the fourth-century historian of Attica and its religious practices, records (fr. 171 Jacoby), the spectators prepared themselves by drinking throughout the days of dramatic performance... The wine drunk was called *trimma*, like the one drunk at marriages, apparently so named for the fortifying additives that were 'ground' into it (Hesychius, *s.v. trimma*)."[459] Dioscorides, a contemporary of Paul from Tarsus, prescribes, in his legendary *De materia medica,* various mixed wines, from mild relaxants and cough syrups to surgically effective anesthetics.[460]

"Julian in his northern campaign saw and no doubt tasted with compunction a wine, made not from the grape but from barley. After the fashion of his age, he wrote an epigram....: 'Who and whence art thou, Dionyse? Now by the Bacchus true/Whom well I know, the son of Zeus, say - "Who and what are you?"/*He* smells of nectar like a god, *you* smack of goats and spelt,/For lack of grapes from ears of grain your countryman the Celt/Made you. Your name's Demetrios, but never Dionyse,/Bromos, Oat-born, not Bromios, Fire-born from out the skies.'"

"The emperor makes three very fair puns...: *bromos* oats, *bromios* of the thunder; *pyrogeni* wheat-born, *pyrigeni* fire-born; *tragos* goat and *tragos* an inferior kind of wheat, spelt....Julian propounds as an elegant jest the simple but illuminating mythological truth that the title Bromios points to a god born not of the lightning and thunder but of an intoxicant made from the cereal *bromos*. Bromios is Demetrios, son of Demeter the Corn-Mother, before he becomes a god of the grape and son by adoption of Olympian Zeus."

"Julian is not precise in his discrimination between the various edible grasses. His epigram is headed, 'To wine made of barley (*krithes*); the god, he says, smacks of *spelt* (*tragos*), he is *wheat*-born (*pyrogeni*) and he is of *oats* (*bromos*). It matters to Julian nothing, nor is it to our argument of first importance, of *what* particular cereal this new-old Dionysos is made. The point is that it is of some cereal, not of the grape. The god is thus seen to be the son of Semele, Earth-goddess in her agricultural aspect as Demeter, Corn-Mother. We shall later see that he was worshipped with service of the winnowing fan, and we shall further see that, when he-of-the-cereal-intoxicant became he-of-the-wine-of-grapes, the instrument that had been a winnow-ing-fan became a grape-basket."[461] By 'corn' Harrison meant 'barley-corn' or 'grain'; the Greeks had no maize.

The song for the slaughter of the sacramental goat at the February Anthesteria (Spring comes earlier in Greece) was the *tragodia*. "It is an odd fact that the ancients seem to have called certain *wild* forms of fruits and cereals by names connecting them with the goat. The reason for this is not clear, but the fact is well-established. The Latins called the wild fig *caprificus* ['goat-fig']; Pausanias expressly tells us that the Messenians gave to the wild fig tree the name *tragos*, goat. Vines, when they ran wild to foliage rather than fruit, were called *tragan*. I would conjecture that the inferior sort of spelt called *tragos*, goat, owes its name to this unexplained linguistic habit. It is even possible that the beard with which spelt is furnished may have helped out the confusion [the psychoactive *Claviceps purpurea* of the *kykeon*]. Tragedy I believe to be not the 'goat-sing,' but the 'harvest-song' of the cereal *tragos*....When the god of the cereal...became the god of the vine, the fusion and confusion of *tragodia* the spelt-song, with *trugodia*, the song of the winelees, was easy and indeed inevitable. The *tragodoi*, the 'beanfeast-singers,' became *trugodoi* or 'must-singers.'"[462]

The confusion was, of course, intentional, like that between *melon* and *melon*, 'sacrificial goat' or 'apple.' An engraved gem from Crete, above, c.1600 BC, shows a winged goat handing a pitcher of liquid to a communicant, who is standing on sacral horns. Floating in the air next to him, indicating the state he is about to achieve on ingestion of the drink, is another winged horned goat.[463] A gold ring from Mycenae, below, shows a worshipper adoring live sacramental plants growing out of an altar while the same plants grow out of the back of the large horned goat that stands behind him.[464] The goat, and the communicant, are about to suffer their own *drama*.

ORPHEUS

"Diodorus in speaking of ceremonial wine-drinking makes a characteristically Greek statement: 'They say that those who drink at banquets when unmixed wine is provided invoke the Good Genius, but when after the meal wine is given with water they call on the name of Zeus the Saviour; for they say that wine drunk unmixed produces forms of madness, but that when it is mixed with the rain of Zeus the joy of it and the delight remain, and the injurious element that causes madness and license is corrected....Charops, grandfather of Orpheus, gave help to the god, and Dionysos in gratitude instructed him in the orgies of his rites; Charops handed them down to his son Oiagros ['wine-grower'], and Oiagros to his son Orpheus....Orpheus, being a man gifted by nature and highly trained above all others, *made many modifications in the orgiastic rites*: hence they call the rites that took their rise from Dionysos, Orphic.'"

"Like the god he served, Orpheus is at one part of his career a Thracian, unlike him a magical musician. Dionysos...played upon the lyre, but music was never of his essence....In Pompeian wall-paintings and Graeco-Roman sarcophagi it is as magical musician, with power over all wild untamed things in nature, that Orpheus appears. This conception naturally passed into Christian art and it is interesting to watch the magical musician transformed gradually into the Good Shepherd. The bad wild beasts, the lions and lynxes, are weeded out one by one, and we are left, as in the wonderful Ravenna mosaic, with only a congregation of mild patient sheep."[465]

"Both on the kotylos of Hieron [5th cent.BC] and on the Tyskiewicky vase [4th cent.BC] Dionysos at Eleusis is represented as a full-grown man, not as a mystery babe. This fact is highly significant. The son has ceased to be a child, and growing to maturity forgets his relation to his mother....the Son is, as is natural in a matriarchal civilization, at first but the attribute of motherhood....But if that cult is to advance with civilization, if the god is to have his male worshippers, he must grow to be a man; and as the power of the Son waxes and he becomes more and more the Father, the power of the Mother wanes, and she that was the Great Mother sinks to be Semele the thunder-stricken."

"Diodorus....says[466] 'The Cretans in alleging that they from Crete conferred on other mortals the services of the gods, sacrifices and rites appertaining to mysteries, bring forward this point as being to their thinking the principal piece of evidence. The rite of intitiation, which is perhaps the most celebrated of all, is that which is performed by the Athenians at Eleusis, and the rite at Samothrace and that in Thrace among the Cicones, the country of Orpheus, inventor of rites, all these are imparted as mysteries; whereas in Crete at Cnossos the custom from ancient times was that these rites should be communicated openly and to all, and things that among the other peoples were communicated in secrecy among the Cretans no one concealed from any one who wished to know.'"[467]

"Diodorus, quoting local tradition, knows the very route by which the rites of Crete went northward, by way of the islands, by Samothrace home of the mysteries, up to the land of the Cicones. There, it would seem, Orpheus the sober met the raging wine-god, there the Maenads slew him, and repented and upraised his sanctuary. Thence the two religions, so different yet so intimately fused, came down to Greece, a conjoint force, dominant, irresistible. Mysticism and 'Enthusiasm' are met together, and, for Greek religion, the last word is said."[468]

"We shall find that the complete human-nature god is, roughly speaking, what we call an Olympian. What are his characteristics? It will be seen...that they are strangely, significantly negative, that an Olympian is in fact in the main the negation of an Eniautos-daimon. (1) *The Olympian sheds his plant or animal form....*Zeus Ktesios was once a snake. Zeus Olbios in local worship long preserved his bull's head....On the beautiful archaic metope of Selinus...we have Europa seated on the bull. 'No whit like other bulls is he, but mild and dear and meek;/He has a wise heart like a man's, only he cannot speak.' Moschos of course, in his lovely idyll, thinks that Zeus took upon him the form of a bull, but...we know this to be a mere late etiological inversion. The Sun-God of Crete in Bull-form wooed the moon-goddess, herself a cow; their child is the young bull-god the Minos-Bull, the Minotaur."[469]

"The shedding of plant and animal form marks of course the complete close of anything like totemistic thinking and feeling. It is in many ways pure loss....There are few things uglier than a lack of reverence for animals. The well-born, well-bred little Athenian girls who danced as Bears to Artemis of Brauronia, the Bear-Goddess, could not but think reverently of the great might of the Bear. Among the Apaches to-day, Bourke states, 'only ill-bred Americans, or Europeans who have never had any "raising," would think of speaking of the Bear or indeed of the snake, the lightning or the mule, without employing the reverential prefix "Ostin,"meaning "old man,"and equivalent to the Roman title "Senator."'"[470]

"Anyone who turns from Minoan pottery with its blossoming flowers, its crocuses and lilies, its plenitude of sea life, its shells and octopuses and flying fish...to the monotonous perfection of the purely human subjects of the best red-figured pottery, must be strangely constituted if he feels no loss. He will turn eagerly for refreshment from these finished athletes and these no less accomplished gods, to the bits of mythology wherein animals still play a part, to Europa and her bull, to Phrixos and his ram, to Kadmos and his snake, and he will turn also to the 'attributes' of the humanized Olympian, he will be gladdened by Athena's owl and by the woodpecker of Zeus; glad too that Dionysos Dendrites still deigns to be a tree and Apollo to carry his living branch. The mystery gods...are never free of totemistic hauntings, never quite shed their plant and animal shapes. That lies in the very nature of their sacramental worship. They are still alive with the life-blood of all living things from which they sprang."[471]

"Olympian Greece turned Apollo Lykegenes, 'born of the she wolf,' into Apollo Lykoktonos, 'the one who slew the wolf.'[472] "*All the canonical denizens of the underworld are heroic or divine figures of the older stratum of the population*....Tityos and Salmoneus are beings of this order. Once locally the rivals of Zeus, they paled before him, and as vanquished rivals become typical aggressors, punished for ever as a warning to the faithful."

"Pausanias saw him [Tityos] on the fresco of Polygnotus at Delphi, a 'dim and mangled spectre,' and Aeneas in the underworld says: 'I saw Salmoneus cruel payment make,/For that he mocked the lightning and the thunder/Of Jove on high.' It was an ingenious theological device, or rather perhaps, unconscious instinct, that took these ancient hero figures, really regnant in the world below, and made the place of their rule the symbol of their punishment. According to the old faith all men, good and bad, went below the earth, great local heroes reigned below as they had reigned above [to become *Demetreioi*, Demeter's people]; but the new faith sent its saints to a remote Elysium or to the upper air and made this underworld kingdom a place of punishment; and in that place significantly we find that the tortured criminals *are all offenders against Olympian Zeus*."[473]

"(2) *The Olympian refuses to be an Earth-daimon.* In discussing the sequence of cults from Gaia to Apollo it has been seen that, even when he has left totemistic ways of thinking behind him, when he has ceased to base his social structure on supposed kinship with animals and plants, man tends, in his search after food, to focus his attention first on earth and only later on heaven. His calendar is at first seasonal, based not on observation of the heavenly bodies but on the waxing and waning of plants, the fruits of the earth. The worship of Earth in a word comes before the worship of Heaven. This worship of Earth and the daimonic powers of the earth is...closely and even inextricably mixed with the cult of the dead. The daimonic power of the dead is figured under the form of a snake."

"When the Olympians mounted from Olympos to the upper air they were, it seems, ashamed of their earth-origin and resolved to repudiate their snake-tails. This is very clearly seen on the vase-painting... To the right is an old Earth-daimon... He is winged, and his body ends in two snake-coils. He is obviously as benevolent and as civilized as Cecrops himself. But he is earth-born, and Zeus of the upper air, the completely human Zeus, will have none of him, will blast him with his thunderbolt."[474]

"Pandora ['All-Giver'] is in ritual and matriarchal theology the earth as Kore, but in the patriarchal mythology of Hesiod her great figure is strangely changed and minished. She is no longer Earth-born, but the creature, the handiwork of Olympian Zeus....there gleams the ugly malice of theological animus. Zeus the Father will have no great Earth-goddess Mother and Maid in one, in his man-fashioned Olympos, but her figure *is* from the beginning, so he remakes it; woman, who was the inspirer, becomes the temptress; she who made all things, gods and mortals alike, is become their plaything, their slave, dowered only with physical beauty, and with a slave's tricks and blandishments. To Zeus, the archpatriarchal *bourgeois*, the birth of the first woman is but a huge Olympian jest: 'He spake and the Sire of men and of gods immortal laughed.'"[475]

Hesiod: "But the noble son of Iapetos outwitted him and stole the far-seen gleam of unwearying fire in a hollow fennel stalk. And Zeus who thunders on high was stung in spirit, and his dear heart was angered when he saw amongst men the far-seen ray of fire. Forthwith he made an evil thing for men as the price of fire; for the very famous limping god formed of earth the likeness of a shy maiden as the son of Cronos willed. And the goddess bright-eyed Athene girded and clothed her with silvery raiment, and down from her head she spread with her hands a broidered veil, a wonder to see; and she, Pallas Athene, put about her head lovely garlands, flowers of new-grown herbs. Also she put on her head a crown of gold which the very famous Limping God made himself and worked with his own hands as a favour to Zeus his father. On it was much curious work, wonderful to see; for of the many creatures which the land and sea rear up, he put most upon it, wonderful things, like living beings with voices: and great beauty shone out from it. But when he had made the beautiful evil to be the price for the blessing, he brought her out, delighting in the finery which the bright-eyed daughter of a mighty father had given her, to the place where the other gods and men were. And wonder took hold of the deathless gods and mortal men when they saw that which was sheer guile, not to be withstood by men."[476]

The mythological devolution from inspirer to temptress, from shamanic ecstacy to sexual excitement, is an infantilizing step down the psychological ladder, equivalent to replacing spontaneous ecstatic singing with masturbation. It's a circus trick for the *laoi*, 'the laity,' as the bowl below, by Makron, c.490 BC, seems to suggest.

The ongoing evolution from shamanic to patriarchal culture is explained, in pharmaco-shamanic terms, in the *Hymn to Apollon*, which dates to the eighth century BC. 'Our Lady of Athana' is first found at Knossos in Crete, Athana originally, apparently, being a cult-place of the Goddess when Zeus was still an infant. The hymn is a rationalization of Athene's new incarnation as Zeus' daughter, that is, of Apollon's (the Dorians') acquisition of Delphi.

In a fury at Zeus for giving birth to Athena without the intercession of her womb, Hera " ... bare one neither like the gods nor mortal men, fell, cruel Typhaon ['stupefying smoke'], to be a plague to men. Straightway large-eyed queenly Hera took him and bringing one evil thing to another such, gave him to the dragoness; and she received him. And this Typhaon used to work great mischief among the famous tribes of men. Whosoever met the dragoness, the day of doom would sweep him away, until the lord Apollon, who deals death from afar, shot a strong arrow at her....And the holy strength of Helios made her rot away there; wherefore the place is now called Pytho ['Snake'], and men call the lord Apollon by another name, Pythian; because on that spot the power of piercing Helios made the monster rot away." The South Italian vase below, c.350 BC, depicts, Jason, *'Iason*, attacking Telphusa with his lance. The serpent guards the Golden Fleece hanging in the Tree. Medea, upper right, supervises.

"Then Phoibus Apollon saw that the sweet-flowing stream had beguiled him, and he started out in anger against Telphusa; and soon coming to her, he stood close by and spoke to her:/'Telphusa, you were not, after all, to keep to yourself this lovely place by deceiving my mind, and pour forth your clear flowing water: here my renown shall also be and not yours alone.'/Thus spoke the lord, far-working Apollon, and pushed over upon her a crag with a shower of rocks, hiding her stream: and he made himself an altar in a wooded grove very near the clear-flowing stream. In that place all men pray to the great one by the name of Telphusian, because he humbled the stream of holy Telphusa."

"Then Phoibos Apollon pondered in his heart what men he should bring in to be his ministers in sacrifice and to serve him in rocky Pytho. And while he considered this, he became aware of a swift ship upon the wine-like sea in which were many men and goodly, Cretans from Knossos, the city of Minos, they who do sacrifice to the prince and announce his decrees, whatsoever Phoibos Apollon, bearer of the golden blade, speaks from his laurel tree below the dells of Parnassos." "Conquering gods their titles take, from the foes they captive make."[477]

"The fight...helps us to realize one cardinal factor in the making of an Olympian. Euripides (*Iphigeneia in Taurus*) gives us the fight in two traditional forms: first the slaying of the snake, and second the dream oracle of Earth and Night as against Phoibos the Sun....The snake, the guardian of the old Earth oracle, is killed, but the general apparatus of the cult, the cleft in the earth, the tripod and the omphalos, is kept. 'And there, behold, an ancient Snake,/Wine-eyed, bronze-gleaming, in the brake/Of deep-leaved laurel, ruled the dell,/Sent by old Earth from under/Strange caves to guard her oracle,/A thing of fear and wonder./ Thou, Phoebus, still a new-born thing,/Meet in thy mother's arms to lie,/Didst kill the Snake, and crown thee King/In Pytho's land of prophecy;/Thine was the tripod and the chair/Of golden truth; and throned there,/Hard by the streams of Castaly,/Beneath the untrodden portal/Of Earth's mid-stone there flows from thee/Wisdom for all things mortal....He slew the Snake; he cast, men say,/Themis, the child of Earth, away/From Pytho and her hallowed stream;/Then Earth, in dark derision,/Brought forth the Peoples of the Dream/And all the tribes of Vision./ And men besought them; and from deep/Confused underworlds of sleep/They showed blind things that erst had been/And are, and yet shall follow./So did avenge that old Earth Queen/Her child's wrong on Apollo.'"

"The chronological sequence at Delphi was as follows: Gaia, Themis, Phoibe, Phoibos. Zeus is not given as fifth, he is the crown and climax of all. Phoibos reigns fourth in time but only as viceregent, as *'Dios prophetis,'* not of course as prophet in our sense, but utterer, exponent of his father's will....In the figure of Themis...we have the utterance, the projection and personification, of *the* religious principle itself....She is the daughter and bye-form of Gaia. She delivers oracles, *themistes, ordinances* [commandments], rather than prophesies in our sense, for both Phoibe and Phoibos; she even ultimately ascends to high heaven and becomes the counselor and wedded wife of Zeus himself."[478]

"(3)*The Olympian refuses to be a daimon of air and sky*....Titaia was a title of Earth....Special Titans specialize into Sun-Gods. The Titan Sisyphos who climbs the steep of heaven rolling his stone before him, only to fall adown the steep and climb it again next morning, is the Sun, the Titan Phaethon is the Sun, the Titaness Phoebe is the Moon, but Titan himself is rather Ouranos, the whole might of the upper air....In Homer and Hesiod they, unlike the Giants, are always gods, *Titenes Theoi*. They are constantly being driven down below the earth to nethermost Tartarus and always re-emerging. The very violence and persistence with which they are sent down below shows that they belong up above. They rebound like divine india-rubber balls. Their great offense in Olympian eyes is that they will climb up to high heaven, which the human-shaped Olympians had arrogated to themselves. The fight between Titans and Olympians always takes place in mid air. In the Theogony the Titanomachia is but a half-humanized thunderstorm, where Zeus as much and perhaps more manifestly than his opponents is but a Nature-Power."

"The stuff of which Zeus is made is clear enough. He too was a Titan, he too was Ouranos and Aither, and his nature retains more of *ta metarsia* [power, exaltation, thunder and lightning] than of *ta meteora* [sky, the heavenly bodies]. But he has emerged into humanized form, and his old form is made to appear, not like the chrysalis from which he evolved himself, but rather as an alien foe opposed. It is strange and interesting that Zeus, king and father of all the other Olympians, should be the last to shed his elemental nature. He who is always boasting that he is Father and Councilor remains to the end an automatically explosive thunderstorm. He has none of the achieved serenity of the Sun-god Apollo."[479]

Ruck: "The eagle that once was symbolic of Prometheus's flight toward the celestial realm has been expropriated as an emblem for Zeus. Prometheus no longer flies. Instead, chained to the eastern mountains that in the Iranian tradition were the home of the magical herb, he is tormented by the eagle who feasts repeatedly on the liver that was the seat of the Titan's power of divination."[480]

Nonnos: "'On one of them [the floating Ambrosial Rocks] grows a spire of olive, their agemate, selfrooted and joined to the rock, in the very midst of the waterfaring stone. On the top of the foliage you will see an eagle perched, and a well-made bowl. From the flaming tree fire selfmade spits out wonderful sparks, and the glow devours the olive tree all round but consumes it not. A snake writhes round the tree with its highlifted leaves, increasing the wonder both for eyes and for ears....the fire keeps to the middle of the tree and sends out a friendly glow: the bowl remains aloft, immovable though the clusters are shaken in the wind.../You must catch this wise bird, the high-flying eagle agemate of the olive, and sacrifice him to Seabluehair. Pour out his blood on the seawandering cliffs to Zeus and the Blessed. Then the rock wanders no longer driven over the waters; but it is fixed upon immovable foundations and unites itself bound to the free rock. Found upon both rocks a builded city, with quays on two seas, on both sides.'"[481]

"(4) *The Olympians refuse the functions of the Eniautos-daimon....*We know now what manner of beings these pre-Olympian potencies were; they were Year-daimones, all alike in shape and function, all apt to take on plant or animal shape, the business of each and all monotonously one, to give food and increase to man and make the year go round. But the Olympian will have none of this, he shakes himself loose of the year and the produce of the year. In place of his old *function*, his *timi* ['value'], his *geras* [ripeness, 'age'], he demands a new honour, a service done to him, himself as a personality. Instead of being himself a sacrament he demands a sacrifice....The real true god, the Eniautos-daimon, lives and works for his people; he does more, he dies for them. The crowning disability and curse of the new theological order is that the Olympian claims to be *immortal (athanatos)*."

"In examining sacrament and sacrifice we have seen that the Year-daimon in the form of a Bull lived his year-long life that he might die, and died that he might live again. His whole gist and nature was absorbed and expressed by the cycle of periodic reincarnation. Out of this cycle came all his manifold, yet monotonous life history, his Births, his Re-births, his Appearances and Disappearances, his Processions and Recessions, his Epiphanies, his Deaths, his Burials, his Resurretions, his endless Changes and Chances."

"Together with this conception of a dead and barren immortality there grew up the disastrous notion that between god and man there was a great gulf, that communion was no more possible. To attempt to pass the gulf was *hybris*, it was *the* [original] sin against the gods. Pindar again lends himself to this pitiless, fruitless doctrine. The dull, melancholy mandate runs through his odes: 'Seek not thou to become a god.' In this mandate we see the door closed finally on the last remnants of totemistic thinking; it is the death warrant of sacramentalism. The only possible service now is the gift-sacrifice; and by that service alone, history has shown, the soul of man cannot live....To the mystery-god Dionysos *phthonos* ['envy'] is unknown: 'No grudge hath he of the great,/No scorn of the mean estate;/But to all that liveth, his wine he giveth,/Griefless, immaculate.'(Eur:*Bac*)...'And any one may follow who can and will, for jealousy stands ever without the heavenly choir.'"[482]

"Until man learns to think of himself as an individual, that is until the hold of the group is weakened, he will not sharply individualize his gods. They will be not clear cut personalities but functional daimones. Now it would seem at first that a clear cut personality is a higher and better thing than a vague impersonal daimon or functionary. So he is from the point of view of art and intellect, but all experience goes to show that his emotional appeal, save to the very highly educated, is feebler. The sight of a great discoverer or great thinker will touch the imagination of a few, but if you want to move the great heart of the people to hysteria, to almost frenzy, you must produce a daimon-functionary, as little individualized as may be, you must crown a king. The reason is clear, the king, the daimon-functionary, is the utterance of the group and each individual in the group claims him as in part himself."

"Here we seem to trace one cause of the chill remoteness of the Olympians. They are...concepts thrown out of the human mind, looked at from a distance, things *known*, not like the mystery gods *felt* and lived. The more clearly they are envisaged the more reasonable and thinkable they are, the less are they the sources, the expression, of emotion....the Olympians not only cease to be sources of emotion but they positivley offend the very intellect that fashioned them. They are really so many clear-cut concepts, but they claim to have objective reality. This is the rock on which successive generations of gods have shattered. Man feels rightly and instinctively that a god is a real thing - a real thing because he is the utterance of a real collective emotion, but, in progress of time, man dessicates his god, intellectualizes him, till he is a mere concept, an *eidolon*. Having got his *eidolon*, that *eidolon* fails to satisfy his need, and he tries to supply the place of the vanished *thymos*, the real life-blood of emotion, by claiming objective reality....But it was only to the Greek that the Olympian lived, a great and beautiful reality. Seen through Roman eyes, focussed always on action, he became the prettiest and emptiest of toys."[483] The literal meaning of *eidolon* is 'ghost,' as in Klytaimnestra's *eidolon* in Aischylos' *Eumenides*.

The *pharmakon*, Dionysos, was the herb eaten, sacrificed, to satisfy the soul. The *pharmakos*, Pentheus, the herb's mythic double, atavistically, psychologically, identified with the herb, became the scapegoat sacrificed to satisfy the community, once the *pharmakon* was prohibited, once the community was convinced that healing and rebirth were second hand, not entheogenic, not sacramental, but sacrificial, political. The psychological transition was simultaneously political, religious and medical - none of the elements can be separated from one another.

The *eidolon* became the focus of the lost group emotion and identity, the *pharmakon athanasias*, the 'medicine of immortality' to use Ignatius'phrase. The *pharmakos*, the official scapegoat identified with the *pharmakon* - the Slave, the Judas, the Witch, the Nigger (a perfect *pharmakos*, embodying, historically, a close connection to tribal culture) - became the living example of what happens to practitioners of the now prohibited shamanism. The emotive meaning, the archetypal apprehension of the originary shamanistic imagery is intentionally used against itself by the fascist high priesthood, the industrial state. Much of the unconscious hostility of racism and misogyny can be understood in terms of neurotic hostility to shamanism, that is, to nonconformity to the official cult, emotionally misunderstood, as intended, as a betrayal of the sacred.

According to Harpocration, "'Istros (circ BC 230), in the first book of his Epiphanies of Apollo, says that Pharmakos is a proper name, and that Pharmakos stole sacred *phialae* ['vials'] belonging to Apollo and was taken and stoned by the men with Achilles, and the ceremonies done at the Thargelia are mimetic representations of these things."[484] Representations of the ethos of industrial conformity, in which the practioner of unauthorized shamanism is ritually slaughtered for the good of the army, which assumes the role of 'legitimate community' or 'symbolic tribe.' The vials are so damn sacred that we aren't even told what was in them, since Apollo kills anyone who shares his food. Goodbye Phoibe.

Ruck: "So too, the magical plant of the Hyperboreans became identified in Hellenic traditions with various substances that were, in one way or another, appropriate to the religious and symbolic context, but which did not share the original's physical properties for inducing mantic inspiration. Such was the case...with the *daphne* at Delphi and the olive at Olympia and Delos. Both are clearly not the plant actually recalled in the traditions of the Hyperborean entheogen, which more poetically could also be metamorphosed into the golden fruit or flowers, subterranean honey, the Gorgon's head, or the creatures with a single eye."

"It became, above all, the god's victim, to be appeased and offered in sacrifice, for the plant belonged to the wilderness that has preceded the growth and evolution of the superior Olympian age of assimilated and reconciled divinities who presided over the perfection of Hellenic culture. Thus it became also the *pharmakos* offering, either the actual giving of human lives or, as became increasingly appropriate to the god's own civilized persona, the token offering of the same."[485]

The communal catharsis by ritual slaughter, of course, strikes very deep chords: "The pharmakos was not a sacrifice in the sense of an offering *made to appease an angry god.* It came to be associated with Apollo when he took over the Thargelia [First Fruits-June], but primarily it was not intended to please or to appease any spirit or god. It was, as ancient authors repeatedly insist, a *katharmos*, a purification. The essence of the ritual was not atonement, for there was no one to atone, but riddance, the artificial making of an *agos*, a pollution, to get rid of all pollution."

"Lydus says 'Mysteries are from the separating away of a pollution (*misos*) as equivalent to sanctification.'" "That the leading out of the 'pharmakos' was part of the festival of the Thargelia we know from Harpocration. He says in commenting on the word: 'At Athens they led out two men to be purifications for the city; it was at the Thargelia, one was for the men and the other for the women.' These men, these pharmakoi, whose function it was to purify the city, were...in all probability put to death, but the expression used by Harpocration is noteworthy - they were led out. The gist of the ceremony is not death but expulsion; death, if it occurs, is incidental.... the cleansing of the city by the expulsion of the pharmakos was regarded as *the* typical purification of the whole year."[486]

"Helladius the Byzantine, quoted by Photius, says that 'it was the custom at Athens to lead in procession two pharmakoi with a view to purification....The pharmakos of the men had black figs round his neck, the other had white ones, and he says they were called 'syBacchoi'['pig-Bacchoi']. Helladius added that 'this purification was of the nature of an apotropaic ceremony to avert diseases, and that it took its rise from Androgeos the Cretan, when at Athens the Athenians suffered abnormally from a pestilential disease, and the custom obtained of constantly purifying the city by pharmakoi."[487]

The flowering branches of the wild fig were originally hung in fig groves to facilitate pollination by the fig wasp, the cthonic Goddess, hence the figs, the fruit, signify regeneration from death. Their branches were not, originally, used to beat anyone to death. The pharmakoi, then, are human sacrifices designed to fructify the Athenian earth, fertilizer. They were chosen for their ugliness or nonconformity.

The implied propaganda of the civic sacrifice thus identified 'cthonic,' shamanic, with pollution, the need for cleansing by ritual slaughter: Ruck: "The verb for sacrifice when directed to a celestial god was typically *thuo* (or *thyo*) and meant basically 'to make smoke.' A different verb was used for cthonic sacrifice, *enagizo*, which implies involvement with 'pollution' and 'curse' by association with the dead....The human sacrificial offering may have been reserved by the classical Greeks for times of extraordinary peril, such as pestilence or war, when the more sinister aspect of the healing Apollo would need special appeasement...."[488]

"Servius...notes that *sacer* may mean accursed as well as holy....To our modern minds pure and impure stand at two opposite poles, and if we were arraying a scape-goat we certainly should not trouble about his preliminary purification. But the ancients...knew of a condition that combined the two, the condition that the savage describes as 'taboo.' [Tongan for 'holy,' 'untouchable.'] For this condition the Latins used the word 'sacer,' the Greeks...the word *agos*.... It is satisfactory to find that the etymology of the word confirms this view, *pharmakos* means simply 'magic-man.'...in Latin it appears as *forma*, formula, magic spell; our *formulary* retains some vestige of its primitive connotation. *Pharmakon* in Greek means healing drug, poison, and dye, but all, for better or worse, are magical. To express its meaning we need what our language has lost, a double-edged word like the savage 'medicine.'"[489]

Ios, 'snake's poison,' also means 'arrow.' Apollo's arrow becomes a 'winged glistening snake' in a latent word-play on *ophis*, 'snake,' and *ios* in Aischylos'*Eumenides* (181). Greek bows were made of the wood of the resilient yew, *taxus*; the bow was a *toxon*; the poison with which the arrows were tipped was a *toxikon*, 'bow medicine,' as distinguished from *pharmakon*, 'healing medicine'; an *eikon*, then, is totemic medicine, from *eidos*, form, shape. Artemis, in the Law Code of Gortyn, Crete, c.500 BC, is referred to as *Toxia*, 'the archer-goddess,' when a woman is required to swear by her, the implication being that the truth will avoid divine vengeance.[490]

"This primitive notion of release from *taboo*, which lay at the root of the Orphic and Christian notion of spiritual freedom, comes out very clearly in the use of the word *aphosiousthai*....'to purify by means of an expiatory offering.' Plato in the *Laws* describes the ceremonial to be performed in the case of a man who has intentionally murdered one of his near kin. The regular officials are to put him to death, and this done 'let them strip him, and cast him outside the city into a place where three ways meet, appointed for the purpose, and on behalf of the city collectively let the authorities, each one severally, take a stone and cast it on the head of the dead man, and thereby purify (*aphosiouto*) the city.'"[491]

"The significance of this ritual is drastically explicit. The taint of the murder, the taboo of the blood guilt, is on the whole city; the casting of the stones, on behalf of the city, *purifies it off* onto the criminal; it is literally conveyed from one to the other by the stone. The guilty man is the *pharmakos*, and his fate is that of a *pharmakos*; 'this done let them carry him to the confines of the city, and cast him out unburied, as is ordained.' Dedication, *devotion* of the thing polluted, *aphosiosis*, is the means whereby man attains *hosiosis*, consecration."[492]

"Consecration (*hosiotes*), perfect purity issuing in divinity, is...the keynote of Orphic faith, the goal of Orphic ritual....Zagreus is the god of the mysteries, and his full content can only be understood in relation to Orphic rites. Zagreus is the mystery child guarded by the Kouretes [Initiates], torn in pieces by the Titans....the Titan myth is a 'sacred story'(*hierologia*) invented to account for the ritual fact that Orphic worshippers, about to tear the sacred bull, daubed themselves with white clay, for which the Greek word *titanos*: they are Titans, but not as giants (*Titanes*), only as white-clay men (*titanoi*)."

"The Orphics faced the most barbarous elements of their own faith and turned them not only qua theology into a vague monotheism, but qua ritual into a high sacrament of spiritual purification....From the time the neophyte is accepted as such, i.e. performs initiatory rites of purification and thereby becomes a *Mystes*, he leads a life of ceremonial purity (*hagnon*). He accomplishes the rite of eating raw sacrificial flesh and also holds on high the torches of the Mountain Mother." Thereafter, he never eats flesh again.[493]

"The word *hagnon*, i.e. 'pure,'in the negative sense, 'free from evil,'marks...the intial stage - a stage akin to the old service of 'aversion'(*apotropi*). The word *hosiotheis*, 'set free,' 'consecrated,' marks the final accomplishment and is a term of positive content....In ancient curse formularies, belonging to the cult of Demeter and underworld divinities, the words *hosia kai eleuthera*, 'consecrated and free,' are used in constant close conjunction and are practically all but equivalents. The offender, the person cursed, was either 'sold' or 'bound down' to the infernal powers; but the cursing worshipper prays that the things that are accursed, i.e. tabooed to the offender, may be to him *hosia kai eleuthera*, 'consecrated and free,' i.e. to him they are freed from the taboo. It is the dawning of the grace in use today 'Sanctify these creatures to our use and us to thy service.'"[494]

"The person cursed or bound down was in some sense a gift or sacrifice to the gods of cursing, the underworld gods: the man stained by blood is 'consecrate'(*kathieromenos*) to the Erinyes. In the little sanctuary of Demeter at Cnidos the curse takes even more religious form. He or she dedicates (*anieroi*), or offers as a votive offering (*anatitheti*, for *anatithesi*), and finally we have the familiar *anathema* of St Paul. Here the services of cursing, the rites of magic and the underworld are halfway to the service of 'tendance,' the service of the Olympians, and we begin to understand why, in later writers, the pharmakos and other 'purifications' are spoken of as *thisiai* [sacrifices]."[495] The *anathemata* were little inscribed statues set up by votaries in shrines.

"Demosthenes pleads with his fellow citizens to honour Fair Order (*Eunomia*), who loves just deeds and is the Saviour of cities and countries, and Justice (Dike), holy and unswerving, *whom Orpheus who instituted our most sacred mysteries declares to be seated by the throne of Zeus....* The Orphic could not rid himself of the notion of Vengeance. Dike as avenger finds a place...in the Orphic Hades. Hosia, the real Heavenly Justice, she who is Right and Sanctity and Freedom and Purity all in one, never attained a vivid and constant personality; she is a goddess for the few, not for the many."

"It was Euripides, and perhaps only Euripides, who made the goddess Hosia in the image of his own high desire, and, though the Orphic word and Orphic rites constantly pointed to a purity that was also freedom, to a sanctity that was by union with rather than submission to the divine, yet Orphism constantly renounced its birthright, reverted as it were to the old savage notion of abstinence (*hagneia*). After the ecstacy of 'I am Set Free and named by name/A Bacchos of the Mailed Priests,' the end of the mystic's confession falls dull and sad and formal: 'Robed in pure white I have borne me clean/ From man's vile birth and confined clay,/And exiled from my lips alway/Touch of all meat where Life hath been.' He that is free and holy (*hosiotheis*) and divine, marks his divinity by a dreary formalism. He wears white garments, he flies from death and birth, from all physical contagion, his lips are pure from flesh-food, he fasts after as before the Divine Sacrament. He follows in fact all the rules of asceticism familiar to us as 'Pythagorean.'"[496]

"The conception of Phanes Protogonos [the hermaphroditic First Light] remained always somewhat esoteric, a thing taught in mysteries, but his content is popularized in the figure of the goat-god who passed from being *o Paon* the feeder, the shepherd, to be *to pan* Pan the All-God.... Dionysos the Bull-god and Pan the Goat-god both belong to early pre-anthropomorphic days, before man had cut the ties that bound him to other animals; one and both they were welcomed as saviours by a tired humanity. Pan had no part in Orphic ritual, but in mythology as the All-god he is the popular reflection of Protogonos. He gave a soul of life and reality to a difficult monotheistic dogma, and the last word was not said in Greek religion, until over the midnight sea a voice [Plutarch] was heard crying 'Great Pan is dead.'"[497]

"When we realize that the *liknon* is, as it were, a cornucopia that for human fruit becomes a cradle, we naturally expect that, in its mystical sense, it will be a symbol of new birth, that *Liknites* will be connected with a doctrine of *palingenesia*, a sort of spiritual resurrection. The Orphics had their doctrine of *palingenesia*, but the symbolism of the *liknon* was to them mainly of purification, to which they added that of rebirth.... It is remarkable that the *liknon* in this representation, unlike those previously discussed, contains no fruits. This can scarcely, I think, be accidental. When the artist wishes to show fruits in a sacred vessel, he is quite able to do so, as is seen in the dish of poppy heads held by the priest [above]..., where perspective is violated to make the content clear. The absence of the fruits is best, I think, explained on the supposition that the *liknon* is by this time mysticized. It is regarded as the winnowing fan, the 'mystic fan of Iacchos,' rather than as the basket of earth's fruits. It is held empty over the candidate's head merely as a symbol of purification. This explanation is the more probable, if the scene be, as is generally supposed, a representation of Eleusinian mysteries, but...held not at

Eleusis but at Alexandria."[498]

"The shift of Maenad to Muse is like the change of Bacchic rites to Orphic; it is the informing of savage rites with the spirit of music, order and peace....Orpheus, it has been established in the mouth of many witnesses, modified, ordered, 'rearranged' Bacchic rites....Did this man...in whose saintly and ascetic figure the early Church saw the prototype of her Christ, effect nothing more vital than modification?.... In the course of the excavations on the west slope of the Acropolis....was discovered an inscription giving in great detail the rules of a thiasos of Iobacchoi in the time of Hadrian [117-138 CE]....and thoroughly Orphic rather than Dionysiac are the regulations as to the peace and order to be observed. 'Within the place of sacrifice no one is to make a noise, or clap his hands, or sing, but each man is to say his part and do it in all quietness and order as the priest and the Archibacchos direct.' ...if any member is riotous an official appointed by the priest shall set against him who is disorderly or violent the thyrsos of the god. The member against whom the thyrsos is set up, must...leave the banquet hall....The thyrsos of the god had become in truly Orphic fashion the sign not of revel and license, but of a worship fair and orderly."[499]

A worship, that is, acceptable to Hadrian. As power shifted from Greece to Rome, the Greek *mysterion* was replaced by its Roman synonym, *sacramentum*, and the meaning changed from participatory mystery to legal oath, "solemn engagement, caution-money deposited in a suit, military oath."(Oxford) Thus was the thyrsos turned into a billyclub, the fennel stalk into a crooked shepherd's crook , and the sacraments into confused symbols not for consumption.

A century earlier, Mark Antony was the 'New Dionysos,' 'Father Liber' to the Romans: Paterculus: "Then, as his love for Cleopatra became more ardent and his vices grew upon him...he resolved to make war upon his country. He had previously given orders that he should be called the new Father Liber, and indeed in a procession at Alexandria he had impersonated Father Liber, his head bound with the ivy wreath, his person enveloped in the saffron robe of gold, holding in his hand the thyrsus, wearing the buskins, and riding in the Bacchic chariot."[500]

As totemic groups became more artificial and culture industrialized, mass hypnosis, based on the archetypal imagery, replaced participatory shamanism: "Ion, like Cecrops, like Erechtheus, is the *megistos kouros* of his tribe, but, expressing as he does an artificial rather than natural group, he is emptied of all vital content."[501] That is, the rites of imperial municipalities are no longer entheogenic, proprioceptive, transformative, creative; they are symbolized, politicized, standardized, apologetic.

"The coin [below]...gives us the clearest possible answer. Here we have a great coiled snake surrounded by emblems of fertility, ears of corn and the poppyhead with its multitude of seeds. The snake's name is clearly inscribed; he is the New Agathos (good) Daimon (NEO. AGATH. DAIM.). On the obverse...is the head of Nero; it is he who claims to be the New Agathos Daimon. Cecrops the hero-king was a snake, Nero the Emperor is the new snake; it is not as private individuals that they claim to be fertility-daimons, it is as functionaries. Cecrops the modest old tribal king was content to bring fertility to the

Cecropidae, Nero as imperialist claims to be the '*Good Daimon* of the whole habitable world.'"[502]

Thus were the dancing snakes of Grandmother Earth turned into Nero's golden idol, barley and poppy into minted metal, a prohibitive substance. God help the shaman who claimed to be *Soter* of any part of Nero's Empire. Captured rebels were slain in Nero's arena with all the trappings of a *pharmakos* sacrifice of a Greek *polis*, but much more regularly. This coin type, showing the *cista mystica* and the snakes, originated in Ephesus, c. 200 BC, as a direct reference to the popularity of Dionysos. It took the likes of Nero to add implications that never would have occurrd to the Ephesians.

"The notion of punishment, and especially eternal punishment, cannot be fairly charged to the account of Homer and the Olympian religion he represents. This religion was too easy-going, too essentially aristocratic to provide an eternity even of torture for the religious figures it degraded and despised. Enough for it if they were carelessly banished to their own proper kingdom, the underworld. It is, alas, to the [Roman] Orphics, not to the Achaeans, that religion owes the dark disgrace of a doctrine of eternal punishment. The Orphics were concerned...with two things, immortality and purification; the two notions to them were inseparable, but by an easy descent the pains that were for purification became for vengeance....The Hades, then, of the Lower Italy vases [4th cent.BC] is a popular blend of Orphism and of Olympian theology, or rather of ancient Pelasgian figures viewed through the medium of Olympianism. The old stratum provides the material, the new stratum degrades it, and Orphism moralises it."[503]

"The mud and the sieve to which the impious were condemned....can only be understood in relation to Orphic ritual...Daubing with mud was...an integral rite in certain Orphic mysteries. The rite neglected on earth by the impious must be performed forever in Hades. The like notion lies at the bottom of the water-carrying. He who did not purify himself on earth by initiation must forever purify himself in Hades. But the vindictive instinct, always alive in man, adds, it is too late, he carries water in a pierced vessel, a sieve, and carries it for ever."

"The word used by Plato [*Republic*] for those who carry the water in the sieve is...*anosioi*, ...'unconsecrated ones.'....What was justified by the old order was criminal in the new. Here was an opportunity for the moralist. Of old the Danaides carried water because they were well-nymphs; the new order has made them criminals, and it makes of their fruitful water-carrying a fruitless punishment - and atonement for murder. It will readily be seen that the well-nymphs, regarded by the new order as guilty maidens seeking purification, offered just the mythological prototype needed for the uninitiated water-carriers. Once the analogy was seized, many further traits of resemblance would eagerly be added....It has already been seen that one special rite of purification, the *Liknophoria*, was common to marriage and the mysteries. The same is true of the *Loutrophoria*, carrying of the bath. Is it surprising that in the figures of the well-nymphs some ingenious person saw the Danaides as *ateleis gamou*, 'uninitiated in marriage,' and therefore condemned in Hades to carry for ever in vain the water for their bridal bath?"[504]

A *hydria* was a ritual water container carried by a *hydrias*, a water priestess, a Danaid. The *hydria* was often a sieve, a rain-bringing charm, beautiful examples of which, as above, with snakes crawling all over them, come from Knossos.[505] The magical *hydrias* was turned into the *Hydra*, the demonic octopus of the old order. *Diana Nemorensis*, Diana of the Grove, went through the same evolution, holding an apple (*pharmakon*) bough in one hand and her calendar wheel promising the revolution of the seasons in the other. The *pharmakon* was turned into snake venom and the seasonal turning into a promise of divine vengeance on the transgressor of Hadrian's bourgeois taboos, *Nemesis*.[506]

"Religion has....within it two factors indissolubly linked: ritual, that is custom, collective action, and myth or theology, the representation of the collective emotion, the collective conscience. And - a point of supreme importance - both are incumbent, binding, and interdependent...When the religious man, instead of becoming in ecstacy and sacramental communion one with Bacchos, descends to the chill levels of intellectualism and asserts that there is an objective reality external to himself called Bacchos, then comes a parting of the ways. Still wider is the breach if he asserts that this objective reality is one with the mystery of life, and also with man's last projection, his ideal of the good." Below is Orpheus, from a Pompeiian painting.

"This idea that religion may be defined as a relation to a god is sufficiently refuted by the simple fact that one of the most important and widespread of religions, Buddhism, knows no god. Religion is to the Buddhist not prayer, the worship of an external being, but the turning in upon himself, the escape from the sorrow that comes of desire, the gradual attainment of Nirvana. Yet no one will deny to Buddhism the name of religion."[507] Nor to Judaism, which divinized none of its prophets and considers all images of God vain idolatry. All we know of God are His Laws, his *themistes*.

"Themis was before the particular shapes of the gods; she is not religion, but she is the stuff of which religion is made. It is the emphasis and representation of herd instinct, of the collective conscience, that constitutes religion....Out of many *themistes* arose Themis. These *themistes*, these fixed conventions, stood to the Greek for all he held civilized. They were the bases alike of his kingship and his democracy. These *themistes* are the ordinances of what must be done, what society compels; they are also, because what must be will be, the prophesies of what shall be in the future; they are also the dues, the rites, the prerogatives of a king, whatever custom assigns to him or any official...It was the boast of Aegina that more than any other city she honoured 'Saviour Themis who sitteth by Zeus, God of Strangers.' Themis like *Doom* begins on earth and ends in heaven. On earth we have our Doomsday, which, projected into high heaven, becomes the Crack of Doom, the Last Judgement."[508]

"Dike in her origin is very like Themis, only always a little more alive, less stationary. In common Greek parlance...she is the 'way of life,' normal habit....Like a wolf, like a foal, like water. Here we have the difference between *Themis* and *dike*. The one, *Themis*, is specialized to man, the social conscience, the other is the way of the whole world of nature, of the universe of all live things. The word *dike* has in it more life-blood, more of living and doing; the word *Themis* has more of permission to do, human sanction shadowed always by *tabu*; *fas* [fate, destiny] is unthinkable without *nefas*....Dike then is the way of the world, the way things happen, and Themis is that specialized way for human beings which is sanctioned by the collective conscience, by herd instinct. A lonely beast in the valley, a fish in the sea, has his Dike, but it is not till man congregates together that he has his Themis.

"And now we understand the link between Dike and the Horai....Dike is manifest in the changes of the rising and setting of constellations, in the waxing and waning of the Moon and in the daily and yearly courses of the Sun....By the side of Theseus a woman is seated holding a drawn sword. She is Dike in her later Orphic aspect of Vengeance....What has this Dike with the drawn sword, this Vengeance incarnate, this denizen of Hades, to do with that Dike we already know, the fixed order of the world, the Way of Nature?...in the light of Eury-dike we understand Dike herself. Eurydike, She of the

Wide-Way, is...but the ordered form of Earth herself, in her cyclic movement of life and death, her eternal wheel of palingenesia. She, the young green Earth, has...her yearly Anodos, as Kore, as Semele, as Eurydike. At first she rises of her own motion and alone...Later, when the physical significance of her rising is no longer understood, when patriarchy has supplanted matrilinear earth-worship, a human and patrilinear motive is provided. She needs a son or lover to fetch her up, to carry her down. So we get the rape of Persephone by Hades, of Basile by Echelos, of Helen by Theseus and Peirithoos, the descent of Dionysos to fetch his mother Semele, and, latest and loveliest, the love-story of Orpheus and Eurydike. Here on the Orphic vase-painting we have a reminiscence of the fact that Eurydike really and primarily returned to the upper world alone. Orpheus is there, but he sings on, untouched by, irrelevant to, her going. Dike then, like her prototype Eurydike, represents the eternal cycles of the life of the earth, the temporal sequence of the Horai."[509]

"Fortune (Tyche) is the goddess who brings - brings forth, brings to accomplishment. But we add to this the notion of retribution....Just such a degradation awaited Dike. From being the order of the world, the way of the world, she became the Avenger of those who outstep and overpass the order of the world....Dike...became in Orphic hands Vengeance on the wrong doer, on him who overstepped the *way*....This notion of Dike explains...a grouping of criminals that might otherwise be unmeaning....The Danaides are filling their cask, and by their side is Sisyphos rolling his pitiless stone up the hill. Sisyphos is the ancient Titan, the Sun himself. His labour is no penalty, it is the course of Dike, it is periodic, eternally incumbent. So too with the Danaides; they are well-nymphs, but also projections of the ancient rain-making ceremonies, they carry water to make rain. Their labour too is ceaseless, periodic. They are part of the eternal *dike* of nature....To Olympian theology, in its ignorance and ineptitude, 'recurrent' had come to spell 'fruitless'; the way of life was envisaged as an immutable sterility and therefore rejected."[510]

"Deep-rooted in man's heart is the pathetic conviction that moral goodness and material prosperity go together, that, if man keep the *rta* [Vedic for Dike, The Way], he can magically affect for good nature's ordered going. When the Olympians became fully humanized, and sacramentalism was replaced by gift-sacrifice, the notion slightly altered its form. The gods it was now felt were bound in honour to bestow on their faithful worshippers a *quid pro quo*. The idea is nowise confined to the Greeks. The Psalmist, whose sheltered outlook on life was traditional and religious rather than realistic, says confidently, 'I have been young, and now am old/And yet saw I never the righteous forsaken,/Not his seed begging their bread'(37:25)....Then, when the social life finds its focus in the figure of a king, on his goodness and the justice of his ruling, on his Dike, his Way, the prosperity of his people depends."[511]

This comfortable idiocy assumes that the thousands of forsaken children who have died in agony in the countless holocausts weren't righteous, an assumption I am unwilling to make. Granted those that don't cross Caesar are less likely to be decimated by him.

The archetypes of fascist indoctrination, then, are of an Olympian nature. They are negations, theocratic caricatures of the tribal consciousness that is reborn in each new baby, symbolic walls built by the industrial theocracy to suppress access to the shamanic state. The most powerful propaganda is implicit, assumed, hence the inversion of the shamanic imagery using its own emotive meaning against itself, that it might not survive to show the way to the dream state, the Paleolithic state, the state in which our emotions, our genius, lives. The Mother of Emotions can no longer prophesy in public, her stream is buried beneath Apollon's landslide, he of the Bulldozer Brain. Henceforth, we are to feed the Genius of the Emperor, our Saviour, or his mandatory iconic equivalent, with the gift of a symbolic entheogen, rather than our own with a real one. Thus sayeth Augustus. The silver quinarius below, 30 BC, celebrates Augustus' victory over Antony and Cleopatra at Actium. Victory, holding a wreath, stands on a *cista mystica* between two sacred snakes.

ASSAYA

The New Testament is a study in imperial cooptation. Since the Roman religio-political philosophy it espouses is the chief engine of industrial conformity in contemporary Euroamerica, my real subject, it is necessary to understand this seminal manipulation of human mythology in order to understand the Drug War. Psychologically, the archetypal shaman, the gateway to the eternal, the Son of the Mother, is Jesus (Dionysos), and his Twin, his *Pharmakos*, his official industrial scapegoat, is Judas (Pentheus). But it's not the ethnicity or the philosophy of Judas that's important in the Drug War. It is the implicit demonization of non-conformity *per se*, and of shamanism in particular, that sticks psychologically, politically, in contemporary EuroAmerica, as in Augustan Rome or medieval Europe.

The originary Inquisition, the archetypes of industrial conformity, descend to the unconscious level, since the archetypal frame of reference has been carefully manipulated, through succeeding historical stages, to destroy conscious, cultural, knowledge of the ancient shamanism. When conscious memory (*mnemosyne*) is destroyed, what is left is emotion, irrational attitudes dictated by 'parentally' inculcated compulsions: God-the-Father as Pavlov. It's not for nothing that the great shaman Plato said that all learning is remembering. The greatest crime of the nonconforming shaman is that she or he struggles to bring to conciousness that which the authorities, and their compulsive sheep, want forgotten.

Jesus was such a shaman. The historical Jesus has about as much in common with the Pauline Jesus as a horse has with a unicorn. The Roman Empire's most prestigious and effective non-Hellenic theology, *de facto religio licita* to the Romans for centuries, was coopted by some of the Empire's most talented syncretists and turned into a dogma capable of filling the void left by the bankrupt post-tribal pseudo-shamanism that Imperial Graeco-Roman religion had become. The syncretists understood organization better than the Imperial government itself, because they understood the people better, and so were able to evolve a credible Graeco-Roman salvationism capable of appealing to the vast majority in the Empire, using, as their foundation, the subtle and cohesive mythology of a still-tribal Israel.

The trick, as Paul well understood, was to turn the nationalist Israeli ghost dancer Joshua into a Greek mystery god, Orpheus. 'Saviours' were turning into mystery gods all the time, but never before with the foundation of the Empire's legendary and prestigious network of Hellenized synagogues as a starting point. Never before with the one holy book capable of replacing Homer and Hesiod, *The Septuagint*, the Greek translation of the Hebrew Bible, created 250 years before by Alexandria's Greek-speaking Jewish community and now read all over Alexander's Empire, the Greek Empire Rome conquered. The worst, the most amnesiac aspects of Israeli theology were used, brilliantly, against itself, to destroy what remained of the ancient *mnemosyne*.

Habiru communities and troops are mentioned in texts from Hammurabi and Zimri-Lim of Mari, c.1700 BC. "Your fathers lived of old beyond the Euphrates, Terah, the father of Abraham and of Nahor; and they served other gods."(Joshua:24:2) In Genesis Abraham (c.1700 BC?[512]) is associated with the Canaanite town of Hebron, identified with El Shaddai, and Jerusalem (EL Elyon). "Thus says the Lord God to Jerusalem: Your origin and your birth are of the land of the Canaanites; your father was an Amorite, and your mother a Hittite."(Ez:16:3) Isaac is associated with Beersheba (EL Olam), and Jacob with Shechem (El) and Bethel (El Bethel). In Canaanite myth Yahweh (Elohim) is El's son.

Many other texts from 1700-1200 BC mention the Habiru as an ethnic group in the area of Babylonia and Assyria. The grandfather of a 14th century BC North Syrian king was an Habiru, as was a powerful prime minister in the 12th century Assyrian court, and many Habiru soldiers, serfs and slaves are recorded as well. The Habiru are also mentioned frequently in the Amarna tablets as marauding raiders from Syria and Canaan, and Egyptian texts from the 15th to the 12th century also mention them.[513]

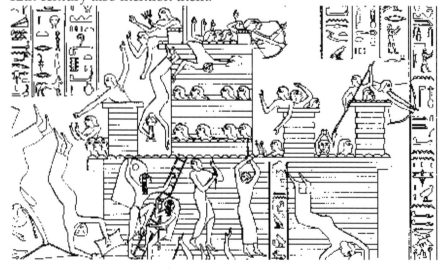

Above is a detail from Ramses II's depiction of his conquest of Tabor in 1295 BC, in which he netted quite a few Canaanite slaves. To be nearer his sea lanes, this grandiose builder transferred his capitol from Thebes to the Delta near Tanis. We have two payprii from Ramses (c.1295-1224) providing for the distribution of grain to 'Apiru slaves erecting a pylon at Tanis. The Bible confirms Israelite residence at 'Zoan,' the Hebrew name for Tanis.[514] "Therefore they set taskmasters over them to afflict them with heavy burdens; and they built for Pharoah store-cities, Pithom and Raamses."[515]

The Egyptian prince Moses, *Moshe*, is the original Hebrew Messiah, *Moshiy'a*. The words are related, both apparently related to the Egyptian *mose*, 'is born,' as in Thutmose, 'Thoth Is Born.' The Egyptian *mose* is derived, according to Professor Gordon, from the Canaanite *moshe*, 'sacred calf.'[516] *Moshiy'a* apparently means 'Salvation Is Born' in Hebrew. The Hebrew use of the word, without a prefix, is Canaanite, not Egyptian.

That Moses' family were dedicated to the cult of the calf is obvious not only from the behavior of his brother Aaron while Moses was communing with God on the Mountain, but from the behavior of Moses himself, who sprinkled 'the blood of the covenant,' bull's blood, on the children of Israel as a sanctification.[517] El was the Canaanite Bull, Moses was the Son of the Bull, the sacred calf, *Moshe*.

It is a commonplace for Jews to say that Moses was not regarded as divine, simply a prophet with a divine message, but that is a political conceit. Israel refused to divinize its kings and prophets, insisting that they live up to the law of the one true king, God. Moses, the archetypal Israelite king, was therefore said not be be divine. But *the word* of Moses became as much an *eikon* to Israel as the *liknon* of the Mysteries became to the Graeco-Roman world. He was as much a *pharmakos* as the calf, a divine child of the river, floating in a *liknon*, a harvest basket, pulled from the rushes by the Queen.

These were universal symbols for godhead in the ancient world. "Sargon, the mighty king, king of Agade, am I./My mother was a changeling, my father I knew not./....My changeling mother conceived me, in secret she bore me./She set me in a basket of rushes, with bitumen she sealed my lid./She cast me into the river which rose not over me./The river bore me and carried me to Akki, the drawer of water./....Akki the drawer of water appointed me as his gardener./While I was a gardener, Ishtar granted me her love,/And for four and...years I exercised kingship."[518]

The Romans derived their word for holy mysteries, *arcana*, from the contents of the *liknon*, the *arca* as they called it, and the Ark of the Covenant, Israel's ineffable sacrament, came from God through Moses. Every synagogue has a *genizah*, a storeroom, for worn copies of the Torah, because the sacred word could not be burned (let alone smoked).

From the outset Israeli culture was inherently multi-ethnic, containing former Egyptian slaves of all colors and backgrounds. The great genius of the Israelite approach to religio-social organization was to do what native cultures of the great slave states were incapable of doing. Israel rejected the unconscious worship of the ancient tribal totems, with which Pharaoh now identified himself for purposes of enslavement. Warrior Israel substituted a patriarchal monotheism that stressed conscious mysticism and democratic social organization, rather than a coopted communal shamanism, a 'mystery' religion. The mystery, to the Israelites, was how anyone could take Pharoah and his Queen seriously as Amon and Mut. *SHE*, after all, for the Israelis, wasn't a loving village Great Mother, but She Who Must Be Obeyed, matriarch of Ramses'murderous clan. Below is Ramses' beautiful depiction of his confrontation with Fate under the Tree of Life.

Israel freed itself from the thrall of totemic magic, losing, of course, important points of contact with its shamanic roots, but gaining an *athanatos* God Almighty that stressed compassion, conscious mysticism, empiricism, group cohesion and personal responsibility. Israel's conception of social organization was centuries ahead of its time. The books Israel produced, *Torah* ('Outpouring'), *Nevi'im* ('Prophets') and *Ketuvim* ('Writings'), the Holy Bible, though varied, are so powerful, self-confident and brilliant, such a consistent and effective combination of cosmology, historiography and morality, that they became the most influential writings of the ancient world, eventually supplanting Homer and Hesiod as the basic texts.

Naturally, as a beleaguered group in a state of almost constant warfare, wild shamanic nonconformity was frowned upon, in favor of effective group action. There was, and is, a powerful ethos of conformity in Israel's mandatory monotheism that Rome was eventually to find quite useful when it became 'the true Israel.' Moses' brother Aaron, the *kohen*, saw two of his sons struck dead for celebrating the Lord with 'illicit fire' (Lev:10), and Judges attributes Israel's defeat in battle to serving 'the baalim and the ashtaroth.' (2:13) Jeremiah promises divine vengeance upon those who worship the popular 'Queen of Heaven,' and archeology proves that she was indeed popular. (44:15-25) As Gordon and Patai point out, if we had no Bible, but only the evidence of Israeli archeology, we would conclude that Israelite religion, until the destruction of the Temple in 586 BC, was mainly the worship of Astarte, Asherah.[519]

That they may believe him, Moses had to take the oracular snake from Asherah's belly: "And God said unto Moses, I AM THAT I AM: and he said, Thus shalt thou say unto the children of Israel, I AM hath sent me unto you....And Moses answered and said, But, behold, they will not believe me, nor hearken unto my voice: for they will say, The Lord hath not appeared unto thee. And the Lord said unto him, What is that in thine hand? And he said, A rod. And he said, Cast it on the ground. And he cast it on the ground, and it became a serpent; and Moses fled from before it. And the Lord said unto Moses, Put forth thine hand, and take it by the tail. And he put forth his hand, and caught it, and it became a rod in his hand: That they may believe that the Lord God of their fathers, the God of Abraham, the God of Isaac, and the God of Jacob, hath appeared unto thee."[520]

"'I am he who speaks,' says the Mazatec shaman. 'I am he who speaks. I am he who speaks with the mountains. I am he who speaks with the corners. I am the doctor. I am the man of medicines. I am. I am he who cures. I am he who speaks with the Lord of the World. I am happy. I speak with the mountains. I am he who speaks with the mountains of peaks. I am he who speaks with the Bald Mountain. I am the remedy and the medicine man. I am the mushroom. I am the fresh mushroom. I am the large mushroom. I am the fragrant mushroom. I am the mushroom of the spirit.'"[521] Or, as a more famous shaman once said, "I am the vine, ye are the branches: He that abideth in me, and I in him, the same bringeth forth much fruit..."[522] Say I AM sent me.

Genesis acknowledges the serpent's maternal oracular powers while prohibiting their use to mortals: "And the serpent said unto the woman, Ye shall not surely die: For God doth know that in the day ye eat thereof, then your eyes shall be opened, and ye shall be as gods, knowing good and evil. /And when the woman saw that the tree was good for food, and that it was pleasant to the eyes, and a tree to be desired to make one wise, she took the fruit thereof, and did eat, and gave also unto her husband with her; and he did eat. And the eyes of them both were opened....And the Lord God said, Behold, the man is become as one of us, to know good and evil: and now, lest he put forth his hand, and take also of the tree of life, and eat, and live for ever; Therefore the Lord God sent him forth from the garden of Eden, to till the ground from whence he was taken. So he drove out the man: and he placed at the east of the garden of Eden Cherubims, and a flaming sword which turned every way, to keep the way of the tree of life."[523]

Used to be all Tsistsistas could taste the fruit of the Tree of Life, but that was long ago. The fruit was now forbidden to "they who do sacrifice to the prince and announce his decrees, whatsoever Phoibos Apollon, bearer of the golden blade, speaks from his laurel tree below the dells of Parnassos." There is no difference between the 'flaming sword' of Elohim and the 'golden blade' of Apollon. The ancients understood this: a drachma from Gaza, c.400 BC, depicts a solar Zeus labeled 'Yahu' in Aramaic letters.[524]

As among the Greeks, participation in Israel's culture was circumscribed by carefully prescribed group ritual. As the most famous prayer in Judaism puts it, 'Sh'ma Yisra'el, Adonai Eloheinu, Adonai Ekhad - Hear, O Israel, the Lord is our God, the Lord is One.'(Deut:6:4) For Israel, God is King, and the earthly King, the anointed one, the Messiah, derived his powers from just rule under the laws of God. In a relatively democratic Iron Age culture 'fear of God' helped liberate people from fear of man, and was used to protect the weak from the powerful, as well as to enforce group cohesion.

To bully the poor was as heinous to the prophets as idolatry,[525] but that was by no means a unique moral innovation, as rabbinic roman-tics would have it. Ur-Nammu of Ur, in the oldest law code known, c.2000 BC, eight hundred years before Moses, worried that "the or-phan did not fall a prey to the wealthy....the widow did not fall a prey to the powerful....the man of one shekel did not fall a prey to the man of one mina."[526] Hammurabi made the same points 300 years later.[527]

And, as with Ur-Nammu, Hammurabi or the ruthless Hittites, idolatry was equated by the Israelites with any unlicensed shaman-ism, as if it were that of a military enemy: "Thou shalt not suffer a witch to live. Whosoever lieth with a beast shall surely be put to death. He that sacrificeth unto any God, save unto the Lord only, he shall be utterly destroyed."(Ex:22:18-20)

Hammurabi wrote that, though he put it more legalistically: "2. If a man brought a charge of sorcery against another man, but has not proved it, the one against whom the charge of sorcery was brought, upon going to the river [the Euphrates], shall throw himself into the river, and if the river has then overpowered him, his accuser shall take over his estate; if the river has shown that man to be innocent, and he has accordingly come forth safe, the one who brought the charge of sorcery against him shall be put to death, while the one who threw himself into the river shall take over the estate of the accuser."[528] The Israelis added the nauseating association of sorcery with screw-ing animals, but one can hardly call that a moral innovation. Bits of Hammurabi's Code are reproduced word for word in Exodus, Leviticus and Deuteronomy.[529] Maybe Moe wasn't burning the right bush after all.

Just as Psalm 104 preserves, almost word for word, parts of Akhenaten's *Great Hymn to the Aten*, so Israel preserved elements of the organizational ruthlessness of the 'monotheism' Akhenaten taught it when it was on the wrong end of his crook: "And thou shalt set bounds unto the people round about, saying, Take heed to yourselves, that ye go not up into the mount, or touch the border of it: whosoever toucheth the mount shall be surely put to death."(Ex:19:12)

Israel's moral advance over Hammurabi and Akhenaten was only incremental until the brilliant Pharisees of the Roman era. Israel was born as a tribal army on the move, and the rules were brutal. Said Moses: "Now therefore kill every male among the little ones, and kill every woman that hath known man by lying with him. But all the women children that have not known a man by lying with him, keep alive for yourselves."[530] That is not different than Agamemnon.

The substitution of infant circumcision for 'child sacrifice' is the logic of a Bronze Age warrior, symbol of a 'Covenant' with God-the-Father, rather than an acknowledgement, as it always had been, of the sexual and psychological hegemony of a now murderous Holy Mother. As slaves who had to fight for their freedom, the Israelites faced the Late Bronze Age Egyptian Mother Terrible, who demanded 'sacrifice,' ownership, of the children, described in Genesis as the most ruthless mass murder. The overthrow of this *ersatz* 'Goddess' was therefore an act of liberation. The God of Israel demanded a blood oath from His faithful warriors-to-be in exchange for a square deal. Instead of cutting Isaac's throat at the behest of God, Abraham had circumcised him, as Zipporah did to Moses' son in Exodus.[531]

As Maccoby shows, this is an etiological myth which emphasizes that circumcision was originally a matriarchal tribal rite usually performed at puberty, as a fertilizing act of obeisance to the Goddess before entering her field, an acknowledgement of the fact that the tribe is the Mother. The Divine substitution of a ram for Isaac under Abraham's knife (Gen:22) is the Hebrew equivalent of Artemis' substitution of a deer for Iphigeneia under Agamemnon's knife.[532] In both cases the mother's consent to the sacrifice was deemed unnecessary, though, revealingly, in the Greek legend it is the daughter who is the sacrifice and the Goddess who intervenes.

Abraham's reward for his acceptance of circumcision (Gen:17) and for his blind obedience to God-the-Bronze-Age-Warrior in the binding of Isaac was the divine outpouring vouchsafed to his offspring Moses, the Torah. "Surely a bridegroom of blood art thou to me....for the circumcision,"growls the flint-wielding Zipporah to Moses, resentfully acknowledging the primacy of God-The-Father in a newborn Israel, as she cuts off the foreskin of their newborn son, a blood-sign of the New Deal.[533]

Moses' warriors were every bit as capable of pillage and rape as any Greek, and the Bible is full of brutal tales, but as the migratory warfare subsided into national settlement, the warriors' priorities changed. The gang rape-murder by some Benjaminites from Gibeah of a young woman, recounted in Judges, is cause for full-scale warfare by all the tribes of Israel against Gibeah. (19-21) The story reveals that women were as much a prize of competing warriors as at Troy, but the objective was equal tribal relations, legitimate marriage, not rape or enslavement, a profound distinction.

Leviticus sanctions a woman's post-birth seclusion this way: "If a woman have conceived seed, and born a man child; then she shall be unclean seven days....But if she bear a maid child, then she shall be unclean two weeks....And when the days of her purifying are fulfilled...she shall bring...a burnt offering, and...a sin offering....and the priest shall make an atonement for her, and she shall be clean."[534] Obviously a Neolithic priestess would have had a different way of sanctioning the woman's release from social obligations than by calling it 'uncleanness,' nor would a male child have been valued over a female, but the seclusion was ended by the simplest of ritual acts performed by the woman herself along with the priest, and was turned into an excuse for a feast.

The fourteen day period of purification after childbirth is mentioned in *King Kheops and the Magicians*, an Egyptian text dating to c.1600 BC, and so was reflective of the ancient tabu associated not with pollution, the later perversion of meaning, but with power, the originary meaning, the instinctive apprehension, of childbirth and menstrual blood.[535] Fourteen is a moon-number, the lucky first half of a lunar month. It was as if the birthing woman had taken a prohibited entheogen, had celebrated with 'illicit fire.' In rural Lithuania, recounts Gimbutas, women going for their ritual sauna a month after giving birth are called 'the Bear,' an ancient power-name of the Goddess. 'Bear'and 'birth' have a common Old European linguistic ancestor, *bher*. *Burdh*, in Old Norse, means 'birth,' and *beran* in Germanic means 'to bear children.'[536]

"Wild indeed are the stories told of the mysterious and awful power of the menstruous discharge,"writes Pliny. "They say that hail-storms and whirlwinds are driven away if menstrual fluid is exposed to the very flashes of lightning." Since the moon, the 'Queen of the Stars,' "saturates the earth and fills bodies by its approach and empties them by its departure...the blood even of humans increases and diminishes with its light, and leaves and herbage...are sensitive to it, the same force penetrating into all things....if this female force should issue when the moon or the sun is in eclipse, it will cause irremediable harm; no less so when there is no moon. At such seasons sexual intercourse brings death and disease upon the man."[537] Josephus mentions that some magical plants can't safely be picked without the application of menstrual blood.[538] This is awe, not disgust - fertility magic, inseparable from the pharmaco-shamanism that accompanied it.[539]

Delphi was taken very seriously by the ancients. When Inanna was raped as she rested, "the woman, because of her vulva, what harm she did! Inanna because of her womb, what she did do! All the wells of the land she filled with blood..."[540] Clearly, Inanna taught Moses. Reflecting the greater cultural milieu, and the territorial value of warfare, Israel pushed the demonization of the originary matristic associations along, but by Early Iron Age standards it was actually quite egalitarian. Abraham is told by God: "Whatever Sarah tells you, do as she says."[541] One of the things Sarah (Asherah, the Laughing Goddess) told Abe was to name their firstborn 'he shall laugh,' Isaac. Isaac's wife Rebecca is clearly shown to be the more prescient as to the character and destiny of their sons Esau and Jacob.[542]

The seminal event in the rise of Pharisaic Judaism, of course, is the sacking of Jerusalem by Nebuchadnezzar in 598 BC and the subsequent destruction of the First Temple in 586. Above is part of Nebuchadnezzar's cuneiform account of the end of ancient Israeli power. Cyrus the Great of Persia, a brilliantly liberal imperialist, broke Babylonian power in 539 BC, but it wasn't until Ezra, a century later, that Israel began to rebuild itself. The Pharisees, the 'Separate Ones,' inspired by the stubborn example of Ezra, led the revivification of Israel after the Babylonian Captivity.

This was, obviously, a warrior-dominated world. The Pharisees, a thousand years after Moses, evolved a patriarchal rulebook for 'wives' and 'daughters,' but not a misogynistic one. It is true that of the more than two thousand rabbis mentioned in *The Talmud*, none are women, but they provided their women with clearly defined independent rights. It became almost as easy for unhappily married women to sue for divorce, remarry and keep their property as for unhappily married men, but it wasn't particularly easy for either, and even this wasn't really an innovation, just a throwback to one of the more matristic aspects of Hammurabi's Code (142). It is no accident that the two most important Pharisee additions to the canon are the lovingly sexual, and sexually balanced, Song of Songs (lifted in part from Egyptian New Kingdom love poems) and the Book of Esther, which celebrates the heroine of Israel's most joyous holiday.

Pharisaic tradition insists that it is equally incumbent on parents to educate their daughters as their sons, since the spiritual life requires education. (Deut:6:7) *The Mishnah* puts this rather strangely: "Whoever teaches Torah to his daughter is as if he teaches her sexual satisfaction."[543] These were men, one hastens to add, who had no tolerance whatever for incest or pedophilia, crimes as serious as murder to them. What is being said is that intellect and body don't separate, that both are necessary for a successful spiritual life, and that a married woman was expected to enjoy both.

Pharisaic Judaism, as in the Song of Songs, regards sexuality itself as the blissful and mystical gift of God, an empowerment of the individual, not a humiliation. Pauline-Augustinian Christianity regards sexuality as a 'curse,' chastity as a 'gift,' and self-abnegating virginity as a virtue. The denigration of sexuality, to Jews, smacks of sadistic domination and infantilization, as does the Pauline denigration of women and the doctrine of Original Sin itself.

Control of reproduction is the primary domestication technique farmers use on their sheep. Selection for submissiveness results in a generational decrease in the production of adrenocortical steroids, producing not only infantile physiological characteristics, but genetically ingrained submissiveness and lack of creativity. The first commandment in the Torah is "Be fruitful and multiply, fill the earth and master it."(1:28) The body and soul are a continuum; there is a sacred logic to procreation, to the use of the body, made 'in the image of God'- the functional image, not the *eidolon* - which entails both a guiltless ecstacy and personal responsibility. Most Jews couldn't conceive how an unmarried rabbi, devoid of sexual responsibility, could give personal advice to the married.

Jesus, as opposed to Paul, talked constantly of adherence to Mosaic Law, because personal responsibility is the whole point of Hebrew mysticism, and acceptance of that responsibility finds the love of God. As Deuteronomy puts it: "For this commandment which I command thee this day, it is not hidden from thee, neither is it far off. It is not in heaven, that thou shouldest say: 'Who shall go up for us to heaven, and bring it unto us, that we may hear it, and do it?'...But the word is very nigh unto thee, in thy mouth, and in thy heart, that thou mayest do it."[544]

This is directly contrary to the Pauline doctrine of Original Sin, in which Salvation is unavailable without an external Saviour, a blood offering to a Pharaonic God, an Orphic *Pharmakos*, without whose agonizing death we are lost, regardless of our own understanding and efforts. Israel's God demands no human sacrifice, but submission to Divine Law, Themis, which reveals Divine Love. Classic Pharisaism, that is, classic post-Mosaic Judaism, provides a flexible karma yoga involving study and ritual that is by no means rigid and legalistic, but, on the contrary, acknowledges gradual progress in the spiritual life on the part of those willing to exert the intellectual effort and assume the moral responsibility. Like the *I Ching*, Israel says, 'No Blame.'

But Israel's rejection of Pharoah's golden *pharmakon* implied the equation of all sacramentalism, golden, animal or vegetal, with Pharaonic idolatry, an historical, or is it hysterical, myopia that Orthodox Christianity would find quite useful in its own inquisitorialism. Pharoah had reviled this world, promising freedom in the next, providing, when necessary, a temporary bloody *orgiazo,* a pseudo-shamanic holiday for slaves, free meat. Israel's daily life, a thousand years after Pharoah, rejected this manipulative trickery, stressing the sanctity of this world. Prophesy belonged only to the Millenium. The age of the prophets had ended for Israel with the last of the Biblical prophets. There was no *pharmakon* that would reveal the mystery of prophesy. Sacrifice, for Israel, wasn't sacramental. The flesh wasn't eaten, the wine wasn't drunk as a universal transformation, but was offered as a gift to the King of Heaven, a mystical communion to call down a blessing in this world.

Israel replaced Pharoah's, or Caesar's, inculcated group terror, the need for magical communal salvation, with individual responsibility within a group that had already been saved. It eliminated the humiliating Pharaonic concept of Original Sin, which requires a *Deus Ex Machina* to take life's responsibilities from our shoulders, to rescue us from our Pauline despair: "I do not even acknowledge my own actions as mine, for what I do is not what I want to do, but what I detest...Wretched man that I am! Who shall deliver me from this body of death? Who but God? Thanks be to him through Jesus Christ our Lord! For I myself serve the law of God with my mind, but with my flesh the law of sin."(Romans:7:15-25) That is certainly an understandable emotion, but it is completely contrary to the Hebraic personal responsibility preached by Jesus.

Israel proceeds from an acknowledgement of good inclination (*yetzer ha-tov*) and evil inclination (*yetzer ha-r'a*) in all of us, but it is the 'inclination' that is stressed, not the 'evil.'[545] A natural inclination needing social direction, sexual behavior, for instance, isn't a Promethean curse, an inherent guilt, an Original Sin. Eve may have eaten too much serpentine fruit, but that didn't communicate a curse to all her descendants, it simply explained the human condition. Properly directed, sexual passion was procreative - evil, or simply unhealthful, only if misdirected.

The New Testament constantly talks of 'hell,' a perverted image derived from *hohle*, 'cave,' the sacred abode of *Holla*, the Indo-European White Goddess of Death and Resurrection. 'Hell' is actually related to 'heal' and 'whole.'[546] The Old Testament has no hell, no Satan, no eternal damnation, even in the face of divine wrath. To show his love for the world, the Pauline God tortures his Only Begotten Son to death, demanding an expiation that would have satisfied Moloch, whereupon Paul blames 'the Jews' for the cruelty of the salvific sacrifice, not God or the Romans, thus freeing the Graeco-Roman faithful to enjoy their *eucharisto* without too much guilt. This is Roman Orphism, *hosia kai eleuthera*, 'consecrated and free' to me, but, since you are the *pharmakos*, accursed to you. The Pauline God seems to be more Janus than Yahweh the Son of Asherah.

There is a very unpleasant, a very Roman schizophrenia here, like watching a reenactment of the rape of Persephone by Hades in the arena, with a young girl from Jerusalem cast in the role of Persephone opposite Crassus' favorite trooper as Hades. I see nothing entheogenic in the blood of the virgin, though most of the *laoi* walked away satisfied.

It was Crassus, in 71 BC, who lined the Appian Way with the crucified remains of Spartacus' slave army, some 6,000 souls. At this time Rome's great wholesale slave market, the island free port of Melos, was processing some 15,000 people a day. Crassus ruled the Roman Empire along with Pompey and Caesar, becoming Syrian proconsul in 54 BC. The 10,000 gold talents he stole from the Temple in Jerusalem, as well as all the money he made selling Israelis into slavery, didn't help in his war against Persia. Crassus lost his army and his life in the contest for Armenia, giving Israel one more reason to love the Persians.

The politic Julius Caesar then took over in Syria, winning an Empire of Jewish allies with his *de jure* recognition of Israel's *religio licita*. As the silver denarius below, from 47 BC, indicates, Caesar himself claimed descent from Venus through Aeneas, who is pictured carrying his father Anchises, and the magical statue of Pallas, from the ruins of Troy. Caesar's murder, of course, touched off the war between his first in command, Marcus Antonius, and his chosen heir, his nephew Octavian.

Virgil, in the Fourth Eclogue, prophesied that Antony's first child, by Octavian's sister Octavia, would be the immortal whose coming marked the birth of the millenium. But Antony rejected Octavia in favor of Cleopatra, and her huge army. Cleopatra was half Macedonian and half Greek, Egyptian only by politics and religion. Her fluent command of Egyptian, rare in a Ptolemy, and her genuine love of Egyptian religion, made her enormously popular. She was portrayed as Hathor in the temple at Dendera, the daughter of Amon-Re. She was a brilliant organizer and international operative, able to converse in many languages - and an expert dynastic murderess, 29 when she met Antony at Tarsus.

Antony married her in 37 BC, giving her all central Syria as a wedding gift. To the Greeks they were Dionysos and Aphrodite; to the Egyptians, Osiris and Isis. Antony ruled his Asian realm as the New Dionysos, which is as much a comment on contemporary politics as on Antony's proclivities or Cleopatra's influence. Friendly oracles, Greek and Jewish, recorded in the Sibylline books stored in the Roman temple of Apollo, told of the arrival of the millenium and the coming of the Messiah on their victory.[547] As contemporary coins show, these ideas were common throughout the Empire, and weren't dependent on any particular personality.

Cleopatra's famous ring, depicitng the goddess *Methe* (Drunkenness) on an amethyst, an *amethistos*, a 'not drunk' stone, signified Sober Drunkenness (*methe nephalios*). That is, the wineless enthusiasm of the Bacchae, indicating that Cleopatra was an initiate of Dionysos, like Alexander's mother Olympias herself. Olympias was world famous as the snake wielding Shaman Queen of Macedon.

Cleopatra, as she herself proudly insisted, was the New Olympias. As Homer put it, of the Shaman Queen of the Hellenes, "But now it entered Helen's mind/to drop into the wine that they were drinking/an anodyne, mild magic of forgetfulness./Whoever drank this mixture in the wine bowl/would be incapable of tears that day -/though he should lose mother and father both,/or see, with his own eyes, a son or brother/mauled by weapons of bronze at his own gate./ The opiate (*nepenthes*) of Zeus's daughter bore/this canny power. It had been supplied her/by Polydamna, mistress of Lord Thon,/in Egypt, where the rich plantations grow/herbs of all kinds, maleficent and healthful;/and no one else knows medicines as they do,/Egyptian heirs of Paian, the healing god."[548]

Cleopatra's spell, of course, proved fatal to Antony. July was named after Antony's old boss, the Divine Julius, as August was named for the time of year that Antony's conqueror, Octavian, entered Alexandria in triumph. The Senate rewarded Octavian with the title *Augustus,* 'the revered,' in 27 BC on the achievement of a compromise that left the Senate in control of some of the less militarily powerful provinces. The term was connected to *augere* and *augurium*, and was traditionally used to describe the mysteries; it implied *auctoritas*.

In the great decree of the province of Asia that adopted the Julian calendar, Augustus is referred to as "The god whose birthday was the beginning of the good news for the world that has come to men through him. From his birthday a new era begins." Good fortune, *evangelion*, leading to salvation, *soteria*, began for Greek Asia (Minor) on Augustus' birthday. "The Providence which rules over all has filled this man with such gifts for the salvation of the world as designate him as Saviour for us and for the coming generations; of wars he will make an end...the hopes of our forefathers fulfilled..it is impossible that one greater than he can ever appear."[549] The young Paul read this inscribed in marble on the wall of the official marketplace of every major city as he made his way from Tarsus to Jerusalem. Little wonder that many canonical Christians identified Augustus as the earthly alter-ego of Christ, who paved the way, politically, for the victory of the Church.

Augustus, of course, was simply following pompous imperial convention, as, ultimately, did Paul. The first Ptolemy to rule Egypt, Alexander's Egyptian commander, became Ptolemy Soter, 'The Saviour,' as did innumerable other 'saviours,' 'gods,' 'manifestations,' 're-deemers,' 'conquerors,' 'liberators' and 'shepherds.' The eastern tradition of emperor worship, as an aspect of civic life, spread throughout the Empire. The *numen Augusti* was celebrated with offerings of incense and wine on propitious anniversaries of the Saviour's life, such as his birthday or the day he entered Rome triumphant after Actium.[550] The offering of wine, incense and flowers, adopted by the Church, was the same ceremony performed for the Genius of the household and was also the formula of legal oath. The bay leaves of Apollo on Augustus' head on the coinage likewise suggested the closest possible association between the revered Genius of the Emperor and the God; he was *Theou ek Theou*, 'God from God,' the Son of God.[551]

The earliest writings of the New Testament are Paul's letters, 50-60 CE. The Gospels, more prominent in the canon, were written between 70-110, in the context of the Church, outside Israel, that Paul was largely responsible for creating. Although the four Greek Gospels bear the names of the Apostles, obviously none were written by them. All the original Hebrew and Aramaic writings of the real Israelite Apostles, the Nazarenes, were destroyed as heretical by the Roman Church in the second and third century.

We know virtually nothing about the Greek authors of the canons ('guidelines') except that Paul's Christology was, more or less, canonical to them. Since Paul left no Cliffs Notes, revealing inconsistencies abound. Mark, the earliest Gospel, contains none of the mythological cliches of the later Gospels: there is no birth in Bethlehem (to fulfill Micah's prophesy), no Massacre of the Innocents (after Moses), no journey of the Magi, no virgin birth, no birth in a manger or greeting by the shepherds.[552]

Paul was born in Tarsus, the Roman capitol of Cilicia (South Turkey-North Syria), the rich seaport where Antony first met Cleopatra. The city was named after the *pharmakos* Baal-Taraz. Paul would have grown up with Aramaic as well as Greek, and apparently, according to Epiphanius, converted to Judaism there as a young man before leaving for Israel.[553]

Paul claimed to be one of Israel's legendary 'Separate Ones,' the Pharisees, who were famous throughout the Roman and Parthian world as courageous and just sages. The claim increased his authority among his correspondents, the Greek-speakers of the greater Empire. It was a transparent lie; he never was a Pharisee, apparently didn't even have fluent Hebrew. Never once, in 160 quotations, did he quote the Hebrew Bible, always the Greek *Septuagint*. Command of the Bible, in its original Hebrew, was the basis for all further Pharisaic studies.

No Pharisee rabbi, that is, master of learning (literally 'my great one'), would ever quote the Greek over the canonical, and often different, Hebrew. Paul's famous quote (I:Cor:15:55) from Hosea (13:14), 'O death, where is thy victory? O death where is thy sting?' is from the Greek *Septuagint*; the Hebrew reads: 'Oh for your plagues, O death! Oh for your sting, O grave!'[554] Paul left not one word in Hebrew, all in fluent *koiné* Greek, his native tongue, the *lingua franca* of the Empire. Most modern experts (Maccoby, Graves, Schonfield, Vermes, etc.) agree with Kaufmann Kohler, the great Talmudic scholar and editor of the *Jewish Encyclopaedia*, who wrote in 1902 that "nothing in Paul's writings showed that he had any acquaintance with rabbinical learning."[555]

The Pharisees, the 'Separate Ones,' were leaders for no other reason than their learning. They were able to prove their fluent command not only of the Hebrew Bible, but of the vast body of homiletic, legal, historical and scientific literature accumulated in their academies. It was traditional that these lay teachers not take money for communicating wisdom, therefore most worked a regular job, say, carpenter, although that word was also used as a synonym for 'wordsmith,' 'wise-man.'

The rather unconscious stress on the ceremonial animal and vegetable gift-sacrifices of the Temple, emotionally recalling a participatory tribal shamanism now long past, wasn't the focus of Judaism for most of the Pharisee sages. They were concerned with the practical creation of a just society on earth, a 'kingdom of heaven' based on compassion and conscious wisdom. Thus the synagogue of the local congregation actually had more practical importance than the pomp and circumstance of the Jerusalem Temple. The synagogues were concerned with education and logical moral analysis far more than with unconscious ecstacy. It is in the synagogue that the roots of Christian congregationalism can be traced, as well as the roots of the Orthodox Christian prejudice against pharmaco-shamanism.

The warning that Matthew puts in the mouth of Jesus, that "they will flog you in their synagogues"[556] is sheer antisemitic fiction, the synagogues had no such function. As the canon itself shows, Jesus was invited in for a stimulating chat, not flogged for his 'Essene' views. By the time 'Matthew' was writing, however, about ten years after the destruction of Jerusalem, c. 80 CE, probably in Antioch, there may well have been intense hostility in the synagogues to pro-Roman turncoats.

The charismatic *Hasidim*, 'the devout,' were concerned with Holy Spirit far more than with social structure, whereas the mainstream

Pharisees were as political as they were religious, concerned with building an effective national structure with which to confront Israel's enemies and build community. It is from the Pharisees that Israel's greatest Senators sitting in the Sanhedrin were chosen. Great charismatics make bad politicians, so naturally there was the usual disagreement over values between Pharisees, Hasids, Essenes, Melchizedekians and what have you. These categories were almost meaningless, however, since Judaism itself teaches iconoclasm, 'image-breaking,' originality.

Free speech, dissent, logical moral analysis and creative thought are organic elements of Hebrew tradition. The 613 positive and negative strictures in Genesis, Exodus, Leviticus, Numbers and Deuteronomy, the Torah, left much to further interpretation. They say nothing about the specifics of sabbath celebration or marriage ceremonies, and so many strictures are vague or uselessly primitive that a contemporary intepretation, an Oral Law, was required. The living law thus produced a literature, *The Mishnah* and *The Talmud*, which records disagreements on every possible aspect of life.

The Mishnah, 'What is Repeated,' is the codification of the memorized oral tradition finally put in writing about 200 CE by Rabbi Judah the Prince. Its sixty-three tractates organize the scattered references in the Torah by category and adds the evolved wisdom on Agriculture, Appointed Times, Women, Damages, Holy Things, and Purities.

'Law' has relatively little to do with *The Mishnah*, since specific punishments for spiritual infractions are rarely, or only metaphorically, mentioned. *The Mishnah* is concerned with clean and unclean, with the difference between the pure and impure approaches to the events of ordinary life. It is the rabbis' idea of spiritual yoga, and the stress is on the achievement of a spiritual community of ordinary people, not on punishment. *The Jerusalem Talmud*, put together about 400 CE, is a collection of rabbinical commentaries on *The Mishnah*, as is the much larger and more basic *Babylonian Talmud*, put together a century later.

Leviticus, for instance, says, "You shall, therefore, keep My statutes and My ordinances, which if a man do he shall live by them." *The Babylonian Talmud* interprets this to mean, "'You shall live by them' and not die by them." Thus, when life was at stake, it became *mandatory* to break the sabbath in order to save the life.[557] Of course, that was an easy judgement call; many ritual and social obligations, rules dealing with marriage and divorce, for instance, were subject to much greater debate. The rabbis struggled, then, with what the Greeks called *themis*, custom, and *epikeia*, appropriate behavior, to come up with *dikai*, statements or judgements.

Friendly intellectual argument was and is a method of logical analysis and a way of life. It is this 'Buddhist' attitude of Judaism ("If you meet the Buddha on the road, kill him."), that every Jew grows up with, that Jesus inherited and so obviously practiced. In Genesis, Abraham challenges God himself to justify the destruction of Sodom and Gomorrah: "Shall not the judge of all the earth act with justice?"[558] Intellect and soul don't separate in Hebrew tradition. There never has been a dogmatic concept of heresy in Hebrew culture, and intellectual effort or moral analysis, even analysis of the moral responsibilities of God, has always been regarded as a form of spiritual ecstacy, hence the disrespect for Dogma.

"A scholar takes precedence over a king of Israel, for if a scholar dies no one can replace him, while if a king dies, all Israel is eligible for kingship."[559] When Jacob finally pins the angel of God with whom he wrestles in his nightmare, the angel rewards him with the name *Yisra'el*, and the descendants of his twelve sons are *B'nai Yisra'el*, the children of *he who wrestles with God*.[560] Like Odysseus wrestling with the shape-changing prophetic sea-lion, Jacob offered neither submission nor faith, but active *participation mystique*.

It took little for the Pauline redactors to insert an element of hostility into Jesus' learned wrestling with his fellow sages where none would naturally have existed. Debate and dissent (*aggadah* - 'telling') were enjoyed in the culture, but in matters of law (*halakhah* - 'going') the majority ruled. The majority decisions in the assemblies of the sages were rarely invested with divine authority, hence to disagree with a decision of the sages would rarely bring a charge of heresy, as it would in Rome. Scriptural infallibility was a form of stultifying conceit these subtle and flexible professors never sanctioned.

Paul accuses Israel of murdering its prophets, but that is precisely what it did not do. It made the most excruciating criticism part of its holiest books, canonizing the likes of Jeremiah and Amos, political dissidents whom other cultures would have burned along with their books. This, of course, doesn't mean that political warfare among the Jews didn't sometimes have a theological aspect. The Samaritan alternative Temple on Mt Gerazim in Shechem was destroyed by the Maccabees, but that was territorial politics, theology only secondarily. Theological dissent, short of outright rejection of the Ten Commandments or intentional abuse of the Holy Name, was rarely viewed askance. Thus Jesus' shamanic or mystery associations, as those of the Essenes or other wild men with whom he was associated, would have been cause for learned debate, not charges of heresy.

The charismatic Galilean Hasid, Honi the Circle-Drawer, who used his magic circle of concentration to make rain and heal the sick, paid little attention to the legal and ritual prescriptions of the Pharisee rule-makers, the political leaders, of his day, seventy years before Jesus. Honi was a grandfather figure to Jesus. The Pharisee leader's reaction to Honi is typical Israel: "What can I do with you, since even though you importune God, he does what you wish in the same way that a father does whatever his importuning son asks him?"[561]

Refusal to acknowledge a majority legal decision was a breach of law, not dogma. The followers of Rabbi Shammai were often over-ruled by the more liberal followers of Hillel in Jesus' day, but that neither affected their standing in the community nor the legitimacy of Jesus' agreeing with the Shammaites on stricter rules of divorce, per his ascetic 'Essene' outlook. Although Jesus' position wasn't the law, it was tenable.

Preoccupation with 'heresy,' a Graeco-Roman word that quislings would have used when addressing their masters, *haeresis*, 'wrong choice,' is a projection laid on the Israelis in the New Testament by Graeco-Roman antisemites who knew next to nothing about the culture. Wildly eccentric theological views about an earthly or heavenly messiah are recorded in the near-contemporary Hebrew literature, all without any hint of persecution because of their nonconformity. In fact, it is the freewheeling and utterly 'uncanonical' mystical specula-tions of the rabbis that gave birth, as much as Graeco-Egyptian mys-ticism, to Gnosticism, the mother of Christianity.

The Pharisee movement came to political maturity during the Maccabean revolt, at the height of recent Israeli power, just prior to the Roman conquest begun by Pompey in 63 BC. Josephus: "The Phari-sees have delivered to the people a great many observances by suc-cession from their fathers, which are not written in the law of Moses; and it is for this reason that the Sadducees reject them, and say that we are to esteem those observances to be obligatory which are in the written word, but are not to observe what are derived from the tradi-tion of our forefathers. And concerning these things it is that great disputes and differences have arisen among them, while the Sadducees are able to pursuade none but the rich, and have not the populace obsequious to them, but the Pharisees have the multitude on their side."[562]

The Hellenizing Sadducees, who claimed to be the true 'Sons of

Zadok,' David's High Priest, controlled the Temple through the High Priest's office, a political appointment. In Jesus' day the appointment was made by the Romans. The Sadducees rejected Oral Law and the popular Pharisee sages that went with it. Their Judaism was a matter of aristocratic control. They valued an archaic interpretation of Written Law, literally 'an eye for an eye,' the Temple, and their place in the ancient Temple ritual; as such they became the party of the pro-Roman rich. They saw nationalist resistance as futile, and regarded themselves as an aristocratic priestly caste, the true descendants of Ezra the Scribe, natural leaders of the Kohanim and the Levites. Most of the Levites, however, were themselves Pharisees or Pharisee supporters, anti-collaborationist nationalists who rejected in principle the right of the Romans to appoint the Sadducee High Priest. As Josephus, who was there, indicates, the political division between the nationalist Pharisees and the collaborationist Sadducees was bitter.

By the time of the Roman-serving Idumaean king Herod the Great's death in 4 BC, 'Israel' had become a romantic dream. It had been reduced to a confusing array of Roman administrative districts, many of them Greek, Syrian, Idumaean, Palestinian or Samaritan. On Herod's death, Varus, the Roman Legate of Syria, allowed his first in command, Sabinus, to plunder Herod's palace and the Temple, sitting next to one another in Jerusalem. Sabinus sparked a nationwide rebellion that saw the Zealots coalesce around Judah, son of the Galilean rebel Hezekiah whom Herod's son Antipas had murdered when he was serving the Romans as governor of Galilee.

Judah took and held the Galilean capitol of Sepphoris, four miles from Nazareth and the three-year-old Jesus. Varus sped south with two experienced legions to support Sabinus and Herod Antipas, burned Sepphoris to the ground, and crucified 2000 captured Israeli rebels. Judah of Galilee lived to fight on.

Crucifixion, originally a *pharmakos* sacrifice designed to fructify the earth with the slow drip of the victim's blood, was so agonizing that Rome reserved it exclusively for rebels and slaves. Ten years later, during the census of 6 CE, the thirteen year-old Jesus saw another 4000 Israelis crucified, among them their leader, Judah of Galilee, who had objected to the census on religious as well as political grounds.[563]

Joshua, as his family called him, was an implacably courageous Galilean nationalist, like his immediate predecessors, Honi the Circle-Drawer, Judah of Galilee and Judah's second-in command, his 'High Priest,' who took the name of Zadok. It is strange that Joshua never once condemns the Romans for the mass murder of his own people, in fact never once mentions the warfare into which he was born, the Roman occupation of Israel or contemporary politics at all. The New Testament portrays Jesus' birth in the midst of general guerrilla warfare as a romantic idyll. He is never once shown in Sepphoris, within walking distance of his birthplace, or any other major center in Galilee, home of Israel's best guerrilla fighters. Instead, we see him in the Roman lakeside resort of Capernaum. This Greek doesn't ring true, especially in light of Joshua's nationalistic attitudes: "Go nowhere among the Gentiles, and enter no town of the Samaritans."[564]

The only reason that such Israeli nationalism would have been included in the Greek Gospels is that it was too well-known to omit, part of the Nazarene tradition held canonical by the first Christians, the Empire's Hellenized Jews. This, of course, forced the 'allegorical' method of interpretation on all later Christians, like Origen and Augustine, who concluded that Jesus was really talking about the 'true Israel,' not the 'old Israel.'

During the census of 6 CE Rome took direct military control of Judaea, south of Galilee, using its tabulation of people and property to institute a head tax (*tributum capitis*), produce taxes (*tributum soli*), and various indirect taxes (*vectigalia*) including sales taxes, custom duties and transport tolls.[565] The Zealots, despite the death of Judah, kept fighting. Just three years later their faith in guerrilla war seemed justified when Arminius, prince of the Cherusci, completely destroyed three of Rome's best legions in a German forest and cut off the head of Varus, destroyer of Sepphoris. Israel, unfortunately, wasn't densely forested.

The Roman Procurator appointed and dismissed Sadducee High Priests at will. Valerius Gratus (15-26 CE), who was Procurator just before Pontius Pilate, made four appointments. His fourth was Caiaphas, the High Priest who arrested Jesus. To call Caiaphas a representative of 'the Pharisees' or 'the Jews,' as the virulently antisemitic John repeatedly does, is like calling Quisling a representative of 'the Norwegians.'

The High Priest functioned much like any other Hellenistic autocrat, with his huge tax-based income, his tax-farmer (publican) allies and reservation police. Free thought was not the Sadducee strong suit; Written Law, that is, autocratic precedent, kept the power where it belonged. Phony charges of blasphemy, for political purposes, were the Sadducee stock in trade. *The Mishnah* records the contemporary Pharisee view of the situation: "a bastard who is a disciple of a sage takes precedence over a High Priest who is an ignoramus."[566]

Paul was one of the High Priest's reservation police. He began his career by "harrying the Church; he entered house after house, seizing men and women, and sending them to prison."[567] In Acts 9 we are told that he "was still breathing murderous threats against the disciples of the Lord. He went to the High Priest and applied for letters to the synagogues at Damascus authorizing him to arrest anyone he found, men or women, who followed the new way, and bring them to Jerusalem." The High Priest's hostility would have represented that of the Romans, not the nationalist Pharisees, virtual blood enemies of the Quisling Sadducee High Priest. Paul was working for the Romans.

Damascus was ruled independently of Rome by King Aretas of Nabataea, east of the Dead Sea, who had gone to war with Herod Antipas, Rome's trusted ally. Obviously, Paul's mission for the High Priest wasn't one of legal extradition, since Nabataea wouldn't recognize Roman letters of extradition, but kidnap: "When I was in Damascus, the commissioner of King Aretas kept the city under observation so as to have me arrested; and I was let down in a basket, through a window in the wall, and so escaped his clutches."[568] That is, Aretas protected his fugitive Israelites from Roman agents.

The Roman agent Paul wrote that, Corinthians, between 55-60 CE. In Acts, written about 90 CE, the same story turns into one of Paul fleeing not Aretas but 'the Jews' for *his* advocacy of the Messiahship of Jesus, despite the fact that the Jews for Jesus were the very people Paul had been sent by the High Priest to kidnap. In Acts,[569] Ananias, who cured Paul's blindness and baptized him into the Christian faith, is portrayed as both an enthusiastic Christian and a pious practicing Jew "well spoken of by all the Jews of that place." Why, if Ananias could combine his popular, pious Judaism with Christianity, should Paul's recent conversion to Christianity bring on the murderous hostility of the same Damascus Jews? Clearly, Acts did some *ex post facto* editing of Paul's more truthful original story in Corinthians. The evidence is overwhelming that the followers of Jesus were a) anti-Roman nationalists, and b) a legitimate Jewish sect, aligned with the Essenes. Like the Essenes, and unlike the Orthodox, they were sacramentalists.

The earliest assertion of the Eucharist, that is, of Jesus as sacrament, *pharmakon*, is in Paul's Corinthians: "For I have received of the Lord that which also I delivered unto you, That the Lord Jesus the same night in which he was betrayed took bread: And when he had given thanks, he brake it, and said, Take, eat: this is my body, which is broken for you: this do in remembrance of me. After the same manner also he took the cup, when he had supped, saying, This cup is the new testament in my blood: this do ye, as oft as ye drink it, in remembrance of me. For as often as ye eat this bread, and drink this cup, ye do show the Lord's death till he come."[570]

This is the Greek *dais omophagos*, the divided feast of the sacrificial bull of the new year, in whose resurrection we share through ingestion of the sacramental flesh and blood. At Greek rites, round cakes were actually shared after the sacrifice. Mark (c.70 CE), Matthew (c.80 CE), and Luke (c.85 CE) then quote Paul's dream of Jesus' words, dutifully placing them where Paul said they belonged, at the Last Supper.

John (c.100 CE), however, the latest of the Gospels, places these words in the Capernaum synagogue, not at the Last Supper, and is emphatically Hellenic in his emphasis: "The Jews therefore strove among themselves, saying, How can this man give us his flesh to eat? Then Jesus said unto them, Verily, verily, I say unto you, Except ye eat the flesh of the Son of man, and drink his blood, ye have no life in you. Whoso eateth my flesh, and drinketh my blood, hath eternal life; and I will raise him up at the last day. For my flesh is meat indeed, and my blood is drink indeed. He that eateth my flesh and drinketh my blood, dwelleth in me, and I in him."[571]

This is Orpheus talking, apparently to a group of idiots. As John indicates, the sacramentalism being espoused was clearly contrary to Orthodox Hebrew tradition since even animal blood was forbidden at a Jewish meal, let alone the symbolic blood of a *pharmakos*.[572] John asserts that it is precisely over this issue that "many of his disciples went back, and walked no more with him."[573]

'Canaanite' Israel, however, would have understood perfectly well the pharmaco-shamanism Jesus was talking about, if not as idolatrously as Paul. It is possible, as Maccoby asserts, that John, by placing Jesus' assertion of the Eucharist not at the Last Supper but in Capernaum, inadvertently indicates that it wasn't part of the original tradition, that it was fiction added by Paul to an already established 'Orthodox Hebrew' Nazarene tradition that never included sacramentalism. But that is inconsistent with the Dead Sea Scrolls, the writings of the Essene community that John the Baptist and Jesus were almost certainly associated with. The Dead Sea Scrolls include extensive references to overt, sacramental pharmaco-shamanism. It is far more likely that the Gospel of John simply indicates that we are dealing with Paul's reinterpretation of genuine Nazarene tradition, as was his wont. John's sacramental dispute, wherever it took place, rings true to contemporary attitudes.

John's sacramentalism is also consistent, of course, with the rest of the Greek New Testament, which would have had no power among the early Hellenized Nazarenes unless it adhered fairly closely to the original Hebrew Nazarene Gospels. All the Gospels agree that the Hebrew Nazarenes gathered around Jesus were practicing shamans, *Assaya* in Aramaic, 'healers,' Essenes - that is, Gnostics who believed in sacramentalism, just as the earliest Christian Gnostic tradition insisted. It is precisely this Hellenism that made possible the conquest of the Graeco-Roman Empire by a form of Judaism.

Gnosticism dates to the century before Christ, as do the Essenes. Christianity didn't invent Gnosticism, Gnosticism invented Christianity. Alexandrian Gnosticism was heavily influenced by Alexandria's enormous and powerful Greek-speaking Jewish community, the authors of Paul's Greek Bible, *The Septuagint*, legendarily written by 'The Seventy' representatives of Israel's twelve tribes. Paul's writings are full of Alexandrian Gnostic terminology, and the most influential of Paul's early constituents were the Greek-speaking Jews of the greater Empire, among whom Judeo-Hellenic Gnosticism was very popular. The whole issue, as Jesus said, hinges on sacramentalism, actual or symbolic entheogenic ingestion. As we shall see, many Gnostics practiced actual entheogenic ingestion, and came to identify the entheogen with *Iasius*, 'the Healer,' Jesus. The canonical fascists, bent on political conquest of the Empire, insisted on symbolic entheogenic ingestion, murdered both the original Nazarenes and their early Gnostic followers, and burned their writings.

As with the Essenes and many other less famous religious dissenters, such as the Melchizedekians, Jesus' sacramentalism would in no way have prevented him from regarding himself as a practicing Jew, although many of the more orthodox, as recorded, would have rejected such 'Hellenism.' Israel, of course, since its conquest by Alexander in 332 BC, had lived in a Hellenistic world. Although sometimes disruptive, well developed religious dissent was, and is, regarded as a form of ecstacy in Hebrew tradition, not treason or heresy. The Melchizedekians, mentioned in *The Talmud*, communed with Adam, 'the red man' who was the oracle of the cave at Machpelah. Their originary sincerity garnered respect, not hostility.[574]

The Essenes, whose Dead Sea Scrolls we have, were Gnostic theological dissenters who celebrated Sunday as the Sabbath, and were quite 'Pythagorean' in their soul-body dualism. Nonetheless, their surviving writings show that, aside from creating their own original literature, they immersed themselves in traditional Hebrew scripture and the writings of the Pharisee sages.[575] They were regarded as sincere Jews, and their communities and prophets were accorded profound respect, especially since they were fierce nationalists. They were never murdered by their own; it took Romans, or their reservation police, to do that.

Aside from his sacramentalism, all four Gospels show Jesus teaching, like his fellow Essenes, traditional, established Pharisee wisdom in the same language as recorded in surviving contemporary and near-contemporary Hebrew sources. The schizophrenia this produced in the Graeco-Roman antisemites who wrote the Greek Gospels is transparently obvious. The Pauline Gospels chooses to call the sages 'lawyers' or 'scribes' as often as 'Pharisees,' as if they were Roman *pontificis*, and consistently portrays even Pharisee members of the Great Sanhedrin, that is Senators, like Nicodemus, as rather stupid children.[576] In order to be a member of the Great Sanhedrin, sages had to qualify not only in Torah, but in general science, mathematics, medicine and languages.[577] Few modern scholars could match their power.

Mark[578] and Matthew[579] record the same incident, in which 'one of the scribes' asks Jesus which commandment is first of all. Jesus answers with the *Sh'ma*, the passage from Deuteronomy[580] that is the central feature of the Hebrew liturgy created by the Pharisees: "Hear O Israel (*Sh'ma Yisra'el*): the Lord our God is the only Lord; love the Lord your God with all your heart, with all your soul, with all your mind, and with all your strength." As Maccoby's astute textual analysis shows, the older Gospel, Mark, is a friendly, mutually respectful exchange which ends with 'the scribe' complimenting Jesus with these meaningful words: "'Well said, Master. You are right in saying that God is one and beside him there is no other. And to love him with all your heart, all your understanding, and all your strength, and to love your neighbor as yourself - that is far more than any burnt offerings or sacrifices.' When Jesus saw how sensibly he answered, he said to him, 'You are not far from the kingdom of God.'"

Recitation of the *sh'ma*, the Pharisees said, comprised "the acceptance of the yoke of the kingdom of God." Hillel, who predates Jesus, and Akiba, the two greatest figures of Pharisaism, both regarded the exhortation from Leviticus, "Love your neighbor as yourself," Jesus' second most important commandment in answer to the scribe's question, as the single greatest principle of Judaism.

Significantly, and this is the pattern throughout these carefully manipulated manuscripts, the later Gospel, Matthew, omits the mutual respect and the friendly exchange of Mark so as to become "just one more story about an envious Pharisee being silenced by the superior wisdom of Jesus."[581] (Maccoby) As Eusebius, Constantine's court historian, put it, "Matthew first collected the oracles in the Hebrew language [the original Nazarene Gospels] and each interpreted them as best he could."[582]

Hillel (b.75 BC) was concerned with the 'kingdom of heaven' on earth, that is, with *tikkun olam*, 'perfecting the world.' His philosophy was anti-legalisitic and pragmatic, with compassion, justice and spiritual peace as the practical goals. Hillel was a grandfather figure to Jesus, the recognized sage who taught the rabbis who taught Jesus. Hillel's proverbs are found in the *Pirkei Avot*, the Sayings of the Fathers, the most famous book of *The Mishnah*, 'What Is Repeated,' the Oral Law finally set down in writing some two hundred years after Hillel.

Many of Hillel's sayings, and those of the other sages recorded in *The Mishnah*, are similar, of course, to Jesus' sayings. In Jesus' day, the sages' proverbs were memorized: "And do not judge your fellow until you are in his place." "Anyone whose deeds are more than his wisdom, his wisdom will endure." "A fence for wisdom is silence." "Who is honored? He who honors everybody." "He who avoids serving as a judge breaks off the power of enmity, robbery, and false swearing." "Do not serve as a judge by yourself, for there is only One who serves as a judge all alone." "And better is a single moment of inner peace in the world to come than a whole lifetime spent in this world."[583]

Jesus'contemporary, Johanan ben Zakkai, the founder of rabbinic Judaism, sole survivor of the Jerusalem Sanhedrin, explained that the fall of the Temple meant that acts of loving kindness now superceded sacrifice as the preferred method of achieving divine grace. That is, virtually everything Jesus says in the Gospels, aside from his sacramentalism and some gratuitous antisemitism, is traditional contemporary Pharisaic teaching enunciated by him in the contemporary Pharisaic phraseology, as recorded in contemporary or near-contemporary Pharisaic sources.

Hillel, when asked for a capsule definition of Judaism, replied, "What is hateful to you, don't do to your neighbor. The rest is commentary - now go and study."[584] Jesus: "So whatever you wish that men would do to you, do so to them; for this is the law and the prophets."[585] Both sayings are obviously based on the Law of Moses: "Thou shalt love thy neighbor as thyself," and can be found repeated through-out the Bible, for instance in Micah.[586]

Tanhuma: "When thou hast mercy on thy fellow, thou hast One to have mercy on thee; but if thou hast not mercy on thy fellow, thou hast none to have mercy on thee." Jesus: "But if you do not forgive men their trespasses, neither will your Father forgive your tres-passes."[587] Nearly all the parables Jesus uses in the Gospels are con-temporary Pharisee teaching devices, as are his pithy phrases such as "a camel going through the eye of a needle"or "take the beam out of your own eye."(*Talmud*) Jesus' parable of the Prodigal Son,[588] in which he says, "I say unto you, that likewise joy shall be in heaven over one sinner that repenteth, more than over ninety and nine just persons, which need no repentence," is a paraphrase of the Talmudic saying: "Where the repentent sinners stand in the World to Come the per-fectly righteous are not permitted to stand."[589]

Mark,[590] Matthew[591] and John[592] assert that the 'Pharisees' plotted Jesus' death for committing the heinous crime of healing on the sab-bath. That is as idiotic, and as antisemitic, as asserting that Jewish sabbath wine is the blood of Christian babies. In fact, Jesus' attitude on the matter is the recorded contemporary Pharisee position. The phrase, attributed as some great insight to Jesus, that "The sabbath was made for man, not man for the sabbath,"comes from a Pharisee source, recorded in *The Babylonian Talmud*,[593] where it is used precisely to justify the saving of life on a day meant for quiet meditation. *The Talmud* is discussing the Pharisee Oral Law that predates Jesus. Sab-bath law, which in the Pharisee tradition simply means sabbath doc-trine, advises that trivial complaints should be left for another day so as not to interrupt one's meditations.

The Pharisee Sabbath is joyful, intellectual and musical, and stresses spontaneity. It was the Pharisees who added the joyful Ecclesiastes and the orgiastic Song of Solomon to the canon, and the festivals of Chanukah and Purim. During Purim, which celebrates Esther's victory over the archetypal antisemite Haman, the rabbis in-structed everyone to get so drunk that they couldn't distinguish be-tween "Cursed be Haman"and "Blessed be Mordechai."As the late medieval codification of Jewish tradition, the *Shulchan Aruch*, explains "The whole miracle was occassioned through wine: Vashti was troubled in the wine feast and Esther was put in her stead; also the downfall of Haman was due to wine, therefore the sages made it obligatory on one to become drunk,"[594] whereupon the scroll of Esther, written in about 130 BC, was read with much revelry and theatricality.

Paul portrays Jesus' supposed substitution of the law of love for the law of revenge as if the sages were in the habit of knocking people's eyes out. In fact, Pharisee Oral Law substituted trial by jury and monetary compensation for the old savagery, which, by the way, wasn't uniformly savage to begin with. The principles of jury trial and monetary compensation were established by Hammurabi and company, not Israel, although the ancient Babylonian code was quite brutal. A literalist interpretation of the Hammurabian eye-for-an-eye rule enshrined in Exodus[595] was derided by one Pharisee scholar who asked: "What happens if a one-eyed man knocks out someone's eye?" Justice, *tzedek*, which included both kindness and just compensation, was the sages' concern.

It was the Pharisee reformers of Hillel's generation who virtually outlawed the death penalty in Israel, requiring two eyewitnesses and evidence of premeditation of heinous wrongdoing. Even confession wasn't enough, and if the Sanhedrin voted unanimously for the death sentence, it wasn't carried out, on the theory that such a vote could indicate that the accused hadn't been properly defended. Judges in capital cases had to fast and refrain from alcohol on the day of voting.

The reason that the Pharisees made capital punishment so difficult was the doctrine, first set down in Genesis[596] in relation to Cain and Abel, that the murder of one man is the murder of all his offspring as well: "The *bloods* of your brother cry unto Me." That is, the blood of Abel and of all his would-be descendants. A commentary in *Mishnah Sanhedrin*[597] says that whoever murders one soul "is deemed by Scripture as if he had destroyed a whole world." Paul caricatures this sensitivity as if the Pharisees were in the habit of putting people to death for trivialities: "Anyone who flouts the law of Moses is put to death without mercy on the evidence of two or three witnesses."[598] Paul is simply quoting Deuteronomy,[599] Israel's ancient pre-Exilic scripture, as if it were still in effect. Paul's neurotic hostility and rank ignorance are obvious on every page.[600]

Jesus tells the leper he has cured, "Go and show yourself to the priest, and make the offering laid down by Moses for your cleansing."[601] Jesus was a practicing Jew, quoted by Matthew as saying: "If any man therefore sets aside even the least of the Law's demands, and teaches others to do the same, he will have the lowest place in the kingdom of Heaven, whereas anyone who keeps the Law and teaches others so, will stand high in the kingdom of Heaven."[602] As *The Mishnah* puts it: "If he has gotten teachings of Torah, he has gotten himself life eternal."[603] Matthew is certainly no Judaizer; it is he who stresses the guilt of Israel for the death of Jesus.[604] If Matthew included this and other orthodox Hebrew sayings of Jesus, it must be because they were too well known to omit, that is, because they were an established part of the Nazarene canon.

Matthew compensates for Jesus' unavoidable Pharisaism by putting in his mouth[605] a nauseating, and world famous, antisemitic diatribe ('scribes and Pharisees, hypocrites!') that would have pleased Sejanus himself. Oddly enough, the diatribe would make perfect historical sense if the word 'Sadducees' was substituted for 'Pharisees,' as it no doubt was in the original Hebrew, since the Pharisees were poor defenders of the poor, hardly the hypocritical rich aristocrats excoriated, no doubt in somewhat less antisemitic terms, by Jesus. This is confirmed by Jesus himself, who begins the diatribe with these extraordinary words: "The scribes and the Pharisees sit in Moses' seat. All therefore whatsoever they bid thee observe, that observe and do."[606] Jesus would then have gone on to excoriate the Sadduccess for not following the Pharisee example, thus accurately reflecting the bitter contemporary divisions - and revealing the political Jesus. As it now stands, Jesus is a raving schizophrenic.

Nonetheless, even as written, the diatribe is diametrically opposed to Paul's Christology, in which Christ was supposed to have abrogated the Law of Moses; according to Matthew, Christ excoriated the 'Pharisees' for not following it. This unavoidable schizophrenia is found throughout the Greek Gospels, as in Luke,[607] when Jesus says: "The law and the prophets were until John: since then, the good news of the kingdom of God is proclaimed, and everyone forces a way in." His very next sentence is: "It is easier for heaven and earth to come to an end than for one letter of the law to lose its force." If he is saying anything, he is saying that the kingdom of God is consonant with the law of Moses, but that the enlightenment of John's Essene baptism is to be preferred to constant study.

The Essene Qumran community, in which John may have been raised, gave us the Dead Sea Scrolls, the greatest manuscript find of the twentieth century. They comprise fragments of almost 1000 compositions, written in Hebrew, Aramaic and Greek, dating from about 250 BC to 68 CE. Much of the Hebrew is an extinct form of paleo-Hebrew that evolved into both modern Hebrew and Samaritan script. Part of the reason for their survival is that the scrolls were penned on sheep or calf skins, rather than the usual papyrus linen. This indicates their canonical character, as does the superb penmanship of these accomplished scribes.

'The Sect' also called itself the 'New Testament' or the 'New Covenant,' claiming themselves to be the true Sons of Zadok, the genuine Keepers of the Covenant. The Essenes reserved their bitterest apocalyptic denunciations for the politicized Sadducee collaborators: "Cities and families will perish through their counsel, nobles and rulers will fall because of what they say." They looked forward to when "the Messiah of Righteousness comes, the Branch of David." He was associated with the resurrected founder of The Sect. Whether he was to be identified with the Priest-Messiah, the King-Messiah, or the Prophet-Messiah is not clear; the Messiahs would divide the temporal and spiritual powers between them, as was traditional in Israel.[608]

Before its discovery at Qumran, all we knew of the apocryphal *Book of Enoch* were scattered Greek quotes from the early Church fathers. The far more ancient Aramaic original found at Qumran has the Messiah as a white bull with huge horns. The Qumran *Manual of Discipline*, c.100 BC, says that the Messiah "will renew for Him the Covenant of the Community to establish the kingdom of His people for ever....May the Lord lift thee up to an everlasting height like a fortified tower on a high wall, that thou mightest smite the peoples with the might of thy mouth, with thy sceptre devastate the land, and with the breath of thy lips kill the wicked...And righteousness shall be the girdle of thy loins, and faith the belt of thy reins. And may He make thy horns of iron and thy hooves of brass to gore like a young bull...and tread down the peoples like the mire in the streets. For God has established thee as a sceptre over rulers."[609] It is this Bull of Righteousness that was the Essene *pharmakos*. As with the sacred Bull of

El, *Moshe*, the *Moshiy'a* here is a war shaman, a bull "with horns of iron and hooves of brass," no lamb. Jesus also "kills the wicked with the breath of his lips."[610]

The Essenes, says *The Manual*, were "those who choose the Way." Says Paul, "according to the Way, which they call a sect, I worship the god of our fathers..."[611] "The New Covenant"and "the New Testament"are oft-repeated Essene phrases lifted by Paul, obviously, as he says, from the Nazarenes.[612] John's First Epistle refers constantly to Light and Darkness, Truth and Error, all standard Essene phrases, as is Peter's "cornerstone, elect, and precious."

We have only a miniscule fraction of the Essene writings, almost all predating Jesus, preserved by an archeological miracle. But even the small sample we have gives us dozens of direct quotes lifted from their writings to the canonical Greek 'New Testament,'obviously by way of the Hebrew and Aramaic speaking Nazarenes. The early Church's baptism, communal meals, communal property and organizational structure, with the Twelve Apostles leading the twelve tribes, were almost identical to Essene ritual and structure.

Joshua spoke Hebrew and Aramaic, not Greek. The Aramaic word for the Greek 'Essene' is *Assaya*, healer. The Sumerian root of *Assaya*, A-ZU or I-ZU, 'physician,' literally means 'water,oil expert.'[613] Josephus: "They...single out in particular those which make for the welfare of soul and body; with the help of these, and with a view to the treatment of diseases, they make investigations into medicinal roots and the properties of stones."[614]

Another contemporary, Philo, called these healing shamans *Therapeutae*: "Thus they preserve an unbroken memory of God, so that even in their dream-consciousness nothing is presented to their minds but the glories of the divine virtues and powers. Hence many of them give out the rhythmic doctrines of the sacred wisdom, which they have obtained in the visions of the deam-life....just as in the Bacchic rites men drink the wine unmixed....Thus drunken unto morning's light with this fair drunkenness, with no head-heaviness or drowsiness, but with eyes and body fresher even than when they came to the banquet, they take their stand at dawn, when, catching sight of the rising sun, they raise their hands to heaven, praying for sunlight and truth and keenness of spiritual vision."[615]

"I prayed for him...and I laid my hands on his head, and the affliction left him and the evil spirit was driven out,"says Abraham in the Essene *Genesis Apocryphon* found at Qumran. The Essenes sought "healing and abundant peace, length of life and fruitful seed with everlasting blessings, and eternal joy in immortality, a crown of glory and a robe of majesty in eternal light."[616] (*Manual of Discipline*)

The angels, says the original Hebrew *Book of Jubilees* found at Qumran, were instructed by the Lord "that we should teach Noah all the medicines...We explained to Noah all the medicines of their diseases, together with their seductions, how he might heal them with herbs of the earth. And Noah wrote down all things in a book as we instructed him concerning every kind of medicine....And he gave all that he had written to Shem, his eldest son."[617] For Noah read Utnapishtim; for Shem read Gilgamesh.

The Essenes were concerned to preserve their own seasonal solar Jubilees calendar of 364 days, rather than the stilted Graeco-Roman lunar calendar of 354 days, the calendar generally in use in a Hellenized Israel. That common calendar was based on 12 actual lunar months of $29^{1/2}$ days, requiring a cycle of intercalation based on eight-year Graeco-Roman festivals. Calendrical mysticism, combining astronomy and astrology with religion and medicine, was as Jewish as it was Greek or Roman, a direct inheritance from Sumer, Akkad and Crete, a pedigree referred to often and shared by all.[618] Pliny: "After the rising of each star, but particularly the principle stars, or of a rainbow....drugs (*medicamenta*) are produced, heavenly gifts for the eyes, ulcers, and internal organs. And if this substance is kept when the dog-star is rising, and if, as often happens, the rise of Venus or Jupiter or Mercury falls on the same day, its sweetness and potency for recalling mortals' ills from death is equal to that of the Nectar of the gods."[619]

One of the Qumran *Thanksgiving Hymns*, c.50 BC, is overtly pharmaco-shamanic: "For Thou didst set a plantation of cypress, pine and cedar for Thy glory, trees of life beside a mysterious fountain hidden among the trees by the water, and they put out a shoot of the everlasting Plant. But before they did so, they took root and sent out their shoots to the watercourse that its stem might be open to the living waters and be one with the everlasting spring....And the bud of the shoot of holiness for the Plant of Truth was hidden and was not esteemed; and being unperceived, its mystery was sealed. Thou didst hedge its fruit, O God, with the mystery of mighty Heroes and of spirits and holiness and of the whirling flame of fire. No man shall approach the well-spring of life or drink the waters of holiness with the everlasting trees, or bear fruit with the Plant of heaven, who seeing has not discerned, and considering has not believed in the fountain of life, who has turned his hand against the everlasting bud."[620]

As the *pharmakos* himself said, he was the *pharmakon*: "I am the vine, ye are the branches: He that abideth in me, and I in him, the same bringeth forth much fruit..." The "Plants of Truth" became a Christian Gnostic expression, repeatedly used in the Nag Hammadi manuscripts and the early heresiologists.

Baptism, of course, was central to the Essene rite of initiation. The Hebrew word translated as 'Baptist' is *Tabbal*, 'dipper' or 'dyer.' As Allegro shows, this is cognate with Akkadian *tabarru*, 'red dye,' and Latin *tablion*, 'purple fringe,' all derived from the Sumerian TAB-BA-LI, 'mushroom,' literally 'twin cone.'[621] The only red mushroom that has, historically, caused religious excitement in the Near East, is Soma, *Amanita muscaria*. The Bible is indicating just what kind of 'baptism' John gave Jesus. The play on *guba*, 'edible locust,' John's food, and *gab'a*, 'mushroom,' is just one of many word-plays in the John story typical of the mystery religions. Locusts and honey are mentioned in the food laws of the Essene *Damascus Document*, and the mention is by no means necessarily literal.

Essene, the Greek cognate of the Aramaic *Assaya*, was the ancient Greek word for 'drone.' It was used as the appelation of the eunuch priests at the sanctuary of Artemis at Ephesus in classical times.[622] 'Drone' is obviously an appropriate description of male companions of the *melissai*, the 'bees,' as the transformed 'honey' priestesses were called.

Shamanism by now was overtly prohibited by the senatorial de-cree of 186 BC and the *Lex Cornelia de sicariis et veneficiis*, the 'Corne-lian Law against assassins and poisoners,' dating to the time of Pompey, under which Apuleius would later be charged.[623] In 186 BC a Campanian priestess led a virtual uprising of the slaves and *plebs urbana* in the name of Dionysos and Proserpina, 'The Bacchanalia' as it was called. This prompted Cato the Censor's Senate to decree that "If any person considered such worship to be ordained by tradition (*sollemne*)" he could apply for permission to hold a ceremony, but only five people could congregate at one time, without an officiant.[624]

The Essenes had nothing but disdain for Roman law, and consis-tently promised the *Kittim*, the 'Coppermen,' divine vengeance from the Messiah. Executions for 'sorcery,' legally equated with treason, were common, so codes and puns, to hide the 'mystery,' became a refined art. The Drones' interest in word-play also had to do with respect for etymology, in the Greek sense of elucidating the true mean-ing. This deeply felt Essene connection to Hellenic mysticism can most easily be seen in Jesus'contemporary Philo, Alexandria's great

Greek-speaking Jewish leader.

In *The Talmud*, Jesus is sometimes called *Bar Pandera*, 'Son of the Panther,' a reference to his fierce nationalism and/or his relationship to the spotted red mushroom, called 'the panther' both for its looks and the state it induces, just as in the Amazon with other entheogens. The word comes from the Sumerian, BAR-DARA, 'spotted, variegated skin,' into Greek as *panther*.[625] Panthers are shown, in association with giant flowers, obviously entheogens, leading ecstatic Maenads and Satyrs in Dionysiac processions on numerous Greek and Italian vases.[626] In fact panthers first appear as psychopomps at Catal Huyuk, and were prominently worn on the head of the Queen of Knossos. As the Gnostics, who claimed to be Jesus' true disciples, said, "the Beast is the teacher." Above Dionysos, dressed in his panther skin, celebrates Passover the old fashioned way.

'Dionysos,' 'Joshua' and 'Jesus' were understood by the ancients to be the same name. Joshua, *Yehoshua* in Hebrew, understood as 'Jah-saves,' is, ultimately, Sumerian, IA-U-ShU-A, a combination of the name of the Exalted Dove, Iahu, meaning 'juice of fertility' and ShU-A, meaning 'fulfilment,' 'restoration,' 'healing' or 'life.' *Dionysos*, in Sumerian, is virtually the same name: IA-U-NU-SHUSH, the NU meaning 'seed,' and the SHUSH being a synonym of SHU.[627] *Iasius*, Jesus, has the same Sumerian etymology as *Yehoshua*. 'Healer' in Greek is *iatros*, 'drugger.' Epiphanius, bishop of Salamis in Cyprus, c.375 CE, says that Christians were first called *Iassai*, 'healers,' 'Essenes,' 'Jesuses.'[628] *Iasius*,'Shaman-Healer,' literally means 'the man of the drug.'

Iasius, Joshua, and five of his twelve disciples had recorded war shaman names, and he and his brothers were all named after Israel's great nationalist warriors.[629] Joshua himself was named after Israel's most legendary warrior, and his brother, Judah,[630] was named after a long line of warriors, including Judah Maccabee and Judah of Galilee, who stubbornly continued the revolt throughout Joshua's childhood. The other brothers were James, Joseph (John) and Simon Peter. Joseph is a father of Israel. Simon is the name of the great Maccabee war leader, Judah's brother, and James is a Romanization of either Jacob or 'Yanni,' Jonathan, the other great Maccabee brother. Mary is a Romanization of Miriam. Jesus' sisters, apparently at least three, aren't named by the Greeks.[631]

Just as Red Cloud, Crazy Horse, Geronimo, and Quanah combined their fierce warlike nationalism with very active pharmaco-shamanism, so too, apparently, did Joshua and his Zealots. Simon Peter, known as 'Barjonah,'[632] more correctly *bariona* in Aramaic, 'Outlaw,' 'Freedom Fighter,' comes, as Allegro points out, from the Sumerian, BAR-IA-U-NA. That evolved not only into the Aramaic word for liberator, but also into the Greek words *Paionia*, plant of the epiphany, literally 'capsule of fecundity, womb' and *Paian*, our paeon. The name can also mean 'son of a dove,' that is, son of Iahu, the Exalted Dove.[633]

'Peter,' it is a commonplace to say, means 'the rock,' *petra* in Greek, but Jesus didn't speak Greek, he spoke Hebrew, as all rabbis do, and Galilean Aramaic, according to both contemporary sources and the Aramaic preserved in the New Testament.[634] 'Peter' is cognate with Hebrew *kotereth* and Akkadian *katarru*, coming from the Sumerian GU-TAR, 'mushroom' - in Arabic *phutr*, in Aramaic, *pitra*, Peter. Simon Peter's other title, Cephas, is cognate with Latin *cepa*, onion, and French *cépe* or *ceps*, 'mushroom,' as well as the related Aramaic word for stone, *kepha*.[635]

Jesus' name for Jonathan ('James') and Joseph ('John'- Jesus didn't speak Latin either), 'Boanerges,' can be derived, as Professor Allegro shows, from the Sumerian PU-AN-UR-GESh, 'mighty man (holding up) the arch of heaven.' Mark[636] translates this as 'sons of thunder.' Although that is spurious Aramaic, it is a direct reference to, and cognate with, the Greek *keraunion*, 'thunder-fungus,' an epithet of the 'lightning-born' Bakkhos, called Yawe by the Canaanites.

In Psalms, Yahweh rides on a fierce, bestial cherub, originally an Egyptian transformation beast, a winged hawk-headed lion, a *Seref*, 'swiftly upon the wings of the wind.'[637] The word 'carob' has the same Sumerian root as 'cherub,' used to describe the 'seed of life' plant, Yahweh's vehicle. This is 'St. John's bread.' The tail of the female transformation beast, the *Saha*, a guardian of Twelfth Dynasty tombs (c.2300 BC), often ends in a full-blown lotus, the symbolic entheogen and symbol of the kingdom.[638]

Judas Iscariot's last name is said to be a bastardization of *sicarius*, which means 'dagger man' in Latin (*sica*). It was the Roman epithet applied to all the Zealots. A derivation of the name from the shamanic Sumerian, USh-GU-RI-UD, yields 'erect phallus of the storm,' something like 'lightning man,' thus giving *sicarius* a double-edged meaning. The name is cognate with *Diaskourai*, the Goddesses sprung from the Minoan Dia, and *Dioskouroi*, the immortal twins, the *pharmakon* and *pharmakos* born from the egg of the swan Leda.[639] Iscariot is thus clearly both a shaman name and a reference to the Israelite *Dioskouroi*, the brothers Joshua and Judah.[640]

Abba Sikra, 'Father Dagger,' *resh barionei*, ' chief of the rebels,' was another famous dagger-man, nephew of Johannan ben Zakkai. Abba Sikra smuggled his uncle out of fortress Jerusalem, thus enabling him to go on, with Vespasian's personal permission, to found the academy that was responsible for the survival of rabbinic Judaism. As Maccoby points out, some early New Testament manuscripts leave out the 'I' in Iscariot, producing names like Skarioth and Scariota, even more directly like *sicarius*. Third and fourth century Coptic New Testament manuscripts call the Judas in John[641] *Kananites*, the Canaanite, which was a common mistranslation of the Hebrew *Qan'ai*, the Zealot. These same manuscripts also lack the 'not Iscariot' of the canonical John, indicating that 'Judas the Zealot' was the same as 'Judas the Dagger-Man.' In fact some early Latin manuscripts call the Judas in Matthew 'Judas Zelotes,' Judas the Zealot. Simon's name is also 'the Zealot.'[642]

Considering that Jesus' four brothers were named Judas (Roman for Judah), James (Roman for Jonathan), John (Roman for Joseph), and Simon,[643] that is, were disciples (despite the invention of doubles) who bore war-shaman names, it seems likely that, like Judah Maccabee, *Yehoshua Ben Yosef* was a family war leader. The three 'pillars' of the Jerusalem Church[644] coincidentally all have the names of Jesus' brothers: Simon Peter, James and John, and we are explicitly told that James was Jesus' brother. We also know that the next two leaders of the Nazarenes, Symeon and Judah, were also blood kin to Jesus, as would be expected in an Israeli monarchical movement, as with the Maccabees.[645]

In an attempt to defend Mary's mythical virginity and disparage the anti-Roman nationalism of 'the Jews,' the Greek Gospel writers denigrate and confuse Jesus' relationship with his family, and clearly falsify the role of his brothers in the movement. They fail, for instance, to mention James as a disciple despite the fact that he was the first leader of the Nazarenes after Jesus' death. It is highly unlikely that a sceptical late convert would be handed the prestigious leadership by the original disciples.

The first thing the disciples ask the resurrected Jesus in Acts is: "Lord, is this the time at which you are to restore sovereignty to Israel?"[646] This had to be included in the Gospel this way because it was a famous part of the Nazarene canon, unalterable. Jesus was Joshua, Phinehas the Zealot, David, Elijah, Judah Maccabee, Judah of Galilee, the Bull of Righteousness - a war shaman.

The word 'Messiah,' 'saviour,' 'anointed one,' is the traditional title given to King David, a war shaman, and to all kings of his line. To claim to be the *Moshiy'a*, in Greek *Khristos*, was in no way blasphemous in Hebrew eyes. The Greek *Khrestos*, meaning 'good,' was an appellation of the mystery gods, and is obviously cognate with *Khristos*, 'anointed one.' The anointing ceremony was performed for both the King and the High Priest, who had the title, even in Roman times, of 'Priest Messiah.' With the Roman abolition of the Israelite monarchy the claim to be the next Davidic king of Israel was an invitation to religio-political rebellion that sat very well with most Israelis, who hated the Romans guts. It wasn't theological dissent Israel worried about, it was the murderous foreign bastards in its streets.

Like Judah Maccabee (Judah the Hammer), Jesus was anointed King. On the death of John the Baptist, Jesus, for the first time, is called the 'Messiah'[647] when he asks "'who do you say I am?' Peter replied: 'You are the Messiah.'" This Salutation is followed by the Transfiguration: "Six days later Jesus took Peter, James and John with him and led them up a high mountain by themselves. And in their presence he was transfigured; his clothes became dazzling white, with a whiteness no bleacher on earth could equal. They saw Elijah appear and Moses with him, talking with Jesus. Then Peter spoke: 'Rabbi,'he said, 'it is good that we are here! Shall we make three shelters, one for you, one for Moses, and one for Elijah?' For he did not know what to say, they were so terrified. Then a cloud appeared, casting its shadow over them, and out of the cloud came a voice: 'This is my beloved Son; listen to him.'"

As Maccoby shows,[648] this is a mythologized version of the Israeli coronation ceremony. The phrase 'This is my beloved Son' is taken from the Coronation Psalm[649] which was recited at the anointing of every Israelite king: "The kings of the earth set themselves, and the rulers take counsel together, against the Lord and his anointed....He who sits in the heavens laughs; the Lord has them in derision....'I have set my king on Zion, my holy hill.' I will tell of the decree of the Lord: he said to me, 'You are my son, today I have begotten you. Ask of me, and I will make the nations your heritage, and the ends of the earth your possession.'" Thus said the Lord to King David, and to all Israelite kings after him.

The tradition that the King was crowned by a prophet was fulfilled by the presence of Moses and Elijah, Israel's greatest, both of whom were war shamans.[650] It was Elijah, eight hundred years before Jesus, who first multiplied food and brought the dead back to life, and who ascended to heaven in a chariot of fire.[651] The making of the 'shelters' fulfills the tradition of making a *succah* or tabernacle in which to crown the King, as was done in the Exodus for Yahweh, the King of Israel.[652]

The Transfiguration took place six days after the Salutation, which is the prescribed interval between the Proclamation of a king and his Coronation. The 'high mountain' near Caesarea Philippi is Mount Hermon, the highest mountain in Israel, Zion for all practical purposes. The twelve tribes of Israel were symbolically represented by the representatives of the twelve disciples.

'Transfiguration' was a term applied to the newly crowned king, to signify the sacred burden he had assumed. Here is the Anointment and Transfiguration of Saul, which was combined with the Transfiguration of Moses on Mount Sinai to give us the Transfiguration of Jesus: "Then Samuel took a vial of oil and poured it on his head, and kissed him and said, 'Has not the Lord anointed you to be prince over his people Israel?....And this shall be the sign that the Lord has anointed you....you will meet a band of prophets coming down from the high

place with harp, tambourine, flute and lyre before them, prophesying. Then the spirit of the Lord will come mightily upon you, and
you shall prophesy with them and be turned into another man."[653]
The Transfigured Saul became the Messiah, the anointed one.

Maccoby points out[654] that the series of events from the Trium-
phal entry to the Crucifixion: the Cleansing of the Temple, the preach-
ing in the Temple, the inquiry before the High Priest, the trial before
the Sanhedrin, the trial before Herod Antipas, the trial before Pilate
and the Last Supper, couldn't possibly have all taken place within six
days, from Palm Sunday to Good Friday.

For one thing, there were no palms available in Jerusalem in the
early Spring, Passover time. Jesus would hardly have been greeted
with withered palm branches from the Festival of Tabernacles of the
previous autumn. The cry of 'Hosanna,' *hosha-na* in Hebrew, with
which Jesus was greeted on his Entry, meaning 'save, please,' is used
only in the Festival of Tabernacles. It is a cry addressed to God to save
the nation through the King, the *Moshiy'a*, who had a special role in
the Autumn Festival, and in no other religious festival.

John, at least, unlike all the Synoptic ('see-alike') Gospels, has Jesus
in Jerusalem for six months. Once every seven years the King, during
Tabernacles, entered the Temple Court and read aloud the 'paragraph
of the king'[655] enumerating the constitutional duties and sacred limits
of royal power in Israel. Solomon dedicated the first Temple on the
Feast of Tabernacles.

By entering Jerusalem on an ass, that is, by committing himself to
the vision of Zechariah which would have been familiar to many in
the crowd, Jesus was saying that the Apocalypse was at hand: "Any
survivors among the nations which fought against Jerusalem are to
go up year by year to worship the King, the Lord of Hosts, and to
keep the pilgrim-feast of Tabernacles. Should any of the families of
the earth not go up to Jerusalem to worship the King, the Lord of
Hosts, no rain will fall on them."[656]

Likewise his evening prayers on the Mount of Olives, where King
David prayed and where Ezekiel saw the 'glory of God,' was a reference to Zechariah: "Then the Lord will go out and fight against the
nations, fighting as on a day of battle. On that day his feet will stand
on the Mount of Olives, which lies to the east of Jerusalem, and the
mount will be cleft in two by an immense valley running east and
west; half the mount will move northwards and half southwards....then
the Lord my God will appear attended by all the holy ones....It will be
one continuous day, whose coming is known only to the Lord; there

will be no distinction between day and night; even in the evening there will be light....The Lord will become king over all the earth; on that day he will be the only Lord and his name the only name....The Lord will strike with this plague all the nations who warred against Jerusalem: their flesh will rot while they are still standing on their feet, their eyes will rot in their sockets, and their tongues will rot in their mouths."[657]

This ain't no peaceful vision. When Jesus entered the Temple at the end of the Year of Release, the seventh year, he was attempting the divine overthrow of the government of Rome. His reading of the paragraph of the king couldn't be included in the Greek canon since that would have been a transparent admission that Jesus, *Moshiy'a*, was political as all hell.

Despite the fact that we are constantly told about the slaughtering of Passover lambs, the Last Supper clearly wasn't a Passover Seder, since there is no mention of any of the elements of a Seder, which is a ritual reenactment of the liberation from Egypt and the forty years of wandering in the desert. There is no eating of the unleavened bread, bitter herbs or *kharoset*, the symbolic brick mortar made of nuts and apple.

There also is no Paschal lamb, unless were are to believe in a symbolic 'thyestian feast,' as the Greeks called cannibalism. Chrysostom understood Christ to be consuming himself, magically, as it were, but that turns him into an alchemical illusion, not an historical figure, as indeed he is for Orthodox Christianity.[658] No cup is poured for Elijah, there is no reading of Exodus, there is no repeated asking of the question *"Ma nish tana halilah hazeh?,"* "Why is this night different from all other nights?," or anything like it - there is no Passover.[659] There is, however, a mention in Mark[660] of what appears to be a Succah, a "room upstairs strewn over"(*estromenon*) with branches, the ritual booth often constructed on the flat roofs of the houses, indicating the Feast of Tabernacles, the Fall harvest.[661]

It was ritually convenient to the Graeco-Roman church to telescope the time frame to Passover week so that the world could have its Passover Lamb, which, in the mystery cults, was eaten and resurrected in early Spring. Instead of the paragraph of the king from Tabernacles and the apocalypse according to Zechariah and Joel, we have Jesus, in a Greek Gospel written after 70 CE, excoriating not the Romans but the Jews for *their* disobedience to God and predicting the destruction of the Temple by God's agents, the Romans.

Ex post facto prophesy was very popular in the Sibylline Oracles and other prophetic books, given the slow pace of the media and the reputation to be gained. The original Nazarene Hebrew or Aramaic of Revelation:11, preserved in the 'allegorical' Greek, predicts the *preservation* of the Temple, not its destruction. Jesus' Cleansing of the Temple would have been a direct challenge to the Sadducee High Priest for political control, which the Gospels admit was greeted by overwhelming, riotous support from the Jerusalem crowd.

There is no record of Jesus appointing another High Priest, which, as King, would have been the first order of business, but that is precisely what the violently anti-Roman Zealots did first when they took control of the Temple in 66 CE. The Zealots of the rebellion were originally led by Menachem, grandson of Judah of Galilee, after whom Jesus' brother was probably named. Another grandson of Judah, Eleazar, led the final defense of Masada. John of Gischala was another great Galilean guerrilla whose fighters were famous for their "mischievous ingenuity and audacity."[662]

Their short-lived coinage featured the chalice, pomegranates, an amphora, the vine, the palm, the inscriptions 'Jerusalem the Holy' and 'The Freedom of Zion.' The silver shekel above, dated to year three of the rebellion, 69 CE, features a chalice on the obverse with the inscription 'Shekel of Israel.' The reverse features three pomegranates mounted on a stem with the inscription 'Jerusalem the Holy.' These are cult objects from the Feast of Tabernacles, not Passover.[663] As the Essene *Damascus Rule* put it, 150 years before, "The Books of the Law are the tabernacle of the king; as God said, I will raise up the tabernacle of David which is fallen."[664]

On taking control of the Temple, Jesus would have had available, for the first time, the Temple's holy anointing oil, of spikenard, which apparently was used in Bethany, on the Mount of Olives, to complete the Coronation ceremony. To hide the political character of yet another Coronation, and this an apocalyptic one, the second anointing was turned into an antisemitic anecdote about Jews too cheap to sanction the use of costly oil on Our Greek Saviour.[665]

By an extraordinary coincidence, Jesus' Cleansing of the Temple coincides with an uprising in Jerusalem, and, coincidentally, Jesus is thrown into Pilate's prison along with the rebels. Here is where the interval between Tabernacles and Passover would actually have taken place, while Jesus languished in prison awaiting his trial before the Roman Governor. The Romans timed their executions for maximum impact; between Tabernacles and Passover Jerusalem would have been relatively deserted.

The Greek Gospels show a mild, pliable, good-natured Procurator Pilate anxious to let Jesus off the hook. Philo and Josephus show a murderous thief actually dismissed by his own murderous government for senseless massacre: "bribes, vainglorious and insolent conduct, robbery, oppression, humiliations, men often sent to death untried, and incessant and unmitigated cruelty."[666] This from Philo, one of the most respected eyewitnesses of the age. Six years after Jesus' death, 36 CE, Vitellius, the Legate of Syria, dismissed Pilate for unnecessarily slaughtering Samaritans. Even Luke refers to "the Galileans whose blood Pilate had mixed with their sacrifices."[667]

Why would such a man, protege of Tiberius' antisemitic Praetorian Prefect Sejanus, who was virtually emperor at this time, with Roman troops at his back, be intimidated by a crowd of unarmed provincials? Pilate's coinage at this time, 29-32 CE, which was the only legal tender in circulation in Judaea, showed the Roman ladle for pouring the sacrifical wine (*simpulum*) and the crook-handled augur's staff (*lituus*), objects of pagan cult calculated to offend the Jews.[668]

Why, in a province with an ongoing guerrilla insurrection, would a disdainful Roman governor defend a 'King of the Jews,' a title all knew to be the equivalent of 'revolutionary leader'? 'King of the Jews' was a Roman senatorial title originally given to Herod the Great when he was Antony's ally. It was a title the Senate jealously reserved for itself, as Jesus proved the hard way.

According to the Synoptists, Jesus was tried before the Sanhedrin for blasphemy. According to John, Jesus was interrogated by the High Priest Caiaphas alone, after a preliminary interrogation by Annas, Caiaphas' father-in-law, and then turned directly over to the Roman Governor, Pilate. John doesn't mention a trial before the Sanhedrin or even blasphemy; that is, Caiaphas was acting in his capacity as Roman police officer.

The Synoptic Gospels show their artificiality by claiming that the Sanhedrin trial of Jesus for blasphemy took place in the High Priest's private house in the middle of the night, at Festival-time, and that the members of the Sanhedrin spat on and struck Jesus. As Maccoby points out, this proves that the whole scene is fiction. Meetings of the Sanhedrin, the Senate and Supreme Court of Israel, took place only in the Chamber of Hewn Stone in the Temple, in daylight. Night meetings, as well as Festival meetings, were expressly forbidden, due to the moral requirement of sobriety and serious contemplation of the charges.[669] It is as absurd to picture these Justices of the Court spitting on a defendant as it is to picture members of the U.S. Supreme Court behaving that way. Clearly the Greek writers of the Synoptic Gospels knew nothing about real Sanhedrin procedure or tradition.

Since there was absolutely nothing in Jesus' claim to be the Messiah that was heretical to Jewish ideas in the first place, but, on the contrary, was a radical expression of the fondest Israeli hopes, the only ones who would have had a motive for bringing Jesus to trial would have been the High Priest's clique and the Romans, as John, Acts, and Luke say: "We found this man perverting our nation, and forbidding us to give tribute to Caesar, and saying that he himself is Christ [*Moshiy'a*] a king."[670] That is the complaint of Sadducee collaborators, not Pharisee nationalists or apocalyptic Essene revolutionaries. John the Baptist, the most famous Essene revolutionary, died for his hatred of Roman taxation. Perhaps Jesus was a tad on the ironic side when he advised Israel to "render unto Caesar that which is Caesar's," or perhaps the whole incident was pure antisemitic fiction, fixating as it did on money.

A charge of political treason, incitement to armed rebellion, not blasphemy, is the only reason Jesus would have to have been turned over to the Romans for execution. If Jesus had been tried before the Sanhedrin for blasphemy, it would not have been necessary to turn him over to the Romans for execution. The Sanhedrin itself could legally have ordered his execution for blasphemy, as the trials of Peter and Paul in Acts show, as well as Josephus.[671]

John notices this inconsistency, and therefore has 'the Jews' say, "It is not lawful for us to put any man to death."[672] This is another instance of overt historical falsehood, since the ratification of the Sanhedrin death sentence by the Procurator was not only lawful but automatic. So far as the Romans were concerned, the Jews could execute any Jews but their Jews, and even those were usually expendable. The Sanhedrin, in fact, actually had the right to execute Romans in the case of Temple trespass.[673]

At Jesus' trial, suddenly, out of nowhere, we are introduced to Barabbas, whose name, in the earliest Gospel manuscripts, is Jesus Barabbas, a fact which had Origen insisting it was a mistake. Expunged from most later Gospel manuscripts, the name Jesus Barabbas has been reinstated in the New English Bible and the Revised English Bible. As Maccoby points out,[674] Jesus addressed God as 'father,' 'abba,'[675] earning himself the nickname Barabbas, Son of the Father. With a double r, the name can also mean 'son of a rabbi,' also an appropriate title for Jesus. The early name for Barabbas, Jesus Barabbas, now makes sense, and it is clear for whose release the Jerusalem crowd was howling, Jesus the Son of the Father, "then in custody with the rebels who had committed murder in the rising."[676] A rising, obviously, instigated by Jesus Barabbas.

Since, of course, the Graeco-Roman Gospel writers couldn't admit that it was the Romans and not the Israelis who wanted their lamb dead, Jesus and Barabbas became two persons, the latter conveniently released by a mushy Pilate who caves in to verbal hounding by those pesky Jews. Pilate was supposedly motivated by the 'Passover Privilege,'[677] which was pure *ex machina* fiction, mentioned in no other source and done for no other people. The Romans were not in the habit of providing religious 'privileges' to rebels who murdered Roman troops; they tortured them to death, by the tens of thousands, with crucifixion, the cruelest punishment they knew. Jesus was crucified for insurrection, uh, heresy, uh, for claiming to be King of the Jews, "by sentence,"as Tacitus put it, "of the procurator Pontius Pilate."[678]

The blood of the original Passover lamb, spread on the lintels of Israelite houses as a sign to the Angel of Death, is an entheogenic memory of the ancient Spring rite. *Pesach* means 'to appease, quieten,' and is a reference to the peace that comes after parturition, after the Goddess gives birth to the new year, the new *pharmakos*.[679] The *pesach* lamb was traditionally spitted on the wood of the pomegranate, Persephone's guarantee of Death and Resurrection. Pomegranate was the only fruit allowed within the Holy of Holies, and its image was sewn into the ceremonial robe of the High Priest as he made his yearly entrance on the Day of Atonement, Yom Kippur, prior to the joyous feasting of Succoth, Tabernacles, the fall harvest.

The brush with which the prophylactic blood of the *pharmakos* lamb was spread was made of hyssop[680] a medicinal herb used as a curandero's sign, the traditional tool of ritual executioners. The leper-cleansing ritual in Leviticus[681] likewise has the bird's blood spread with "cedar-wood, and scarlet thread, and hyssop," and the sacrifice of the Red Cow[682] also couples cedar and hyssop. "He spoke of trees, from the cedar that is in Lebanon to the hyssop that grows out of the wall."[683] This is a reference, as Graves shows, to the Israelite tree-alphabet, in which hyssop, the plant of the winter solstice, IA, was combined with cedar, the tree of the summer solstice, HU, giving IAHU, indicating that Solomon was a master of pharmaco-shamanic oracular techniques.

'Hyssop' (probably the wild caper, says Graves) is described as growing hemiparasitically on cedar as mistletoe grows on oak. Its sacrifice was taken by the Israelites, in their most ancient rites, to represent the turning of the year, as was the sacrifice of mistletoe in Europe. This hyssop brush would likely have been the 'sign' given Cain by God when he slew Abel,[684] "lest any finding him should smite him," just as mistletoe was the sign and weapon of Loki, with which he killed Balder. Loki killed Balder on the advice of the old shaman woman Frigg (Freia, Venus, Ishtar), who knew that mistletoe, the symbolic entheogen of the prophetic tree, "which they call all-heal in their language...which falls from heaven upon the oak"(Pliny), was Balder's one weakness (that is, the means by which he may be 'reached'). Without the death of Balder (Christ), the crops would fail, so Loki (Judas) had his magical purpose, he was the eternal evil twin, as Israel became the eternal evil twin of the Empire.[685]

Like Balder and Loki, Romulus and Remus, Jesus and Judas, Cain and Abel are King and Twin, *Pharmakon* and *Pharmakos*. Far from killing Cain for his sacrifice, God tells him almost exactly what he told Adam and Eve on their expulsion from Eden: "When thou tillest the ground, she shall not henceforth yield unto thee her strength."[686] Cain "dwelt in the land of Nod, on the east of Eden," which is precisely where the cherubim and the flaming sword "guard the way to the tree of life."

The dispute, it should be remembered, was sacramental: Cain brought a vegetable offering for the Lord whereas Abel brought "the firstlings of his flock," whereupon Cain topped Abel by offering him. Cain, despite the murder, then went on, with God's protection, to found civilization, which, of course, makes Abel a Passover lamb, only apparently a human sacrifice. Another lamb-eater, below, suckles the founders of Roman civilization. The Capitoline She-Wolf dates to the sixth century BC and is the canonical Roman image.

The post-exilic Pharisee redactors, anti-sacramental and anti-shamanic, carefully edited the ancient texts, but intentionally preserved much of the original Hebrew. The Greek *Septuagint* humanized, Euhemerized, the already disguised pharmaco-shamanic language completely, thus cutting all connection to the ancient meaning. The amnesiac Sicilian Euhemerus of Messene (*fl.*315 BC) had the likes of Demeter and Zeus as originally just plain folks: "Euhemerus lists those who have been treated as gods in recompense for benefaction or valor; he enumerates...Jupiter of Dicte, Apollo of Delphi, Isis of Pharos, Ceres of Eleusis."[687] (Minucius)

The Greek *Septuagint* has 'Cain,' but the ancient original Hebrew has *Qayin*, which means 'smith.' He was the eponymous Kenite shaman,[688] what the Greeks called a Telchine, a magical metalsmith who transformed matter.[689] *Qayin* fathered "Jubal; he was the ancestor of those who played the harp and pipe. Zillah, the other wife, bore Tubal-cain, the master of all coppersmiths and blacksmiths..."[690] Tubal-qayin, the son of Zillah, is Bar-Zillah in Aramaic, the language of the Kenite community. *Barzela* means 'axe-head,' a reference to the ubiquitous ancient symbol of the power of the Goddess.[691]

The Septuagint, Euhemeristically, has 'Abel,' but the original Hebrew has *Hevel*, and this means, remarkably enough, 'vapor,' 'smoke.' *The Telchine sacrificed smoke to join the Angel of Death for the Spring Resurrection. That* would make perfect sense to any Greek or Essene, as would the equation of the blood of Christ with the blood of the lamb: "A jar stood there full of sour wine; so they soaked a sponge with the wine, fixed it on hyssop, and held it up to his lips. Having received the wine, he said, 'It is accomplished!' Then he bowed his head and gave up his spirit." "Christ our Passover lamb has been sacrificed."[692]

"Any animal in close relation to man, whether as food or foe, may rise to be a god, but he must first become sacred, sanctified, must first be *sacrificed*....the dedication (*anadeixis*) of the bull takes place at the beginning of the agricultural year; the bull's sanctified, though not his actual, life and that of the new year begin together."[693] As the *pharmakos* himself said, he was the *pharmakon*.

Halfway between the bull and Jesus, historically and psychologically, was Chiron, the Centaur, who taught the Saviour Asklepios, as he was called, the art of medicine. Hermes tells the archetypal Telchine Prometheus, "Look for no ending to this agony/until a god will freely suffer for you,/will take on your pain, and in your stead/descend to where the sun is turned to darkness,/the black depths of death."[694] The Centaur Chiron, inventor of medicine, was Prometheus' Saviour. Aischylos wrote those words, legendary throughout the Greek world, 450 years before Jesus. After Aischylos, but before Jesus, the Greek world often said that Asklepios himself was the Saviour of Prometheus, that is, of all us Telchines.

Paul, then, was plausibly recalling Essene 'mystery' shamanism in his equation of Jesus and the Passover lamb, *hevel*, the smoked entheogen, and recalling it every bit as Euhemeristically as *The Septuagint* itself. Just as human pychology is atavistically carnivorous, so it is atavistically shamanic. The conscious awareness of these symbols is lost to most contemporary communicants in childlike Euhemeristic or idolatrous confusion. But their unconscious power is awesome, releasing in some cases the same neurochemicals as the entheogens themselves, especially in combination with other archaic techniques of ecstacy, such as music and prayer. Since the symbology remains unconscious, devoid of *mnemosyne, gnosis*, it is susceptible to political manipulation. Israel became, to a fascinated but unconscious Orthodox Christendom, both the evil twin and the originary Telchine, Cain. This equation was then used by the industrial fascists who institutionalized it to provoke an orgy of sacrifices to Caesar.

In grief, "Joseph of Arimathaea, a respected member of the Council, a man who looked forward to the kingdom of God, bravely went in to Pilate and asked for the body of Jesus."[695] Luke[696] has Joseph of Arimathaea as a dissenter in the Sanhedrin, not a "respected member," and John[697] takes the logic one step further and has him "a secret disciple for fear of the Jews," who, however, is joined in his reverence for Jesus by Nicodemus, another voting member of the Sanhedrin, obviously not one of the Jews Joseph needed to fear.

Mark, the earliest Gospel, has Joseph as a member of the Sanhedrin majority, who needed courage to approach the murderous Pilate for the body of Jesus the Son of the Father, whose death was so painful to his Israeli supporters that he became equated with Elijah, who would rise again. If Mark is right about Joseph, then Jesus was beloved by mainstream Israeli nationalists, as Acts intimates when it speaks of "some of the Pharisaic party who had become believers."[698]

"Just before he was taken into the barracks Paul said to the commandant, 'May I have a word with you?' The commandant said, 'So you speak Greek? Then you are not the Egyptian who started a revolt some time ago and led a force of four thousand terrorists out into the desert?'"[699] The Egyptian and Theudas were Ghost-Dance Messiahs, like Jesus, who hoped, like the Paiute Prophet Wovoka, for divine intervention against an enemy that couldn't be defeated militarily. Wovoka was no pacifist, but an apocalyptist who expected the divine destruction of his enemies, in the absence of earthly means, and the establishment of the Kingdom of Heaven, on Earth. Far from wishing the Romans well, The Egyptian and Theudas hoped God would utterly destroy them. As Josephus and Acts indicate, both had wide popular support.[700]

The real situation in Israel, c.30 CE, is revealed in Acts, when "the high priest and his colleagues, the Sadducean party, were goaded by jealousy to arrest the apostles and put them in official custody."[701] In the Synoptic Gospels only the Sadducee High Priest accuses Jesus of blasphemy for claiming to be the Messiah, never the Pharisees. The High Priest, a Roman appointee, was president of the captive Great Sanhedrin by virtue of his office, but his political powers derived mainly from his own separate Roman police court, which empowered him to examine for sedition, not heresy. In the event of arraignment for sedition the High Priest turned the defendant over to the Romans for punishment, as happened to Jesus.

"So Judas, procuring a band of soldiers and some officers from the chief priests and the Pharisees went there [to arrest Jesus] with lanterns and torches and weapons."[702] The 'band of soldiers' was a *speira*, in Latin a *manipulus*, a unit of the Roman army, which obviously didn't take orders from anyone named Judah.[703] The Pharisees and Sadducees had been in a state of virtual civil war over Sadducee cooperation with the Romans for the past sixty years. It is impossible that Pharisee Senators, fierce nationalists, would march with the Roman army and Sadducee turncoats to arrest an Israeli nationalist revolutionary. This is further proof that the word 'Pharisee' was thrown in where convenient to the Greek redactors of the Hebrew Nazarene Canon.

It also explains, of course, the political hostility of the early Roman Church to the nationalist Nazarene writings, which wouldn't have substituted 'Pharisee' for 'Sadducee,' but, on the contrary, would have stressed the distinction. The word 'Zealot' was virtually synonymous with 'Nazarene.' In his angry defense in the Council of the Sanhedrin, the Nazarene Peter specifically accuses the Sadducee High Priest of putting Jesus to death.[704] In this he is supported by the Pharisee leader Gamaliel, the most prominent political ally of the Zealots.

Peter is appearing before the Sanhedrin itself, not the High Priest's police court, so the issue is left to 'the Seventy,' the full council of the Sanhedrin, by majority vote. It is the legendary Pharisee Gamaliel, a great figure in *The Mishnah*, who saves the Apostles' lives with this warning: "Men of Israel, be very careful in deciding what to do with these men. Some time ago Theudas came forward, making claims for himself, and a number of our people, about four hundred, joined him. But he was killed and his whole movement was destroyed and came to nothing. After him came Judah the Galilean at the time of the census; he induced some people to revolt under his leadership, but he too perished and his whole movement was broken up. Now, my advice to you is this: keep clear of these men; let them alone. For if what is being planned and done is human in origin, it will collapse; but if it is from God, you will never be able to stamp it out, and you risk finding yourselves at war with God."[705]

Likewise when Paul is put on trial (58 CE): "Well aware that one section of them were Sadducees and the other Pharisees, Paul called out in the Council, 'My brothers, I am a Pharisee, a Pharisee born and bred; and the issue in this trial is our hope of the resurrection of the dead.' At these words the Pharisees and Sadducees fell out among themselves, and the assembly was divided. (The Sadducees deny that there is any resurrection or angel or spirit, but the Pharisees believe in all three.) A great uproar ensued; and some of the scribes belonging to the Pharisaic party openly took sides and declared, 'We find no fault with this man; perhaps an angel or spirit has spoken to him.'"[706]

Both Peter and Paul, according to Acts,[707] were under attack from the Sadducees, that is, the Romans, and both were saved by the Pharisees, that is, 'the Jews.' In both instances, it is the spirituality of the Nazarenes that is defended by the Pharisee leaders, thus further indicating that they were regarded as a legitimate Jewish sect. The mainstream Pharisees would have been delighted to be divinely liberated by Elijah, Phinehas, Jesus or anyone else. In his canonical defense of Peter, Gamaliel specifically equates Jesus'Apostles with Judah of Galilee, founder of the Zealot guerrilla fighters, and Theudas, both of whom were killed for attempting to overthrow the Roman government.[708] Theudas actually flourished 15 years after Gamaliel's speech, and so is representative of an apparently common type.

The Nazarene Apostles, it seems, weren't as apolitical as represented, at least not according to Gamaliel, "held in high regard by all the people," that is, political leader of the majority Pharisee voting block in the Great Sanhedrin. Other pro-Jesus Pharisees with Sanhedrin votes mentioned in the New Testament include Joseph of Arimathaea and Nicodemus. Thanks to the need for a majority vote, Gamaliel, a direct descendant of Hillel himself, was able to prevent the judicial murder of the Apostles, whom he saw, according to Acts, as potential political allies, anti-Roman nationalists.

Peter's synagogue believed that Joshua, like Enoch, Eliezer, Elijah, the Teacher of Righteousness and others, had entered Paradise while alive and was the Messiah, the King whom God would eventually use to rescue Israel. This was a variation of the Zealot belief that Phinehas the Zealot, the son of Aaron who was "zealous for his God,"[709] had never died and was coming back to announce the liberation. This apocalypticism was as consistent with Nazarene pharmaco-shamanism as it was with Sioux pharmaco-shamanism. Among the Essenes such herbal sacramentalism was considered completely consistent with orthodox Judaism, though of course, it would have been easy to get an argument on that point from the likes of Gamaliel, who regarded Peter as another rash Galilean extremist, even if a potential military ally.

James, Jesus' brother, leader of the Jerusalem Nazarenes, was a devout Pharisee rabbi who undertook the Rechabite and Nazirite vows that only the most orthodox undertake, and was famous for his devotion to the Temple and the minutiae of Jewish observance.[710] In one of the acts that led to the Zealot rebellion, James was executed by the Sadducee High Priest Ananus (Annas) in 62 CE, whereupon, according to the excellent historian and eyewitness Josephus, the Pharisees rose in protest and succeeded in having Ananus dismissed.[711] That is, as Acts says, the Pharisees were active supporters of the Nazarenes.

James' successor, Symeon, son of Jesus' cousin Cleopas, was himself executed for high treason by the Romans; as Hegesippus put it, for "being of the house of David and a Christian." Obviously, the Romans regarded the Jerusalem Nazarenes as pro-Zealot revolutionaries whose claim to Davidic descent was itself treason. Eusebius, the first great historian of the Church, in discussing the persecution of the family of Jesus, says: "Vespasian, after the taking of Jerusalem, gave orders that all the members of the family of David should be sought out, so that none of the royal tribe might be left among the Jews."[712] Jesus, in other words, was held to be at least spiritually responsible for the Zealot War by the Romans. Cleopas confirms this, saying to the resurrected Jesus himself, whom he doesn't recognize (consistent with the denigration of Jesus' family throughout): "But we had been hoping that he was to be the liberator of Israel."[713]

The Nazarenes became known as the Ebionites, 'the poor ones,' a traditional name of the Essenes recorded at Qumran. They were excommunicated by the Roman Catholic Church in the third century. "For there are some sects who do not accept the [Greek] epistles of the apostle Paul, such as the two kinds of Ebionites [Virgin Birth and normal birth] and those who are called Encratites," wrote Origen in about 248.[714] All Nazarene writings were ordered destroyed, one more of the Church's great literary crimes, since their writings would have included the genuine Hebrew and Aramaic Gospels of the genuine Apostles - Israelites, not Greeks, about whom, now, we can only guess.

As Leviticus puts it: "And Aaron shall present the goat upon which the lot fell for the Lord, and offer him for a sin-offering. But the goat, on which the lot fell for Azazel, shall be set alive before the Lord, to make atonement for him, to send him away for Azazel into the wilderness."[715] Israel, of course, sacrificed goats instead of people, and the scapegoat was allowed to escape, to live a life of freedom in atonement for the taking of the life of its double. Rome sacrificed people instead of goats, and the scapegoat was never allowed to escape, but was made to suffer like Prometheus, eternally, Orphically. Jesus was slain for a sin-offering, and his brother Judas was set alive before Rome, as if *he* had done the slaying. As Israel became the scapegoat, the Evil Twin of the Roman Empire, the *pharmakos* of Augustine's universal Graeco-Roman City, so Judas became Israel in the Canon.

Judah or Yehudah, Jacob's son, the founder of his tribe, is the eponymous hero of 'the Jews.' David is of the tribe of Judah; Israel's greatest revolutionaries, Judah Maccabee and Judah of Galilee, bore the name: "Judah a lion's whelp, you have returned from the kill my son; you crouch and stretch like a lion, like a lion no one dares rouse. The sceptre will not pass from Judah, nor the staff from between his feet, until he receives what is his due and the obedience of the nations is his. He tethers his donkey to the vine, and its colt to the red vine; he washes his cloak in wine, his robe in the blood of grapes. Darker than wine are his eyes, whiter than milk his teeth."[716] Judah is here, in this most ancient of Israelite passages, the *pharmakon*, described as a living entheogen. Jesus, as claimant to the Davidic throne, claimed to be the new Judah.

Paul, the founder of the Christian Church, who knew the Apostles but not Jesus, had never heard of the betrayal of Judas; he never mentions it. In fact, he mentions just the opposite, that Christ appeared to 'the Twelve' after his resurrection.[717] This is also what the 'Gospel of Peter' says, a second century fragment found in Egypt in 1886, mentioned by Serapion, Bishop of Antioch (190-203); it too talks of 'the Twelve.' The canonical Gospel writers are careful to correct Paul, referring to 'the Eleven.'

Considering, of course, that Jesus' brother Judah is probably the disciple known as Judah the Dagger-Man, Judas Iscariot, his betrayal of his own brother to his own mortal enemies does seem a bit far-fetched. This is supported by the fact that the canonical Epistle of Jude is purportedly written by 'Judas the brother of James' ('Judas of James' in Luke), that is, by Jesus' brother Judah. Judah is named by both Mark[718] and Matthew[719] as a leader in good standing when the Gospels were in their formative years. This is further confirmed by the *Apostolic Constitutions* and Epiphanius, who names 'Judas of James' as the successor to Symeon as head of the Jerusalem Church. Eusebius further confirms this, but Romanizes the name to Justus.[720]

Was the Judas who sheltered the newly-converted Paul in Damascus[721] Jesus' brother, on the run from the Romans? He was certainly no traitor to the Damascus Christians. Was his outlaw status the reason that Judas was the third and not the second leader after Jesus of the Jerusalem Nazarenes? Is the friendliness of Judas the reason why Paul never heard of his betrayal? Is this the same Judas Barsabbas, "a leading man in the community" and a "prophet"[722] who accompanied Paul to Antioch from Jerusalem on order of the Jerusalem Nazarenes? Is Judah Barsabbas a prophetic war name, like Joshua Barabbas, Judah Sicarius, Simon the Zealot, Peter Bariona, Jonathan Boanerges and Abba Sikra? That, of course, would explain both the Epistle of Jude and the outlaw status.

Given the fact that at the time of his arrest Jesus was one of the most recognizable figures in all Jerusalem, why did Judas have to identify him to the High Priest's henchmen, whom Jesus had just finished humiliating in the Temple? Were they idiots? Complains Jesus to the temple guards: "Day after day I have been with you in the temple, and you did not raise a hand against me. But this is your hour - when darkness reigns."[723] Judas, then, served no practical purpose in 'identifying' Jesus to people who already knew him. This is one more sign of the artificiality, and the unconscious rituality, of the story.

Paul moved freely among all classes, Antioch's Hellenized Jewish merchants and the Graeco-Roman aristocracy at Ephesus and Corinth. In all three cities, as in many other cities of the Empire, bitter street wars were in progress between the Jews and the Greeks for control of the city. The separate Jewish political entities, the *politeumata*, gave the Jews an independent, and international, base of action while depriving them of citizenship, and power, in the legally Greek cities. The Jews pressed the Romans for *isopoliteia*, political equality with the Greeks, and the Greeks insisted that they give up their independent rights to get it. Ethnic friction was at a fever pitch, exploding into full scale warfare in many parts of the Empire; tens of thousands died. After Antioch, Paul broke with 'the Jews,' declaring "Your blood be on your own heads! My conscience is clear! From now on I shall go to the Gentiles."[724]

Paul then begins the demonization process, cursing "the Jews, who killed the Lord Jesus and the prophets and drove us out, and are so heedless of God's will and such enemies of their fellow-men that they hinder us from telling the Gentiles how they may be saved."[725] This is just what the Greeks wanted to hear; it was the only way any kind of Graeco-Judaism could be made palatable to them. Other contemporary or near contemporary Graeco-Roman writers, such as the Alexandrians Manetho and Apion and the Romans Tacitus and Seneca, make virtually identical use of the rebellious Jews, though the Son of God they resent the Jews rejecting is the Emperor. The Jews, to the Romano-Christians, were becoming what the Canaanites had been to the Jews.[726]

Paul is no doubt telling the truth, at least, when he asserts that "those dogs"[727] threw him out of Israel. Paul's clash with the Jerusalem Nazarenes was their attempt, as the canon indicates,[728] to reign in his overt Graeco-Roman cooptation of their Messiah: "Men of Israel, help: This is the man, that teacheth all men everywhere against the people, and the law, and this place: and further brought Greeks also into the temple, and hath polluted this holy place."(Acts:21:28)

John, who has two Judas', has Jesus tell 'the Jews,' "Your father is the devil."[729] In Acts[730] Judas dies in the 'Field of Blood' by the bursting of his entrails, thus fertilizing the field. In Matthew[731] Judas hangs himself. Obviously, he couldn't have done both. Both images, however, are classic methods of death for the Evil Twin, who fertilizes the earth with his blood.

As Acts puts it: "By the deliberate will and plan of God he was given into your power, and you killed him, using heathen men to crucify him." That is the precise equivalent of accusing the Zealots of using Vespasian and Titus to destroy Israel. Although ridiculous, it made the Romans happy enough to allow the early Church fathers relative political freedom. Above is the last Zealot fortress to fall, in 73 CE, Herod the Great's forbidding Masada. The white line on the right is the ramp built by the Romans for the final siege.

The Pauline thrust was the peaceful conversion of the Graeco-Roman bourgeoisie, some of whom Titus pictured above, on his celebratory Arch, 81 CE, parading the spoils of Zealot Jerusalem through Rome.

Paul's Roman citizenship, a political advantage the Nazarenes disdained, guaranteed him freedom of action throughout the Empire for years. By the time of the Revelation of John, c.100 CE, we have "the synagogue of Satan."[732] Orthodox Christians resented Judaism's status as *religio licita* and the continued Roman recognition of the Jewish *politeuma* in most major cities of the Eastern Empire, even in the face of continual rebellion, while Christianity itself remained *prava*, 'depraved' (new). Traditional Jewish legitimacy, of course, proved unable to compete with the wide appeal of Christianity's simple Greek communion.

BALSAM

Israel reacted to the vicious human sacrifices from which it suffered under Pharoah by institutionalizing compassion - and burying all memory of the ancient tribal shamanism which Pharoah had coopted. Abel, *hevel* in Hebrew, means 'smoke,' but mainstream Israel smoked nothing, outlawed the smoke when it outlawed Pharoah's viciousness. It threw out the baby with the bathwater, as, apparently, Jesus was trying to say: "I am the true vine, and my Father is the vinedresser."[733] That may be just exactly what it sounds like - sacramental pharmaco-shamanism copied straight out of the Nazarene gospels.

The epiphany of the *Prophetis* growing out of the Vine was a standard shamanic device of Cretan and Greek potters for millennia.[734] This was the widely understood pharmaco-shamanic code, relating to the 'Plants of Truth' spoken of by Jesus' sect, the Essenes, who were the most Hellenized, the most sacramental, of Israel's mystics.

As Harrison tried to make clear, originary tribal religion can be understood only by calling up an accurate paleo-neolithic shamanic experience that takes one past the Euhemeristic pseudo-shamanism of the Late Bronze Age, in which *pharmakon* became indistinguishable from *pharmakos*, *hevel* from Abel. This was, of course, precisely the distinction made by Jesus, who insisted that he was the *pharmakon*, not the *pharmakos*.

Emperor Constantine's Jesus, of course, the Roman idol, was indistinguishable from Emperor Constantine, the Roman slaver. That

Israel, like Joshua, insisted on pointing that out only turned Israel into an enemy of all that was holy, according to Constantine. As his laws prove, Constantine used the image of a crucified shaman as a mortal threat, the same way Pharoah used the sacred snake. *He* would let you know what was sacred and what was not. And what was not was punished by enslavement or death. For an enslaved Israel, the equation of the Roman Emperor with Pharoah was not difficult.

But all calves are not golden. Even so great a modern Talmudist as Maccoby, after using the original Hebrew *Qayin* to demonstrate that Cain was an originary Kenite shaman, explains *hevel* as a meta-phor for 'emptiness.' The metaphor was designed, explains Maccoby, to distance Cain from a sacrifice even more painful than that of a brother, possibly that of his son, like Abraham.[735] His argument is "common [post-shamanic] linguistic usage." This awesome scholar displays absolutely no pharmaco-shamanic sophistication or experi-ence whatsoever, even when his own analysis leads him to a smoking shaman, inventing his own device to distance himself from the smoke. When forced to consider the meaning of the 'illicit fire' of Aaron's two sons, Maccoby can only throw up his hands, "whatever that means."

Sometimes, instead of catching young sharks —man-eaters or the thick-headed variety at the right —the Quelpart fisherman goes up into the mountains after mushrooms. There he wears greased dogskin and spends the night in a cave of the extinct volcano

Moses, whose father-in-law Jethro was a Kenite, is never under-stood as a shaman burning a bush on a mountain, despite the fact that that is literally what is being said: "the bush speaks, the mush-room speaks." The anthropological literature is full of examples of the traditional pharmaco-shamanic practice of retiring to a mountain for an extended period to smoke, eat sacramental herbs and induce rev-elation, as the *Bacchae*, and the Quelpart fisherman above, did.

Many Jewish scholars are as unempirically fixated on Abraham's near-sacrifice of Isaac, the binding, the *akedah*, as many Christian schol-ars are on the Crucifixion. Both are archetypal images of the Whole Self, or at least legendary images built upon archetypes, symbolizing the union of consciousness with the collective unsconscious, or, if you will, the human condition. They reflect the relationship of the indi-vidual to the group and to the natural processes of individuation, the search for the "psychic center of the personality not to be identified with the ego."[736] (Jung)

Both images are capable of great spiritual extrapolation, and con-fusion, but to proclaim either to be the only legitimate image of the Self, as both Israel and Christendom have done, is to practice idola-try, not alchemy (*Aurum nostrum non est aurum vulgi.*[737]). Jesus did not preach idolatry, he preached the Essene-Pharisee 'Way.' Like any rabbi, he would have been nauseated to be used as a Roman idol: "Why do you call me good? No one is good but God alone. You know the commandments..."[738] He was teaching yoga, not posing for sculp-ture.

The great contemporary Christian scholar, W.H.C. Frend, suffers from the same anthropological myopia, in which history is given a Mosaic rather than an empirical analysis, and God is viewed as a sa-distic Bronze Age male despot, or, at best, a stern overlord rejecting "anti-social individualism."[739] The result of the iconic fixation is a gull-ibility that causes both great scholars to accept the Euhemeristic meta-phors, confusions or exaggerations of the ancients at face value far too often. Maccoby's caricature of the *Bacchae* is cartoonish, as if he had never read any Greek scholar's description of the Great Dionysia. And both Frend and Maccoby accept Bishop Irenaeus' idiotic carica-ture of the 'orgiastic' Gnostics, the Carpocratians, at face value, as if Irenaeus' political hostility need not be taken into account.

Akiba, last of the great Pharisees, insisted that while most com-mandments could be violated to save one's life, three which could not, even at the cost of one's life, were the laws which forbid idol worship, murder and adultery or incest. These were adopted as the *tria capitula* of Tertullian, violation of which could only be forgiven by God himself. The Church then went on, as Israel did before it, to equate all shamanism with idol worship or witchcraft: "with your sorcery you deceived all the nations."[740] This equation was then used to justify the arbitary *prohibitio* of all sacraments other than its own and the most horrible torture for the practice of unauthorized shamanism, including arbitrary imprisonment, a torture commonly practiced today.

The 'faithful' seem unable to accept the ecstatic, the matristic Paleolithic, which is, of course, where both procreation and dreams take place. 'Good inclination' and 'evil inclination' is a woefully simplistic dualism in the face of the ecstatic creativity of children and shamans. Most people know that their dreams are filled with meaningful spontaneous imagery. We use the symbolism of our remote ancestors every time we dream, and that contact is curative. The age of the Prophets is past only if you think they were more alive than you are.[741]

Israel would do well to remember the sacramental Herb as well as the sacred Word. Moe's mountain ain't that far off - just say I AM sent me. The original *pharmakos* wasn't a human sacrifice demanded by a savage male despot, as Pharoah would have it, and as Abraham apparently thought. It was a *pharmakon, hevel,* a leaf which was smoked, medicine, Dionysos, Ploutos, Wealth, vegetal son of the Holy Mother of us all, reborn every spring. We come from tribal peoples who did not distinguish their blood from the blood of the ivy or the blood of the ox, and who joined both in ecstacy.

Hesiod: "Demeter, noble among goddesses, gave birth to Wealth, in union of intimate desire with the hero Iasius ['the man of the drug'] in a thrice-fallow field, in the rich Cretan land: broad back of the sea, and whoever encounters him, into whosoever hands he comes, he makes him rich and bestows much fortune on him."[742] The Essenes were the *Iassai,* the 'Jesuses.' Mousaios, of course, is as effective a psychopomp as Iasius - come to think of it, so is Diana.

Gnosticism, the Mother of Sacramental Christianity, is a very broad category of Judeo-Hellenic-Egyptian mysticism.[743] Many Gnostics used the Hebrew canon as a starting point in their cosmology, but insisted that the Hebrew God, the Demiurge, the 'Workman,' the 'Creator,' was a material illusion, behind which the originary Platonic archetypes, the Pleroma, the 'fulfillment,' could be experienced directly. This *gnosis*, this 'acquaintance' with the spirit, was often achieved through a sacramentalism that was nothing short of Paleolithic.

Since they were concerned far more with genuine entheogenic

sacraments than with iconic substitutes, many Gnostics expressed a proprioceptive disdain for the Church's *eidololatreia*. The early Church was driven crazy by ecstatic, iconoclastic Gnostics who felt free to pick and chose from the canon like hungry tokers from a Chinese menu. Jesus, they said, only seemed (*dokeo*) to suffer, so as to demonstrate the sacramental mystery, the Secret of Salvation. This, of course, meant that Judas was innocent and that Jesus pretended to die only to get everybody high and creative, not to atone by his agony for our Original Sin. Original Sin was simply a trap of the Demiurge, who used threat, guilt and sex to bring us down to the material level.

Some Gnostics, notably the famous Alexandrian teacher Basilides (fl.130), insisted that sex was to be enjoyed without any sense of guilt, as a sort of baptism in the material world which prepared one for the next level. Basilides was a teacher of Valentinus, the most popular and influential Christian Gnostic.

Among the Valentinians women were completely equal, prophesying, healing and officiating right alongside the men. "Some said, 'Mary conceived by the holy spirit.' They are in error. They do not know what they are saying. When did a woman ever conceive by a woman?"[744] Bishop Irenaeus of Lyon (130-200) was infuriated by the Valentinians among his congregation who enjoyed the fleshly delights of life, and who insisted that they were, like Paul, above the law - the law of the 'true Israel' as well as that of the 'old Israel': "where there is no law, there is no transgression."[745]

"The Gospel of Truth is Joy," wrote Valentinus (c.140 CE), "for those whom the Father has given the Word from the pleroma, providing the grace and the power of the Father of Truth, the Saviour who dwells in the mind of the Father. When he was nailed to the Tree of Life he became a fruit of the *gnosis* of the Father. When that fruit was eaten, those who consumed it became ecstatic, having discovered the Saviour in themselves and themselves in the Saviour. But first they passed through the terrifying empty space, stripped naked to the soul, contacting their pure emotions. This is the wisdom of the living book of the ages, composed of letters each of which expresses a whole thought, a complete book, known only to the speaker. Each letter expresses the Unity of the *Logos* of the Father, the fruit of His heart of His will. Each automatic thought purifying the soul, bringing it back into the Father, into the Mother, Jesus of the infinite sweetness."[746]

Here we have a shaman's sacramental letters, not *pistis*, 'faith,' but a very active *participation mystique*, a "psychedelic experience," and the consequent originality and matristic ideology that was anathema to the Bishops of Lyon and Rome. Valentinus understood *Iasius*, as he called him, as the "fruit of the knowledge of the father" - an hermaphroditic combination of Adam, Eve, the serpent and the fruit - offering an original gift, not an original sin.

The fruit, the sacrament, the *pharmakon*, was the major point of Gnostic disagreement with the Orthodox church, since the Gnostic apotheosis consisted not of the ordinary symbolic communion, but of a second pharmacological sacrament of *apolytrosis* (deliverance, liberation, redemption). That is, the Gnostic *Iasius* or *Iason* was the Greek hero, whom the Romans called Jason. Jason's *apolytrosis*, after an apparently exhausting trip, is pictured above on a fifth century BC ceremonial vase. The pharmacological serpent, with vine and golden fleece, ushers *Iaion* (*Ia-ion* - see p.129 for *ion*) into the presence of 'the Mother.' Athena holds the prophetic owl she inherited from Lilith the Transformer. She also wears the Gorgoneion, symbol of the terrifying mysteries through which the naked soul must pass before it is admitted "into the Father, into the Mother, Jesus of the infinite sweetness."

Aldous Huxley used the ancient Sanskrit equivalent of *apolytrosis*, *moksha*, to describe the central sacrament - entheogenic mushroom juice - of his utopian *Island*. That, of course, is an historically accurate reference to the *Rg Veda*. Bishop Irenaeus, in a fit of empiricism, seems to have helped Huxley write his novel. He described the Gnostic rites fairly accurately: "And he [Valentinus] says that the Holy Spirit was produced by the Truth to inspect and fructify the Aeons, entering them invisibly, through whom the Aeons produced the *plants of truth*....For some of them prepare a *nuptial couch* and perform a *sacred rite* for those who are 'perfected'....'O Saviour of Truth.' This is what those who initiate invoke, while he who is initiated replies, 'I am strengthened and redeemed, and I redeem my soul from this age, and from all things connected with it in the name of Iao who redeemed his soul to full redemption in the living Christ.'"

"Then they *anoint the initiate with balsam*, for they say that this *ointment* is a type of the sweet fragrance which is above all things....There are others who keep on 'redeeming'the dying up to the moment of death, pouring oil and water on their heads, or the ointment mentioned above mixed with water, and with the invocations mentioned above, that they may not be grasped or seen by the principalities and powers, and that their inner man may ascend even above the invisible things....And they claim that he who says this will avoid and escape the powers...'I am a precious vessel, more than the female being who made you. Though your mother does not know her origin, I know myself, and I know whence I am, and I call on the incorrupt Wisdom, who is in the Father, who is the Mother of your mother, and has no Father nor any male consort; for a female, made of a female, made you, not knowing her own Mother, and thinking that she was alone; but I call upon her Mother.'"[747] (Italics mine)

The *sacred rite* with the *plants of truth* on the *nuptial couch* is a reference to the sacred marriage of the mystery religions, the *hieros gamos*, as mentioned in the Essene *Thanksgiving Hymn*. The Mahayana Buddhists of Tibet also 'redeem the dying,' calling their shamanic initiation 'the little death.' They use the *Book of the Dead*, the *Bardo Thodol* ('Liberation by Hearing on the After-Death Plane') to guide the initiate through the 'Gnostic' levels of ascent and descent. The Gnostics and their 'Hermetic' brethren were the inspiration of the medieval alchemists, who elaborated spectacularly on the 'precious vessel.'

Jung explains a comment on the 'balsam' by the greatest of the alchemists, Paracelsus (1493-1541), the prototype of Goethe's *Faust* and the inventor of modern chemistry: "'Life, by Hercules, is nothing other than a certain embalsamed Mumia, which preserves the mortal body from the mortal worms and corruption by means of a mixed saline solution.'" That solution, of course, being blood. 'Mumia,' supposedly the pulverized parts of real mummies, had the reputation in the Middle Ages as a sort of prophylactic against all disease. "Paracelsus attributed incorruptibility to a special virtue or agent named 'balsam.' This was something like a natural elixir, by means of which the body was kept alive or, if dead, incorruptible. By the same logic, a scorpion or venomous snake necessarily had in it an alexipharmic, i.e., an antidote, otherwise it would die of its own poison."

"This is the balsam, which stands even higher than the *quinta essentia,* the thing that ordinarily holds the four elements together. It 'excels even nature herself' because it is produced by a 'bodily operation.' The idea that the art can make something higher than nature is typically alchemical. The balsam is the life principle, the *spiritus mercurii,* and it more or less coincides with the Paracelsan concept of the Iliaster. The latter is higher than the four elements and determines the length of life. It is therefore roughly the same as the balsam, or one could say that the balsam is the pharmacological or chemical aspect of the Iliaster.... In the microcosm the balsam dwells in the heart, like the sun in the macrocosm."[748]

The alchemists compared the balsam to their other "fruits and powers of paradise and heaven,"Aniada, Cheyri, Thereniabin, Nostoch and Melissa, all of which they compared to the Communion substances, that is, they asserted that they caused transformation. These were often ancient pharmacological recipes preserved by Europe's tribal midwives. The Church's inquisitors, Paracelsus' enemies, hunted the curanderas; Paracelsus, as he repeatedly wrote, went to them to learn.[749] Paracelsus named himself after Celsus and Theophrastus, two of the most legendary medical empiricists of the ancient world.

Resurrection, insisted the Gnostics, was spiritual and sacramental. The Gnostic Sethians denied bodily Resurrection as an idolatrous delusion foisted on fools by materialist politicians anxious to coopt the tradition by claiming descent from one particular physical body. Christ was really a 'guide' to "lead the soul which is invisibly being saved" into the Pleroma, from whence it came, therefore to argue that physical death "would have overcome the savior himself...is absurd."[750] (Theodotus)

Gnostic texts like *Pistis Sophia* constantly talk of Christ revealing the mysteries to 'the Twelve.' "In the place where I shall be, there also will be my twelve ministers, but Mary Magdalene and John the virgin shall be higher than all the disciples."[751] There is no Eleven, no Judas, no betrayal, no fascist scapegoat, no evil pharmacological serpent, only *gnosis*, with an accent on the feminine, on the Holy Spirit *as* feminine. That is, with an accent on that which gives birth and rebirth: "I will tell you all mysteries from the exterior of the exteriors, to the interior of the interiors. Hearken, I will tell you all things which have befallen Me....The Mystery which is beyond the world, that whereby all things exist: It is all evolution and all involution..."[752]

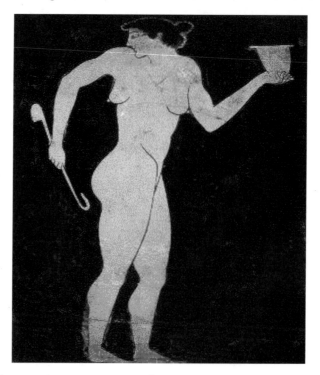

Gnosis, experience, was everything; external imagery, canon, meant nothing. All that mattered was the digestion of the fruit, the balsam, the creative voice of the inner being: "If you bring forth what is within you, what you bring forth will save you. If you do not bring forth what is within you, what you do not bring forth will destroy you."[753]
(*Gospel of Thomas*)

This *docetism* (from *dokeo*, 'to seem, appear,' a reference to the delusion of *eidololatreia*) eventually provoked the Church to inquisitorial savagery, hence the burial of the Nag Hammadi manuscripts, numbering among them *The Gospel of Truth* and *The Gospel of Thomas*. In 1945, some 1600 years after their burial in central Egypt, the Nag

Hammadi manuscripts were rediscovered. Were it not for that archeological miracle, none of Valentinus' writings would survive, despite the fact that between 136 and 165 he was one of the most popular teachers in Rome. All his works were systematically sought out and burned by the Church, as were those of Basilides, Cerinthus, Heracleon, Ptolemy, Theodotus and the rest.

Gnostic ideas pervaded the Graeco-Roman world, and what little of their literature survives is easily the best and most original of the era, proving that many were uninhibited geniuses. The legendary Basilides' 24 books of *Exegetica* were no doubt extraordinary; we'll never know. Nor will we know how many Gnostic women set down their thoughts, since they were a special target of the inquisitors because of their Original Sin, that is, because Demeter, Persephone, Asherah and Miriam were women.

IDOLATRY

As the Roman ecology became industrial, so did the rites of passage. Experience of the original tribal rites of transformation became buried in the overlay of politicized legend upon legend, which overlay included, inherently, rules restricting the shamanic experience. Politically acceptable - that is, mandatory - legend replaced *mythos*, the transforming words of the Mother, so that rites of passage became rites of submission. Symbology replaced experience; idolatry replaced ecstacy. This is the psychological equivalent of ecocide, since what is being peddled is servitude, not freedom; guilt, not creativity; repentance, not ecstacy; supplication, not dance; a wafer, not a mushroom; rote, not song. The pump don't work cause the Vandals took the handles.

Paul, as he himself emphasized, aimed at control of the Roman Empire. He combined manipulative Roman idolatry, political servility and misogyny with genuine Graeco-Judeo Gnosticism, producing an instinctively brilliant syncretism that literally seduced the Empire.

"Be it known unto you therefore, men and brethren, that through this man is preached unto you the forgiveness of sins: And by him all that believe are justified from all things, from which ye could not be justified by the law of Moses."[754] The new remnant is "chosen by grace...no longer on the basis of works."[755] Well, that certainly is a *new* remnant. Zechariah's remnant, which, according to his canonical words included Jesus, defined themselves by their good works.

But Paul, unlike Jesus, let Rome's slavers off the hook: "Let every person be subject to the governing authorities. For there is no authority except from God, and those that exist have been instituted by God."[756] No Israeli nationalist, facing Roman enslavement, would have a polite answer to that one. Jesus, of course, was executed by the Romans for trying to overthrow them. Murderous slavers come to power all the time, and they are overthrown by rebels inspired by God's dream of freedom. Thus sayeth Jesus' true disciple, Shimon Bar Kokhba, Simon the Son of the Star, who led the last great rising of ancient Israel.

Nor would the Drones forget the Buzzing of the Bees, as Paul did: "Let a woman learn in silence with all submissiveness. I permit no woman to teach or to have authority over men; she is to keep silent. For Adam was formed first, then Eve; and Adam was not deceived, but the woman was deceived and became a transgressor."[757] Christian Rome burned the writings of women simply because they were women, just as Pagan Rome did. Paul's misogyny is indistinguishable from Cato's.

But Paul could also wax poetic, with great proselytic power, about the Holy Spirit in life, though too often his vision was predicated on a manipulative rejection of the body combined with his redemptive idolatry, as if only adoration of the *eidolon* would release us from the unavoidable guilt our God-given appetites confers on us: "For if we have become identified with him in his death, we shall also be identified with him in his resurrection. We know that our old humanity has been crucified with Christ, for the destruction of the sinful self, so that we may no longer be slaves to sin, because death cancels the claims of sin....When he died, he died to sin, once and for all, and now that he lives, he lives to God. In the same way you must regard yourselves as dead to sin and alive to God, in union with Christ Jesus; we look forward eagerly to our adoption, our liberation from mortality. It was with this hope that we were saved."[758]

Apuleius, about 80 years after Paul, who had thoroughly indulged his God-given appetites, described his salvation by Isis from his life as *The Golden Ass* in almost the same terms: "I approached the very gates of death and set one foot on Proserpine's threshold, yet was permitted to return, rapt through all the elements. At midnight I saw the sun shining as if it were noon; I entered the presence of the gods of the under-world and the gods of the upper-world, and stood near and worshipped them."[759] This was called the *apathanatismos*, the 'proof against death,' the 'immortalization.' "Therefore baptism is called 'death,' and an 'end of the old life,'"said the Gnostic Theodotus.[760]

The Roman catacombs of Domitilla and Priscilla, third century, represent Christ as Orpheus more than any other mythical figure.[761] As wine was the blood of Orpheus/Dionysos, so it was the blood of Jesus. Egyptian magical texts have wine as the blood of Osiris, the ancient Egyptian Orpheus.[762] Diodorus: "'Charops, grandfather of Orpheus, gave help to the god, and Dionysos in gratitude instructed him in the orgies of his rites; Charops handed them down to his son Oiagros ['wine-grower'], and Oiagros to his son Orpheus....Orpheus, being a man gifted by nature and highly trained above all others, *made many modifications in the orgiastic rites*: hence they call the rites that took their rise from Dionysos, Orphic.'"[763] Obviously, the water of Paul's baptismal font, or even the communion wine, when the communicants were allowed to imbibe, was something less than the *oinos* of the Gnostic Plants of Truth, but a Graeco-Roman Orphic could understand and use them.

The many cults of Orpheus, Demeter-Dionysos, Herakles, Artemis, Aphrodite-Adonis, Isis-Osiris-Sarapis and Cybele-Attis were established in the dominant culture, many of their figureheads appearing as civic deities on coins from time to time. Unlike Christianity, however, their organization was local and congregational - they had no ability to act in a coordinated way throughout the Empire. Nor could the Empire use them in a coordinated way, except one at a time, city by city. There was no Imperial 'Vatican' before the Vatican.

Attis met his seasonal death under a pine tree by self-castration, that is, he ate his *phallos*, his mushroom, whereupon he hung his body in the tree to fertilize the earth for the Resurrection. Although the memory of these cults was shamanic, their practice was often symbolic, Euhemeristic, disconnected. Castration was actually taken to mean castration by some hysterical devotees of Cybele, and Christ, the vegetal ecstacy replaced by physical agony. The aristocratic Romans, who were often Eleusinian initiates, found this perverted 'enthusiasm' disgusting and dangerous, and banned it under the *Lex Cornelia de sicariis et veneficiis*, as they did the circumcision of non-Jews.[764]

As Apuleius shows, the genuine entheogenic 'initiations' were often quite expensive, and necessarily surrounded by a wall of exclusivity and secrecy. But a wall easily and often pierced by those who could afford it or who had the knowledge. As their lush wall paintings show, the mysteries were celebrated at Pompeii. The rather hermaphroditic Pompeiian conception of Hermes, above, was little different than its Greek prototype, Korykia/Nike. As the Roman glass mosaic above indicates, the association of a rabbit with a Soma mushroom was common 'mystery' code. There was a lively trade in dried medicinal and 'sacred' mushrooms,[765] but their overt connection to religious rites had become downright dangerous.

The wrong rites became *maiestas, crimen laesae maiestatis humanae,* 'injuring the majesty of humanity,' high treason. When forced into an *inquisitio* by a military uprising in Germany in 89 CE, Domitian demonstrated for the locals a lesson in torture they never forgot. Domitian, like Sejanus before him, used the *inquisitio* solely on the assertion of informers to institute a reign of terror. Typical is the case of Mettius Pompusianus, who lost his life for having an imperial horoscope and a map of the whole empire. Hermogenes of Tarsus was killed for lampoons against the Emperor and his slave-copyists crucified. In 83 CE the Chief Vestal, Cornelia, was buried alive for having sex, and her lover beaten to death with rods. The Greeks, who thought of virginity as renewable, like the Spring, disdained this simplistic savagery, but the symbolism of State control of sexuality proved irresistible to Domitian, who killed a few other Vestals as well.

Domitian despised original thought, either killing or exiling the likes of Epictetus, Artemidorus and Apollonius of Tyana. As a test of loyalty Domitian demanded religious sacrifice before his image, and insisted on being addressed as *Dominus et Deus,* 'Master and God,' charging those who refused with *atheotes,* neglect of the State religion. Conversion to Judaism was prohibited, but Judaism by descent was tolerated, since the 'Jewish tax,' now paid to Rome since Jerusalem no longer existed, was worth too much to the Imperial exchequer. Vast estates were confiscated for trivialities. Nobles were forced to fight in the arena, and if they survived were banished. Books and rites were arbitrarily subjected to *prohibitio.*[766]

Dio reports[767] that on Trajan's return to Rome in 107, ten thousand Dacian prisoners took part in games lasting 123 days, and eleven thousand animals were slaughtered, along with about half the Dacian gladiators. The most famous of Trajan's arena victims wasn't a prisoner of war, but a dangerous *atheos,* Ignatius, Bishop of Antioch (fl.115 CE), 'the father of orthodoxy,' who rejected Trajan's gory *pietas* to his face.

Ignatius directly analogized the symbolic *eucharisto* with the ancient shamanic *pharmakon*: "At these meetings you should heed the bishop and presbytery attentively, and break one loaf, which is the medicine of immortality (*pharmakon athanasias*) and the antidote which wards off death but yields continuous life in union with Jesus Christ....Thus no devil's weed will be found among you; but thoroughly pure and self-controlled, you will remain body and soul united to Jesus Christ."[768]

"I urge you, therefore, - not I, but Jesus Christ's love - use only

Christian food. Keep off foreign fare, by which I mean heresy. For those people [Gnostics] mingle Jesus Christ with their teachings just to gain your confidence under false pretenses. It is as if they were giving a deadly poison mixed with honey and wine, with the result that the unsuspecting victim gladly accepts it and drinks down death with fatal pleasure....And if, as some atheists (I mean unbelievers) say, his suffering was a sham (it's really *they* who are a sham!), why, then, am I a prisoner? Why do I want to fight with wild beasts? In that case I shall die to no purpose. Yes, and I am maligning the Lord too!"[769]

Many Gnostics would have agreed completely, insisting that the ecstacy of spontaneous creativity was far more important than suffering and religio-political witness (*martyria*). This attitude uniformly enraged the early Church fathers, who felt that they earned the authority they suffered for; they were "Maccabees of the true Israel,"and *auctoritas* was their spiritual goal.

Ignatius could easily have avoided the Coliseum by prostrating himself before the image of the Emperor-Saviour or Juppiter, saying a ritual prayer and burning some incense, but such a course was unthinkable to this mystic politician, whose implacable courage magnified the influence of his Church throughout the Empire. Jesus was a real mystery god, a living one, whose *eucharisto* had enormous power in the face of the pseudo-tribal alternatives, precisely because he was post-tribal, neither Jew nor Greek (Roman), a 'third race,' *katholikos,* 'universal.'

Some Gnostic Christians, or aristocratic initiates of the mysteries like Ovid and Apuleius, might call the symbolic *pharmakon 'vicarius,'* a 'substitute,' but for many of the bulk of the population, for whom the mysteries weren't an option, the body and blood of Christ were far more genuine than the idols of the Emperor, whose shamanic posing was simply an insult. For Ignatius, Bishop of Antioch, control of the powerful symbolism was everything: "It is not lawful apart from the bishop either to baptize or to hold a love feast; but whatsoever he shall approve, this is well pleasing also to God....He that honoureth the bishop is honoured of God; he that doth aught without the knowledge of the bishop [the vicar] rendereth service to the devil."[770] The canonical word for sin is *hamartia,* an archer's term, 'missing the mark,' failing to toe the line.[771]

Consistent with its authoritarianism, the Church evolved a sacramental ritual in which the priest imbibed the wine on behalf of the congregation, everyone partaking of the symbolic blood vicariously.

That is political theology, authoritarian organizational genius which the Romans themselves refined and quite rightly perceived as a political threat. As Frend put it: "orthodoxy produced no leaders of the intellectual range and status of its opponents. The orthodox were often of an administrative cast of mind, ones to whom rules of behavior necessary to win salvation seemed more important than the fulness of Christ's grace."[772]

Most of the Church fathers were so unoriginal and repetitive that reading them is painfully boring. They understood, however, the unique power of the Empire-wide organization they were building, and their mysticism is psychologically indistinguishable from their politics. That, of course, was precisely the Gnostic complaint. Many other early Orthodox Christians, such as Justin and Tatian (*flor*.160), also directly challenged Rome in organizational terms; wrote Tatian: "I reject your legislation also; for there ought to be one common polity for all. But now there are as many different codes as there are states, so that things held disgraceful in some are honourable in others."[773]

Melito of Sardes, one of the later Apologists, felt free to address this explanation of Christianity to Marcus: "A philosophy which formerly flourished among the barbarians, but which during the great reign of your ancestor Augustus sprang up among the nations which you rule, so that it became a blessing of good omen to your Empire....To this power you have succeeded as men have desired; and in this power you will continue with your son, on condition that you guard that philosophy which has grown with the Empire, and which came into existence under Augustus."[774]

From the early to the later Apologists ('Defenders'), no Orthodox ('straight-thinking') Christian ever raised the standard of revolt in the Empire, ultimately penetrating its social fabric completely. Athenagoras of Athens, c.177, wished Marcus a peaceful succession in these words: "For who are more deserving to obtain the things they ask than those who, like us, pray for your government that you may, as is most right, receive the kingdom son from father, and that your empire may extend and increase, all men becoming subject to your sway? And this is also for our advantage that we may lead a peaceable and quiet life and may ourselves readily perform all that is commanded of us."[775]

By this time the Church of Rome had become the authoritative center of Imperial Christianity. It founded the *Aedicula*, marking the site of Peter's burial on Vatican hill, in which were collected 'trophies' of the apostles for pilgrims to revere. An enormous amount of property and cash flowed into the Church's hands. Warned Bishop Irenaeus, "Each church must be in harmony with this church because of its outstanding pre-eminence, that is the faithful from everywhere, since apostolic tradition is preserved in it by those from everywhere."[776] The Empire-wide system of monarchical episcopacy, giving each *episkopos* ('inspector,overseer') enormous power, became the sole form of Church government. Early schisms, such as those of Marcion, Montanus and Gnosticism, "rending the seamless robe of Christ," had been branded heretical and crushed or outmaneuvered.

Athenagoras' prayer for a happy succession for Marcus wasn't realized in his egomaniac son Commodus, who inherited the Empire at the age of eighteen, like Alexander so he thought, in 180. He styled himself the new Hercules, slaying a lion from horseback in the arena by way of demonstration. He made the Persian Mithra, with its *sacramentum*, sacred oath, and sacramental bread and wine, the official religion of the Empire.

Mithra's thousands of sanctuaries throughout the Empire were peopled largely by soldiers and slaves. The Mithraic *taurobolium*, the bull-chase and bathing in the bull's blood, resulted in an initiate 're-born for eternity.' Unlike the ancient Cretan rite, however, the *kernos* no longer contained an herbal entheogen, just a soup made from the bull's balls, which about sums up the difference between Crete and Rome.[777] The rite was often performed officially for the health of the Empire by the soothsaying head druid (*vaticinatione archigalli), pro salute imperatoris sacrum.*

Mithraism was a combination of the Persian prophet Zoroaster's (b.c.570 BC) solar monotheism, which depicted Ahura' Mazda as a winged disc with a human head, quite like Akhenaten's Aten, and Graeco-Roman sacramentalism. Mithra, the Persian genius of celestial light, was the slayer of the bull, from whose blood the crops arose. Hellenes could recognize the archetype of Nike sacrificing the bull.[778]

The *apotheosis* of Mithra was the sacred meal, the communion of bread and wine, body and blood of the Bull, shared with the Sun: "Us too, thou hast saved by shedding the blood that grants eternity." Mithra was "the Logos that emanated from God and shared His omnipotence."[779] He was friendly to all the gods: in Gaul, Apollo; in Spain, Mercury and Oceanus; in Greece, Zeus; in Rome, Juppiter and Oceanus. Hermes Trismegistos could be shown as psychopompic guide in the Mithraeum; Attis could be shown as the Good Shepherd; Herakles overthrew the evil powers, and Ulysses quested for bliss and immortality. Above Mithra stood Ahura Mazda, Juppiter Caelus;

behind him Zervan akarana, infinite time, Kronos; Ahriman represented death, decay, a negative but not evil principle.

Mithra was the Unconquered One, God of Time, Lord of the Planets, whose cult combined mystery and awesome ceremony with comradeship and a sense of achievement. The branded initiates, all men, 'born' and 'sealed,' worked their way up the seven planetary spheres from *corax* to *nymphus, miles, leo, Persa, heliodromus* and finally *pater*, that is, from Saturn (Kronos-lead), to Venus (Aprhrodite-tin), Jupiter (Zeus-bronze), Mercury (Hermes-iron), Mars (Ares-a mixture), the Moon-silver, and the Sun-gold.[780]

At this time Mithraism was the most popular single cult, with thousands of small *Mithraea* dotting the Empire. Justin Martyr and Tertullian regarded Mithraism as a "diabolic imitation"[781] of Christianity, in the Roman Christ is the iconic combination of Mithra and the Bull, and both religions employed almost identical baptism, communion, ritual meals and local hierarchical structure. Mithraism's outright exclusion of women (it was the religion of the army), lack of an Imperial vision and an effective international hierarchy marked it for extinction in the face of Christianity.

As commercial power shifted to the provinces, the loyal provincial gods took their place beside Roman deities. Druidic shamanism was suppressed, while its memory, in the form of a domesticated Teutates, 'God of the Tribe,' identified with Mercury, was encouraged. Mercury was identified with Rosmerta and the ancient *Matronae* - the Celtic nature spirits, as Apollo with Sirona. Although Caesar had made it his business to cut down sacred groves in newly-conquered territory, the ancient Celtic wild horse, Epona, remained as powerful in Europe as the Magna Mater, Cybele, in Asia Minor. The lusty Hercules was readily adopted by the Gauls and Germans, Sulis Minerva evolved in Britain and Juppiter Dolichenus, from the town of Doliche, represented Anatolia.

The Empire encouraged hundreds of local 'divine marriages.' Mithra traveled West with the troops, as did the Alexandrian Sarapis. "I therefore think that it makes no difference whether we call Zeus the Most High, or Zen, or Adonai, or Saboath, or Ammon like the Egyptians, or Papaeus like the Scythians,"said Celsus, c.178.[782]

The fourteen most frequently mentioned deities in the corpus of Latin, Western, inscriptions, after Juppiter, are, in order, Mercury, Hercules, Fortuna (Tyche), Liber (Dionysos), Diana, Mars, Aesculapius, Apollo, Silvanus, Venus, Mithra-Sol, Isis-Sarapis, Juppiter Dolichenus and Cybele. In the East the Greeks stressed Zeus, Apollo, Athena,

Dionysos, Artemis, Hera, Aphrodite, Asclepius ('the Saviour'), Tyche, Hercules and Cybele. We find inscriptions like 'Zeus Helios the Great All-God Sarapis,' 'Zeus Greatest Helios Olympian, the Saviour,' or this Orphic verse: 'Zeus is One, Hades is One, Helios is One, Dionysos is One.'[783]

Septimius Severus ('The Severe'-193-211), legate of the Western armies based at Carnuntum, near Vienna, took the Principate by force after the death of Commodus. "For, more than any of his predecessors, Severus made the imperial house, as a *domus divina*, the centre of the religion and discipline of the army and indeed of the whole militarized structure which the State had now become."[784]

His *consilium principis*, run like a general staff and peopled by such legendary jurisconsults as Papinian, Plautianus, Paulus and Ulpian, asserted that the decisions of the emperor had the force of law (*legis vigorem*). Justification was found in the traditional legislative power inherent in the emperor's *imperium*, as promulgated by the Senate for Augustus and codified in the *lex de imperio Vespasiani*.[785]

Augustus had simplified the legal system by appointing a single magistrate who handled the case from start to finish. The magistrate could institute an *inquisitio* without the accuser that had previously been necessary. This was a *cognitio extra ordinem*, which, despite its name, became the ordinary form of criminal trial, such as the one Jesus was subjected to before Pilate. The likes of Domitian could then promulgate a *prohibitio* and instruct his magistrates to institute inquisitions on their own initiative, operating under the Emperor's *legis vigorem*.

It was these seminal legal thinkers who institutionalized the concept of *sacrilegium* ('stealing of sacred things') as *maiestas*, treason, in Western law, via Justinian's Code, the violation of a *prohibitio* being a sacrilege. This is quite literally the originary legal precedent upon which contemporary American Prohibition is based. Justinian's Code, adopted as canonical 'ancient law' by the medieval Church-State in the twelfth century, became the basis of the legal system of all Western nations. It is sickening to see contemporary Justices of the American Supreme Court cite this Roman inquisitorial law, which overthrew the aristocratic Greek libertarianism, as originary legal precedent, just as the Church courts of the Inquisition did.

The 'liberal' Ulpian, who contributed more than any other jurist to both Justinian's *Corpus* of laws and *Digest* of opinions, explained that "No one can be condemned to the penalty of being beaten to death or to die under rods or during torture, although most persons, when they are tortured, lose their lives."[786] That is, to put it in contemporary American terms, no one is accused of treason for violating contemporary American Prohibition, although the punishment is the same.

Julia Maesa, like her powerful sister Julia Domna, wife of Severus, became Augusta, a powerful independent force. She often acted officially for her Emperor-grandson Elegabalus, whose acquisition of the throne she engineered after the death of Severus. The teenage Elagabalus, *Summus Sacerdos*, 'High Priest' as his coins had it, made a serious attempt to Syrianize the Roman government. He tried to replace Juppiter with the Sun God of Emesa, *Dei Solis Elegabalus*, married to the Punic Tanit. To this end he married a Vestal Virgin, declaring that the two were Baal and Tanit incarnate. The sacrilege only earned him the contemptuous nickname 'the Assyrian' and the lethal hatred of the Senate.

In 222, seeing the writing on the wall, Julia Maesa encouraged Elegabalus to adopt his fourteen year-old cousin, son of her other daughter, Julia Mammaea, as Marcus Aurelius Alexander Severus. She then promptly helped the Praetorians murder Elegabalus and his mother. This gave Rome what it longed for, a Roman emperor, or at least a more Roman Syrian, thus preserving the Severan dynasty and the power of the surviving Augustae, Maesa and Mammaea. The Augustae were portrayed on the coins as Cybele - *Mater Deum, Matri Magnae*, or as Juno - *mater Augustorum, mater senatus, mater patriae*. Young Alexander Severus did not mess with his Augusta Mammaea, a veritable Livia, '*mater Augusti et castrorum et senatus atque patriae et universi generis humani*.'

The imperial *Lararium*, house-chapel, was said (*Augustan History*) to include a statue of Christ along with those of Apollonius of Tyana, Abraham and Orpheus. Ulpian, apparently under orders from Mammaea, arranged in the lawbook he prepared for imperial proconsuls for Christians to be arraigned under the more lenient minor treason law rather than the severe sacrilege law.[787] Although Mammaea may not have been a Christian, as Eusebius asserts, her polite reception of Origen, c.232, and the dedication to her by Hippolytus of his treatise *On the Resurrection* certainly indicate an interested sympathy, the same interest, at least, that she displayed in Gnosticism and the mysteries.

We get some idea of their discussions from this warning Origen penned at about the same time: "Today under the pretext of Gnosis, heretics rise against the Church of Christ. They pile on their books of commentaries. They interpret the Gospel and the apostolic texts. If we are silent, if we do not oppose them, famished souls are fed with their abominations."[788] (John's Gospel)

Tertullian (c.160-240) concurred: "What then has Athens to do with Jerusalem? What does the Academy have to do with the Church? What do heretics have to do with Christians?....Away with those who have introduced a Stoic, a Platonic, a dialectical Christianity!/We do not need this kind of curiosity now that we have Jesus, nor do we need inquiry now that we have the gospel."[789] (Adversus Marcionem)

Clement in Alexandria agreed with his student Origen, and with Tertullian in North Africa and Hippolytus in Rome, and all wielded enough power to cooperate with one another across the entire Empire; each literally had an army of priests, deacons and communicants at his disposal. Latin Rome and Carthage, and Greek Antioch, Alexandria and Ephesus were not only Imperial power centers, they had become Church power centers.

Origen thought Augustus was a Godsend, "reducing to uniformity, so to speak, the many kingdoms on earth so that he had a single empire. It would have hindered Jesus'teaching from being spread through the whole world if there had been many kingdoms..."[790]

Origen's pagan contemporary, the Bithynian Roman consul Dio Cassius, agreed with him completely. There is no discernable difference in their attitudes, despite the fact that one helped to rule the Empire and the other, as yet, only helped to rule the Church: "Those who attempt to distort our religion with strange rites you should abhor and punish not merely for the sake of the gods (for if a man despises these he will not pay honour to any other being), but because such men by bringing in new divinities in the place of the old, persuade many to adopt foreign practices from which spring up conspiracies, factions and cabals which are not profitable to a monarchy. Do not therefore permit anyone to be an atheist or a sorcerer."[791]

Christ, insisted Origen's mentor Clement, was both man and God, "becoming man in order that such as you may learn from man how it is even possible for man to become a god...And shall we not even at the risk of displeasing our fathers, bend our course towards the truth and seek after him who is our real Father thrusting away custom as some deadly drug."[792]

Clement agreed completely with Dio Cassius on 'sorcery' as a political threat. The *pharmakon* was now deadly, as if it were arrow poison, but sheer childlike obeisance to Our Father who art in Church could effect the ecstatic liberation, in the next life. In the meantime, be satisfied with your chains, which are the will of God. This is simply the Imperial theology with a different *eidolon,* as Origen so clearly understood when he asserted that the Church was an *imperium in imperio,* a state within a state.[793]

The Gnostic Philo, elucidating the rationalism Plato derived from Eleusinian shamanism, metaphorized the Manna given to the Israelites in the Sinai as the Divine *Logos* bestowed on man for his sustenance. This is obviously a prototype of the eucharistic wafer.[794] "Now the house of Israel called its name manna; it was like coriander seed, white, and the taste of it was like wafers made with honey."[795] The Manna was symbolized by the unleavened bread, matzo, *matsoth,* which, interestingly enough, simply means 'dehydrated,' and is cognate with the *mazones* of the Dionysiac feasts, which included dehydrated entheogenic mushrooms.[796] The word is related to *matzevot,* stones, used by the ancients, as in the *Epic of Gilgamesh* (p.82), to denote 'stoned' just the way we do today, and as a synonym for mushrooms, as the Aramaic *kepha* (stone) and *pitra* (mushroom). We also have Sumerian medical tablets from c.2250 BC which prescribe 'the manna-plant' in conjunction with fir and pine, indicating entheogenic mushrooms.[797] The ritual use of both matzo and the eucharist, of course, also give the impression of an entheogenic substitute.

Justin Martyr, in the *Dialogue with Trypho* (c.160), identified Christ as the same *Logos* of God that appeared to Moses as the burning bush: "In Canaan the prime oracular tree was the acacia - the 'burning bush'..."[798] (Graves) The memory of the ancient entheogenic ecstacy is there, but now the *pharmakon* must needs be symbolic, since the *pharmakos* must replace the Emperor in the worship, if the Church is to conquer the Empire. 'No Salvation outside the Church,' 'One God, One Bishop,' declared Ignatius, Clement, Irenaeus, Tertullian and every other Church father *ad nauseum.*[799] The magic was no longer in the entheogenic ecstacy induced by the fruit of Eileithyia, but in the political institution of the holy fathers. They insisted that God appeared on earth in Euhemerized form as Jesus and now worked as Holy Spirit *only* within the Church. That is, they insisted on *pistis,* 'faith,' a literal, unconscious adoration of the iconography, generally discarding *gnosis,* conscious mystic experience, as irrelevant, or at least esoteric, Hellenic antiquarianism.

Says the Bishop in the *Church Order* of Hippolytus of Rome, the oldest surviving record (c.230), and the model, of the Sunday celebration of the Eucharist: "We thank Thee, God, through Thy beloved Servant Jesus Christ whom in the last times thou hast sent us as Saviour and Redeemer and Messenger of thy counsel, the Logos who comes from Thee, through whom thou hast made all things, whom Thou wast pleased to send from heaven into the womb of the virgin, and in her body he became flesh and was shown forth as Thy Son, born of the Holy Spirit and the virgin....And when he delivered himself to a voluntary passion, to loose death and to break asunder the bands of the devil, and to trample hell and to enlighten the righteous and to set up the boundary stone and to manifest the resurrection, he took a loaf, gave thanks, and spake, 'Take, eat, this is my body which is given for you.' Likewise also the cup and said, 'This is my blood which is poured out for you. As often as you do this, you make my commemoration.'"

"Remembering therefore his death and resurrection, we offer to Thee the loaf and the cup and give thanks to Thee that Thou hast counted us worthy to stand before Thee and to do Thee priestly service./And we beseech Thee, that Thou send down Thy Holy Spirit upon this offering of the church. Unite it and grant to all saints who partake of it to their fulfilling with Holy Spirit, to their stengthening of faith in truth, that we may praise and glorify Thee through Thy Servant Jesus Christ, through whom to Thee be glory and honour in Thy holy church now and ever. Amen"[800]

"The fact that the Eucharist was also celebrated with water shows that the early Christians were mainly interested in the symbolism of the mysteries and not in the literal observance of the sacrament."[801] (Jung) The symbolic *pharmakon*, the bread and wine, the body and blood of *Soter* Jesus, *restitutor orbis*, bringer of the *saeculum novum*, is offered by the priest as a gift-sacrifice upon the altar, which, through the prayer of thanksgiving (*Eucharistia*), is filled with the Holy Spirit and symbolically shared by all.

The pagan gift-sacrifice to the image of Juppiter or the Emperor involved the actual killing of an animal, for which the symbolic body, the bread, and the symbolic blood, the wine, or water, were substituted; in this Christianity imitated the bloodless sacrifice of Demeter. Aside from this ritual difference, the Christian rite was identical to the gift-sacrifice of animal and wine consecrated by the image of the Imperial Saviour in an atmosphere perfumed by priestly benedictions and holy incense; even the Latin terminology was the same. *Jesus Invictus* meant to coopt Juppiter and Mithra and bury Demeter.

Athens elected Emperor Gallienus 'eponymous archon' and initiated him at Eleusis in 267. The contemporary Roman aurei show this fierce warrior as a veiled transvestite, *Galliena Augusta*, Shaman Son of the Virgin, an image that equated the ancient Holy Mother, and her

Eleusinian sacraments, with the government of Rome.[802] Given the choice, it's not hard to see why the *eidolon* of an *athanatos* prophet offering community and comfort was preferred by so many to the *eidolon* of a murderous Imperial landlord claiming to be *athanatos*. Many Gnostics, of course, found the dichotomy a false one, preferring *gnosis* to either kind of *eidololatreia*.

The Church, in these war-torn days, was penetrating the Empire politically. When Kabyle raiders made off with hundreds of Cyprian's flock near Carthage in 254, it was Cyprian, not the Empire, that ransomed them. At the episcopal council in Carthage in 256, eighty-seven bishoprics were represented.

Gallienus' father, Valerian, had reacted to his repeated losses to Parthia's King Shapur by unleashing as much irrational persecution of the Christians, and seizing as much Christian property as possible, apparently crediting the power of their prayers in the reverse. As the governor of Africa put it to Cyprian: "*qui Romanum religionem non colunt, debere Romanas caerimonias recognoscere.*"("who doesn't practice Roman religion, must acknowledge Roman ceremony.")[803] Cyprian, though he lost his life in Valerian's three-year terror, calmly responded that Valerian ought to be grateful for prayers to the 'one true God' rather than to some 'strange new god,' himself.[804] Valerian's capture and execution by Shapur in 260 was reckoned by Christians as his just deserts. His son Gallienus, a brilliant field general, wisely mollified his many Christian troops.

In general, Imperial persecution of Christians was disorganized, sporadic, half-hearted and reactive. For the most part Christians, a productive and increasingly influential lot, were left in peace. Christianity cherishes its martyrs, and incredibly courageous they were, but they were few and far between, and they taught Imperial Christianity nothing.[805]

The great Church issues of the third century, before the Church actually took power, were organizational and formulaic, not spiritual, as for instance the great debate between the bishops in 256 over the need to re-baptize those who had recanted during persecution. Cyprian of Carthage, Firmilian of Cappadocian Caesarea and other bishops influential at the Synod at Antioch argued that rebaptism was necessary to reinstill the Holy Spirit, which apparently left the body when an unkosher ritual, such as obeisance to the *eidolon* of the Emperor, was performed. To make his point, Firmilian mentioned the consecration of the Eucharist by a *woman*, who had baptized many according to the accepted rite: surely such an abomination required rebaptism! Stephen of Rome and the other conservatives held sway, insisting that the original baptism in infancy was good for life, but eventually compromised on a repeat baptism 'as a precaution.'[806]

The candidate for rebaptism must renounce Satan and then give his or her oath of allegiance (*sacramentum*) to Jesus by recitation of the creed. After the cleansing baptism and the receipt of the Holy Spirit from the hands of the bishop, the communicant could join in the Eucharist. The attitude revealed was in no way different than that of the Roman governor who insisted that all citizens *debere Romanas caerimonias recognoscere;* the only difference was the substitution of the *episkopos* and his *eidolon* for the Imperial governor and his. Imperial slave-state law remained unchallenged and unchanged.

The Church fathers went on at great length, with deadly seriousness, the control of whole sees at stake by majority vote, over iconic issues such as whether or not Jesus was three substances in one body or 'of the same substance.' Was He God manifest, did He suffer? Was He a man visited by a preexisting God, or was He an aspect of the preexisting God on a mission? 'Christology' occupied these enormously powerful politicians in their joust for control of Church machinery. There was bitter division over whether or not Jesus "ate and drank in a manner peculiar to himself and that the food did not pass through his body."[807] A few sincere souls really did care about an honest definition of Holy Spirit, but most could no more distiguish manipulative iconography and power politics from religion than Chaldean astrologers could distinguish astrology from astronomy.

When he took Antioch in 272 from Zenobia, Aurelian recognized "the bishops of the doctrine in Italy and Rome"as the legitimate owners of the property-holding corporation known as the See of Antioch, since the Bishop of Antioch, Paul, had been Zenobia's chief financial officer. The Church Synod of 268 found a theological way to support Aurelian. It excommunicated Zenobia's Paul for insisting that Christ was a prophet visited by a preexisting God (Adoptionist), not himself preexistent (Origenist); this was deemed 'Judaizing,' as indeed it was.[808] Control of Antioch went to the loyal Rome-Alexandria axis as soon as it came within Aurelian's grasp. The Church synods may have decided by majority vote, but it was most unwise to vote against the *consensus ecclesiae.* The literature produced by these men is nothing short of stultifying, a competition in conformity.

When he built his temple to *Sol Invictus* in 274, Aurelian declared December 25 *natalis Invicti*, the birthday of the Unconquerable, a national holy day. The winter solstice was the time, when the days started getting longer, that the Goddess gave birth the Sun, or the Son. Cybele, the only Oriental Goddess for whom Roman municipalities built temples, was celebrated March 15-27. The celebrations began with the *dies Sanguinis* in which Attis, the *phamakos*, was sacrificed, and then resurrected in the *Hilaria*. That was followed by the passage of the Great Mother to her *Lavatio*, the renewal of her virginity and power of procreation, over the flower-strewn streets.[809] It was, essentially, Aurelian's *Sol Invictus* that became the imperial *Jesus Invictus*, through the agency of Constantine.

During the chaotic civil war between Constantine, Galerius, Maxentius, Licinius and other generals for control of the Empire after the retirement of Diocletian, Diocletian's second-in-command, Galerius, in the East, instituted 'The Great Persecution' in an attempt to rally his forces behind Imperial Paganism.[810] In 304, just before Diocletian's official retirement, Galerius rammed through the famous Fourth Edict, demanding that all Christian men, women and children publicly sacrifice a small animal, offer libation and burn incense before an image of the Emperor or face death. Since *eidololatreia* was viewed by many with deadly serious awe, the edict meant Inquisition.

Many Gnostics, of course, simply went along with the public mummery and then returned to their *ekstasis*, untouched by outward forms. This attitude infuriated the Orthodox Christians, who regarded them as traitors to Holy Mother Church. The official exemption of the Jews from the requirement of sacrifice, recognizing, as usual, their traditional licit nonconformity, also, as usual, infuriated the Christians.[811] The Imperial government well understood that the universalistic, internationally-organized Christians were a threat to the Imperial religion in a way that the nationalistic, aniconic Jews never could be. Heralds called everyone to the temples while soldiers used the tax rolls to register compliance to the order to sacrifice. But so much of the Empire had already become Christian that the strategy backfired, causing a groundswell of support for Constantine in the West.

By 310 Constantine controlled the mints at London, Trier and Lyon, striking tens of thousands of folles marked *Soli Invicto Comiti*, 'The Unconquered Sun My Companion.' This is Constantine's first conversion, identifying him with the *Sol Invictus* of Aurelian and the Apollonian heraldry of the old Flavian dynasty of Vespasian, Titus and Domitian, from which he had just discovered his descent. It was Vespasian and Titus, in 70 CE, who had destroyed Jerusalem.

In 311 Galerius repealed the Fourth Edict after he was persuaded, probably by his pro-Christian wife Valeria, that his severe illness was the vengeance of the Christian God. A few days after issuing the 'Edict of Toleration' Galerius died, ending the Great Persecution on a suitably mystic note. The whole thing cost less than 3500 lives throughout the Empire, and was great only in its political consequences.[812]

In his battle with that son of Roma, Maxentius, for control of Italy, Constantine actively sought the support of Italy's numerous Christians, the Sun evolving into a political symbol of Christ, the solar lion now accompanied by a Greek Cross, a plus sign in which all the arms are of equal length. The Greek Cross is an archetypal symbol recurring throughout the Paleo-Neolithic remains. It was used to represent the stars of heaven at Catal Huyuk and on the body of Hathor, also in Native American pictographs. A beautiful solid marble Greek Cross, above, almost 9 inches high, representing the celestial body of the Goddess, was the central feature of the Shrine of the Snake Goddess found at Knossos. It is also, of course, a basic element of most originary alphabets.[813] The power of this archetypal imagery is awesome. It is unconsciously rooted in the feminine.

Immediately after his victory in Rome, Constantine ordered all provincial finance officers to give to the Catholic Church whatever monies it might need. Constantine eventually organized the return of all confiscated Church and private Christian property, indemnifying those who had bought confiscated property out of public funds. Licinius, from Nicomedia near Byzantium, contested control of the

Empire with Constantine, finally losing the long civil war in 324.

Constantine converted Byzantium into Constantinople, the New Rome, ruled by bishops professing allegiance to the unifying creed of the Council of Nicaea, 325: "We believe in one God, the Father All-sovereign, maker of all things visible and invisible. And in one Lord Jesus Christ, the Son of God, begotten of the Fatherly, only begotten, that is from the substance of the Father. God of God, Light of Light, true God of true God, begotten, not made, of one substance with the Father, through whom all things were made, things in heaven and things on earth: who for us men and for our salvation, came down and was made flesh, and became man, suffered, and rose on the third day, ascended into the heavens; is coming to judge the living and the dead. And in the Holy Spirit. And those who say, 'There was when he was not,' and 'Before he was begotten he was not,' or those that allege, that the son of God is 'of another substance or essence,' or 'created,' or 'changeable,' or 'alterable,' these the Catholic and Apostolic Church anathematizes."[814] 'Anathema' often included judicial torture and execution. A simplified form of this, the 'Nicene or Apostles' Creed,' became the canonical assertion of what 'I believe.'

The unity of the Church, said Constantine repeatedly, was the guarantee of the prosperity of the Empire he ruled with power that came directly *ek Theou*, 'from God,'[815] part of the pregnant phrase used to describe the Divine Augustus in Egypt, *Theou ek Theou*.[816] Constantine claimed, like Diocletian, and *Jesus Invictus*, to be *Parens Aurei Saeculi*, Father of the Golden Age. His figure, bedecked in gold-embroidered *purpura*, sometimes wearing a jeweled flower garland, a diadem, image of the ennobling entheogen, holding the eagle-topped sceptre, was approachable in the *nimbus* of his *sacrum palatium* only in the position of *proskynesis*, not only kneeling in *adoratio*, but kissing the corner of his robe. This regal figure appeared on the coinage. These unrepublican images and ceremonies, instituted by Diocletian, were inherited from the vanquished Persian autocrats.

Like his predecessor Diocletian, Constantine was a book burner. The Gnostic and alchemical treatises were a special target of both.[817] Much is made of the difference between the 'pagan' Diocletian and the 'Christian' Constantine, but they burned the same books and enslaved the same people.

Like Diocletian, Constantine's imperial title of address was *Dominus*, Lord; he was *Pontifex Maximus*, chief priest, God's Vicar, a title that derived from the Roman keeper of the Capitoline Trinity of Juppiter, Juno and Minerva. That title devolved to the Pope in time, the 'Chief Pontiff.' The imperial council, mostly powerful generals, became the *consilia sacra,* below which served the *duces* and *comites,* dukes and counts. Correspondence became *sacrae litterae* and *theia epistole.* Laws, written in gold on purple paper, became *sacrae constitutiones. Moneta* was *sacra,* even Constantine's rooms were *sacri cubiculi.*[818] During his thirty-year anniversary, celebrated in Jerusalem with Eusebius, the cleric hailed the Emperor as "imitator and representative on earth of the Divine Word himself,"ruling as "vice-gerent of God."[819] His coinage shows the chi-rho, the first two letters in *Christos,* destroying paganism, aptly depicted as a snake.[820]

By recognizing the reality of the culture, and the army, which had become Christian, Constantine was enabled to leave Imperial ritual and law, including the laws relating to Emperor-worship ('vice-gerant of God'), slavery, penal servitude, confiscatory taxation and torture, completely untouched. In this he won the wholehearted support of the bishops of the Church, whom he released from all taxation and encouraged to go into business. Constantine's bishops achieved civil powers equal to governors on the Imperial investiture of the Church.

Church organization, which effectively spanned the entire Empire, had been a positive inspiration to the Imperial bureaucracy, so Constantine coopted the vast Church machinery by conferring judicial powers on it, putting Church courts on a par with civil courts. The result was that ecclesiastical ordinance had the force of civil law, which wasn't really that much of an innovation. Cicero had said that there were no private unrecognized worships, sanction being given only to civic rites in temples or recognized groves or to family rites.[821] Legal worship was thus sanctity, *sanctitas,* and sanction, *sanctio,* at the same time, just as *sacramentum* was either legal escrow or a compact with the gods. Unsanctioned worship, *sacrilegium,* 'sorcery and heresy,' were, as they had always been, equated with high treason, *maiestas,* the punishment for which was death and confiscation of all property, much of which flowed into the Church's hands.

50-60% of Constantine's subjects were slaves or indentured serfs.[822] Most of the rest were debt-ridden smallholders. Control of rural land was about equally divided between the aristocrats, the Empire and the Church, and all ran their great estates with equal ruthlessness, despite the occasional pious exhortation. Magnificent churches were built with public funds in key cities throughout the Empire, with the bishops left in control of enormous annual subsidies and bequests. Constantine gleefully encouraged the destruction of priceless ancient temples such as that of Asclepius in Agis in Cilicia and Venus Ourania near Mount Lebanon, turning the plundered wealth over to the Church. Clerics were allowed to use the Imperial carriage system just as if they were government officials.

Under Constantine's son, Constantius, who closed all pagan temples in 356, the Church was given a fixed portion of the confiscatory taxes in kind (*anonna*). These were so severe that they caused open rebellion in many parts of the Empire: "the insensate extortion of the tax-collectors...brought him more hatred than money," wrote one contemporary.[823]

In 380 Emperor Theodosius (379-395) declared a position halfway between 'same' and 'like' to be "the form of religion handed down by the apostle Peter to the Romans"; all other positions were "heretical poison."[824] As the list of proscribed philosophies grew longer, inquisitors were organized into strike forces, and a large class of professional bounty hunters, *delatores*, 'denouncers,' were encouraged to help the official secret police. They got 25% of the take.

Gratian (375-383), in the Western half of the Empire, supported Theodosius in the East. The most famous Western victim of this early Inquisition was an aristocratic Galician bishop named Priscillian. He was a charismatic Gnostic-Manichaean who threw the power elite of Spain into an uproar with his enthusiasm for mystic rites, spontaneous prophesy, nude prayer and talk of a 'one-horned Christ.'[825] The Gallic and Spanish bishops appealed to the new Western Emperor, Gratian's killer, an 'orthodox Nicene' soldier named Magnus Maximus, who obligingly executed 'the sorcerer' and six of his fellow nude dancers in 386, by way of a demonstration of piety.

In 392, when he gained control of both halves of the Empire, Theodosius issued an official proscription of paganism, forbidding anyone anywhere, even in private, to practice the ancient religion. Possession of the ancient sacraments, of course, was de facto proof of illegal worship, that is, treason. Landowners, bailiffs and tenants were held responsible for any heretical activity that took place on their lands.

'Saint' Augustine's (354-430) vast preserve, ruled from the great Roman port of Hippo Regius, Algeria, contained five large church complexes scattered among the villages. Augustine's own church complex, overlooking the harbor, was in the residential suburbs of the great nobles and merchants who ran the town.[826]

Like the senators he socialized with, Augustine thought slavery was just dandy, as 'divinely ordained' as marriage: "The prime cause of slavery, then, is sin, so that man was put under man in a state of bondage; and this can be only by a judgement of God, in whom there is no unrighteousness, and who knows how to assign divers punishments according to the deserts of the sinners....Yet slavery as a punishment is also ordained by that law which bids us to preserve the natural order and forbids us to disturb it; for if nothing had been done contrary to that law, there would have been nothing requiring the check of punishment by slavery."[827] As Paul put it: "Every person must submit to the authorities in power, for all authority comes from God."[828]

Augustine was one of the tiny minority of rulers of grain-, grape- and olive-rich Roman Numidia who had no direct contact with the land. The overwhelming majority of serfs and slaves were subjected to such regular starvation and brutality that revolt was an endemic problem for the elite.[829] 'Gardening,' for Augustine, was just 'bracing exercise,' not the brutal ordeal of the field hands.[830]

Augustine's first major appointment, in 382, was as the professor of rhetoric for the city of Milan, then the seat of the Imperial Court. His duty was to deliver the official panegyrics on the Emperor and the consuls of the year. That is, he was Minister of Propaganda. He was appointed by Symmachus, Prefect of Rome and former Carthaginian Proconsul, cousin of Augustine's mentor, Milan's former civil governor Ambrose, Bishop of Milan, a Roman lawyer.[831]

Augustine was surrounded by aristocratic Roman lawyers. They linked political radicalism, challenging the *potestas* of the state, to heresy, so that heresy, challenging the *auctoritas* of the Church, which sanctioned the power of the state, became a form of political radicalism.[832] Both heresy and radicalism, therefore, hindered the Church from saving the human race, "conceived in iniquity,"and so deserved what they got from the state, death.

This, of course, is simply traditional Roman law, in which Augustine had been trained before he took up rhetoric. Grace in communion within the Church alone can overcome the 'great sin,' because "humanity itself must be treated like an invalid, that is, with authority (*auctoritas*)."[833] Augustine placed his faith in *eruditio, admonitio* and *disciplina*, teaching, warning and punishment.[834] These traditional Roman ideas were first outlined in Christian terminology by Bishop Irenaeus in *Adversus omnes haeresus* two hundred years before and simply embellished, *ad nauseum*, by Augustine. *Qui Romanum religionem non colunt, debere Romanas caerimonias recognoscere.*

When he returned to North Africa from Milan, Augustine founded a monastery. It had seemed a logical step to quite a few members of the dreaded secret police to become Augustinian monks in the service of the great North African landlords.[835] These monks became Roman Africa's bishops in time. As a great landlord and magistrate himself, Augustine worried about "rural audacity contrary to apostolic discipline."[836] He equated the populist Donatist Christian rebels who threatened his domain with "Heretics, Jews and pagans - they have come to form a unity over and against our Unity."[837]

The Edict of Unity, 405, legally branded the Donatists as 'heretics.' The Donatists were a 'Church of Judas,' bound only by the 'original taint' of their founders, and as such Augustine helped in their judicial execution.[838] "The mass of men keep their heart in their eyes, not in their heart. If blood comes spurting out of the flesh of a mortal man, anyone who sees it is disgusted; but if souls lopped off from the peace of Christ die in this sacrilege of schism or heresy...a death that is more terrifying and more tragic, indeed, I say plainly, a more true death than any other - it is laughed at, out of force of habit."[839]

Augustine is the father of the medieval Inquisition, insisting that it is better to burn to death in this world than to burn eternally in the next. The Imperial Edict he lobbied for in 408 is virtually word for word Augustinian 'theology,' although written by his friend the Emperor's lawyers: "Assuredly that force of evil, which mingles together the human with the divine, deceives very many people with evil persuasion, and impels them to their ruin, in the present life and in the future....the Donatists, who are also called Montenses, the Manichaeans, the Priscillianists, and the Gentiles, and also the Heaven-fearers [converts to Judaism] shall be absolutely forbidden to hold feasts or carry out any cult in honor of a sacrilegeous rite in abominable places. Furthermore, we grant the local bishops the competence to prohibit all these through the ecclesiastical authority."[840]

Bishop Augustine had a great deal of human blood on his hands, although he preferred forced conversion to the last resort of execution. As Luke himself said,[841] 'compel people to come in': "No one is indeed to be compelled to embrace the faith against his will; but by the severity, or one might rather say, by the mercy of God, it is common for treachery to be chastised by the scourge of tribulation...for no one can do well unless he has deliberately chosen, and unless he has loved what is in free will; but the fear of punishment keeps evil desire from escaping beyond the bounds of thought."[842] "Let constraint be found outside; it is inside that the will is born." "For the rod has its own kind of charity."[843] This fascist crap has been peddled as great theology for centuries.

The high school history texts say Augustine is famous for his profound discussion of 'free will,' that is, for his confused, *ad hoc* insistence that we both do and don't have it: "...the woman would not have believed the serpent spoke the truth, nor would the man have preferred the request of his wife to the command of God. The wicked deed, then - that is to say the transgression of eating the forbidden fruit - was committed by persons who were already wicked."[844] "And thus, from the bad use of free will, there originated that whole train of evil which, with its concatenation of miseries, convoys the human race from its depraved origin, as from a corrupt root, on to the destruction of the second death, which has no end, those only being excepted who are freed by the grace of God."[845] The 'predestined elect' were so often, of course, the aristocratic rulers of the *laoi*.[846]

Augustine's mentor, the aristocratic Roman lawyer Ambrose, the Bishop of Milan, also insisted on rote conformity, dutiful tax remittance and acceptance of enslavement as the road to divine grace. Like Augustine, he backed up his theology with ruthless judicial murder. Bishop Ambrose is also a 'saint,' remembered for bravely defending the right of his see to burn down the local synagogue, against Emperor Theodosius' insistence that it be rebuilt (388).

Augustine had no Hebrew but based his entire philosophy on the Hebrew Bible, or at least on his fanciful interpretation of the Latin, the one language he had. In *Contra Judaeos* he saw the Jews as Cain (how original! what a theologian!), and explained that the greats of the Bible, Moses, David, Elijah and Isaiah were really part of the 'true Israel,' Christians, a Pauline commonplace set down by Justin in 155 (*First Apology*) and parroted by every Christian 'thinker' ever since, in relation to all those, before Jesus, who followed the divine *Logos*. "Isaac's words are law and prophesy: even by the mouth of a Jew Christ is blessed by prophesy through one who knows not, because the prophesy itself is not understood."[847]

'History,' for Augustine, was a solipsistic fairytale: "Moreover, how much wisdom could there be in Egypt before Isis, whom the Egyptians thought fit after her death to worship as a great goddess, gave them letters? Now Isis is said to have been the daughter of Inachus, who became the first king of the Argives at a time when we find that Abraham already had grandsons sprung from him."[848]

Wrote the extraordinary aristocrat Julian of Eclanum to Bishop Augustine: "You ask me why I would not consent to the idea that there is a sin that is part of human nature? I answer: it is improbable, it is untrue; it is unjust and impious; it makes it seem as if the Devil were the maker of men. It violates and destroys the freedom of the will...by saying that men are so incapable of virtue, that in the very wombs of their mothers they are filled with bygone sins....what is as disgusting as it is blasphemous, this view of yours fastens, as its most conclusive proof, on the common decency by which we cover our genitals."[849]

Despite his horror of 'genitals' in the Garden, Augustine was capable of prolix spiritual masturbation. Since his demonology became the theoretical basis of the medieval Inquisition, which itself is the basis of our wildly unempirical contemporary drug laws, Augustine is the original Harry Anslinger:

"Because of the demands of their detestable superstitions, their Elect are required to eat a sort of eucharist sprinkled with human seed. They claim the divine essence may be liberated from that just as it is from other foods of which they partake. They deny they do this, claiming that is a practice of the Manichaeans....They gather their sacramental flour by sprinkling it beneath a couple in sexual intercourse, which they commingle with their seed."

"Surely they use the same holy books as do the Manichaeans, books which describe the diabolical transformation of males into females and females into males. Thus, through their concupiscence, the powers of the princes of darkness of both sexes are released to pollute the world. This is the source of the obscene practices which some of the Manichaeans refuse to admit pertain to them. They imagine they are imitating higher powers when they attempt to purge a part of their god, which they truly believe is held befouled just as much in human seed as it is in all celestial and terrestrial bodies, and in the seeds of all things. And for this reason, it follows that they are just as much obliged to purge it from human seed by eating, as they are in reference to other seed which they consume in their food. This is the reason they are called Catharists, that is, Purifiers, for they are so attentive to purifying this part that they do not refrain even from so horrifying food as this."[850] So much for Demeter's *Panspermia*. "The Greek classics, I abominated. Not one word did I understand."[851] I don't doubt it for a moment.

Augustine was canonical to Emperor Honorius in the West and Theodosius II (408-450) in the East, as he was to Justinian, thus his 'reasoning' and language became enshrined in Western law. Justinian's Code (529-534), the *Corpus Iuris Civilis*, incorporated the *Codex Theodosianus* in its reorganization of Roman law going back to the Divine Hadrian. It was adopted as canonical 'ancient law' by Western Europe's Church-State in the twelfth century, and became the basis of the legal system of all European countries.[852] It insisted that "priesthood and empire" were "the twin gifts of God"ordained for the Emperor to manage, and that "all roads that lead to error were to be closed."[853]

Contemporary American inquisitors, heirs of Cotton Mather and Harry Anslinger, would deny that their attitude is theological or inquisitorial; the fact that their law is identical to the *Codex Theodosianus* (438) is just coincidence: "The rest, however, whom We adjudge demented and insane, shall sustain the infamy of heretical dogmas, their meeting places shall not receive the name of churches, and they shall be smitten first by divine vengeance and secondly by the retribution of Our own initiative, which we shall assume in accordance with the divine judgement....We determine that to these, indeed, that is the Manichaeans, Borborits and pagans, as well as the Samaritans, Montanists, Tascodrogits and Ophyts, all testimony as well as all other legal actions are prohibited." That is, my opinion of my sacraments is legally irrelevant, since they are deemed demented and insane and therefore subject to *prohibitio*; *all evidence to the contrary shall be inadmissable* and I shall be smitten with retribution at the State's initiative; that is *de facto* contemporary American law.

Religio meant the canonical Christian religion and its canonical sacraments; all others were *superstitio*, and "every superstition must be entirely uprooted."Justinian's Code prescribes confiscation of property and death by torture for soothsaying, sorcery, magic, divining, heresy, poisoning, unnatural lusts, adultery, Christian conversion to Judaism and many other kinds of nonconformity, on grounds of *maiestas*, treason.[854] The legal definitions of these heinous crimes were left to the churchmen. Trial by jury disappeared. Marriage between Christian and Jew was defined as adultery. Using the ancient herbal sacraments was, of course, deemed to be 'poisoning' or 'sorcery,' the punishment for which was the same as for adultery - forfeiture of all property, torture and death.[855] Today it's just forfeiture of all property and an agonizing prison term.

Both Justinian's *Corpus* of laws and *Digest* of opinions go on at length 'Concerning Torture' and 'On Punishments.' They became the model of the *Malleus Maleficarum*, the official handbook of torture of the medieval Inquisition. Burning alive or the forced drinking of boiling oil or molten lead replaced the traditional Roman crucifixion and branding on the face - far more Christian, obviously.

As *honestiores* themselves, the churchmen, even if they broke the law, weren't subject to torture, but the testimony of the vast bulk of the population, *humiliores*, wasn't valid in capital cases, or against *honestiores*, without torture. This 'legal principle' degenerated into indiscriminate torture for many minor offenses. The methods employed included the rack, which tore the joints apart, the *lignum*, which pulled the legs apart, the *ungulae*, which ripped the flesh, the *mala mansio*, a metal body-suit, the bodily insertion of red hot metal, slow strangulation, and, as the *Digest* put it, "castigation with rods, scourging, and blows with chains."[856] The only thing Christian martyrdom taught Imperial Christianity was methodology. "We call heretic everyone who is not devoted to the Catholic Church and to our Orthodox and holy Faith."[857] The Inquisition had begun.[85]

By Justinian's time (527-565), episcopal sees coincided with civil territories, the bishop of a rich see earning as much as the procurator. The personal wealth of the Church patriarchs, who controlled whole industries, was rivalled only by the richest senators. The patriarchs were those bishops that controlled the great see of an imperial territory: Alexandria controlled Egypt and Cyrenaica; Jerusalem controlled Palestine; Antioch controlled Syria; Constantinople controlled Asia Minor, Thrace and Greece; and Rome controlled Western Europe. Some of Justinian's favorite bishops and troops are pictured with him below in the famous mosaic on the wall of the church of San Vitale that he built in Ravenna, Italy, c.547. The Archangel Michael, opposite, dates to the same time. Above is Justinian's wife, Empress Theodora, offering a gilded communion.

The Roman and Alexandrian sees tried to break the power of Constantinople by attacking the orthodoxy of its bishops. To actually follow the 'theological' arguments in detail is both nauseating and stultifying, since behind them the most grotesque hypocrisy was at work: "begotten, unbegotten, preexistent, sole from sole, perfect from perfect, like in all respects, in all things, of the same substance, individualities, hypostases, manifestations," blah, blah, blah.

In a savage battle for control of vast wealth and influence, council after high council condemned one or another clerical politician for incorrectly using one pin-headed term after another. Whole sees actually depended on the difference between *homoousios* and *homoiousios*, 'of the same substance' and 'like in substance.' The dueling clerics actually divided into the *homoousian* party and the *homoiousian* party and fought it out for decades.

Apollinaris of Laodicea, in 375, was concerned to stress that Christ, God, could not possibly have had a human mind, "a prey to filthy thoughts, but existing as a divine mind, immutable and heavenly."[859] Someone noticed that this radical *homoousian* position made Mary redundant, so Apollinaris was condemned. Mary, of course, despite all those children, was 'perpetually Virgin.' By Justinian's time the Church had made enormous theological progress: "The Word in the last times, having himself clothed with flesh his hypostasis [reality] and his nature, which existed before his human nature, and which, before all the worlds, were without human nature, hypostasized human nature into his own hypostasis."[860]

GNOSIS

Eusebius, Constantine's court theologian, explained Gnosticism this way: "These claimed to transmit Simon's magic arts, not secretly like Basilides but quite openly, as if this was something marvelous, preening themselves as it were on the spells which they cast by sorcery, on dream-bringing familiar spirits, and on other goings-on of the same sort. In keeping with this they teach that all the vilest things must be done by those who intend to go through with their initiation into the 'mysteries'or rather abominations, for in no other way can they escape the 'cosmic rulers'than by rendering to them all the due performance of unspeakable rites."[861]

The virtually canonical Bishop Irenaeus, writing in Lyon c.180, complained that they "put forth their own compositions....They really have no gospel which is not full of blasphemy. For what they have published....is totally unlike what has been handed down to us from the apostles....Let those persons who blaspheme the Creator...as [do] the Valentinians and the falsely so-called 'Gnostics,' be recognized as agents of Satan by all who worship God. Through their agency Satan even now...has been seen to speak against God, that God who has prepared eternal fire for every kind of apostasy."[862]

Clement, third Bishop of Rome, put it succinctly in the oldest Orthodox Christian document outside the canon, *Clement's First Letter*, c.96 CE: "Those, therefore, who act in any way at variance with His will, suffer the penalty of death. You see, brothers, the more knowledge we are given, the greater risks we run."[863]

The Church organized the Imperial murder of many leading Gnostics and the systematic destruction of nearly all their writings. The lost Gnostic writings were known only by their titles and distorted legend for the better part of two millennia, but by a spectacular archeological miracle fifty-two Gnostic texts, thirty of them complete and unknown except by legend, were rediscovered on leather-bound papyrus scrolls in 1945 at Nag Hammadi in central Egypt. They were written in Coptic, phonetic Egyptian, Greek transliterations of the original Greek.

The scrolls had been buried in jars, about 370 CE, in meditation caves, obviously in fear of their discovery. Since there was no war going on at the time, it is assumed that the regular authorities were involved. In his Easter letter of 367, the supreme regular authority, Archbishop Athanasius of Alexandria, condemned heretics and their "apocryphal books to which they attribute antiquity and give the name of saints."[864] That, of course, is a perfect description of the Nag Hammadi texts, many of which are copies of works hundreds of years older.

The care with which the Nag Hammadi texts were copied and bound indicates that they were canonical to the copyists. As Abbot Shenoute of Panopolis near Nag Hammadi put it about forty years later, to a group of 'kingless' Gnostics who worshipped the 'demiurge' at the nearby temple of Nuit using 'books full of abomination' and 'every kind of magic,' refusing to acknowledge Archbishop Cyril, Patriarch of Alexandria, as their 'illuminator': "I shall make you acknowledge ... the Archbishop Cyril, or else the sword will wipe out most of you, and moreover those of you who are spared will go into exile."[865]

Cyril, of course, had his text: "A good many of those who formerly practiced magic collected their books and burnt them publicly, and when the total value was reckoned up it came to fifty thousand pieces of silver. In such ways the word of the Lord showed its power, spreading more and more widely and effectively."[866]

The ancient world's greatest collector of magical books was Ptolemy III of Egypt (246-221 BC). He had the profound insight to order all travelers who disembarked at Alexandria to deposit any books in their possession at the Royal Library for copying, the traveller then receiving the copy, the Library keeping the original. This rule applied even to official state copies of classical tragedies from Athens, the Library preferring to forfeit the large pledge rather than part with the original. The Royal Library, thus, over the course of hundreds of years, became the greatest library in the world, possessed of hundreds of thousands of priceless volumes, easily the greatest cultural treasure of the ancient world.

The Ptolemies made this vast treasure available to the scholars studying at or visiting the Museum. These included Erasistratos (medicine), Theocritus (poetry), Euclid (geometry), Archimedes (mathematical physics), Ctesibius (mechanics), Eratosthenes (mathematical geography), Callimachus (poetry), Apollonius (mathematical astronomy), Apollonius Rhodius (poetry), Herophilus (anatomy and pharmacology), Hero (mechanical physics), Aristarchus (astronomy), Hipparchus (astronomy) and Strato (physics, natural science).

Erasistratos discovered the valves of the heart, the nervous system, peristalsis and the capillary system. Eratosthenes calculated the circumference of the earth to within an error of less than one percent.

Hero invented the steam engine and the mechanical windmill. Hipparchus invented trigonometry. Ctesibius invented the force pump and the constant-head water-clock. Aristarchus of Samos propounded an accurate picture of the heliocentric universe nineteen centuries before Copernicus. Euclid, of course, and Archimedes virtually invented geometry and physics, or, at least, are the effective vehicles for the transmission of the technical tradition they inherited at Alexandria and Syracuse.

Zenobia, in a bid for Christian and Egyptian support in her fight with Aurelian, incinerated most of the work of these seminal geniuses when she sacked the Royal Library. Alexandria's Christian authorities, shortly after the Nag Hammadi texts were buried, destroyed most of what remained. Nothing at all survives from Ctesibius, Aristarchus, Herophilus, Erasistratos, Strato, and many of the legendary predecessors of Euclid and Archimedes, and only fragments survive from most of the others. We know of them from surviving writers like Aristotle, Theophrastus, Galen and Ptolemy.

It took human culture more than a millennium to recover the science burned at the Museum, and most of the poetry, drama and mythology, the spectacular genius of Classical Greece, including most of Aristotle's huge library, is lost forever. Imagine having the books used by Aristotle. We have about a tenth of the plays of Aischylos, Sophokles and Euripides, and they're nearly all masterpieces.[867]

In 391 Archbishop Theophilus of Alexandria and his strong-arm monks destroyed the Sarapeum, the ancient chapels and equally ancient library of Ausar Hapi, Sarapis, who was the Bull Osiris (Apis) in the Underworld. Ptolemy I had combined Sarapis with Zeus to form a Gnostic psychopomp.[868] Theophilus' orchestrated riot was also used to burn more of the Royal Library.

In 415 Archbishop Cyril of Alexandria arranged the savage murder of Hypatia by a mob led by his Nitrian monks. She was the daughter of Theon, a legendary philosopher and mathematician who "interpreted astronomical works, and the writings of Hermes Trismegistus and Orpheus."[869] Hypatia was reputed, by her student Synesius of Cyrene, Bishop of Ptolemais, to be the greatest astronomer and mathematician alive. Her murder had precisley the effect Cyril intended; the best of the remaining scholars at the Museum left Alexandria, never to return. We know Hypatia only by legend because 'the city of the orthodox' coordinated the destruction of all her writings, along with numerous other legendary, and popular, Hermetic and alchemical tracts.

In 431 Archbishop Cyril of Alexandria allied himself with Rome and the sees of Asia Minor to secure the condemnation of the Patriarch of Constantinople, Nestorius, in the Council of Ephesus. The issue was Nestorius' condemnation of the popular term 'Mother of God'(*Theotokos* - 'God-bearer') as applied to Mary. Nestorius became 'the new Judas' and Constantinople went to an ally of Cyril. The Church, Roman or Greek, reserved the powerful image of the Holy Virgin Mother for its own use, even against its own.

A century later Justinian's spectacular cathedrals of Hagia Sophia ('Holy Wisdom') in Constantinople and San Vitale in Ravenna depicted the Emperor and Empress under the guardianship of the *Theotokos*. Justinian declared Cyril of Alexandria to be "the almost absolute *regula fidei* ('rule of faith') in christological matters."[870]

It is no coincidence that Imperial Christian culture produced no geniuses on the level of Sappho, Pythagoras, Euripides, Hippokrates or Plato, iconoclastic shamans all, for whom Eleusis and any great library were holy places. Eleusis, after 2000 years of continuous existence, was destroyed in 396 by Alaric the Goth and his Christian monks, "who in their dark garments entered with him unhindered."[871]

Theodosius banned the Olympiad in 393. Under Justinian, pagans and Jews weren't even allowed to teach. He closed Plato's Academy in Athens in 529 and ordered all pagans to convert. At the Second Council of Constantinople, in 691, it was decided that the wine treaders, who wore the traditional masks of satyrs and sileni as they pressed the grapes, should be unmasked, and prohibited from calling out the name 'Dionysos!'[872]

In 250 Origen pointed out that the eclipse in Matthew at the time of the Crucifixion, the day before a full moon, couldn't have happened; in 400 Augustine replied that the very impossibility was proof of a miracle. The relics of martyrs were held to replace herbs in medicine as Constantine's mother Helena discovered 'the true cross' on her visit to Jerusalem, near the defunct Temple of Aphrodite.

For Sappho, of course, the most famous poet of the Ionian renaissance, Aphrodite was far from defunct: "Leave Crete and come to this holy temple/where the pleasant grove of apple trees/circles an altar smoking with frankincense./Here roses leave shadow on the ground/ and cold springs babble through apple branches/where shuddering leaves pour down profound sleep./In our meadow where horses graze/and wild flowers of spring blossom,/anise shoots fill the air with aroma./And here, Queen Aphrodite, pour/heavenly nectar into gold cups/and fill them gracefully with sudden joy."[873]

Sappho's overtly pharmaco-shamanic writings were ordered burned in 380 by Archbishop Gregory of Constantinople. The Joy of Aphrodite's Heavenly Nectar wasn't what Gregory was peddling, though I certainly would like a cup. Sappho of the Ionian island of Lesbos was born about 612 BC. She is mentioned with the utmost respect by Plato ('the beautiful Sappho'), Herodotus, Pausanias, Strabo ('a marvel'), Aristotle, Plutarch ('what charm the songs of Sappho have to hold the listeners spellbound'), Cicero, Lucian ('Sappho gave us refinement'), Philostratos and many others. Plutarch: "And Sappho's words are truly mixed with fire, and through her songs she brings out her heart's warmth, and according to Philoxenos heals the pain of love with the sweet-voiced Muse." Plato called her 'the Tenth Muse.' She was as widely read as Plato, but, since a genuine Maenad, far less friendly to Orthodox mind games than the Athenian word-meister. Thanks to Archbishop Gregory, only four or five of her 500 poems survive to bear witness to Sappho's sacraments.

A 'sacramental' issue to the Orthodox Church, with which it struggled, was put by the powerful Syrian monk Barsumas in c.440: "If the nature of the blood of the crucified only Son had been the same nature as the blood of the sons of Adam, how could it have expiated the sins of the sons of Adam?"[874] The murderous Cyril of Alexandria, the most powerful cleric of that generation, sort of agreed that Christ "being as God life-giving by nature, when he became one with his own flesh he made that flesh life-giving....; through the bloodless sacrifice of the Eucharist we are being made the partakers of the holy flesh and precious blood of Christ, the Saviour of us all."[875]

The meaning and function of the sacraments was precisely the issue between Pythagoras (fl.550 BC), who studied among the Jews and the Egyptians, and the traditional meat-eating Greeks. "The Daktyls of Crete, the initiates of Idaean Zeus...initiated Pythagoras into the thunder-rites of the Idaean cave. If Picus the Bird-King was of their company, small wonder that he could make and unmake the thunder."[876]

The difference between the 'thunder-rites,' the 'bloodless sacrifices' and 'sober offerings,' the *nephalia* shared with Demeter and Aphrodite at Eleusis, and the bloody hecatombs offered to Zeus was recognized by the Greeks to be historical and profound. It was expressed in sacramental terms understood to represent shamanic and historical realities. The significance of the sacraments was also the issue between the Essenes and their more worldly brethren; likewise the issue between the Gnostics and the Orthodox Christians.

For many Gnostics, Jesus' blood was more like Aphrodite's Heavenly Nectar, conceived of the Spirit of God, which is, and always has been, female in Hebrew, as in Genesis: "And the Spirit of God moved upon the face of the waters." Yahweh is the Son of Iahu, the Exalted Dove, who is the daughter of Tiamat, the originary creative waters.[877] The Gnostic Sophia had a lot of Aphrodite, 'risen from sea-foam,' the fish, the unconscious, in her. The Church adopted the archetypal image of the fish as a symbol of baptism and coopted a Gnostic acrostic of Jesus' name which matched the Greek for fish (*ichthys*), but changed the originary feminine meaning to stress the masculine nature of *spiritus* and the Trinity; it was all Solar.

The Quaternity so many of the Gnostics insisted on included the awesome Moon Mother of the Mysteries, whose womb is the sea we swim in. She is the mother of the *pharmakos* in the *liknon*, the mother of the evolved body, instinct. As *The Gospel of Philip* put it: "Some said, 'Mary conceived by the holy spirit.' They are in error. They do not know what they are saying. When did a woman ever conceive by a woman?" The medieval alchemists, who traced their roots to the Gnostics, called her water *succus lunariae*, 'the sap of the moon plant.'[878] This obvious code was understood by many, as was the importance of control of the iconography; the Cross, after all, is an archetypal image of the Goddess, Quaternity, extrapolated from her ancient wheel of life. The Theban sacramental vase above dates to 700 BC.

The Pythagoreans insisted that the soul was a square, not a triangle. Jung points to the reliance of the medieval alchemists on the same symbolism, the quaternity as the symbol of wholeness. "The motif of the double quaternity, the ogdoad, is associated in shamanism with the world-tree: the cosmic tree with eight branches was planted simultaneously with the creation of the first shaman. The eight branches correspond to the eight great gods."[879] Jung stresses that the human mind naturally forms quaternites, such as the four points of the compass, the four elements, the four prime qualities, the four colors, the four quarters of heaven, and that trinities are artificial confabulations of quaternities. As the *Viatorium spagyricum* put it, "All things do live in the three, but in the four they merry be."[880] That fourth was the Mother of God, and the Gnostics insisted that the fruit of her Tree brought forth a *return* to Eden, not expulsion from it.

Despite the best efforts of the canonical fascists, an alternative discussion of 'sober offerings' survived, by the grace of the miracle at Nag Hammadi, to let a genuine shaman have her or his say. Our copy of the astonishing *On the Origin of the World* dates to just before its burial at Nag Hammadi, although the original may be hundreds of years older:

"The tree of *gnosis* has the strength of God. It glows like the moon, and its magical fruit is sweet, like dates. And this tree is to the North of Paradise, so that it might arouse the souls from the torpor of the demons, in order that they might approach the tree of life and eat of its fruit and so condemn the authorities and their angels."

"A droplet of light fell from Sophia's hands onto the waters, immediately producing an androgynous human being. Sophia formed it first into a woman, but an andogynous woman, called Hermaphrodites by the Greeks. Her Mother is called Eve of Life by the Hebrews. She is the female instructor of life. Her progeny is the creature that is called lord. But the authorities called it 'Beast,' so as to tarnish its reputation among their modelled creatures. But 'the beast' is really 'the instructor,' the wisest of all beings."

"Sophia sent her daughter Life, called Eve, to teach Adam, who was soulless, how to become a container of light. Eve felt compassion for Adam, exhorting him to 'Arise! Become a container of light upon the Earth!' Her Word became reality, as Adam opened his eyes to the

Light of Life. He looked upon Eve, telling her, 'You shall be called "Mother of the Living." For it is you who have given me life.'"

"The authorities resolved to rape this luminous woman so as to destroy her power. But Eve laughed. She became one with the tree of *gnosis*. They pursued her in vain, realizing her power had enabled her to become one with the tree. They panicked in their blindness and ran. Then the wisest creature of all, called Beast, came. Addressing the image of their mother Eve, he said to her, 'What did God say to you? Was it "do not eat from the tree of *gnosis*?"' She said, 'He said "Not only do not eat from it, but do not touch it, lest you die."' The Beast then said, 'Don't be afraid. You will not die, but come to life. When you eat from the Tree of Life, your intellect will become sober and you will become like gods, able to see the difference between evil people and good ones. Indeed, it was in jealousy of His power that he said this to you, so that you would be afraid to partake.'"[881]

The authorities surrounded the Tree of Life with fearsome Cherubim and flaming swords, so that all would be afraid to taste the fruit of *gnosis*, now subject to *prohibitio*, as so clearly explained by this brilliant shaman, floating, as they said, on "the cold, flowing waters of the Lake of *Mnemosyne*." One 13th century Gnostic-Christian fresco, above, from Plaincouralt Chapel, pictures Eve, her hands cupped over her womb, with a snake's tail, standing next to a giant *Amanita muscaria*, speckled cap and all, around which curls the sacred snake.[882]

In the Gnostic-Christian frescoes discovered in 1919 in the Tomb of the Aurelii in Rome, dating to c.230 CE, the snake, curled around the Tree of Life, is portrayed the same way, with its mouth open, in the attitude of an instructor. The fifth century BC Greek illustration above, of their Holy Trinity, also portrays the snake as the pharmaco-shamanic instructor.[883] The fourth el;ement in the Trinity, of course, is the snake itself. Canonical Christian tradition projects a different image, "offering them the bitter and evil poison of the serpent, the prince of apostasy"- both evil and masculine.[884]

The snake-women often had an equal place as 'instructor' among the Gnostics, who were very clear about the psycho-spiritual meaning of woman in the pantheon: "She is the Conceiver of all gods and all lords; she is the Gnosis of all invisibles. Thy Image is the mother of all Uncontainables and the power of all Impassables....Praise to Thee, for ever and ever, O Thou Alone-begotten One. Amen."[885]

"And the arrogant ruler cursed the woman....And what she had made became a product in the matter, like an aborted fetus. And it assumed a plastic form molded out of shadow, and became an arrogant beast resembling a lion....'It is I who am God, and there is none other apart from me....If any other thing exists before me, let it become visible to me!' And immediately Sophia stretched forth her finger and introduced light into matter..."[886]

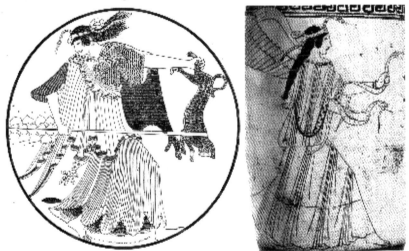

Sophia, of course, is Korykia, the Snake-Bird Goddess, originary ecstatic creativity, which so many Gnostic texts display. But, as they say, she is heretical to the arrogant ruler: Paul: "Their role is to learn, listening quietly and with due submission. I do not permit women to teach or dictate to the men; they should keep quiet. For Adam was created first, and Eve afterwards; moreover it was not Adam who was deceived; it was the woman who, yielding to deception, fell into sin."[887]

That is the aborted fetus talking, the plastic lion, doing what Romans did best, 'dividing and conquering,' fixating not on hermaphro-ditic *ekstasis* but on sexual domination, cursing the ingestion of the entheogenic fruit, cursing the sacred marriage which gives birth to *gnosis*:

"Her lover secretly fetched it for her. He pressed it to her mouth as if it were food, applying the word as medicine to her eyes so that she could see with her mind. She understood her roots and her ancestry. She cleaved to the tree of her origins, so that she might renounce the material world. She reclined on her marriage bed. She ate the ambro-sia, the immortal food she hungered for. She found what she searched for. She found rest from her quest in the everlasting light. To the light belongs the power and the glory of revelation lasting for ever and ever. Amen."[888]

This, from Nag Hammandi, is a clear and literal description of the *hieros gamos*, the sacred marriage, the imbibing of the 'immortal food' leading to the epiphany of Eleusis. Persephone's bridegroom is Aidoneus, Dionysos, Hermes Psychopompos, known as Hermes Trismegistos, Thrice-Great, in the Hellenistic world; he carried magi-cal plants, or their symbol, the snake-staff, the Kerykeion.

Western alchemy was born with such as Harpocration of Alexan-dria, fl.c.160 CE, and Zosimos of Panopolis, c.300, who wrote that Hermes Trismegistos "overpowered me and pierced me through with the sword, and dismembered me in accordance with the rule of har-mony. And he drew off the skin of my head with the sword he was holding, and mingled the bones with the pieces of flesh, and caused them to be burned with the fire that he held in his hand, till I per-ceived by the transformation of the body that I had become spirit....the man of copper...you will not find as a man of copper; for he has changed the color of his nature and become a man of silver. If you wish, after a little time you will have him as a man of gold."[889]

Bodily dissolution and reassemblage in the fire, of course, is traditional shamanic imagery. "But if the mysteries are necessary, it is all the more important that everybody should possess a book of chemistry, which should not be hidden away," wrote Zosimos to Theosebia, the great Syrian priestess.[890]

The late medieval alchemists, who gave birth to the Renaissance, derived their Mercurius from Hermes Trismegistos. The *serpens mercurialis*, the 'mercurial serpent,' was "consubstantial with the parental hermaphrodite." The Hermaphrodite, Hermes-Aphrodite, was the symbol of the sacred marriage between the conscious mind and the mammalian unconscious, and of the androgynous power that invoked. Melusina or Lilith, the serpent or owl who inhabited the shamanistic tree, was Mercurius. The 'medicine to make her see with her mind' was called *spiritus vegetativus, medicina catholica,* and *alexipharmakon.* The 'fire that he held in his hand' was called *ignis mercurialis:* "Take the fire, or quicklime, of which the philosophers speak, which grows on trees, for in that [fire] God himself burns with divine love," wrote one alchemist in 1678.[891]

The Alexandrian world, in its many editions of the *Book of the Dead,* identified Hermes with Thoth, the traditional Egyptian scribe of the Gods. As the heart of the deceased was weighed in the Hall of Osiris, Thoth's baboon, sitting on the balance beam, announced the results to the Ibis-headed 'Measurer.'[892] Thoth was often pictured as the baboon himself, the Beast, the instructor, *phosphoros,* 'light-bringer.'

The Ring of Nestor, p.101, c.1400 BC, has Thoth's function performed by an enthroned Griffin, a winged, hawk-headed lion, another transformation beast.[893] "For the transformation leads from the depths to the heights, from the bestially archaic and infantile to the mystical *homo maximus*."[894] That is, it is primal therapy. Thoth, holding the Kerykeion, was the Egyptian Asklepios. Incubation, primal therapy, was practiced at Thoth's ancient center of Hermopolis: "O Thoth, heal me as thou didst heal thyself."[895]

Paracelsus: "A snake which gets wounded heals itself. Why? Man also seeks his healing in herbs and stones. From where does he have the reason and art? Out of the brutish kind, for that reason he seeks it. If now this is done by the snake, do not be astonished for you are the snake's son. Your father does it, and you inherit his capacity; the snake is a doctor, and therefore you, in a brutish sense, are also a doctor....Now as the snake knows her help and knows the herb, there is also such an understanding in you, that you shall know by the same spirit which teaches the snake and is a brutish spirit and belongs to the brutes. Therefore do not be astonished that the snake knows medicine. She has had it for a longer time than you, and you have had it from her; for you are made out of the matter of brutish nature, and therefore both of you are equal."[896]

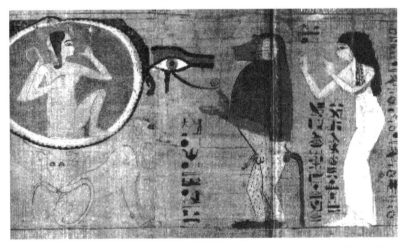

Bishop Hippolytus of Rome, c.230 CE, says that the Gnostics are called 'snake seers,' *Naassenes*. "These say that the serpent is the moist element, as Thales of Miletus also said, and that nothing which exists, whether immortal or mortal, animate or inanimate, could exist without it. They say too that all things are subject to her, that she is good and has something of everything in herself as in the horn of the one-horned bull." Like the 'one-horned Christ,' therefore, the serpent is a cure-all, the *pharmakon* that brings all things to maturity and perfection. Hippolytus says that the power of the snake is in all things and that all temples were named after her (*naous apo tou naas*: a play on the words *naas*:serpent, *naos*:temple).[897] The serpent is the embodiment of the life force in Kundalini yoga. In the myth of Glaukos it is the female serpent who reveals the herb of resurrection.

The Gnostics outraged the canonical fascists by handing 'the cups to women!' and inviting them to prophesy.[898] "Celsus [c.178]," wrote Origen in *Contra Celsum*, c.248, "knows also of Marcellians who follow Marcellina, and Harpocratians who follow Salome, and others who follow Mariamme, and others who follow Martha." "Indeed," snarled Origen, "of the Pythian priestess - the oracle that seems to be more distinguished than the others - it is related that while the prophetess of Apollo is sitting at the mouth of the Castalian cave she receives a spirit through her womb; after being filled with this she utters oracular sayings, supposed to be sacred and divine. Consider, then, whether this does not indicate the impure and foul nature of that spirit in that it enters the soul of the prophetess, not by open and invisible pores which are far purer than the womb, but through the latter part which it would be wrong for a self-controlled and sensible man to look upon or, I might add, even to touch."[899]

The profoundly influential Origen castrated himself early in life, so obviously he had no wife, but did he have a mother? Tertullian referred to a woman teacher of religion as 'that viper,' insisting that "It is not permitted for a woman to speak in the church....nor to claim for herself a share in any masculine function - not to mention any priestly office."[900]

The very real religio-political issue for the Gnostic shamans was the choice between Quaternity or Trinity, Holy Mother or Holy Father, Ecstacy or Supplication, Freedom or Guilt. Historically, Original Sin won. Christian orthodoxy was born inquisitorially, as a function of the Roman world, and compulsively builds social infantility - a communally sanctioned scapegoat reinforcing fear of pharmacoshamanism - into its basic texts. Just as the *Uraeus*, the enraged cobra poised to strike, was an inverted shamanic image used as an hypnotic threat by Pharoah, so the image of a crucified shaman was used by Constantine. Jesus' demonized double, Judas/Dionysos, was both subliminally and overtly - legally - pharmaco-shamanic.

Today's hysterical drug propaganda is permeated with these inculcated fears. Fear, of course, is the very last thing in the world the heroic Joshua wanted to inculcate. The very function of the shaman is psychotherapeutic, release from fear, breaking the evil spell of subjugation. That, of course, is precisely why the Essene Zealot Joshua was executed in the first place. The *Essenes*, the 'Drones,' knew precisely who the *Melissai*, the 'Bees,' were, and paid them the respect that was due the prophetic Honey Priestesses of the ancient world.

The interpretation of the Holy Ghost as Sophia became heretical precisely because Sophia's image evoked the memory of the ancient herbal magic - the familial, bare naked, time-is-no-object tribalism. The inquisitorial process, historically, has played out as cultural geno-cide aimed at the tribal objects of enslavement, precisely because tribal shamans remember what industrial slavers want forgotten. Jah's warriors remember the Shaman Queen of Sheba.

The Drug War, in America, didn't begin with Nixon and the de-monized alkaloids. It began with the slavers, with the Portugese and the Spanish and their demonized tribal sacraments, centuries before the invention of alkaloids. The great psycho-legal trick of the indus-trial fascists has been their successful confusion of the safe sacramen-tal herbs with the dangerous refined alkaloids. The unavailability of the herb popularizes the alkaloid, thereby criminalizing Native cul-ture and strengthening the military fascists that control the trade in the alkaloids. Until Pizarro spitted Incan culture on the sharp edge of his superior wisdom, Mama Coca was their Supreme Deity. The De-ity was named after the Herb that was, and still is, the premier sacra-ment, medicine and health food of the culture.

Psychologically, institutionalized cultural genocide is enforced am-nesia. Forgetting Sophia, as the Gnostic shamans repeatedly insisted, is like forgetting your Mother. Our conscious lives may be ones of sanctioned industrial conformity, but our dreams still perform their ancient Paleolithic function. We still talk to ourselves in primal pic-tures every night, as we swim ecstatically in Aphrodite's ocean. We still awaken with the taste of her Nectar in our mouths, spellbound by the power of our own automatic creativity, as we reach for our morning brew.

BIBLIOGRAPHY

Abel,Ernest L.:*Marihuana*:Plenum Press,1980

Achterberg,Jeanne:1:*Imagery In Healing*:New Science Library ,1985
2:*Woman As Healer*:Shambhala,1990

Aeschylus:*Collected Works*:Herbert Weir Smyth,tr.,Harvard
University Press,1922

Allegro,John:1:*The Sacred Mushroom and The Cross*:Doubleday
& Company,1970
2:*The Dead Sea Scrolls*:Penguin Books,1964

AMA:*The American Medical Association Encyclopedia of Medicine*:
Random House,1989

Anderson,Edgar:*Plants,Man & Life*:University of California
Press,1969

Andrews,George & Solomon,David:*The Coca Leaf And Cocaine
Papers*:Harcourt Brace Jovanovich,1975

Apollodorus:*The Library*:Sir J.G.Frazer,tr.,Harvard University
Press,1921

Apollonius Rhodius:*The Argonautica*:R.C.Seaton,tr.,G.P.Putnam's
Sons,1921

Ardrey,Robert:1:*African Genesis*:Dell Publishing Co.,1961
2:*The Territorial Imperative*:Dell Publishing Co.,1966
3:*The Social Contract*:Dell Publishing Co.,1970

Aristotle:*The Athenian Constitution*:P.J.Rhodes,tr.,Penguin
Books,1984

Arms,Suzanne:*Immaculate Deception*:Bantam Books,1977

Artaud,Antonin:1:*Artaud Anthology*:City Lights Books,1965
2:*The Peyote Dance*:Helen Weaver,tr.:Farrar,Strauss and
Giroux,1976
3:*The Theater and its Double*:Grove Press,1958

Ashley,Richard:*Cocaine*:St.Martin's Press,1975

Athanassakis,Apostolos N.:*The Homeric Hymns*:The Johns
Hopkins University Press,1976

Augustine,Saint:*The City of God Against The Pagans*:David
S.Wiesen,tr.,Harvard University Press,1968

The Badianus Manuscript:Emily Walcott Emmart,tr.,The Johns
Hopkins Press,1940

Bailyn,Bernard,et al:*The Great Republic*:D.C.Heath and
Company,1977

Bakalar,James B. & Grinspoon,Lester:*Drug Control In A Free
Society*: Cambridge University Press,1988

Barber,Elizabeth Wayland:*Women's Work*:W.W.Norton & Company,1994

Barnstone,Willis:*Sappho*:New York University Press,1965

Barrett,Leonard:*The Rastafarians*:Beacon Press,1977

Beowulf:Michael Alexander,tr.,Penguin Books,1973

Boardman,John, Griffin,Jasper & Murray,Oswyn:1:*Greece and the Hellenistic World*:Oxford University Press,1989
2:*The Roman World*:Oxford University Press,1989

Bonomi,Joseph:*Ninevah And Its Palaces*:George Bell And Sons,1875

Bordin,Ruth:*Woman and Temperance*:Temple University Press,1981

Bourke,John Gregory:*On the Border with Crook*:Charles Scribner's Sons,1891

Brecher,Edward M.,ed.:*Licit & Illicit Drugs*:Little,Brown and Company,1972

Broun,Heywood & Leech,Margaret:*Anthony Comstock*:Albert & Charles Boni,1927

Brown,Dee:*Bury My Heart At Wounded Knee*:Henry Holt and Company,1970

Brown,Peter:*Augustine of Hippo*:Faber & Faber,1967

Brunton,T.Lauder:*Pharmacology,Therapeutics and Materia Medica*: Lea Brothers & Co.,1889

Budge,E.A. Wallis:1:*The Mummy*:Collier Macmillan Publishers,1974
2:*The Egyptian Book Of The Dead*:Dover Publications, 1967
3:*Egyptian Magic*:Dover Publications,1971
4:*The Divine Origin Of The Craft Of The Herbalist*:Culpeper House,1928

Burroughs,William & Ginsberg,Allen:*The Yaje Letters*:City Lights Books,1971

Buschor,Ernst:*Greek Vase-Painting*:E.P.Dutton,1910

CAH:*The Cambridge Ancient History*:The Cambridge University Press
1:1:*Prolegomena and Prehistory*
1:2:*Early History of the Middle East*
2:1:*The Middle East and the Aegean Region, c.1800-1380 BC*
2:2:*The Middle East and the Aegean Region, c.1380-1000 BC*
3:1:*The Prehistory of the Balkans, The Middle East and the Aegean*
3:3:*Expansion of the Greek World,Eighth to Sixth Centuries BC*
4:*The Persian Empire and the West*
5:*Athens: 478-401 BC*
6:*Macedon: 401-301 BC*
7:1:*The Hellenistic World*
8:*Rome and the Mediterranean, 218-133 BC*

9:*The Roman Republic, 133-44 BC*
10:*The Augustan Empire, 44 BC-AD 70*
11:*The Imperial Peace, AD 70-192*
12:*The Imperial Crisis and Recovery, AD 193-324*

Cantor,Norman F.:*The Civilization of the Middle Ages*:Harper Collins Publishers,1993

Carter,Howard:*The Tomb of Tutankhamen*:E.P. Dutton & Co., 1972

Carthy,J.D. & Ebling,F.J.,eds.:*The Natural History of Aggression*: Academic Press,1964

Churchland,Patricia Smith:*Neurophilosophy*:The MIT Press,1989

Clark,W.E.LeGros:*History of the Primates*:The University of Chicago Press,1965

Cockburn,Leslie:*Out of Control*:The Atlantic Monthly Press,1987

Cocteau,Jean:*Opium*:Peter Owen Ltd.,1968

Cohn,Norman:*Europe's Inner Demons*:Basic Books,1975

Cook,Arthur Bernard:*Zeus*:Cambridge University Press,1925

Copenhaver,Brian P.:*Hermetica*:Cambridge University Press,1992

Coulter,Harris L.:*Divided Legacy*:Wehawken Book Co.,1975

Coulter,Merle C. & Dittmer,Howard J.:*The Story Of The Plant Kingdom*:The University of Chicago Press,1972

The Creel Report:Da Capo Press,1972

Crystal,David:*The Cambridge Encyclopedia of Language*:Cambridge University Press,1987

Cultural Survival:*Coca and Cocaine*:Cultural Survival,1986

Cumont,Franz:*The Mysteries of Mithra*:Dover Publications,1956

Daniel,Glyn:*The First Civilizations*:Thomas Y.Crowell Company,1968

Darrow,Clarence & Yarros,Victor S.:*The Prohibition Mania*:Boni and Liveright,1927

Dart,Raymond A.:*Adventures With The Missing Link*:The Institutes Press,1967

Dartmouth:*The Dartmouth Bible*:Houghton Mifflin Company,1961

Davies,David:*The Centenarians Of The Andes*:Anchor Press,1975

DeKorne,Jim:*Psychedelic Shamanism*:Loompanics Unlimited,1994

Deno,Richard A., Rowe,Thomas D., Brodie,Donald C.:*The Profession of Pharmacy*: J.P. Lippincott Company,1966

Detienne,Marcel and Vernant,Jean-Pierre:*The Cuisine Of Sacrifice Among The Greeks*:The University of Chicago Press,1989

Dio Cassius:*Dio's Roman History*:Earnest Cary,tr.,MacMillan Company,1914

The Dispensatory of the United States of America,13th Edition:J.B. Lippincott And Co.,1874

The Dispensatory of the United States of America,20th Edition:J.B. Lippincott Company,1918

Dobkin de Rios,Marlene:*Visionary Vine*:Waveland Press,1984

Dodds,E.R.:1:*The Greeks and the Irrational*:University of California Press,1951
2:*Pagan And Christian In An Age Of Anxiety*:W.W.Norton & Company,1965

Drake,William Daniel Jr.:*The Connoisseur's Handbook of Marijuana*: Straight Arrow Books,1971

Dubois,W.E.B.:*The Suppression of the African Slave Trade to the U.S.A., 1638-1870*:Dover Publications,1970

Duke,Steven B. & Gross,Albert C.:*America's Longest War*:G.P.Putnam's Sons,1993

Eisler,Riane:*The Chalice & the Blade*:Harper & Row,1987

Eliade,Mircea:*Shamanism*:Princeton University Press,1974

Ellis,William T.:*Billy Sunday*:The John C.Winston Co.,1914

Ellul,Jacques:*Propaganda*:Random House,1973

Engelmann,Larry:*Intemperance*:The Free Press,1979

Epstein,Edward Jay:*Agency Of Fear*:G.P.Putnam's Sons,1977

Erman,Adolf,ed.:*The Ancient Egyptians*:Harper & Row,1966

Euripides:*Collected Works*:Arthur S.Way,tr.,Harvard University Press,1912

Euripides:*The Bacchae*:Michael Cacoyannis,tr.,New American Library,1982

Eusebius:*The History of the Church*:G.A.Williamson,tr.,Dorset Press,1965

Evans,Sir Arthur:1:*The Palace Of Minos At Knossos*:4 Volumes: Macmillan and Co.,1921
5:*Mycenaean Tree And Pillar Cult*,Macmillan and Co.,1901

Evans-Wentz,W.Y.:*The Tibetan Book Of The Dead*:OxfordUniversity Press,1968

Farnell,Lewis Richard:*The Cults Of The Greek States*:5Volumes: Clarendon Press, 1896-1909

Finegan,Jack:*Light From The Ancient Past*:Princeton University Press,1959

Fleming,Paula Richardson & Luskey,Judith:*The North American Indians*:Dorset Press,1986

Fontenrose,Joseph:*The Delphic Oracle*:University of California Press,1978

Forbes,Thomas R.:*The Midwife and the Witch*:Yale University Press,1966

Fort,Charles F.:*Medical Economy During The Middle Ages*:Augustus
    M.Kelley,1973
Fowden,Garth:*The Egyptian Hermes*:Princeton University Press,1986
Frazier,Jack:*The Marijuana Farmers*:Solar Age Press,1974
Frend,W.H.C.:1:*The Rise of Christianity*:Fortress Press,1984
    2:*Martyrdom and Persecution in the Early Church*:New York
    University Press,1967
    3:*Religion Popular and Unpopular in the Early Christian
    Centuries*: Variorum Reprints, 1976
    4:*The Early Church*:Fortress Press,1982
Freud,Sigmund:*Cocaine Papers*:Robert Byck,ed.,Stonehill Publishing
    Company,1974
Friedman,Milton & Szasz,Thomas S.:*On Liberty And Drugs*:The Drug
    Policy Foundation Press,1992
Furnas,J.C.:*The Late Demon Rum*:G.P.Putnam's Sons,1965
Furst,Peter:1:*Hallucinogens and Culture*:Chandler & Sharp
    Publishers,1988
    2:*Mushrooms*:Chelsea House Publishers,1986
Gaskell,G.A.:*Dictionary Of All Scriptures And Myths*:The Julian
    Press,1973
Gaskin,Stephen:*Jurisdictional Statement*:The Farm,1973
Gelb,I.J.:*A Study of Writing*:The University of Chicago Press,1963
Gervais,C.H.:*The Rumrunners*:Firefly Books,1980
Gibson,J.C.L.:*Canaanite Myths And Legends*:T.&T.Clark,1978
Gimbutas,Marija:1:*The Goddesses and Gods Of Old Europe*:University
    of California Press,1982
    2:*The Language Of The Goddess*:Harper Collins Publishers,1989
    3:*The Civilization Of The Goddess*:Harper Collins
    Publishers,1991
Ginsberg,Allen:*Allen Verbatim*:Gordon Ball,ed.,McGraw-Hill Book
    Company,1974
Goldman,Eric F.:*Rendezvous With Destiny*:Vintage Books,1956
Gordon,Cyrus H.:1:*The Common Background of Greek and Hebrew
    Civilization*:W.W.Norton & Company,1965
    2:*Ugarit And Minoan Crete*:W.W.Norton,1966
Goshen,Charles E.:*Drinks,Drugs,and Do-Gooders*;The Free Press,1973
Goodall,Jane:*In The Shadow Of Man*:Houghton Mifflin Company,1988
Graves,Robert:1:*The Greek Myths*,George Braziller,Inc.,1959
    2:*The White Goddess*:Vintage Books,1959
    3:*Apuleius' The Golden Ass*:Farrar,Strauss & Giroux,1951
The Great Geographical Atlas:Rand McNally:1989

Grieve,M.:*A Modern Herbal*:Dover Publications,1971

Griggs,Barbara:*Green Pharmacy*:The Viking Press,1981

Grinspoon,Lester:1:*Marihuana Reconsidered*:Harvard University Press,1971

2:& Bakalar,James B.:*Psychedelic Drugs Reconsidered*:Basic Books,1979

Grossinger,Richard:1:*Planet Medicine*:Anchor Books,1980

2:*Embryogenesis*:North Atlantic Books,1986

Guignebert,Charles:*The Jewish World in the Time of Jesus*:University Books,1965

Haard,Richard & Karen:1:*Poisonous & Hallucinogenic Mushrooms*:Cloudburst Press,1975

2:*Foraging for Edible Wild Mushrooms*:Cloudburst Press,1974

Haggard,Howard W.:*Devils,Drugs and Doctors*:Halcyon House,1929

Haller,John S.Jr.:*American Medicine in Transition,1840-1910*:University of Illinois Press,1981

Hand,Wayland D.,ed.:*American Folk Medicine:A Symposium*: University Of California Press,1976

Harner,Michael J.:1:*The Jivaro*:Anchor Books,1973

2:ed.:*Hallucinogens and Shamanism*:Oxford University Press,1973

3:*The Way of the Shaman*:Bantam Books,1986

Harris,Bob:*Growing Wild Mushrooms*:Wingbow Press,1976

Harrison,Jane Ellen:1:*Prolegomena to the Study of Greek Religion*: Cambridge University Press,1903

2:*Epilegomena to the Study of Greek Religion*:Cambridge University Press,1921

3:*Themis*:Cambridge University Press,1912

Hass,Hans:*The Human Animal*:Dell Publishing Co.,1970

Hawkes,Jacquetta:*The Atlas of Early Man*:St.Martin's Press,1993

Hawkins,Gerald S.:*Stonehenge Decoded*:Dell Publishing Co.,1965

Heidel,Alexander:*The Gilgamesh Epic and Old Testament Parallels*: Univ. of Chicago Press,1946

Helmer,John:*Drugs and Minority Oppression*:The Seabury Press,1975

Herer,Jack:*The Emperor Wears No Clothes*:Hemp Publishing,1993

Herman,Edward S.:*The Real Terror Network*:South End Press,1982

Herodotus:*The History*:David Grene,tr.,The University of Chicago Press,1987

Hesiod:*The Collected Works,The Homeric Hymns and Homerica*: Hugh G.Evelyn-White,tr.,G.P.Putnam's Sons,1914

High Times:1:*High Times Greatest Hits*:St. Martin's Press,1994

2:*High Times Encyclopedia*:Stonehill Publishing Company,1978

Hill,G.F.:*Illustrations Of School Classics*:Macmillan and Co.,1903

Hoffer,A. & Osmond,H.:*The Hallucinogens*:Academic Press,1967

Hoffman,Abbie with Silvers,Jonathan:*Steal This Urine Test*:Penguin Books,1987

Hofmann,Albert:*LSD,My Problem Child*:J.P.Tarcher,1983

Hogshire,Jim:*Opium for the Masses*:Loompanics Unlimited,1994

Holbrook,Stewart H.:*The Golden Age of Quackery*:The Macmillan Company,1959

The Holy Bible:King James Version:Tyndale House Publishers,1979

The Holy Bible:Revised Standard Version:Meridian,1974

Homer:1:*The Iliad*:Richmond Lattimore,tr.,The University of Chicago Press,1967

2:*The Odyssey*,Robert Fitzgerald,tr.,Doubleday and Company, 1963

Howell,F.Clark & Bourliere,Francois,eds.:*African Ecology And Human Evolution*:Aldine Publishing Company,1966

Hughes,Muriel Joy:*Women Healers in Medieval Life and Literature*:Books For Libraries Press,1968

Huxley,Aldous:*The Doors of Perception*:Harper & Row,1954

Hyams,Edward:*Dionysus*:The Macmillan Company,1965

Inglis,Brian:*The Forbidden Game*:Charles Scribner's Sons,1975

James,Wharton:*Learning from the Indians*:Running Press,1974

Jastrow,Morris:*The Civilization Of Babylonia And Assyria*:J.B.Lippincott Company,1915

Jayne,Walter Addison:*The Healing Gods of Ancient Civilizations*: University Books,1962

Josephson,Emanuel:*Merchants in Medicine*:Chedney Press,1941

Josephus:1:*The Essential Writings*:Paul L. Maier,tr.,Kregel Publications,1988

2:*The Jewish War*:Penguin Books,1967

Jung,C.G.:*The Collected Works*:Princeton University Press,1956

5:*Symbols Of Transformation*

8:*The Structure And Dynamics Of The Psyche*

10:*Civilization In Transition*

11:*Psychology And Religion:West And East*

12:*Psychology And Alchemy*

13:*Alchemical Studies*

14:*Mysterium Coniunctionis*

15:*The Spirit In Man,Art,And Literature*

Kahin,George McTurnan, & Lewis,John W.:*The United States In*

Vietnam:Dell Publishing Co.,1969

Kaplan,John:*Marijuana-The New Prohibition*:Thomas Y.Crowell Company,1975

Karlsen,Carol F.:*The Devil in the Shape of a Woman*:W.W.Norton,1987

Karnow,Stanley:*Vietnam*:The Viking Press,1983

Kennedy,David M.:*Birth Control In America*:Yale University Press,1976

Kennedy,Jospeh:*Coca Exotica*:Fairleigh Dickinson Univ. Press,1985

Kerenyi,Karl:1:*Dionysos*:Princeton University Press,1976

    2:*Asklepios*:Pantheon Books,1959

    3:*Eleusis*:Pantheon Books,1967

    4:*Prometheus*:Thames And Hudson,1963

    5:*The Religion Of The Greeks And Romans*:E.P.Dutton & Co.,1962

    6:*Athene*:Spring Publications,1978

    7:*Hermes*:Spring Publications,1976

Kerr,K.Austin:*Organized For Prohibition*:Yale University Press,1985

King,Rufus:*The Drug Hang-Up*:W.W. Norton & Company,1972

Kluver,Heinrich:*Mescal And Mechanisms Of Hallucinations*:The University of Chicago Press,1971

Kramer,Samuel Noah:1:*The Sumerians*:The University of Chicago Press,1963

    2:*Sumerian Mythology*:Harper & Row,1961

Krauss,Melvyn B. & Lazear,Edward P.:*Searching For Alternatives*: Hoover Institution Press,1991

Krippner,Stanley & Rubin,Daniel:*The Kirlian Aura*:Anchor Books,1974

Krout,John Allen:*The Origins of Prohibition*:Alfred A. Knopf,1925

LaBarre,Weston:*The Peyote Cult*:Archon Books,1975

Lader,Lawrence:*The Margaret Sanger Story*:Doubleday Company, 1955

Lajoux,Jean-Dominique:*The Rock Paintings of Tassili*:Thames and Hudson,1963

Landels,J.G.:*Engineering in the Ancient World*:University of California Press,1978

Lane,Earle:*Electrophotography*:And/Or Press,1975

Latimer,Dean & Goldberg,Jeff:*Flowers in the Blood*:Franklin Watts,1981

Lea,Henry Charles:*The Inquisition*:Russell & Russell,1958

Leakey,L.S.B.:*Adam's Ancestors*:Harper & Row,1960

Leaney,A.R.C.:*The Jewish And Christian World, 200 BC To AD 200*: Cambridge University Press,1984

Leary,Timothy, Metzner,Ralph, Alpert,Richard:*The Psychedelic Experience*:University Books,1964

Levy,G.Rachel:*Religious Conceptions of the Stone Age*:Harper & Row, 1963

Linder,Amnon:*The Jews In Roman Imperial Legislation*:Wayne
     State University Press,1987
Lindesmith,Alfred R.:*Addiction And Opiates*:Aldine Publishing
     Company,1968
Loehr,Franklin:*The Power Of Prayer On Plants*:New American
     Library,1959
Long,James W.:*The Essential Guide To Prescription Drugs*: Harper &
     Row,1977
Lorenz,Konrad Z.:*King Solomon's Ring*:Thomas Y. Crowell Company,
     1952
Lyons,Albert S. & Petrucelli,Joseph R.:*Medicine*:Abradale Press, 1987
The Mabinogion:Jeffrey Gantz,tr.,Penguin Books,1976
Maccoby,Hyam:1:*Revolution in Judaea*:Orbach and Chambers,1973
     2:*The Sacred Executioner*:Thames and Hudson,1982
     3:*The Myth-Maker*:Harper Collins Publishers,1987
     4:*Judas Iscariot and the Myth of Jewish Evil*:The Free Press,1992
MacMullen,Ramsay:*Paganism in the Roman Empire*:Yale University
     Press,1981
Mainage,Th.:*Les Religions De La Préhistoire:L'Age Paléolithique*:
     Desclée,De Brouwer & Cie.,1921
The Malleus Maleficarum Of Heinrich Kramer and James Sprenger:Dover
     Publications,1971
Mangelsdorf,Paul C.:*Corn*:Harvard University Press,1974
Marks,Geoffrey and Beatty,William K.:*The Story of Medicine in
     America*:Charles Scribner's Sons,1973
Marshack,Alexander:*The Roots Of Civilization*:McGraw-Hill Book
     Company,1972
Maspero,G.:*The Dawn Of Civilization*:Society For Promoting
     Christian Knowledge,1901
McKenna,Terence:1:*Food Of The Gods*:Bantam Books,1993
     2:*The Archaic Revival*:Harper Collins Publishers,1991
McCoy,Alfred W.:*The Politics of Heroin in Southeast Asia*:Harper &
     Row,1972
McIlvaine,Charles & Macadam,Robert K.:*One Thousand American
     Fungi*:Dover Publications,1973
Mead,G.R.S.:1:*Fragments of a Faith Forgotten*:University Books,1960
     2:*Apollonius of Tyana*:University Books,1966
Meek,Theophile James:*Hebrew Origins*:Harper & Row,1960
Mellaart,James:1:*Catal Huyuk*:McGraw-Hill Book Company,1967
     2:*Earliest Civilizations of the Near East*:McGraw-Hill Book
     Company,1965

Mertz,Henriette:*Pale Ink*:The Swallow Press,1972

Merz,Charles:*The Dry Decade*:Doubleday,Duran & Co.,1931

Mezzrow,Mezz & Wolfe,Bernard:*Really the Blues*:Doubleday & Company,1972

Mikuriya,Tod H.,ed.:*Marijuana:Medical Papers*:Medi-Comp Press,1973

Millspaugh,Charles R.:*American Medicinal Plants*:Dover Publications, 1974

Milt,Harry:*The Revised Basic Handbook on Alcoholism*:Scientific Aids Publications,1977

Minucius,Marcus:*The Octavius*:G.W.Clarke,tr.,Newman Press,1974

The Mishnah:Jacob Neusner,tr.,Yale University Press,1988

Mizruchi,Ephraim H.,ed.:*The Substance of Sociology*:Meredith Corporation,1973

Morales,Edmundo:*Cocaine*:The University of Arizona Press,1989

Moran,William L.:*The Amarna Letters*:The Johns Hopkins University Press,1992

Morgan,Lewis H.:*Ancient Society*:Harvard University Press,1878

Morris,Desmond:*The Naked Ape*:Dell Publishing Co.,1973

Mortimer,W.Golden:*History Of Coca*:And/Or Press,1974

Murray,Margaret A.:1:*The God of the Witches*:Oxford University Press,1970

2:*The Witch-Cult in Western Europe*:Oxford University Press,1971

Musto,David F.:*The American Disease*:Yale University Press,1973

Myerhoff,Barbara G.:*Peyote Hunt*:Cornell University Press,1976

Nadelmann,Ethan A.:*Cops Across Borders*:The Pennsylvania State University Press,1993

National Formulary XIV:American Pharmaceutical Association,1975

Neihardt,John G.:1:*Black Elk Speaks*:University of Nebraska Press,1961

2:*The Splendid Wayfaring*:University of Nebraska Press,1970

Neumann,Erich:*The Great Mother*:Ralph Manheim,tr.,Princeton University Press,1974

The New English Bible:Oxford University Press,1971

NHL:*The Nag Hammadi Library*:James M. Robinson,ed.,Harper Collins Publishers,1990

Nilsson,Martin P.:1:*The Mycenaean Origin of Greek Mythology*: University of California Press,1972

2:*The Dionysiac Mysteries Of The Hellenistic And Roman Age*: Arno Press,1975

3:*Imperial Rome*:Schocken Books,1967

Nonnos:*Dionysiaca*:W.H.D.Rouse,tr.,Harvard University Press,1952

Oakley,Kenneth P.:*Man The Tool-Maker*:The University of Chicago
  Press,1959
Origen:*Contra Celsum*:Henry Chadwick,tr.,Cambridge University
  Press,1965
Osler,William,ed.:*Modern Medicine*:Lea & Febiger,1925
Oss,O.T. & Oeric,O.N.:*Psilocybin*:And/Or Press,1976
Ott,Jonathan:*Hallucinogenic Plants of North America*:Wingbow Press,
  1976
Ovid:*Metamorphoses*:Frank Justus Miller,tr.,Harvard University
  Press,1916
The Oxford Book Of Food Plants:Oxford University Press,1973
The Oxford Dictionary of English Etymology:Oxford University
  Press,1966
Pagels,Elaine:1:*The Gnostic Gospels*:Vintage Books,1989
  2:*The Gnostic Paul*:Fortress Press,1975
  3:*Adam,Eve,And The Serpent*:Random House,1988
Palmer,Leonard R.:*Mycenaeans and Minoans*:Alfred A. Knopf,1965
Parvati,Jeannine:*Hygieia:A Woman's Herbal*:Freestone Collective,1983
Patai,Raphael:*The Hebrew Goddess*:Ktav Publishing House,1967
Paterculus,Velleius:*Res Gestae Divi Augusti*:Frederick W.Shipley,tr.,
Harvard University Press,1924
Pausanias:*Guide To Greece*:Peter Levi,tr.,Penguin Books,1988
PDR:*Physicians Desk Reference:1989*:Edward R. Barnhart
Pei,Mario:*The Story of Language*:The New American Library,1965
Perowne,Stewart:*Caesars & Saints*:Barnes & Noble,1992
Peters,Edward:1:*Heresy and Authority in Medieval
  Europe*:University of Pennsylvania Press,1989
  2:*Torture*:Basil Blackwell,1986
  3:*Inquisition*:The Free Press,1988
Pindar:*The Odes of Pindar*:Sir John Sandys,tr.:Harvard University
  Press,1915
Plato:*The Dialogues*:Harold North Fowler,tr.,Harvard University
  Press,1914
Plato:*Laws*:R.G.Bury,tr.,G.P.Putnam's Sons,1926
Pliny:*Natural History*:H.Rackham,tr.,Harvard University Press,1942
  2:*A Selection of His Letters*:Clarence Greig,tr.,Cambridge
  University Press,1978
Polybius:*The Histories*;W.R.Paton,tr.,G.P.Putnam's Sons,1922
Porter,Joseph C.:*Paper Medicine Man*:Univ. of Oklahoma Press,1986
Porphyry:1:*On the Cave of the Nymphs*:Thomas Taylor,tr.,Phanes
  Press,1991

    2:*Letter To His Wife Marcella*:Alice Zimmern,tr.,Phanes Press, 1986

Pritchard,James B.,ed.,:*The Ancient Near East*:Princeton University Press,1971

Prouty,L.Fletcher:*The Secret Team*:Prentice-Hall,1973

Rank,Otto:*Art and Artist*:Agathon Press,1968

Reichel-Dolmatoff,G.:*The Shaman and the Jaguar*:Temple University Press,1975

Riedlinger,Thomas J.,ed.:*The Sacred Mushroom Seeker*:Dioscorides Press,1990

The Revised English Bible:Oxford and Cambridge University Presses, 1989

Richardson,Cyril C.,tr.:*Early Christian Fathers*:The Westminster Press, 1953

Riddle,John M.:*Dioscorides on Pharmacy and Medicine*:University of Texas Press,1985

Riis,Jacob A.:*How The Other Half Lives*:Dover Publications,1971

Robbins,Rosell Hope:*The Encyclopedia of Witchcraft and Demonology*: Crown Publishers,1959

Roe,Derek:*Prehistory*:University of California Press,1970

Rorabaugh,W.J.:*The Alcoholic Republic*:Oxford University Press,1979

Rose,Jeanne:*Herbs & Things*:Grosset & Dunlap,1975

Rosenthal,Franz:*The Herb*:E.J.Brill,1971

Rothenberg,Jerome,ed.:1:*Shaking the Pumpkin*:Doubleday & Company, 1972
    2:& Quasha,George:*America a Prophesy*:Random House,1974
    3:*Technicians of the Sacred*:Doubleday & Company,1969

Rowland,Beryl:*Medieval Woman's Guide To Health*:The Kent State University Press,1981

Ruck:2:See Wasson:2
    3:See Wasson:3

Ruspoli,Mario:*The Cave of Lascaux*:Harry N.Abrams,Inc.,1983

Sandoz,Mari:*Crazy Horse*:University of Nebraska Press,1961

Sanger,Margaret:*An Autobiography*:W.W.Norton &Company,1938

Sauer,Carl O.:1:*Seeds,Spades,Hearths and Herds*:The MIT Press,1969
    2:*Northern Mists*,Turtle Island Foundation,1968

Schlieffer,Hedwig,ed.:*Sacred Narcotic Plants Of The New World Indians*: Hafner Press,1973

Schlesier,Karl H.:*The Wolves of Heaven*:University of Oklahoma Press,1987

Schlesinger,Arthur M.:*The Age of Jackson*:Little,Brown & Company,

1946

Schonfield,Hugh J.:*The Passover Plot*:Bantam Books,1971
Schultes,Richard Evans:*Where the Gods Reign*:Synergetic Press,1988
Schultes,Richard Evans & Hofmann,Albert:1:*The Botany and Chemistry of Hallucinogens*:Charles C Thomas,1980
    2:*Plants of the Gods*:Healing Arts Press,1992
Scott,Peter Dale & Marshall,Jonathan:*Cocaine Politics*:University of California Press,1991
Sered,Susan Starr:*Priestess,Mother,Sacred Sister*:Oxford University Press,1994
Siegel,Ronald K.:*Intoxication*:E.P Dutton,1989
Sloman,Larry:*Reefer Madness*;The Bobbs-Merrill Company
Slotkin,J.S.:*The Peyote Religion*:Farrar,Strauss and Giroux,1975
Smallwood,E.Mary:*The Jews Under Roman Rule*:E.J.Brill,1976
Snyder,Charles R.:*Alcohol and the Jews*:The Free Press,1958
Snyder,Solomon H. & Matthysse,Steven:*Opiate Receptor Mechanisms*: The MIT Press,1975
Soren,David,Ben Abed,Aicha & Slim,Hedi:*Carthage*:Simon & Schuster,1990
Spuhler,J.N.ed.:*The Evolution of Man's Capacity For Culture*:Wayne State University Press,1965
Stafford,Peter:*Psychedelics Encyclopedia*:And/Or Press,1977
Starr,Paul:*The Social Transformation Of American Medicine*:Basic Books,1982
Stein,Philip L. & Rowe,Bruce M.:*Physical Anthropology*:McGraw-Hill Book Company,1989
Steinmetz,E.F.:*Kava Kava*:Level Press
Struever,Stuart,ed.:*Prehistoric Agriculture*:The Natural History Press,1971
Sturtevant,Edward Lewis:*Sturtevant's Edible Plants of the World*:U.P. Hedrick,ed.,Dover Publications,1972
Swain,Tony,ed.:*Plants in the Development of Modern Medicine*:Harvard University Press,1972
Szasz,Thomas:1:*Our Right To Drugs*:Praeger,1992
    2:*Ceremonial Chemistry*:Anchor Books,1975
    3:*The Manufacture of Madness*:Dell Publishing,1970
    4:*Ideology and Insanity*:Anchor Books,1970
    5:*The Myth of Mental Illness*:Harper & Row,1974
Szent-Gyorgi,Albert:*The Crazy Ape*:Philosophical Library,1970
Tacitus:*The Histories*:Clifford H.Moore,tr.,G.P.Putnam's Sons,1925
Taussig,Michael:*Shamanism,Colonialism,and the Wild Man*:The

University of Chicago Press,1987

Taylor,Arnold H.:*American Diplomacy and the Narcotics Traffic,1900-1939*:Duke University Press,1969

Taylor,Colin F. & Sturtevant,William C:*The Native Americans*: Smithmark Publishers,1991

Taylor,Norman:*Plant Drugs That changed The World*:Dodd,Mead & Company,1965

Telushkin,Rabbi Joseph:*Jewish Literacy*:William Morrow And Company,1991

Thomas,Lee:*The Billy Sunday Story*:Zondervan Publishing House,1961

Thucydides:*The Peloponnesian War*:Thomas Hobbes,tr.,The University of Chicago Press,1989

Trebach,Arnold:*The Heroin Solution*:Yale University Press,1982

Tuchman,Barbara W.:*A Distant Mirror*:Alfred A.Knopf,1978

Turnbull,Colin M.:*The Forest People*:Simon & Schuster,1962

Ucko,Peter J. and Rosenfeld,Andree:*Palaeolithic Cave Art*:McGraw-Hill Book Company,1967

USDA:*Common Weeds of the United States*:Dover Publications,1971

The United States Dispensatory,26th Edition:J.B.Lippincott Company, 1967

Utley,Robert M.:*The Lance And The Shield*:Henry Holt and Company,1993

Vallance,Theodore R.:*Prohibition's Second Failure*:Praeger Publishers,1993

Vaughn,J.W.:*The Reynolds Campaign On Powder River*:University of Oklahoma Press,1961

Veninga,Louise:*The Ginseng Book*:Ruka Publications,1973

Vermes,G.:1:*The Dead Sea Scrolls in English*:Penguin Books,1987
2:*Jesus the Jew*:Fortress Press,1981

Vogel,Virgil J.:*American Indian Medicine*:University of Oklahoma Press, 1982

Waley,Arthur:*The Opium War Through Chinese Eyes*:Stanford University Press,1968

Washburn,Sherwood L.,ed.:*Social Life Of Early Man*:Aldine Publishing Company,1961

Wasson,R.Gordon:1:*Soma:Divine Mushroom of Immortality*: Harcourt Brace Jovanovich,1968
2:with Ruck,Carl A.P. & Hofmann,Albert:*The Road To Eleusis*: Harcourt,Brace,Jovanovich,1978
3:with Kramrisch,Stella, Ott,Jonathan & Ruck, Carl A.P.:*Persephone's Quest*:Yale University Press,1986

4:*The Wondrous Mushroom*:McGraw-Hill Book
Company,1980

Watts,Alan W.:*The Joyous Cosmology*:Random House,1963

Webster's Third New International Dictionary:G.&C.Merriam
Company,1968

Weil,Andrew:*The Natural Mind*:Houghton Mifflin Company:1972

Weil,Andrew and Rosen,Winifred:*Chocolate To Morphine*:Houghton
Mifflin Company,1983

Wesley,John:*Primitive Remedies*:Woodbridge Press Publishing
Company,1973

Whorf,Benjamin Lee:*Language,Thought & Reality*:The M.I.T. Press,1964

Wilkinson,Sir J.Gardner:*The Manners And Customs Of The Ancient
Egyptians*:S.E.Cassino And Company,1883

Willetts,R.F.:1:*The Civilization Of Ancient Crete*;University of
California Press,1977

2:*Cretan Cults And Festivals*:Barnes & Noble,1962

Williams,Selma R.:*Riding The Nightmare*:Atheneum,1978

Williams,Terry:*The Cocaine Kids*:Addison-Wesley Publishing
Company,1989

Wood,Michael:*In Search of the Dark Ages*:Facts on File Publications,1987

Woolley,C.Leonard:1:*The Sumerians*:W.W.Norton & Co.,1965

2:*Ur of the Chaldees*:W.W.Norton & Company,1965

Young,James Harvey:*The Toadstool Millionaires*:Princeton University
Press,1961

NOTES

[1] Jung:13:253

[2] Jung:13:272

[3] Jung:8:436

[4] Jung:10:29

[5] Robinson in Howell:411

[6] Goodall:197-213

[7] Stein:372

[8] Stein:369-375;Ardrey:1:224

[9] Howell:347

[10] *New York Times*:12/18/94

[11] Siegel:90

[12] Hass

[13] Churchland:36

[14] AMA:405

[15] Snyder & Matthysse

[16] Hogshire:49

[17] Schultes & Hofmann:1:25-27

[18] Goldstein in Krauss:402

[19] Churchland:67-69

[20] Washburn in Spuhler:27-29

[21] Robinson in Howell:410

[22] Crystal:124;261;291;398;Stein:266-269

[23] Ardrey:3:309

[24] Dart:173

[25] DeVore and Washburn in Howell:337

[26] Washburn & DeVore in Washburn:96:101

[27] Blanc in Washburn:133

[28] Oakley in Washburn:179

[29] Oakley in Washburn:184

[30] Oakley in Washburn:182

[31] Wasson:1:216

[32] Schlesier:31

[33] Blanc in Washburn:131

[34] Furst:1:4

[35] Vasilevich in Schlesier:31

[36] Marshack:170

[37] Marshack:209

[38] Marshack:218

[39] Marshack:174

[40] Wasson:3:141

[41] Marshack:238;260;261;277

[42] Marshack:302

[43] Marshack:334

[44] Frolov in Marshack:337

[45] Gimbutas:2:142;3:222

[46] Jung:12:96

[47] Reichel-Dolmatoff:173ff

[48] Marshack:314

[49] Eliade:285

[50] Eliade:268

[51] Eliade:132

[52] Schlesier:85

[53] Hawkins:52;Graves:2:317

[54] Gimbutas:3:296;Finegan:20

[55] Schlesier:143;159

[56] Grinnell in Schlesier:53

[57] Furst:1:9;Schultes & Hofmann:1:157

[58] Harner:1:154

[59] Eliade:107

[60] Eliade:297

[61] Curtis in Schlesier:71

[62] Achterberg:1:44

[63] Eliade:233

[64] Schlesier:36

[65] Eliade:4;299

[66] Ackernecht in Grossinger1::94

[67] Schlesier:24;33;30

[68] Schlesier:175

[69] Sternberg in Eliade:72

[70] Schlesier:39

[71] Grinnell in Schlesier:55

[72] Neihardt:277

[73] Schultes in Reichel-Dolmatoff:xii

[74] Churchland:46

[75] Blake in Huxley:Frontispiece

[76] Eliade:98

[77] Churchland:152

[78] Achterberg:1:49

COPPER

[79] Barber:53
[80] Flannery in Struever:59
[81] MacNeish in Struever:143ff
[82] Mellaart:1:20;2:16;36
[83] Evans:1:14;20
[84] Hole in Struever:274;284
[85] Mellaart:1:211;217
[86] Gimbutas:3:x;9
[87] Gimbutas:3:324-344;Mellaart:1:79;209
[88] Mellaart:1:167;2:89-101
[89] Mellaart:1:65;125;126
[90] Taylor,Colin:171
[91] Mellaart:1:181
[92] Mellaart:1:184;Gimbutas:2:107;307
[93] Mellaart:1:142;157
[94] Mellaart:1:175
[95] Gimbutas:2:265
[96] Gimbutas:3:245;247;1:93
[97] Evans:4:1:25
[98] Gimbutas:2: 271
[99] Gimbutas:2:33;
[100] Gimbutas 2:48
[101] Evans:1:605;499
[102] Gimbutas 3:222
[103] Wasson:4:43
[104] Gimbutas:3:196
[105] Gimbutas:3:144-147
[106] Gimbutas:3:396
[107] Evans:1:414
[108] Wasson:1:47
[109] Gimbutas:2:119
[110] Evans:1:76
[111] Gimbutas:3:223
[112] Graves:2:224
[113] Gimbutas:3:257
[114] Gimbutas:3:178
[115] Gimbutas:3:202-3
[116] Wasson:4:57ff
[117] Wasson:4:62

[118] Gimbutas:1:219
[119] Gimbutas:3:188
[120] Furst:2:18
[121] Evans:1:160
[122] Schultes & Hofmann:1:64;79
[123] Lajoux;McKenna:1
[124] Gimbutas:1:95;2:282;293
[125] Gimbutas:1:101:
[126] Gimbutas:1:201
[127] Gimbutas:2:175
[128] Evans:1:508
[129] Evans:1:;438-440
[130] Jung:10:31
[131] Gimbutas:2:121
[132] Gimbutas:1:216;135;152;196
[133] Gimbutas:2:231;M:292
[134] Gimbutas:3:308
[135] Evans:;2:2:484
[136] Gimbutas:3:320;Evans:1:134;1:2:641
[137] Hawkes:62

KNOSSOS

[138] Palmer:Plate 14

[139] Evans:1:501-507;2:2:748

[140] Evans:4:2:910ff;Palmer:Plate 11

[141] Kerenyi:3:xix

[142] Evans:1:432

[143] Evans:4:2:950

[144] Willetts:1:99

[145] Hesiod:*Theogony*:477

[146] Evans:1:627

[147] Evans:1:97

[148] Willetts:1:79;Evans:4:1:28-43

[149] Evans:3:209-223

[150] Schultes & Hofmann:1:330

[151] Gimbutas:3:346

[152] Webster's:403

[153] Schultes & Hofmann:367

[154] Finegan:25

[155] CAH:2:1:161

[156] Evans:4:1:43

[157] Evans:1:624;Graves:1:76

[158] Evans:4:2:460

[159] Evans:;4:2:392-394

[160] Evans:3:70

[161] Evans:3:68;Gimbutas:1:185

[162] Evans:2:2:842

[163] Wasson:4:151ff;Wasson:4:166

[164] Gordon:3;Mertz;Sauer:2

[165] Ruck:3:189

[166] Evans:2:2:789

[167] Evans:4:2:453;Gimbutas:1:184

BRONZE

[168] Mellaart:1:68-70
[169] Mellaart::2:112;CAH:1:2:363;404
[170] Crystal:299
[171] Gimbutas:3:352-400
[172] Struever:304
[173] Struever:75
[174] Struever:285ff
[175] Mellaart:2:120
[176] CAH:1:1:352
[177] Finegan:39
[178] CAH:1:1:392
[179] Kramer:1:111
[180] CAH:1:2:79
[181] Kramer:1:43
[182] Kramer:1:50
[183] Evans:4:2:813
[184] Woolley:1:35ff
[185] Kramer:1:88
[186] Kramer:1:125
[187] Kramer:1:79
[188] Kramer:1:148;2:40
[189] Evans:1:509
[190] Finegan:81
[191] Budge:1:281
[192] CAH:1:2:35
[193] CAH:1:493
[194] Finegan:fig.28
[195] Finegan:87
[196] Herod:2:124ff
[197] Graves:2:413
[198] Erman:10;85
[199] Erman:5-7
[200] Wasson:45;47
[201] Evans:2:2:740
[202] Erman:9
[203] Evans:4:1:149
[204] CAH:2:1:187
[205] Finegan:61
[206] Pritchard:138ff

THE DOVE

[207] CAH:2:1:205
[208] Allegro:1:74;Pliny:*NH*:22:96;5:9:8
[209] Palmer:131;Willetts:2:172;*Od*:19:183;Str:10:476;Paus:1:18:5
[210] Evans:1:635
[211] Allegro:1:20;91
[212] Finnegan:59
[213] Pritchard:33-35;Finnegan:64
[214] Gordon:1:91
[215] Finnegan:224
[216] Kramer:1:198; Finnegan:33
[217] Pritchard:74; Gordon:1:84

PHOENISSA

[218] CAH:2:2:59; Finegan:105

[219] Budge:1:116;290)

[220] Carter:9-10

[221] CAH:2:2:88

[222] Gordon:1:126

[223] CAH:2:2:626

[224] CAH:2:1:377

[225] Gordon:1:141

[226] Graves:2:255

[227] *Odyssey*:21:391

[228] Willetts:2:12

[229] Pritchard:262

[230] Evans:4:1:167

[231] Soren:123;Diodorus:20:14;Plutarch:*DeSuperstitione*:171C;Jer:7:30;32:35;
2Kings:17:16;23:10

[232] Gordon:2:25;

[233] Allegro:1:58

[234] Gordon:1:131

[235] Graves:2:412

[236] Pritchard:277

[237] Gordon:1:188

[238] Allegro:1:24

PHOINIKEIA

[239] Erman:lxiv
[240] CAH:3:1:800
[241] Erman:169
[242] Gelb:215
[243] Gordon:1:128
[244] Gordon:2:15;1:129ff;CAH:3:1:794-833
[245] Crystal:202
[246] Kerenyi:1:56
[247] Gelb:144
[248] Budge:1:116
[249] Graves:2:236
[250] Herodotus:1:2;5:58
[251] Graves:1:194;Apoll:3:1:1;Paus:5:25:7
[252] Willetts:2:167
[253] Evans:4:2:859;885;Soren:97;Willetts:2:28
[254] Allegro:1:252
[255] Frazier:8
[256] Graves:2:36
[257] Graves:2:310
[258] Hawkes:135
[259] Apollodorus:1:9:16
[260] Graves:2:107
[261] Graves:2:215
[262] Graves:2:199
[263] Graves:2:169;Graves:2:239
[264] Graves:2:29
[265] *The Song of God*:146:in Jung:13:313
[266] Rev:22:2

<u>MYKENAIKOS</u>

[267] Evans:2:2:482;3:153-160

[268] CAH:2:2:828;841

[269] *Iliad*:6:168FF;Palmer:54;55;342

[270] Palmer:133

[271] Palmer:Plate 13

[272] CAH:2:2:;867

[273] Kereny:1:xxvi; 103

[274] Pausanias: 2:16:3

[275] Ruck:3:255

[276] Evans:4:2:733;Pl.69

[277] Palmer:113

[278] Fowden:53

[279] Sturtevant;Rose;Grieve

[280] Palmer:132

[281] Palmer:205

[282] Pliny:*NH*:23:159;24:50;21:126;

[283] Palmer:207

[284] Palmer:325;Crystal:300

[285] Gelb:156;Evans:1:2:654

[286] Gordon:2:33

[287] Pritchard:89

IRON

[288] Finegan:71
[289] CAH:2:2:269
[290] CAH:3:1:714
[291] CAH:3:3:160
[292] *Works*:110-200
[293] CAH:3:1:787;681
[294] Graves:2:256
[295] Detienne:105-118
[296] CAH:3:1:788
[297] Detienne:136-140
[298] Detienne:131-135
[299] *Odyssey*:11:423
[300] *Eumenides*:284
[301] *Eumenides*:658
[302] *Agamemnon*:1234-1412
[303] *Iliad*:8:287
[304] *Iiad*:2:354
[305] Pind:*Nem*;Aisch:*Pers*
[306] CAH:3:1:530
[307] *Iliad*:18:336
[308] Thucydides:1:5
[309] Thuc:1:13:1
[310] Herod:3:82:3;5:92
[311] CAH:3:3:347
[312] *Ath.Pol.*:2
[313] CAH:3:3:;99
[314] Ezekiel:27:13
[315] CAH:3:3:22
[316] CAH:3:3:242
[317] Herod:2:53
[318] Graves:1:20
[319] *Odyssey*:19:560
[320] Graves:2:11
[321] Gimbutas:2:198
[322] Munn in Harner:2:88
[323] Jung:12:25
[324] CAH:3:1:831
[325] Evans:4:1:165

[326] Harrison:2:323
[327] Harrison:2:331
[328] Graves: 2:vi
[329] Jung: 14:97
[330] Jung: 14:177
[331] Jung: 13:347
[332] Eliade:217

DIONYSOS

[333] CAH:2:2:880

[334] Kereny:3:23

[335] Willetts:1:122

[336] Pausanias:1:18:5

[337] Willetts:2:109;170

[338] Athanassakis:73

[339] Evelyn-White:*Hesiod:The Homeric Hymns*:289

[340] Pausanias:1:31:6

[341] Ruck:2:88

[342] *Iliad*:2:508

[343] Graves:1:96

[344] National Archeological Museum, Taranto

[345] Evans:2:341

[346] Ruck:3:187

[347] Vatican Museum

[348] Kerenyi:3:74

[349] *To Demeter*:A:206

[350] Evans: 4:2:626-627

[351] Schultes & Hofmann:1:36

[352] Hoffer:84;216-219

[353] Wasson:2:66-67

[354] Graves:2:164;Jung:14:406

[355] Apollodorus:1:9:12

[356] *U.S. Dispensatory*:26:468

[357] Pseudo-Dioscorides:2:100

[358] Evans:4:2:718-720

[359] Gimbutas:2:208

[360] Evans:4:2:950

[361] Willetts:2:160

[362] Apollonius:*Argon*:3:843

[363] *Iliad*:11:623

[364] *To Demeter*:224

[365] Exodus:3:1

[366] *To Demeter*: 470

[367] Harrison:2:292

[368] Palmer:137

[369] Kerenyi:1:304

[370] Pritchard:85;Gordon:1:90

[371] Eliade:85

[372] Harrison:2:292

[373] Kerenyi:3:135
[374] Ruck:2:118
[375] Euripides: *Bac*:1016
[376] Allegro:1:86
[377] Harrison:2:119
[378] Harrison:2:149
[379] Harrison:2:141
[380] Harrison:2:143
[381] Harrison:2:154;205
[382] Harrison:2:141
[383] Ruck:3:171; Graves:2:276
[384] Harrison:1:26
[385] Allegro:1:34
[386] Harrison:1:394
[387] Kereny:3:51
[388] Plato:*Phaedrus*:229:C
[389] Ruck:2:86
[390] Allegro:1:65
[391] Grieve:1:424
[392] *Bacchae*:88
[393] Ruck:2:121
[394] Wasson:3:50
[395] *Bacchae* :555
[396] *Bacchae*:1
[397] *Bacchae*::268
[398] *Bacchae*::213,265,539,etc
[399] Ruck:3:199
[400] *Bacchae*:550;Kerenyi:3:84
[401] Homer:*IL*:22:94;Virgil:*Aen*:2:741;Pliny:*N.H.*: 22:95;Pindar:*Olympian Odes*:6:43
[402] Ruck:3:163
[403] Ruck:3:196
[404] Kerenyi:1:306
[405] Pausanias:1:2
[406] Hesiod:*Th*:969;*Od*:5:125;Kerenyi:3:127
[407] *Bacchae*:298
[408] *Bacchae*:378;594
[409] Clement in Harrison:1:480
[410] Kerenyi:1:299;3:135
[411] *Bacchae*:695
[412] Harrison:1:426

[413] Kerenyi:3:125;*Fasti*:3:736

[414] Harrison:1:410

[415] CAH:11:77;*Vita Pythag*:14;15

[416] Herodotus:4:74

[417] Graves:1:75

[418] Eliade:400

[419] Wasson:1:164

[420] Antoine Vivenel Museum, Compiegne

[421] Harrison:1:422

[422] Graves:1:118

[423] *Odyssey*:18:193

[424] Harrison:2:24

[425] Harrison:1:441

[426] Harrison:1:443

[427] Ovid:*Metamorphoses*:7:179

MNEMOSYNE

[428] Cornford in Harrison:2:222
[429] Ruck:3:208
[430] Harrison:2:369
[431] Harrison:2:371
[432] Willets:2:143
[433] Harrison:2:108
[434] Ruck:3:233
[435] Kerenyi:3:132
[436] Harrison:1:172
[437] Nonnos:*Dionysiaca*:14:23
[438] Harrison:2:506
[439] Hesiod:*Theogony*:53
[440] Harrison:2:379
[441] Harrison:2:380
[442] Harrison:2:382
[443] Apollodorus:3:3
[444] Ovid:*Metamorphoses*:13:924
[445] Evans:4:1:138-145;151;164;Willets:2:60;Graves:2:360;Gimbutas:2:133;1:74
[446] Harrison:2:271
[447] CAH:8:553
[448] Harrison:2:323
[449] Puhvel in Hand:33
[450] Gimbutas:3:288
[451] Kerenyi:2:73

DRAMA

[452] Harrison:1:568
[453] Harrison:1:569
[454] Harrison:2:331
[455] Harrison:2:334
[456] Harrison:2:335
[457] Harrison:2:339
[458] Harrison:2:346
[459] Ruck 3:221;208
[460] Riddle:146
[461] Harrison:1:415
[462] Harrison:1:420
[463] Evans:4:2:467;1:708
[464] Gimbutas:1:79;2:235

ORPHEUS

[465] Harrison:1:448

[466] Diodorus:5:77:3

[467] Harrison:1:560

[468] Harrison:1:567

[469] Harrison:2:X

[470] Bourke:132

[471] Harrison:2:X

[472] Ruck:3:233

[473] Harrison:1:606

[474] Harrison:2:X

[475] *Works*:59;Harrison:1:284

[476] Hesiod:*Theogony*:565

[477] Evelyn-White:*To Apollon*:350

[478] Harrison:2:394

[479] Harrison:2:X

[480] Ruck:3:174

[481] Nonnos:*Dionysiaca*:40:469

[482] Harrison:2:X;Plato:*Pha*

[483] Harrison:2:X

[484] Harrison:1:102

[485] Ruck:3:249

[486] Harrison:1:103;154;95

[487] Harrison:1:99

[488] Ruck:3:240;Aris:*Knights*:1405;*Lysias*:6:53

[489] Harrison:1:108

[490] Willetts:2:275

[491] Plato:*Laws*:873B

[492] Harrison:1:503

[493] Harrison:1:477

[494] Harrison:1:500

[495] Harrison:1:141

[496] Harrison:1: 507

[497] Harrison:1:650;Plutarch:*The Obsolescence of Oracles*

[498] Harrison:1:525;547

[499] Harrison:1:475

[500] Paterculus:2:82

[501] Harrison:2:259

[502] Harrison:2:277

[503] Harrison:1:612

[504] Harrison:1:614-621
[505] Evans:4:1:155;Gimbutas:2:49
[506] Graves:2:273;469
[507] Harrison:2:486
[508] Harrison:2:483;Pind:*Olympian Odes*
[509] Harrison:2:XI
[510] Harrison:2:XI
[511] Harrison:2:XI

ASSAYA

[512] Finegan:73

[513] Finegan:68ff

[514] CAH:2:2:269

[515] Ex:1:11

[516] Gordon:2:23

[517] Ex:24:8

[518] Pritchard:85

[519] Patai;Gordon:2:31

[520] Ex:3:14-4:5

[521] Munn in Harner:2:121

[522] John:15:5

[523] Genesis:2-3

[524] CAH:6:180

[525] Ex:23:6;Amos:5:7-13

[526] Finnegan:52

[527] Finegan:60

[528] Pritchard:139

[529] For Hammurabi parallels see Ex:21:16:2325:29;22:2;Deut:19:18:21;22:22;24:1; Lev:20:10;also Heidel

[530] Num:31:17-18:also Judges:5:19

[531] Exodus:4:24-6

[532] Euripides:*Iphigeneia at Aulis*

[533] Maccoby:2:88-94

[534] Leviticus:12

[535] Erman:46

[536] Gimbutas:2:116

[537] Pliny:*NH*:28:77;2:221;8:78

[538] Josephus:*War*:7:181

[539] Allegro:1:63-75

[540] Allegro:103

[541] Gen:21:12

[542] Gen:27

[543] *Mishnah:Sotah*:2:6;3:4;*Ketubot*:3:2;12:1-12:4

[544] Deuteronomy:30:11

[545] Maccoby:3:92

[546] Gimbutas:2:319

[547] CAH:10:82;472

[548] *Odyssey*:4:219

[549] Mead:1:4

[550] CAH:10:483
[551] Frend:2:91-92
[552] Maccoby:1:137
[553] Epiphanius:*Heresies*:30:16
[554] Maccoby:3:71
[555] Maccoby:3;209
[556] Matthew:10:17
[557] *Babylonian Talmud:Yoma*:85b
[558] Genesis: 18:25
[559] *Horayot*:13a;See also Psalms:44:24;Habbakkuk:1:2;Job
[560] Gen:32:28
[561] *Mishnah:Taanit*:3:8
[562] Josephus:*Antiq*:10:6
[563] 2:Sam:24
[564] Mat:10:5
[565] Smallwood:159
[566] *Horayot*:3:8
[567] Acts:8:3
[568] 2:Cor:11:32
[569] Acts:9;22
[570] 1:Cor:11:23-27
[571] John:6:52-56
[572] Lev:3:17;7:26;17:10;Deut:12:16;12:23
[573] John:6:66
[574] Graves:2:164
[575] Allegro: 2:74
[576] John:3
[577] *Sanhedrin*:17a;36b
[578] Mark:12:28-34
[579] Matthew:22:34-40
[580] Deuteronomy:6:4
[581] Maccoby:3:30
[582] *Hist.Ekkles*:3:39:16
[583] *Mishnah Avot*:2:4;3:9;13;4:1;7;8;17
[584] *Shabbat*:31a;Telushkin:121
[585] Mat:7:12
[586] Micah:6:8
[587] Mat:6:15
[588] Luke:15
[589] *Babylonian Talmud:B.Ber*:34b;Maccoby:1:266
[590] Mark:3:6

591 Matthew:12:14

592 John:5:16

593 *Babylonian Talmud:Yoma*:85b

594 *Shulchan Aruch* in Snyder:29

595 Exodus:21:23

596 Genesis:4:10

597 *Mishnah Sanhedrin*:4:5

598 Heb:10:26

599 Deuteronomy:17:6

600 Maccoby:3:39

601 Mark:1:43

602 Matthew:5:19

603 *Mishnah Avot*:2:7;4:2

604 Matthew:23:33-6

605 Matthew:23

606 Matthew:23:2

607 Luke 16:16

608 Vermes:1:54

609 Allegro:2;169;Vermes:2:95;133

610 2:Thess:2:8

611 Acts:24:14

612 Heb:8

613 Allegro:2:147;148

614 Josphus:*War*:2:136

615 Philo:*Cont.Life*:1:2:2;Mead:1:70

616 Allegro:2:140

617 Vermes:2:62

618 Willetts:2:93;99;104;Allegro:2;128

619 Pliny:*NH*:11:37;Kereny:1:73

620 Vermes:1:187

621 Allegro:1:122

622 Gimbutas:1:183;Allegro:2:148

623 CAH:8:352;Livy:39:8

624 Frend:2:83

625 Allegro:1:125

626 Kereny:1:1Ilus 70

627 Allegro:1:34

628 Mead:1:126

629 Maccoby:1:159

630 Mat:13:55

631 Mark:6:3

632 Mat:16:17

633 Allegro:1:18

634 Vermes:2:53

635 Allegro:1:40;47

636 Mark 3:17

637 Psalms 18:10

638 Evans:1:709; Allegro:1:94

639 Evans:2:1:342

640 Allegro:1:99-101

641 John 14:22-24

642 Maccoby:4:132;144

643 Mat:13:55;Mark:6:3

644 Gal:2:9

645 *Hist.Ekkles*:4:22:4

646 Acts 1:6

647 Mk:8:27

648 Maccoby:1:167

649 Psalm 2

650 1:Kings:18:40

651 2:Kings:2:11

652 Exodus 38

653 1:Sam:10

654 Maccoby:1:175

655 Deut:17:14-20

656 Zechariah:14:16

657 Zechariah:14:3-12

658 Chrysostom:*In Matthew Homiliae*:72:73

659 Ex:12

660 Mark 14:15

661 Maccoby:1:186

662 Josephus:*War*:4:558

663 Smallwood:300

664 Vermes:1:89;Amos:9:11

665 Maccoby:1:185

666 Philo:*De Legatione*:38;159;Josephus:*Antiq*:18:60;*War*:2:175

667 Luke 13:1

668 Smallwood:162-7

669 Maccoby:1:202

670 Luke:23:2

671 Maccoby:1:204;*Antiq*:20:9:1;*War*:6:334

672 John 18:31

[673] Smallwood:150
[674] Maccoby:1:216
[675] Mark:14:35;Rom:8:15;Gal:4:6
[676] Mark:15:7
[677] Luke:23
[678] Tacitus:*Annals*:15:44
[679] Allegro:1:170
[680] Ex:12:22
[681] Leviticus:14:6
[682] Num:19:6
[683] 1:Kings:4:33
[684] Num:19:18
[685] Graves:2:28;45;283;371
[686] Gen:4:12
[687] Minucius:*Octavius*:21:1
[688] Num:24:22
[689] Maccoby:2:19:24
[690] Gen:4:22
[691] Allegro:1:97
[692] John:19:29;1:Cor:5:7
[693] Harrison:2:149
[694] Kerenyi:3:117-128
[695] Mark:15:43
[696] Luke:23:50
[697] John:19:38
[698] Acts:15:5
[699] Acts:21:38
[700] Josephus:*Antiq*:20:97;167
[701] Acts 5:17
[702] John:18:3
[703] Maccoby:4:76
[704] Acts:5:30
[705] Acts:5:36
[706] Acts:23:6-9
[707] Acts 24:1
[708] Josephus:*Antiq*:20:97
[709] Num:25:13
[710] Acts:2:46;3:1
[711] Josephus:*Antiq*:20:9:1
[712] *Hist.Ekkles*:23:11-18;3:12
[713] Luke:24:21

[714] Origen:*Contra Celsum*:5:65
[715] Leviticus:16:9-10
[716] Gen:49:9-12
[717] 1:Cor:15:5
[718] Mark:6:3
[719] Matthew:13:55
[720] *Apostolic Constitutions*:7:46: in Maccoby:4:88
[721] Acts:9:11
[722] Acts:15
[723] Luke:22:53
[724] Acts:18:6
[725] 1:Thess:2:15
[726] Acts:19:32;18:8;Gen:15:16-21
[727] Philip:3:2
[728] Acts:18:12;21:18
[729] John:8:44;14:22
[730] Acts:1:16-19
[731] Matthew:27:3-5
[732] John 2:9

BALSAM

733 John:15:1
734 Kerenyi:1:illus 67
735 Maccoby:2:24
736 Jung:12:99
737 Jung:13:307
738 Mark:10:18;Luke:18:18
739 Frend on Gnosticism:2:260
740 Rev:18:23
741 *Sanh*:74a;Tertullian:*De pudicitia*:19; Frend:2:45;Jung:12:87-89
742 Hesiod:*Theogony*:969
743 Jung:12:357
744 *Gospel of Philip*:NHL:143
745 Irenaeus *Heresies*:1:6:1-4;Romans:4:15
746 NHL:41
747 Irenaeus:*Heresies*:1:11-21:in Richardson;1:Cor:1:30;Pagels:2:95
748 Jung:13:135-154;Paracelsus:*De vita longa*
749 Coulter:1:350-380
750 Pagels:2:144
751 Mead:1:484
752 Mead:1:462
753 Pagels:1:126

IDOLATRY

[754] Acts:13:29

[755] Romans:11:5-6

[756] Romans:13:1

[757] 1:Timothy:2:11

[758] Romans:6:5-7;8:23

[759] Graves:3:280

[760] Pagels:2:144

[761] Frend:1:417

[762] Jung:14:510

[763] Harrison:1:455

[764] Smallwood:429

[765] CAH:10:401

[766] CAH:11:28

[767] Dio:68:15;CAH:11:215

[768] Ignatius *Ephesians*:20:2;10:3

[769] Ignatius:*Trallians*:9:6;10:1:in Richardson

[770] Ignatius:*Smyrnaeans*:8:2-9:1

[771] Pagels:1:123

[772] Frend:1:231

[773] Tatian:*Address to Greeks*:28

[774] *Hist.Ekkles*:4:26:7

[775] Athenagoras *Plea*:3

[776] Irenaeus:*Ag.Heresies*:3:3:2

[777] CAH:12:424

[778] CAH:12:428

[779] Cumont:140

[780] Eliade:121;Origen:*Contra Celsum*:6:22

[781] Frend:2:225

[782] Celsus in *Contra Celsum*:5:41

[783] MacMullen:6;84;87

[784] CAH:12:34

[785] CAH:12:352

[786] *Digest*:1:4:1;48:19;8:3 in Peters:2:36

[787] Linder:103;Peters:34

[788] *John's Gospel*:GCS:10:8:105:in Frend:1:281

[789] Tertullian:*Adversus Marcionem* in Peters:1:30

[790] *Contra Celsum*:2:30

[791] Dio:52:36:1-3

[792] Clement *Exhortation*:10:73

[793] Origen *Contra Celsum*:2:79
[794] Philo:*Legum Allegoriae*:59
[795] Ex:16:31
[796] Allegro:1:170
[797] Kramer:1:95-97
[798] Graves:2:492
[799] Pagels:1:28-47
[800] CAH:12:525
[801] Jung:11:211
[802] CAH:12:189
[803] Eusebius:*Hist.Ekkles*:7:2:3
[804] *Acta Cypr*:1:2
[805] Frend:2:302
[806] CAH:12:489
[807] *Pap.Oxy*:2332 in Frend:1:372
[808] *Hist.Ekkles*:7:30:19;Smallwood:532
[809] CAH:12:423
[810] CAH:12:665ff
[811] Smallwood:540
[812] Frend:2:394
[813] Evans:1:513-517;Mellaart:1:162
[814] Frend:4:141
[815] CAH:12:707
[816] Frend:2:91
[817] Fowden:174
[818] CAH:12:362
[819] Eusebius:*De laudibus Constantini*:5
[820] Cantor:49
[821] Cicero *On laws*:2
[822] Cantor:117
[823] Ammianus:21:16:17
[824] Frend:1:636ff
[825] Frend:1:711-714;Jung:13:102;Peters:1:44
[826] Brown,Peter:190
[827] Augustine:*City of God Against the Pagans*:19:15
[828] Romans:13
[829] Frend:1:722ff
[830] Brown,Peter:21
[831] Brown,Peter: 69;
[832] Brown,Peter:216

[833] *City*:23;*De moribus eccl.cath*:1:30:63;*Psalmos*:50:6-11;Brown,Peter:225

[834] Brown,Peter: 236

[835] Brown,Peter: 144

[836] Frend:1:671;Brown,Peter:239

[837] Brown,Peter:231

[838] Brown,Peter: 213

[839] Brown,Peter:232

[840] Linder:231

[841] Luke 14:23

[842] Augustine in Peters:1:43

[843] Brown,Peter:223

[844] *City*:14:13

[845] *City*:13:14

[846] Brown,Peter:221;223

[847] *City*:16:37

[848] *City*:18:37

[849] Brown:388; Augustine:*Serm*:151:5

[850] Augustine:*Concerning Heresies*:46

[851] Augustine:*Confessions*:1:14:23

[852] Cantor:126

[853] Frend:1:830

[854] *Cod.Th*:16:1:2;16:8:1;16:8:7;16:8:19;16:10:3;*Code*:1;12;16;48;54;Peters:1:45; Linder:81;258

[855] *Codex Theodosianus* in Linder:258

[856] Peters:2:32-35

[857] Linder:66

[858] *Code*:1:5:21;18;56;64;*Digest*:48:19:7

[859] Frend:1:634

[860] Leontius of Jerusalem,536:in Frend:1:849

GNOSIS

[861] Eusebius:*Hist.Ekkles*:4:7

[862] Irenaeus:*Ag.Heresies*:3:11:9;5:26:1

[863] *Clement's First Letter*:41:3,in Richardson

[864] NHL:19

[865] NHL:20

[866] Acts:19:19

[867] CAH:7:1:321-352;Landels

[868] Budge:1:282

[869] Fowden:178

[870] Frend:1:853

[871] Eunapios, an initiate eyewitness, in Kerenyi:3:17

[872] Kerenyi:1:67

[873] Trans.Willis Barnstone:29;161-186

[874] Frend:1:753

[875] *Letter*:17:7;in Frend:1:757

[876] Harrison:2:108

[877] Kramer:2:70

[878] Jung:12:74;13:226;302-315

[879] Jung:11:167;13:283;305

[880] *Viatorium spagyricum*:1625:in Jung:12:125

[881] NHL:179

[882] Allegro:1:80

[883] Frend:1:201;280

[884] Irenaeus:*Ag.Heresies*:1:27:4

[885] *Untitled Apocalypse*:Mead:1:555

[886] *The Hypostasis of the Archons*:'The Reality of the Rulers,' c.250 CE:NHL:164

[887] 1:Tim:2:11-14

[888] *Authoritative Teaching*:NHL:305-310

[889] Fowden:121

[890] Fowden:125

[891] *Musaeum Hermeticum*,1678, in Jung:13:307; also:12:74;13:226;302-315

[892] Budge:1:276

[893] Evans:2:2:482

[894] Jung:12:134

[895] *Book of the Dead*:71:6 in Jayne:82

[896] Paracelsus in Coulter:1:373

[897] Hippolytus:*Elenchos*:5:9:12 in Jung:12:449

[898] Irenaeus:*Heresies*:1:13:1;1:25:6

[899] Origen:*Contra Celsum*:5:62;7:3
[900] Tertullian:*De Baptismo*:1;*De Virginibus Velandis*:9